British
Theatrical
Patents
1801-1900

TERENCE REES saw his first live theatrical performance at the age of nine and has never been the same since. It was that event which fixed once and for all his prime interest in the theatre: 'How is it done' rather than 'What is it about?' This bias remained with him even throughout his days as a student, when he declined the offer of a speaking part in his college Dramatic Society production (Hortensio in *The Taming of the Shrew*), preferring to involve himself with lighting and sound effects. His studies of infectious diseases were subsequently adjusted to admit an investigation of that little-known Gilbert and Sullivan operetta *Thespis* and the outcome of this was a book on the subject.

Thereafter, Terence's interests returned to theatre lighting, resulting, in the fullness of time, in another book: *Theatre Lighting in the Age of Gas*. This dalliance in the realm of theatre technology brought him, naturally, into contact with the largely unexplored field of theatrical patents. From this point, the next step was the production of this volume.

DAVID WILMORE went to Newcastle University to study Geology and became involved with the restoration of the Tyne Theatre and Opera House, in particular its unique set of wooden stage machinery. From here he undertook a PhD at Hull University, relating to the development of nineteenth century stage machinery. During the final stages of writing it up he was called upon to restore the same machinery a second time, when a disastrous fire on Christmas Day 1985 burnt the stage house of the Tyne Theatre to the ground.

In 1986 he formed *Theatresearch* to undertake theatre consultancy and restoration projects. This has involved work at the Playhouse Theatre, London, the Gaiety Theatre, Isle of Man, and the Royal Hall, Harrogate. *Theatresearch* also undertakes research commissions for films and books and has a substantial archive of photographs, drawings, information and full patent specifications available for consultation.

JOHN EARL is a surveyor who has specialised in building conservation since 1956. He has contributed to a number of publications on theatre and music hall architecture. He was Director of the Theatres Trust from 1986 to 1995 and is now a consultant and researcher in various aspects of theatre buildings.

BRITISH
THEATRICAL
PATENTS
1801-1900

Edited by
Dr Terence Rees
and
Dr David Wilmore

The Society for Theatre Research

First published in 1996 by
The Society for Theatre Research
c/o The Theatre Museum
1E Tavistock Street
Covent Garden
London WC2E 7PA

ISBN: 0 85430 058 9

Printed and Bound in Great Britain by
Woolnough Bookbinding, Church Street,
Irthlingborough, Northants.

Foreword

Theatre is a notoriously chancy business, but there is one event which can be guaranteed to bring expectant crowds thronging through the door of any theatre at any time. It is the backstage tour.

The mystery of the theatre is in no way diminished by knowledge of how it is all done. A peep behind the curtain seems, in fact, to whet appetites for the conventions, illusions and improbabilities of the stage.

As adult theatre-goers, we may regularly suspend our disbelief but we never completely surrender our critical faculties. If we are, for a moment, deceived we are perfectly aware that there has been a deception and we are willing, indeed as eager as children, to be involved as accomplices. Maurice Gorham's book *Showmen and Suckers* (1951 - and only marginally about theatre) examined the pleasures of this paradoxical compact between performer and audience:

'It is fascinating to penetrate to the other side of the curtain, to climb to the dizzy flies at Covent Garden, watch the pantomime from the wings or the circus from the performers' entry ... but I am still in my seat early enough to enjoy the never-failing thrill of the moment when the house lights go down and the lighted curtain begins to go up.'

Words and gesture provide everything needed to make the magic work but, through the ages, mechanical devices and illusions have been pressed into the service of the stage.

Vitruvius, in the first century BC, referred to the conventional scenic device called periaktoi. His description is characteristically spare, not to say obscure, but the principle is demonstrated on hundreds of mechanical, triple-image advertising panels today. A perfectly simple apparatus, it worked on the antique stage and it works now.

Scenic illusions and tricks with sound and light burgeoned in the Renaissance. Serlio was full of ideas for making strange beasts move 'according to their manner' or for lighting scenes with burning camphor 'to show a very good light and smell well'. The tradition of trickery is still alive and, in some ways, curiously hardy. The effects which delighted 1990s audiences for *Into the Woods* were remarkably similar to those of mid-Victorian pantomimes and extravaganzas, but today we can also amaze ourselves with black light, holograms, lasers and synthesised sound, coming at us from all directions in a space which we are prepared to believe is at one moment closely confined, at another, limitless.

The nineteenth century was a wonderfully productive period. The carpentry tradition of the scenic stage had reached its final state of development (what do you do for an encore when you have created the Corsican Trap?) just as new technologies - gas, electricity, focused light, the ability to manufacture large sheets of plate glass - were opening up a range of possibilities previously undreamt of. At the same time, insistence on greater comfort and safety was leading to the development of a host of new devices to extract foul air and contain or extinguish fire.

The dense jungle of patents for this period, in which real horses galloped without moving, 'aeroplanes' (*sic* - in 1895!) flew through the air and stalls seats were tipped up for the first time, has been charted for us by Dr Rees and Dr Wilmore. The patented ideas range from the truly ingenious through the solidly serious to the plainly daft. Here are all the names you would expect to find - Maskelyne, Cinquevalli, Pepper of the famous ghost, the pantomime family of Conquest, Loie Fuller of the swirling, illuminated skirts - and many more previously uncelebrated. My very first dip into the contents produced an old friend, Defries the master gasman, and explained a device for ventilating footlights which I had observed but never fully understood at the private theatre at Normansfield.

This is, of course, a permanent reference work to be quarried by theatre historians, But I fancy it will be dipped into randomly and often by those of us who would willingly have offered a bribe at the stage door to see a Whitechapel Pavilion pantomime from the substage mezzanine - and then climbed a hundred stone steps to see it again from the Gods.

JOHN EARL

Introduction

A patent for an invention is essentially a monopoly granted by the Crown for a limited period, and the earliest known English patent was granted by Henry IV in 1449 to John of Utynam, a Fleming who was to make coloured glass for the windows of Eton College. Over the following centuries, development of the patent system was accomplished within the legislature in the form of judgements and reports for the law officers of the Crown who advised whether patent protection should be granted. This process was not controlled by statute, and it was under their administration that the practice evolved in Queen Anne's time of inserting a clause in the grant that a patent might be declared void if the inventor did not particularly describe the invention and its manner of performance in 'an instrument in writing'. In other words, the patentee was to supply a full account or specification of the invention. Since then, laws have been designed to regulate patent protection from exploitation by unauthorised parties provided it is fully described to the patenting authorities and approved by them. And, as details of all patents are made available to the public in printed form, i.e. the Specification, we have the Gilbertian situation in which inventors are obliged to disclose their secrets in order to protect them.

Over the years an enormous amount of descriptive material has been accumulating in what was formerly known as the Patent Office but is now part of the British Library. This is available to anyone wishing to consult it, though it might at first sight seem to be an unpromising source of information concerning the theatre in the nineteenth century. Every approved British Patent is there, numbered consecutively in order of receipt, irrespective of subject matter, the numbering being renewed annually. The ingenuity displayed by the inventors is staggering, though we can be certain that many of their devices never left the drawing board. There are limelights, fire-proof curtains, vanishing ladies, panoramas, trap doors and stage machinery of many kinds, magic lanterns, trick cycles, and a horse race simulated on stage with live galloping horses, together with a host of other creations, some brilliant, some absurd. Most of the physical aspects of nineteenth century theatre are touched upon at least once by the patents contained in this volume, and some of them were not without considerable influence.

The Patents

The printed descriptive material exists in three forms, each of which has its particular usefulness. The inventor begins by submitting his idea in outline only. This is the Provisional Specification, and it is considered by the patent Examiner to see if it has merit. If so, it is awarded short term protection while the inventor perfects the idea and submits a detailed account of it, with plans and drawings as necessary. This is the Complete Specification. It may include additional information describing the background to the invention together with details of previous related practice, known as 'prior art'.

It is this Complete Specification which is likely to be of greatest use to the theatre scholar, with its detailed descriptions and working drawings. Sometimes the patentee feels the need to give some account of the circumstances in which the invention will be used, and this can be a bonus to the reader where it occurs.

Finally, the patent is published in the form of an *Abridgement* which may be as brief as a single sentence or as long as a whole page with one or more reduced diagrams. These are written by the patent Examiners rather than the patentee, and their purpose is to offer sufficient detail to enable the reader to decide whether or not to consult the Complete Specification. It is the abridgements of theatrical patents that we have assembled here. The acid test for the admission of a patent to these pages is the presence of a claim by the patentee that the invention is suitable for use in the theatre or for some clearly defined theatrical purpose. By this token, patents for opera glasses are included but those for binoculars are not. The claim is usually found stated in some detail at or near the close of the Complete Specification, and it is sometimes part of a larger claim which extends to cover a wide range of possible alternative uses for the invention. In his patent with the unlikely title 'Refrigerating Apparatus for Fluids, Liquids, or Solids.' (No.3725 of 1881), H.D. Cogswell claims that it is '...applicable to the cooling of air for the supply of halls, theatres, steamships for passenger traffic, railway cars, hospital wards, and other apartments for any purposes.' We have also included one or two patents which, exceptionally, make no claim to a theatrical function, but which we know were designed for use in the theatre.

Patent applications sometimes failed to complete the course. Occasionally they were abandoned after the Provisional stage so that the only details available are the printed Provisional specification and the Abridgement of it. Perhaps the patentee has declined to pay the sealing fee once the patent had been approved. Again, interested parties might choose to oppose the patent if they felt that it infringed an invention of their own. For these and other reasons a patent could be declared void, and these, where they occur, have been omitted by us. A very high percentage of those listed weekly in *The Era* and *The Stage* during part of the period under review proved to be void, so that we wasted a deal of time in following them up, particularly as many of them are inaccurately quoted. For the purposes of patent research, these two periodicals should be regarded as very unreliable.

Much that was specifically designed for use in the theatre was never submitted for patent protection. Conversely, many patent devices which have been used widely and successfully in the theatre were never originally designed for it. A good example of this latter is the Argand lamp which was approved by the Examiners in 1784 as a superior type of oil lamp for general use. Years later it was modified for use with coal gas, but the new design was not submitted for patent protection. Thereafter it made its way into the theatre where it found widespread use as 'the patent lamp'. The only patent concerning it, therefore, is the original one, and this, not being designed for the theatre, has no place in this volume. Another example of this kind of patent is, surprisingly, the limelight. It was invented by an English army officer who intended it to be used as a signalling device, and who did not submit it for patent protection. But its subsequent adaptation for use in the theatre stimulated a host of modifications and improvements, most of which were patented and are hence included here. There was much that was new among them, but oddly enough, novelty of idea did not become a point for consideration by the Examiners until the year 1905.

The Patentees

These were drawn from all walks of life, and we have compiled a name index, stating where possible the profession of the patentee. As might be expected, there are among them theatre proprietors and managers, architects, actors, music hall entertainers, scene painters, and members of that little-known group of workers, the stage machinists. Some patentees admit to no other occupation than that of 'Gentleman', or, in a few cases, 'Spinster'.

In their Complete Specifications, some music hall players include a wealth of detail about their acts. For example, in his patent (No.1724 of 1897), Samuel Grogan, an 'artiste... at present on tour', describes his design for a quick-change costume as used in his act. More than this, he gives an account of the act itself, the nature of the dancing in it and even the number of bars of music required. In another patent (No.2432 of 1895) by Harry Stelling, also for a quick-change costume, the bonus is in the illustrations which not only show us two versions of Stelling's design but also his facial make-up. Alas, few patents contain so much additional material.

The exploitation of reflections in one or more sheets of plain glass as ghosts or visions attracted enormous attention in its day, and the original description of Pepper's Ghost is available (No.326 of 1863) in the names of Henry Dircks and John H. Pepper. This gave rise to a large number of subsequent patents which extended and developed the idea; too many to list here, but the Abridgements of all of them are included in this volume. So also is that of John Arrowsmith's original designs for the Diorama, a part of which still stands at the time of writing in Regent's Park.

As an example of stage machinery which led to a change in performance style we can cite the third of George Conquest's patents involved with the art of stage 'flying'. Conquest modestly describes his patent (No.24539 of 1899) simply as an improvement on his previous work, though it was really something quite new. It added another dimension to the range of movement available to the performer at will, in that the movement was directly under the performer's control and not in any way dependent on the operators in the wings. Flying had previously been the province of fairies and other supernaturals, or perhaps became available to mortals through the intervention of magic. This new device allowed a much greater liberty of movement so that forward and backward somersaults and other manoeuvres became possible. A capacity for the merely acrobatic was thus introduced and the consequence of this was that flying was taken up by overtly non-magical characters. We can note in passing another flying patent in the name of a stage carpenter, one George Kirby (No.8559 of 1898), whose identity is preserved to this day in the name of the well-known firm which hires flying equipment to theatres.

Most of the patents listed in these pages were devised for use in association with the English Wood Stage in an era when there was little concern for personal safety and the average life of a theatre was about seven years. It was a time when patents concerned with safety, such as emergency exits or fire-proof curtains, were few and far between. Indeed, with certain exceptions, they averaged out at about one every two years. The exceptions are easily identified as the periods following the occurrence of disastrous theatre fires and concomitant loss of life. The burning of the Vienna Ringtheater on December 8th, 1881, with a catastrophic loss of life, is a case in point. It was widely reported and caught the public imagination on an international scale. During the ensuing twelve months a total of eleven British patents were granted to inventions dedicated to safety in the theatre. A lesser disaster, but one nearer to home, was the fire at the New Theatre Royal, Exeter, on September 5th, 1887, in which 180 people were killed. Over the following year there was another surge of safety patents well in excess of the average, showing the clear influence of events upon the work of inventors.

Not all patentees with theatrical aspirations were people of the theatre. Some of them came from those disciplines in which their inventions were founded. For example, it is hardly odd to find a cabinet maker involved with the design of theatre seats (No.2022 of 1881), or an engineer concerned with safety curtains (No.14556 of 1887). But in contrast with these we also include a stage-struck hay salesman (No.6154 of 1886), a cotton broker (No.5247 of 1888), a minister of religion (No.15292 of 1890), and at least one dentist (No.1049 of 1868). These and other unlikely aspirants also lurk within our pages. Not included here are those 'inventors' and manufacturers who, from time to time, have made dishonest claims that their special product is protected by patent, and it should come as no surprise to students to find the occasional claim which is unmatched by a specification in the Patent Archive.

Some of our patents are of foreign origin, their inventors having employed the services of English patent agents to oversee their applications. Conversely, quite a number of British patents were registered abroad where they enjoyed the protection afforded by the patent legislation of that country, notably the United States of America.

The research for this book took an enormous amount of time and hard work. Yet the discovery from time to time of a patent to make an elephant turn a somersault, or a pair of opera-glasses complete with counterweights which hung behind the ears, made it all worthwhile! Research has, therefore, already begun into the twentieth century ....

The Preparation of the Patents Database

The project to research this book was conceived several years ago, when computer technology and the theatrical researcher were worlds apart. However, as the project progressively grew and grew, the card index to *British Theatrical Patents* became larger and larger, and it became apparent that the only way to complete the book was via the use of a computer database.

Consequently, the information contained within this book is still held on database, and further analysis of the information is possible by contacting the authors via The Society For Theatre Research. If you have any suggestions for alterations or believe that there are omissions, we should also be delighted to hear from you, and would ask you to complete a copy of the form printed in this book on page 190.It should however be noted that additional patents will only be admitted to the British Theatrical Patent Database if they fulfil all the criteria defined in the introduction to this book.

The Patents

1801

STEWART.
3rd Nov. 1801.

2549. A grant unto DAVID STEWART, of Woodlands, in the parish of Greenwich, in the county of Kent, gardener, for his new invented method of ventilating dwelling houses, theatres, hospitals, and other buildings ; and also of ventilating, heating, and constructing of every kind of buildings for forwarding or preserving trees, plants, shrubs, flowers, fruits, roots, and vegetables on an improv'd principle, thereby reducing the consumption of fuel, simplifying the mode of management, and rendering more certain the production of fruit and flowers ; to hold to him, his exors, admors, and assigns, within England, Wales, and the town of Berwick-upon-Tweed for the term of fourteen years pursuant to the statute ; with a clause to inroll the same within one calendar month from the date thereof. W. H. M. at Westmr, the 3d day of Novr, in the year above.   By writ, &c.

1811

STEWART.
22nd March 1811.

3417. A grant unto DAVID STEWART, of Stamford Street, in the parish of Christ Church and county of Surrey, architect, for his invented further improvement in the method of rendering dwelling houses, theatres, hospitals, prisons, shipping, conservatories, greenhouses, hothouses, and every other kind of building, air and water tight, as far as relates to the glazing, by means of a lop made of copper or any other metal, or some metal prepared by machinery for that purpose ; to hold to him, his exors, admors, and assigns, within that part of our united kingdom of Great Britain and Ireland called England, our dominion of Wales, and town of Berwick-upon-Tweed for the term of fourteen years pursuant to the statute ; with a clause to inroll the same within six calendar months from the date thereof ; and also with a clause for supplying His Majesty's service with all such articles of the said invention as shall be required by the master general of the ordnance, the commissioners of the navy, and the elder brethren of the Trinity House for the time being. By writ, &c.

1816

REDDELL.
27th May 1816.

4035. A grant unto ISAAC HADLEY REDDELL, of Orange Court, Leicester Square, in the cõy of Midx, engineer, for his invtd certain improvements in or on the means of lighting the interior of offices, theatres, buildings, houses, or any place where light may be required ; six mos.

1824

ARROWSMITH.
10th Feb. 1824.

4899. A grant unto JOHN ARROWSMITH, of Air Street, Piccadilly, in the county of Middlesex, esq., in consequence of discoveries by himself and communications made to him by certain foreigners residing abroad he is in possession of " An improved mode of publicly exhibiting pictures or painted scenery of every description, and of distributing or directing the day light upon or through them, so as to produce many beautiful effects of light and shade, which he denominates ' diorama ' "; six months.   By writ, &c.

1833

GIBBS.
4th April 1833.

6408. A grant unto JOSEPH GIBBS, of the Kent Road, in the county of Surrey, engineer, of his invention of " Improvements in the means, apparatus, and machinery for exhibiting scenery, paintings, or certain descriptions of pictures "; 6 months.   By writ, &c.

1840

STEPHENSON.
29th Feb. 1840.

8404. A grant unto ROWLAND MACDONALD STEPHENSON, of Upper Thames Street, in the city of London, civil engineer, for his invention of " An improved method or methods of adjusting, shifting, and working theatrical scenery and apparatus "; 6 months.

1846

MYERS.
COOPER.
WANSBROUGH.
31st Dec. 1846.

11,512. A grant unto GEORGE DAVID MYERS, of Bridge Row, in the city of London, engraver and printer, WILLIAM COOPER, of St. Paul's Church Yard, bonnet manufacturer, and JAMES WANSBROUGH, of Southwark Square, in the county of Surrey, hatter, for their invention of " Improvements in the manufacture of caps, bonnets, book covers, curtains, and hangings, show cards or boards, labels, theatrical decorations, and coffins "; 6 months ; colonies.

1855

SPARKHALL.
10th February 1855.

313. EDWARD SPARKHALL, of 142, Cheapside, in the City of London, Printer, for an invention for—" Improvements in the exhibition of pictorial representations of various subjects."   *Letters Patent sealed.*

1856

28. Marsden, C. Jan. 3.

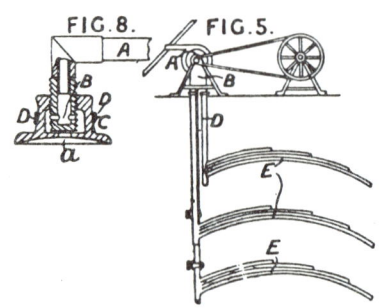

FIG.8.　FIG.5.

Air, drawing-off, methods of; forced ventilation; valves.—Theatres, churches, houses, military huts, &c. are ventilated by branch pipes E, Fig. 5, connected to main pipes D leading to a shaft B provided with a fan A driven by a weight and clockwork, or by gearing. The diameters of the branch pipes are directly proportional to their lengths. Fig. 8 shows an air-admission valve, the orifice a of which is regulated by screwing the body C of the valve along the nozzle B of the air pipe A by means of a cord D, fixed to a spring at one end and within reach of the operator at the other.

807. Abraham, H. R.　April 3.　[*Provisional protection only.*]

Tickets; railway and like tickets; season tickets; theatre and like tickets.—Tickets for checking the numbers of persons travelling on a railway &c. or entering an exhibition, or for indicating and recording the delivery of goods, are made of pieces of pasteboard, card, &c., subdivided by lines, marks, designs, or colours into compartments, one of which is defaced or punched each time a ticket is used. The fares, routes, periods, class, &c. may be indicated by colours or designs on the parts of the tickets.

2751. Brooman, R. A., [*Boulard, —*]. Nov. 20.

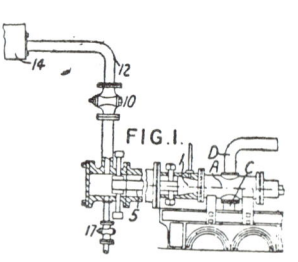

FIG.I.

Fireproof compositions.—Relates to the preparation of soluble glass, and to its use, with or without the addition of colours or other materials, for rendering wood, paper pulp, fabrics, &c., fireproof. A mixture of about 20 lb. of sodium carbonate, 30 lb. of pure white sand, and 2 lb. of charcoal is fused in a furnace, the product is reduced to powder, dissolved in water, boiled down, filtered, and is then ready for use. Fig. 1 shows apparatus for impregnating pieces of timber 1 with the solution. The receiver 5 is exhausted by a pump A provided with a suction valve C, pressure gauges, and an escape pipe D, and the exhaustion is aided by superheated steam admitted through a pipe 17. The solution is then run into the receiver from a reservoir 14 through a pipe 12 fitted with a stop cock 10, and enters the pores of the wood. For external application to wood, paper, fabrics, theatrical decorations, furniture, &c., the solution is boiled down to the required density and boiled with pigments or colouring-matter, such as zinc white, verdigris, ochres, sodium phosphate, barium sulphate, manganese borate, salts of copper or iron, or a composition described in Specification No. 1271, A.D. 1854. The composition is applied like ordinary paint, or it may be deposited by means of a galvanic battery. A salt of magnesium may be used instead of sodium carbonate. A suitable size for application to the surface before the composition consists of 4 lb. of flour, 4 lb. of carbonate of lime, and 2 gallons of water.

1857

478. Moule, J. Feb. 18.

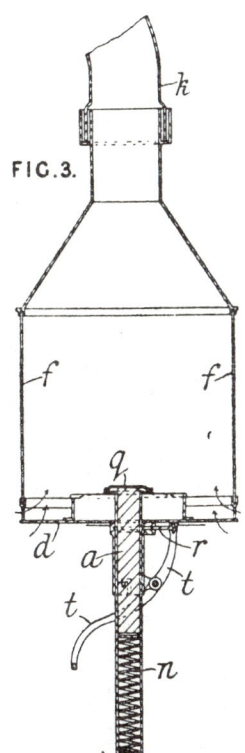

FIG.3.

Pyrotechnics. — Relates to coloured fires, and consists in burning the composition *a* in a lantern, which is provided with glass sides *f* and a chimney *k* to carry off the fumes. Air is admitted through perforations in the base *d*. The composition *a* may be carried in a bed of sand, or, as shown, it may be carried like a candle in a candle lamp, and be forced upward against the wire *q* by a spring *n*. With this arrangement a cut-off slide *r*, operated by a lever *t*, is employed.

1060. Newton, W. E., [a communication]. April 14.

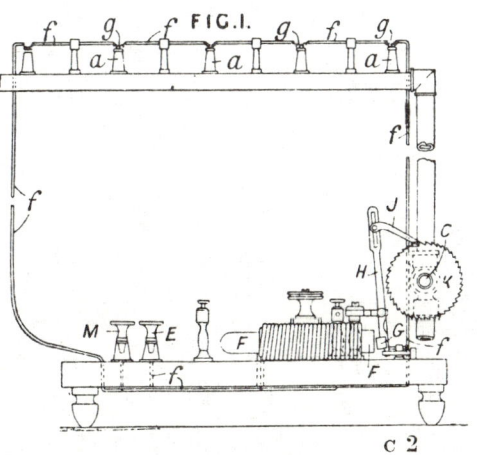

Lighting and extinguishing gas. —Relates to electrical apparatus for actuating gas cocks and for lighting series of burners or burners placed in inaccessible positions, and to means for re-igniting burners which have been accidentally extinguished. The gas cock C is actuated by means of a key M and an electro-magnet F, which attracts an armature G on the spring-controlled lever H of a pawl and ratchet J, K on the cock. A second key E serves to send the current through a conductor *f* and render incandescent coiled wires *g* arranged in proximity to the burners *a*, to which gas has been previously supplied by the cock C. After the ignition of the gas, the flames keep the coils *g* sufficiently heated to re-ignite the gas in the event of the flames being accidentally extinguished. Similarly, platinum re-igniting coils *g*, Fig. 3, may be mounted upon burners to which the electrical igniting-apparatus is not fitted.

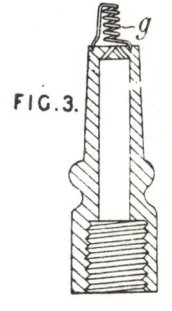

FIG.3.

1400. Vasserot, C. F., [*Trouillet, A.*]. May 19. *Drawings to Specification.*

Theatre and like tickets.—A special hand stamp may be used for making counter marks for theatres or otherwise.

2229. Steell, G., and **Steell, W.** Aug. 22.

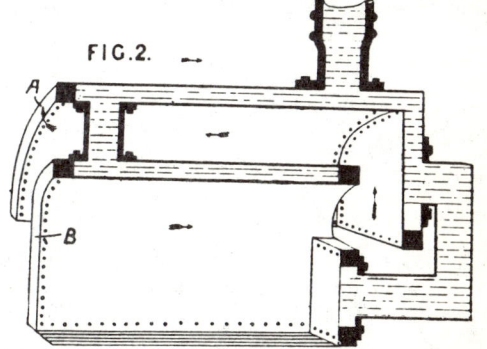

FIG.2.

Heating water. — Water for heating churches, horticultural buildings, mansions, and theatres is heated in a boiler having two arched water chambers A, B, connected together at both ends by flanged pipes of the form shown. The inlet and outlet pipes are connected to the bottom of the inner chamber and the top of the outer chamber. There may be three water chambers and the boiler may be round or square.

1858

2170. Luis, J., [a communication]. Sept. 29.
[*Provisional protection only.*]

Wall and ceiling coverings ; churches ; theatres.—
Relates to a method of "fixing" pastel pictures,
which may also be applied to paperhangings for
rooms and decorations of churches and theatres.

The picture, which is preferably prepared on
printing paper, is laid face upwards on a layer of
almost liquid potassium or sodium silicate, and
when well saturated is placed on a paper to dry,
any spare liquid having been run off. The operation may be repeated until the picture is "fixed."

1859

2334. Prosser, W.   Oct. 13.

Limelight appa-
ratus ; lighting large
areas, systems of.—
According to this
improvement on the
invention described in
Specification No. 2087,
A.D. 1858, the lime or
its equivalent is held
in a frame or case,
which not only enables
several pieces of lime
to be held together
and moved as one
piece, but also pre-
vents parts of the
lime from breaking
away should the lime
become fractured by
heat or otherwise.
The frame comprises
a holder or cart-
ridge B in which the
pieces A of lime are
secured by overlapp-

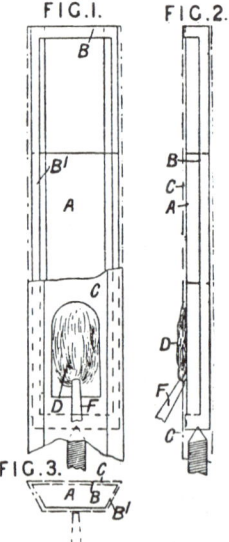

ing edges B¹, and an outer case C formed
with apertures D, which correspond in number,
position, and size with the oxyhydrogen or other
jets F. The displacement of the lime may be
further prevented by placing platinum or other
refractory wires or bands across the apertures D.
The movement of the lime cartridge B may be
effected by attaching it either to a piston working
in a cylinder or to the top of a collapsable
chamber from which liquid, sand, or like material
is allowed to escape under the control of a stop-
cock or through an aperture of definite size. The
cartridge may, however, be actuated by clockwork or by a motor driven by a stream of the gas
which supplies the jet. In the latter case, one of
the gases employed in the jet is passed
alternately through two flexible or other
chambers, which, by means of connecting rods,
impart rotary motion to a crank, from which a
vertical screw carrying the cartridge may be
driven by gearing. In lamps for lighting large
areas in which a number of jets are arranged

around the lime, the jets, instead of being
supplied by separate pipes, are fed from a double
annular chamber, the gas supply to the jets being
controlled by screw valves so connected that they
can be actuated by a single handle. Pieces of
lime of the shape required may be manufactured
by moulding waste and dust which have been
reduced to a uniform state of powder.

2564. Brooman, R. A., [*Demangeot & Co.*].
Nov. 11.

Fireproof compositions. — Fabrics, filamentous
materials, pulp, wood, oil, &c., are rendered non-
inflammable by the application of a substance
obtained by the treatment of ammonium sulphate
in a specified manner. To purify the ammonium
sulphate and combine it with other re-agents, it
is heated in a reverberatory furnace until all the
organic matters are destroyed and sulphuretted
hydrogen is evolved. The cooled mass is next
boiled with specified proportions of calcium
chloride and lime acetate, to obtain a crystalline
deposit. The crystals are heated in a furnace to
a dull red heat, and the compound, when cooled,
is adapted for use in rendering matters non-inflammable. In preparing a non-inflammable starch for
application to muslins, linens, &c., the prepared
salt or compound is dissolved and added with
ammonia to the starch, the whole being treated in
a specified manner. Fabrics, such as those for
theatrical decorations, may be rendered non-
inflammable by coating the back of the material
with size and Meudon white, and, when dry, coating
with non-inflammable starch dissolved in baryta.
In rendering oils, such as linseed, non-inflammable,
hydrated protoxide of manganese is added to the
oil and heated, and when afterwards cooled the
prepared salt is added, and a current of electricity
is passed through the mixture until the salt is
dissolved. In treating tar, a soap solution having
a soda base is prepared, and this being added to
the prepared salt and tar, the mixture is heated
and the supernatant liquid removed. In rendering
filamentous materials non-inflammable, the prepared salt is dissolved in water containing
ammonium sulphate, and to this is added a
solution of carbonate of lime, the solution thus
prepared being adapted for treating the fibres.

1860

187.   Ramspacher, T., and Schmidt, C. F. Jan. 25.

Backing leather.—Metallic gauze, in the form of ordinary wire gauze, gauze without weft, gauze with meshes partly filled with metal, or with metallic warp and weft of vegetable or animal threads, has its meshes more or less filled in, by dipping in metal, or by electrodeposition. It is then covered with india-rubber, gutta-percha, marine glue, linseed oil, fish glue, resins or tar by dipping in a solution or in the molten substance. A backing of leather or india-rubber is then attached by means of rollers. These fabrics are used for making straps or bands, cuirasses, soles of boots and shoes, shakos, helmets, furniture, carpets, roofs, shutters, camp and other bedsteads, girths, hammocks, pipes, cables, screens, vases, tents, reins, traces, gutters, straps for guns, sacks, belts, epaulettes, drapery and decorations for theatres, fire-buckets, washers for steam engines, and beds.

1318.   Dufossé, E. May 29.

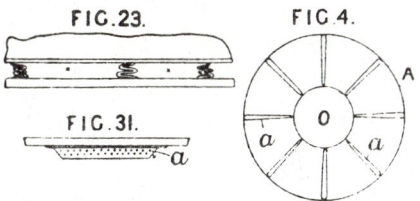

FIG. 23.   FIG. 4.

FIG. 31.

Seats and stools; chairs; sofas; furniture frames; mattresses; hammocks; cushions.—Seats and cushions for stools, chairs, sofas, divans, benches, footstools, and other furniture for theatres concert-rooms, ships, hospitals &c., and also mattresses, hammocks, and upholstery, are constructed on a framework having horizontal channels, for air currents. In one arrangement, the air channels are situated between two wooden boards A which may have a central aperture O. These boards are kept apart by cross-pieces *a*, and one or both sides of the framework may be upholstered with horsehair or other stuffing, or with leather, cloth, or other fabric, and may be fitted with springs. In a modification, the lower board is dispensed with. A second form of framework comprises two concentric double hoops, of iron or iron wire, steel, brass, or copper, secured together by radial pieces. This framework is fitted with springs, which are covered with cloth, and the whole is upholstered with horsehair, and cloth, or leather. If desired, the framework may be made of india-rubber, india-rubber cloth, or other material which will enable the framework to assume a bag-like shape and be airtight; the air channels may be formed as tubular rails. These various arrangements may be adapted to movable or fixed seats. In the case of fixed seats, springs or half springs may be used instead of partitions, as shown in Fig. 23. In a third form of framework, receptacles are substituted for the lower board as shown in Fig. 31; both framework and receptacles are made of wood, iron, perforated tin plate, zinc, wire gauze, matting, twine, netting, fabrics, or other suitable material. Mattresses, especially those for the sick, are fitted with frames having air channels formed therein; the central part of the mattress is provided with a tube or receptacle to serve as a sanitary convenience. The parts of the mattress to which the tube is adapted, may be protected by oilcloth.

1448.   Spence, W., [*Vanderburgh, G. E.*]. June 13. *Drawings to Specification.*

Fireproof compositions.—Consists in using a fluid silicate, obtained by the action of super-heated steam and an alkali, such as soda or potash, upon a silicious substance like sand, for fireproofing planks, boards, timber, articles of wood, theatrical scenery, the canvas of which is soaked in the fluid and then painted with a silicated paint, and as a substitute for size and starch in the manufacture of fireproof roofing.

2080.   Chandler, H., and Hempson, A. Aug. 29. [*Provisional protection only.*]

Seats.—For the purpose of facilitating the passage of spectators between the rows of seats in the pits of theatres or in other places where long rows of benches are used, the seats are supported by cast metal standards which "project at less than half the projection of the "seats." The standards are high enough to carry a back rail. About sixteen inches from the floor a hole is left in each standard, and attached to the underside of each seat are two bolt holders. A rod passes through all the standards and bolt holders, securing the whole in position, or each seat may be secured separately. When the occupants of the seats are required to make way, the seats are raised, and the occupiers of the seats can then stand close to the projecting parts of the standards.

1861

927. Gye, F. April 15.

Oxyhydrogen and like lamps.—The lime is in the form of a disc or plate a carried in a two-part holder c, d secured to a rotating shaft b, which is mounted on a bar traversed by a screw n on a shaft f^1, so that a new surface of lime is constantly presented to the jet. The shaft f^1 forms the upper detachable part of a two-part shaft driven by clockwork, not shown, so that a duplicate carrier apparatus can be substituted when the lime is spent. The shaft b is driven from the shaft f^1 through a face wheel j and a long pinion on an intermediate shaft geared to a toothed wheel i. A more uniform surface speed of the lime with respect to the jet is obtained by the addition of two cones and an endless band in the gearing.

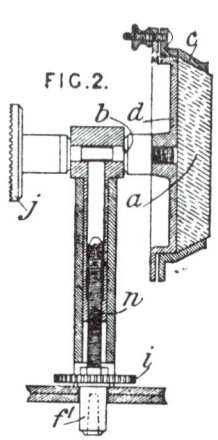

FIG.2.

1711. Pradou, J. E. M. de, and **Lecoq, L. G.** July 5.

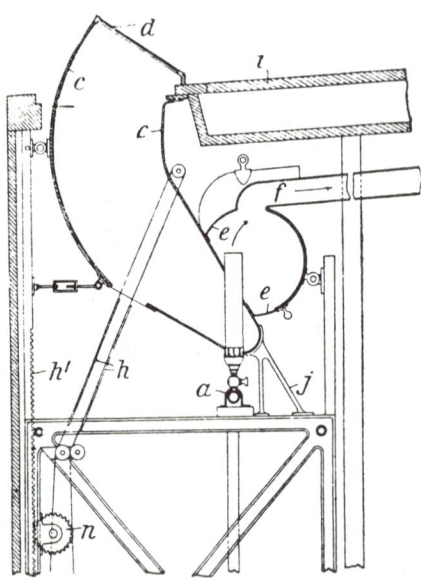

Reflectors; lamp shades; footlights. — Gas-burners employed for lighting the stage and ceiling of a theatre, and for other buildings, are mounted on a pipe a and contained in a reflector c which throws the rays on to a glass surface d. The reflector is held by a support j, and may be moved by a rack and pinion n, h^1, so as to adjust the inclination of the glass with respect to the stage i. A reservoir e receives the combustion products which escape through a pipe f. Screens or shades h may be used to vary the colour of the light.

1784. Clark, W., [*Foucault, T.*]. July 15.

Theatrical appliances.— The back scenery is on a smaller scale, in perspective, and the sky is represented on a spheroidal surface g, h, Fig. 5. Fig. 7 shows a vertical section of the stage parallel to the curtain. Movable platforms or floor sections D can be raised and lowered in frames F, which are mounted on rollers carried by oscillating rods, and can be lowered out of sight on a lift M operated by ropes from a drum O provided with counterbalance weights. The

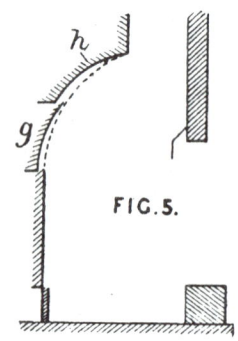

FIG.5.

FIG.7.

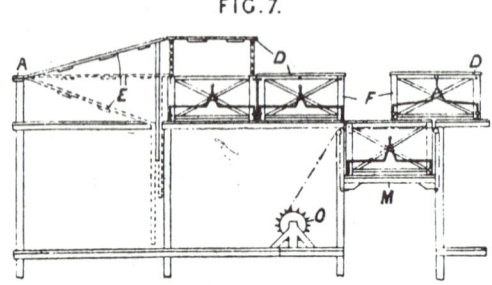

movable stage frames F are connected together by hooks, and hinged bridges E lead from the sides A on to the stage.

2083. Clark, W., [*Douhe, W. F. Count de*]. Aug. 21.

Lenses; reflectors; globes; lighthouse lamps.— Lenses are made hollow and filled with a liquid. An ordinary lantern is "divided into chambers "by means of circular concentric glasses diverging "the one from the other towards the upper part." The chambers are filled with water to effect the dispersion of the light. The lantern, which may be used as a lighthouse lantern, may be polyhedral in shape and be fitted with a reflector, having an equal number of faces. For the electric light, a liquid of an orange tint is employed. By the use of various coloured liquids, decorative effects for public illuminations can be obtained.

2500. Callcott, W. Oct. 7.

Theatres; exhibitions, scenic and spectacular.—Relates to apparatus which produces the effect of water in motion &c. Straight or bent pieces of glass A are supported by a frame

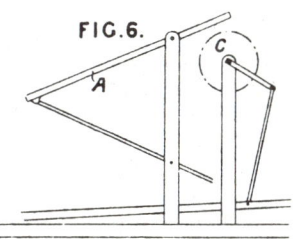

FIG.6.

in front of rollers C. The glass, which is painted or distempered, is adjusted by levers. The rollers are of metal, wood, or glass, the outer face being spiralled or painted. Light is thrown between the two and effects are produced by rotating the rollers. Several sets may be employed, one behind the other, in graduated heights on the stage, and they may be on the stage or above it, or may be worked from below. The glass surface may be covered with gauze and figures introduced into the lighted space to add to the effects.

1862

980. Duncan, C. S. April 7.

Cooling buildings.—Pipes are carried from the water main to the roof of a church, warehouse, theatre or other building, and the water is distributed by means of a horizontal pipe running along the highest point of the roof. This pipe has perforations in its upper side, with an inverted V-shaped trough above it. One or more sets of diffusing-pipes may be taken into the rooms.

1863

31. Keeling, E. B. Jan. 5.

Lighting buildings &c., systems of; lamp shades.—Theatres, halls, and other buildings &c. are illuminated with diffused light by placing a white or coloured screen or curtain of oiled silk or other material, with or without a supplementary glass or other transparent screen, beneath or before an electric, lime, or other intense light arranged in the ceiling or upper part of the building &c.

264. Louit, J. B. E. Jan. 29. *Drawings to Specification.* [*Provisional protection only.*]

Chimneys.—To preserve theatre and other ceilings &c. from heat and smoke, the top of a lamp chimney is made dome-shaped, or is otherwise closed, and openings, for the escape of hot air, are made under the dome, or in the sides of the chimney.

326. Dircks, H., and Pepper, J. H. Feb. 5.

Optical illusions, producing.— A stage phantom or "Pepper's ghost" is produced by an inclined transparent glass plate *f*, which reflects an image of a performer, who stands on a stage or support *b* below the stage *a*, and is strongly illuminated by electric or lime light from lanterns *c*. A sloping screen *k*, arranged at the back of the performer parallel to the plate *f*, is covered with black velvet or other light-absorbing material, and the stage is covered with green baize or dark material. The light from the lanterns can be cut off gradually or instantly by a board *b¹*, or opaque lantern shades, or by cutting

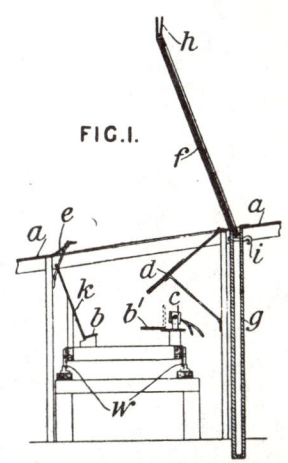

FIG.I.

off the gas or light. The trap door is constructed of hinged sections *d*, which screen the lantern from the audience and the stage when turned into the position shown. The apparatus may be mounted on wheels *w*, and the lanterns are adjustable to follow the movement of the performer on the support *b*. The glass plate is secured in a frame concealed by scenery, and can be raised and lowered by a rope *h* in a box *g* during the performance, and supported by bolts *i*. The proper angle of inclination of the glass plate is ascertained experimentally. The support *b* may be provided with a well or hole through which the actor can rise to produce the appearance of a spectre rising out of the stage *a*. The lanterns may be provided with coloured glasses, and several sheet-glass reflectors may be used on the stage.

351. Hackforth, M. Feb. 7.

Lamp shades ; reflectors.—Shades and reflectors for lamps used in offices, shops, railway carriages, theatres, and other places, or for chandeliers or table lamps, are made of porcelain or china. The shades may be plain or ornamental, and may be held by an internal support of metal, or an external clip, or by any ordinary means.

449. Puntis, J., and Cox, G. Feb. 18.

Gas burners.—In an arrangement for illuminating public gardens, houses, buildings, and other structures, and for displaying designs, mottoes, and announcements, gas is admitted to an air-tight metal chamber A, the walls of which are perforated in any desired manner. The gas passes through the perforations, and is ignited on the outside of the chamber. The design on the outside is painted in japan or distemper colours or

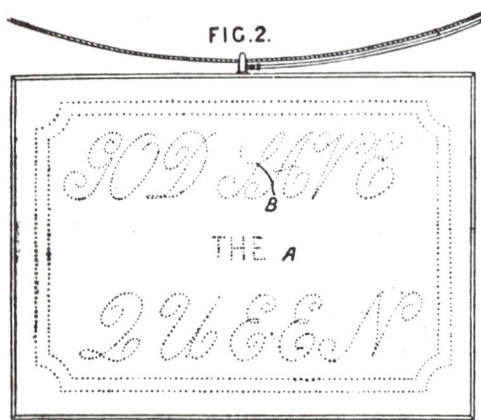

FIG. 2.

is otherwise ornamented. The gas may be supplied through a flexible or rigid pipe.

894. Heath, T. T. April 9. [*Provisional protection only.*]

Ceilings ; roofs ; galleries ; ceiling coverings ; partitions ; theatres.—Ceilings, the under surfaces of roofs and galleries, cabin and similar ceilings, and the lower parts of partitions, theatre

scenes, &c. are made wholly or partially of glass, which is preferably silvered, and may be transparent, opaque figured, or coloured.

1630. Silvester, A. June 30.

Optical illusions, producing.—In order to produce an erect image on the stage and allow the actors to move about freely on the lower stage in an upright position in phantom or "Pepper's "ghost" performances of the kind described in Specification No. 326, A.D. 1863, a silvered glass mirror is arranged below the stage parallel to the inclined transparent glass plate reflector above the stage. Images of scenes, plants, &c. may also be produced by magic-lantern or optical apparatus, and electrical effects as well as pyrotechnic objects may be reflected from below.

1744. King, H. N. July 13. [*Provisional protection only.*]

Optical illusions, producing.—Spectral illusions are produced by persons standing on the floor of an opening in the stage, so that a mirror, resting on the floor, with its upper edge against the front edge of the opening, throws their images onto a sheet of plate glass inclining forward at 45°, parallel to the mirror, with its lower edge against the back edge of the opening. The persons should be strongly illuminated against a dark background.

1917. Munro, J. Aug. 3. [*Provisional protection only.*]

Optical illusions, producing. — Relates to accessory apparatus for illusions of the Pepper's ghost type, and consists in (1) interposing tinting glass and stops or screens between the lantern and the "ghost" to be illuminated ; (2) illuminating different parts independently ; (3) mounting the lantern upon a carriage ; (4) surrounding the "ghost" with screens with adjustable openings ; (5) using a pivoted and movable reflector ; (6) covering the reflector with coloured glass ; (7) using two or more mirrors in series ; (8) supporting the ghost in an inclined position on a wheeled carriage ; (9) placing the "ghost" on one side of the stage and tilting the reflector to suit ; (10) auxiliary apparatus for ensuring simultaneous action between the movements of the ghost and the actor on the stage ; and (11) various arrangements to avoid the difficulties attending the superposition of images upon real objects on the stage.

1998. Dennett, C. C. Aug. 13.

Ceilings ; floors ; arches and domes ; foundations ; roofs ; partitions ; vaults and cellars ; bridges and aqueducts ; fireproof concrete buildings ; theatres ; churches &c. — Buildings and parts of buildings are constructed of concrete, composed of

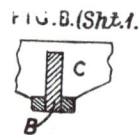

FIG. B. (Sht. 1.

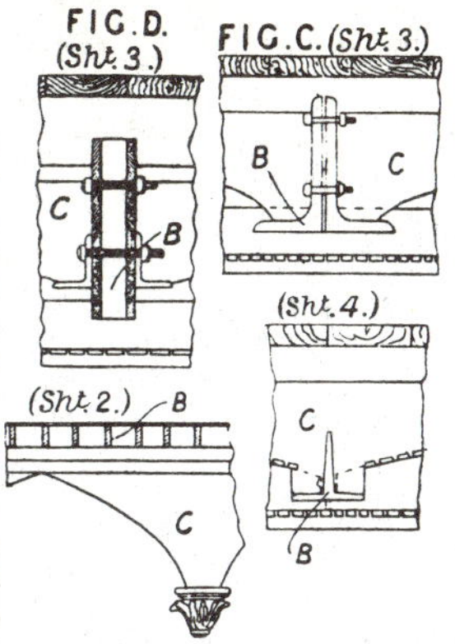

FIG.D.
(Sht 3.)

FIG.C.(Sht 3.)

(Sht.4.)

(Sht 2.)

sulphate or carbonate of lime, broken calcined cinders, bricks, or other porous material, combined with wood or iron beams. The Figures show various applications, the concrete being marked C, and the iron or woodwork B. Ventilating-pipes may be inserted in the arches, or flues may be formed in the concrete.

2019. Hoffman, J. W. Aug. 15. [Provisional protection only.]

Optical illusions, producing.—Relates to reflecting-apparatus of the Pepper's ghost type for producing optical illusions on a stage. Water, rain, hail, snow, fire, and like effects are produced by a glass reflector on the stage, and an inclined mirror out of sight of the audience. Lightning is shown, either with or without a glass on the stage, by a lamp with two superposed caps, an inner fixed one having a forked diametral slit and an outer rotary one with a short straight radial slit. Images of persons or objects are made to follow real persons or objects on the stage, by means of platforms or "traps" connected together and worked by bands and pulleys. A person or object is made to dissolve or fade away by interposing gauze curtains. Scenic effects may be painted on velvet, gauze, or other curtains.

2841. Hughes, De B. Nov. 14. [Provisional protection only.]

Illusions, producing.—Dramatic or like effects reproduced on a stage or in a room by casting shadows or reflecting objects in such a manner that the shadow or reflection is parallel to the object. In one method, the shadow of an object in one of the wings of a stage is thrown by lime-light on a vertical clear glass screen placed obliquely across the stage, the light rays being subdued, while introducing or withdrawing the shadow, by smoked or coloured glasses, or other semi-opaque substance.

3209. Bolton, C. Dec. 19.

Theatrical appliances ; exhibitions, scenic and spectacular.—One form of apparatus for producing ghost illusions comprises a vertical plain glass sheet arranged obliquely across the stage or platform for reflecting the image of actors or objects contained in a portable internally-blackened floorless chamber or an internally-blackened room at the side of the stage. The actors &c. are illuminated by gas lights and reflectors arranged behind glass sheets in the front corners of the chamber, or otherwise screened from the reflector on the stage. In a modification, the chamber is arranged above the stage behind a curtain or drop scene, and the image is reflected by a mirror to an inclined clear glass plate on the stage.

3272. Smith, E. T. Dec. 26. [Provisional protection only.]

Theatrical appliances.—To produce the effect of flowing water and of moving figures on the stage, water is caused to flow over sheets of plate glass arranged in a frame at an angle of 45°, rising and falling figures being placed behind the glass.

3015. Clark, W., [Subra, B.]. Dec. 1.

Heating buildings.—Relates to means in combination with inverted or downwardly-inclined gas lamps, candles, and other lights for siphoning off the products of combustion and thereby maintaining the air supply for combustion and ventilating the room, and applicable to gas or other heating-apparatus. A means in combination with gas burners and applicable on a theatre stage is shown. The burners D are placed at the top of glass chimneys A secured in sockets on a horizontal pipe B, which is connected to a long vertical pipe C. The parts A, B, C constitute an inverted siphon. The pipe C is provided with a valve H and with an auxiliary burner I for starting the draught. In the part B, "any furnace may be "applied, which would possess the advantage of "being placed below the burner or burners, and

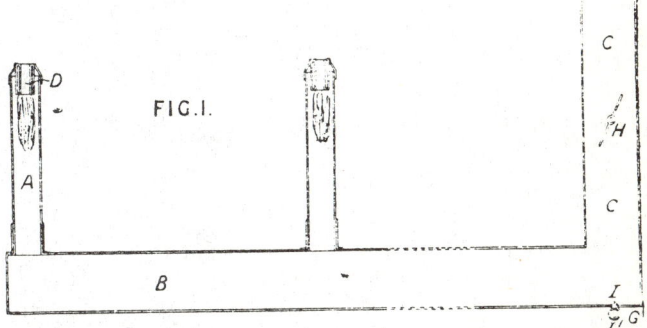

FIG.I.

"thereby heated and lighted at the same time." In heating stoves, the burners are placed in the chimneys, in order to afford light, the products of combustion circulating in tubes for heating purposes.

1864

22. Defries, C. Jan. 4. [*Provisional protection only.*]

Footlights.—The products of combustion from footlights are carried off by means of a dome passing along the entire length of the row and connected by an iron pipe passing beneath the stage to a flue in which a draught is created by a gas burner. Series of coloured glass shades are arranged so that any set can be moved at will, in front of the footlights.

41. Weston, J. H., and **Morton, C.** Jan. 6. [*Provisional protection only.*]

Optical illusions, producing.—The glass reflecting-screen of the phantom-producing apparatus described in Specification No. 326, A.D. 1863, is made adjustable in inclination by supporting it at the top or bottom and connecting the free edge by rope to a winch. By these means, the image may be caused to rise gradually from a fountain &c. on the stage.

498. Pepper, J. H. Feb. 29. [*Provisional protection only.*]

Theatrical appliances.—Relates to the system of producing on one stage spectral and other images of actors and objects on a lower stage, by means of an inclined unsilvered glass. A convex or concave mirror is used to increase or diminish the size of the image.

826. Callcott, W. April 2. *Drawings to Specification.*

Conjuring-apparatus; optical illusions, producing; panoramas.—To produce illusions, such as the ghost effects, sheets of glass are used, painted in transparent colours and having a transparent backing, of white linen or cotton. The glass is sometimes covered in front with painted Italian net or other network, and the lime light may shine through graduated coloured glass so that the figure appears coloured. The apparatus is used in dioramas.

1179. Silvester, A. May 10. [*Provisional protection only.*]

Theatrical appliances. — In connection with Pepper's ghost reflecting-apparatus, an artiste is mounted on a pedestal in the middle of a fountain in a compartment in the ceiling or below the stage, and may be raised and lowered by a rope passing over a drum or pulley.

1643. Defries, C. July 1. [*Provisional protection only.*]

Theatres.—Coloured plates of glass or the like are arranged below the footlights, so that any one of them can be brought between the lights and the stage.

2393. Defries, C. Sept. 29. [*Provisional protection only.*]

Lighting buildings, theatres, &c., systems of.— In a method of lighting and ventilating buildings, theatres, and music halls, the ceiling is divided into a number of compartments by joists. Some of the spaces are filled by panes of glass, some by movable glass prisms, and some by cut-glass lustres, arranged in openwork form. The heated and foul air from the building may thus pass through the interstices of the ceiling. Above the ceiling a series of sun or other gas lights are arranged under funnel-shaped reflectors, which are provided with pipes leading into other and converging pipes which finally enter a horizontal cylinder or cylinders leading to the open air. The exits from the cylinders are provided with cowls or other similar contrivances. The prisms and lustres may be replaced by perforated glass or slips of glass or other transparent material.

2564. Maurice, J. Oct. 17.

Optical illusions, producing.—Relates to the Pepper's ghost type of illusion. A real actor or object on a stage or platform is apparently caused to vanish, or to be replaced by other actors or objects, by reflecting an image of a duplicate stage, hidden from the house, the effects being determined by the relative illumination of the two stages. The duplicate scene is preferably an exact copy of the real stage background and floor; but that portion only behind the object to be hidden need be reflected, so that small reflectors may be used. The image may be continually in view, if the stage background is coloured so as to be easily hidden, and effects, such as an actor vanishing through a solid wall, may be obtained. Also, sham acrobatic performances may be given by hiding a supporting-platform. The Provisional Specification also mentions that a scene, curtain, blind, &c. may be drawn in front of the actor or object.

1865

131. Edwin, W. Jan. 16. [*Provisional protection only.*]

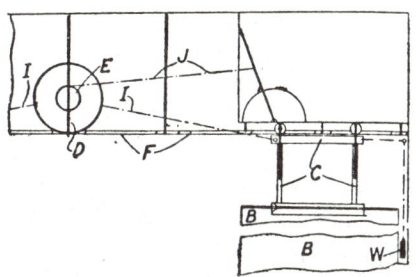

Theatrical appliances.—Stage scenery B in halves, of which one is shown, is fixed to "grooves" C, which run on parallel wooden rails F in the flys. The halves of the scene are drawn together by a lever which, by unwinding the rope J, rotates the small and large drums E, D, fixed together and mounted between the rails, thus winding up the ropes I. The scenes, when brought together, are held by a small wheel on the bottom of each engaging with a slot in the centre of the stage floor, and, when released, are drawn back by weights W. The wings may be worked in a similar way, a long roller enabling a number to be moved together. A windlass in the flys may replace the double drum.

222. Pepper, J. H., and **Tobin, T. W.** Jan. 26.

FIG. 3.

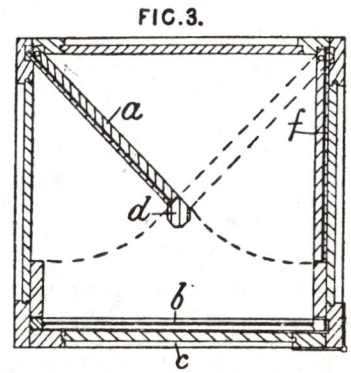

Exhibitions, scenic and spectacular.—A rectangular box for containing subjects for representation and illusory exhibition is shown in horizontal section in Fig. 3. Doors *a*, having mirrors *f* fitted to them, swing from angles of the box, and are capable of either closing on a centre post *d* or lying back in recesses in the sides. An internal door *b* of thick plate glass is covered by an external door *c*. A fresco or design is placed at the upper part of the box and a lamp is hung at the top of the post *d* for lighting and ventilation.

1983. Tobin, T. W., and **Stodare, —.** Aug. 1. [*Provisional protection only.*]

Illusions, producing.—Mirrors are placed under a table or slab at such angles as to reflect images of surrounding scenery or objects, and at the same time serve to conceal persons or objects controlled by a conjurer.

2815. Solomons, S. Nov. 1.

Magic - lantern apparatus. — Magic - lantern, phantasmagoria, and like transparent slides are produced by chromolithography, using transparent colours instead of the ordinary colours. An impression is taken upon a sheet of gelatine or other transparent material, which is afterwards mounted upon or between sheets of glass in a frame; or, an impression is transferred to glass and varnished.

3139. Pepper, J. H., and **Tobin, T. W.** Dec. 6. [*Provisional protection only.*]

Exhibitions, scenic and spectacular.—In the production of illusions, a mirror, large enough to fill the chamber and inclined from front to back, is used, a hole being formed in the glass through which an object may protrude. A second apparatus consists of a box glazed on all four sides and divided diagonally by two mirrors placed back to back and surrounded by curtains so as to appear transparent. Articles may be introduced at one side of the box, and, while temporarily covered, the whole may be revolved so as to appear empty on uncovering. Holes may be made in the mirrors as described above.

3286. Kerr, W. Dec. 20. [*Provisional protection only.*]

Exhibitions, scenic and spectacular. — The strongly-illuminated head of a person is projected upon a semi-transparent screen on a stage, by means of a silvered glass or metallic reflector and a case containing two achromatic lenses.

1866

184. Tanner, G., and **Parkes, G.** Jan. 20.

Theatrical appliances; exhibitions, scenic and spectacular.—An imitation fall of water is produced by vibrating or revolving cylindrical or rectangular frameworks of bright coloured or ornamented wires D, Fig. 3, in a powerful light. The rectangular frames may have a roller at the bottom, so that they can be raised or lowered. Sometimes the wires are arranged in a series of endless bands, and an endless band of canvas, coloured to represent water, revolved below them.

FIG. 3.

442. Stoddart, A. Feb. 13. [*Provisional protection only.*]

Conjuring-apparatus. — A vertical mirror is arranged behind the front legs of a conjuring table, to reflect drapery &c., and the table top is fitted with hinged flaps, through which articles or persons may disappear through a box and a trap door in the stage.

689. Stoddart, A. March 7. [*Provisional protection only.*]

Theatrical appliances.—A column or suspending or supporting bar for supporting a performer above the stage is rendered invisible, to produce the illusory effect of a performer floating in mid air, by means of mirrors set at an angle to one another and the spectators.

1491. Hall, J. May 29.

Targets; theatrical appliances. — An elastic facing secured to a frame is provided with holes or slots, preferably forming together a cruciform shape, and each communicating with a shell at the rear. A ball or other projected object is seized by the elastic facing, or passes completely through. The frame is applicable for theatrical purposes, and may be of any shape. The back may be fixed or movable.

2318. Vinant, W., and **Westcott, G. R.** Sept. 10. [*Provisional protection only.*]

Lighting gas.—Theatrical float lights are lit by lamps arranged to run on rails, or wires, or in slotted tubes, or the lamps may be carried by endless bands.

2301. Defries, C. Sept. 7.

Footlights; reflectors.—Relates to a footlight arrangement for theatres &c. stated to be a "float light." A series of gas burners *f* is arranged along a supply pipe R and in front of a concave reflecting face of a hollow chamber or flue *a* which forms part of an iron framing A. A second flue *a*[1] may also be connected with the flue *a*, and, by means of a reducing piece, with a flue communicating with the open air; a gas burner may be used primarily to create a draught. Combustion products escape through slits *j* formed in the reflector *i*. The frame is preferably made in sections and extends across the width of the stage, the front of which slopes down to the level of the flue. The top of each section is covered by a plate *e*, a space being left between the plate and the top of the frame. This space may be filled with sand or other non-conducting material, or holes *e*[1], *e*[11] may be formed in the plate and frame respectively to allow a current of cold air to pass as indicated. Each burner tap *g* is placed near the supply pipe so that the lights may be adjusted from beneath the stage. In the front of the frame is a sash *b* to receive sheets of glass; through the open bottom *h* of the sash the burners may be supplied with oxygen. The sections are partly supported by brackets D. which carry, at their lower ends, bearings *m* to receive a shaft E. At each section the shaft is provided with a grooved roller, over which passes an endless chain *o* carried by a pulley P at the top of the frame. Coloured glass media *r*, *r*[1] are carried by tubes *q* attached to the chain, and may be raised or lowered as desired. The coloured media may also ride in grooved uprights and be raised or lowered by separate cords. The cords or chains may be actuated from the prompter's box.

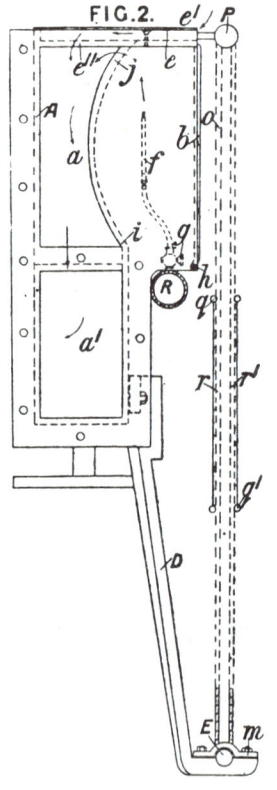
FIG. 2.

2755. Brooman, C. E., [*Bourrieff, J. B. M. A.*]. Oct. 25. [*Provisional protection only.*]

Heating buildings &c.—The products of combustion from hexagonal lanterns, shaped as pyramids at their upper and lower ends, are carried off by a pipe, which, in theatres, may be enclosed in a box and utilized for warming the feet of the audience. When gas is the illuminant, the supply pipe may be arranged within the ventilating pipe, and, in summer, the heat of the ventilating pipe may be neutralized by circulating cool air, by means of fans, through the enclosing box.

3110. Harrison, W. H. Nov. 26. [*Provisional protection only.*]

Theatrical appliances; exhibitions, scenic &c.—In a method of producing optical illusions, the dresses and persons of actors, and lay figures and scenery, are covered with quinine sulphate, uranium glass, aesculin, or other chemical, which appears fluorescent when exposed to violet rays of light.

3278. Pepper, J. H., and **Pichler, S. F.** Dec. 13. [*Provisional protection only.*]

Acrobats, toys imitating; skating toys; walking toys; magnetic toys; cords, suspended, toys travelling on.—To imitate performers on the trapeze, an automatic jointed figure is caused to grip the bar of the trapeze with its hands. The ropes are connected together at their upper ends so that they can be rocked simultaneously, and a light shaft passed down inside one of them; bevel pinions are placed at the top and bottom of this shaft, gearing respectively with a crank-driven pinion and a pinion on the trapeze bar. The bar can thus be caused to rotate partially or completely as the trapeze swings. To form a skating automaton, a figure is mounted on iron skates and placed on a large sheet of brass or other material. Magnets are moved about under the brass sheet, so as to cause the automaton to imitate the movements of a skater. Similarly, an automaton may be made to walk on the underside of a ceiling. To cause an automaton to walk on a tight-rope, the rope is formed of a slotted tube, in which are two screws provided with nuts, to which the feet of the figure are attached. By turning the screws alternately, the figure is caused to traverse the rope with a walking motion.

1867

722. Newton, W. E., [*Cabanes, H.*]. March 13. [*Provisional protection only.*]

Air, purifying, moistening, cooling, and aromatizing.—Relates to the cooling, purifying, and perfuming of air in churches, theatres, and other large buildings. An apparatus is employed consisting of a box containing a wire cage filled with sponge, wool, horse-hair, &c., which is kept saturated by a liquid supplied through perforated tubes from a tank placed above. Coiled steel springs prevent the sponges &c. from becoming compressed. The air is drawn through the cage by a fan.

2631. Porter, P. Sept. 19. [*Provisional protection only.*]

Theatrical appliances.—Relates to rollers and raising and lowering appliances for maps, blinds, scenes, &c., the invention being described with reference to maps. The map &c. has a roller at each end, and is laid across a roller supported lengthways and parallel to an upper frame or moulding of twice the usual breadth to admit of rolling or folding. Room is left for the map to pass up or down between the roller and the frame. The maps, " being reversed, may each be respectively " exhibited while the upper frame remains in " position, by means of a cord attached to each " roller in the centre." The roller is divided lengthways, and has a small groove on the inner side of each half. The lower edge of the map is placed somewhat over and below the groove of one half, and is fastened down by a string brought over from end to end. The edge of the map is then turned over the string, the other half of the roller is applied, the end knobs are replaced, and the halves are fastened together by circular brass bands with pins.

2737. Laine, L. Sept. 28. [*Provisional protection only.*]

Opera and field glasses; eyeglasses; reading-glasses.—A " hand glass, binocle, or spy-glass " is mounted by means of a spring in the stick of a fan, and is projected for use by pressing upon a button connected with the spring.

2902. Tinet, C. Oct. 16. [*Provisional protection only.*]

Chairs and seats; umbrella &c. holders; brackets.—Relates to arrangements for holding umbrellas &c. attached to chairs or seats for concert rooms, theatres, &c. Two rings are attached behind the top-rail of the back, and two corresponding rings below are attached behind the seat. The rings serve to receive sticks or umbrellas. Cross-bars hooked on to the rings are provided for hanging coats &c. upon. Bars are provided under the chair to receive hats and other small articles.

3523. Young, G. A. Dec. 12.

Theatres, curtains and screens for. Consists in the use of wire gauze for constructing stage curtains and other screens, with a view to prevent the spread of fire from one part of the building to another. The wire meshwork is either wound on rollers, or arranged to slide or swing on hinges.

3541. Pepper, J. H., and Tobin, T. W. Dec. 12. [*Provisional protection only.*]

Theatrical appliances.—Relates to a method of sustaining bodies on a stage without visible support. Between two pairs of concealed uprights is placed a sheet of glass, set on edge or girder-wise, and serving as a support for the person or article to be sustained. The glass may be raised or lowered between the uprights by means of cords at the ends. In place of this arrangement the upright guides may be arranged beneath the stage, and the glass slid up through a slit in the flooring, so that it may raise a person &c. standing above. The uprights may be framed and mounted on wheels, so as to produce lateral motion ; or the glass may be mounted on a frame raised and lowered by ropes or rods, and moved laterally over the top of the scene, in which case the object is attached to the lower edge of the sheet.

3617. Simmons, J. Dec. 19. [*Provisional protection only.*]

Theatrical appliances. — A cavern scene is arranged at the back of the stage, and, whilst the performer is entering the cavern, a piece of loose rock falls upon his head, apparently crushing it and severing it from the body. This effect is produced by inserting the head (without the assistance of the hands) into a cap or box, which is coloured similarly to the background so as to be invisible to the audience. In this box is a vessel, or series of vessels, containing blood or its equivalent, which, when the head is inserted in the box and brought to a vertical position, is caused to run down a series of tubes and disperse all over the neck of the performer. On the same principle a person may be otherwise apparently dismembered.

1868

46. Hartley, F. W. Jan. 7. [*Provisional protection only.*]

Magic-lanterns.—A magic-lantern is combined with a "phenakistiscope" or zoetrope for representing on a screen objects in apparent motion. For this purpose, rapidly-moving pictures of the object in successive phases of its motion are so arranged with relation to the lantern as to be successively projected on the screen.

1049. Maurice, J. March 27. [*Provisional protection only.*]

Theatrical appliances for producing scenic effects. Relates to the production of phantom images in motion on a stage or platform, by means of a phanakistiscope, sobroscope, zoetrope, or other like apparatus for exhibiting the effects of persistence of vision, the apparatus being so placed as to be invisible to the spectators. This is effected by placing upon the stage or platform a transparent mirror or glass, arranged at such an angle with the apparatus that, when a strong light is thrown upon the figures, they will be reflected on the glass, and all the effects of motion reproduced on bringing the said apparatus into operation. To facilitate reflection, the figures should be bright in colour, the rest of the apparatus being black, or very dark, so as not to be reflected. In some instances, a silvered mirror is used for transmitting the reflection of the objects on to the transparent mirror on the stage. The "motion apparatus" may be constructed in the form of an endless band working upon rollers, and provided with slots for viewing the objects, which are secured to the inner side of the band.

1487. Hall, F. T., [*Heit, E.*]. May 6.

Railway, omnibus, theatre, and like tickets. — Consists in utilizing railway, steamboat, omnibus, theatre, and like tickets as a medium for advertising. For this purpose the ticket is formed of two strips of cardboard secured at their edges to form a pocket for the advertisement. Two strips, bent over at their edges as shown in Fig. 5, are pasted at the edges and pressed into the form shown in Fig. 6. Return tickets may be made with two pockets. Two large sheets may be pasted at the edges, printed, and then cut into strips, or cut first and afterwards printed.

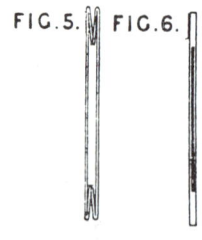

FIG. 5.   FIG. 6.

3542. Sims, J. Nov. 21.

Ornamenting wearing-apparel ; trimmings.—Relates to the ornamentation of woven and felted fabrics, curtains, and garments. A thin sheet of gutta-percha or similar material is laid on the back of a silk, velvet, or other fabric of which the ornamentation or trimming is to consist. The sheet is caused to adhere to the fabric by the aid of moisture, heat, and pressure, which may be applied by means of steam-heated pressing-boxes covered with flannel or other absorbent of water. The backed fabric having been cut up by dies, punches, embossing-rollers, or scissors into the required forms, the pieces are laid upon the fabric or garment to be ornamented, and subjected to dry heat and slight pressure, for which purpose a hot iron may be employed. The process is stated to be suitable for forming borders to woollen petticoats, and to silk and woollen dresses, theatrical costumes, and emblazonments.

1869

447. Taylor, A. W. Feb. 13. [*Provisional protection only.*]

Acrobatic apparatus.—Apparatus for walking on ceilings, walls, or other surfaces, &c. Iron plates are attached to the feet of the performer, and the underside of the ceiling is formed of a large sheet of brass or other material above which is a powerful electromagnet. The electromagnet attracts the iron plates, and keeps the performer in a vertical position. "As the connecting points of "the electromagnet are moved," so the performer is able to walk in a "graceful manner." By a similar arrangement, the performer may walk up a wall, or he may traverse a tube formed to imitate a rope. The iron plates may be attached to the hands of the performer.

1077. Hunter, W. A. April 9.

Street and like lamps ; lighting and extinguishing gas.—Relates to apparatus by which any number of gas lamps in a theatre or other building, or any number of lamps in a town, may be lighted and extinguished simultaneously. Each lamp is fitted with an apparatus which turns on the gas and strikes a match to ignite it. Fig. 1 shows one form of apparatus. A vertical rod h, which terminates in a piston j, working in a cylinder n, is connected to the gas cock by a link i and provided with teeth d for rotating a disc c by means of a pinion e. The disc c is notched to receive a match b from a containing-tube a. When the rod h is raised, the gas is turned on and the disc c is rotated, which causes the match to be rubbed against a roughened plate f and struck to ignite the gas. The rod h is raised by water or other power or by suitable arrangements of gearing &c., or it may be raised by the pressure of the gas. Percussion caps, or substances capable of spontaneous combustion, may be used in place of matches. A three-way cock k is fitted to each lamp to enable the rod h to be lowered in case the match has not struck. The lamps are extinguished when the working fluid is allowed to escape from the cylinders n. The construction and disposition of the rotary disc may be modified, or it may be dispensed with, as shown in Fig. 8, in which case the matches are forced between striking-plates w by the rod h. The matches are moved from the tube a on to the end of the rod h, by a transversely-sliding plate x operated by a slotted link, as shown. In a modification, the matches are laid horizontally in the tube a, and they are forced between striking-plates fixed on the tube a, by the slide x.

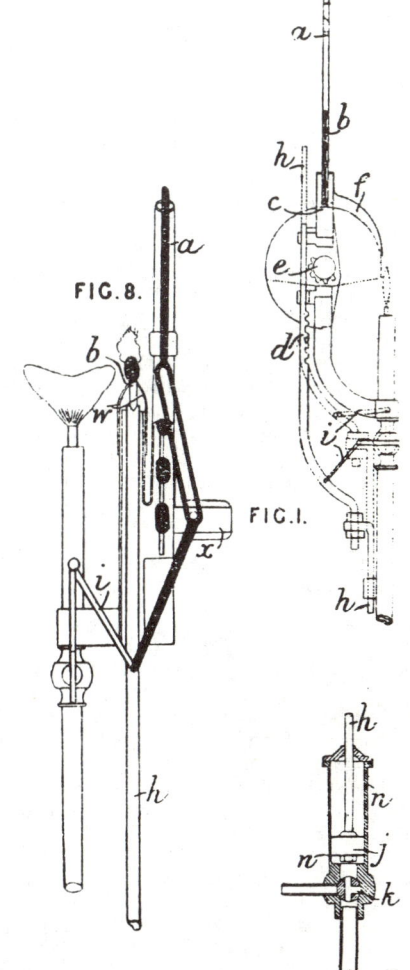

FIG. 8.

FIG. 1.

2996. Barbour, W. Oct. 14. [*Provisional protection only.*]

Lamp shades.—Stage lights are screened from the spectators, and prevented from setting fire to dresses and properties, by means of a curved casing, consisting of a venetian or louvre screen on the side next the audience, the part towards the stage being composed of glass. The lights in the casing are arranged alternately at a higher and lower level, so that the whole stage, and persons and scenery thereon, may be completely illuminated. The back of the casing is made partly double, *i.e.*, with an air space, so as to prevent the heat from being radiated into the orchestra.

1870

178. Calvert, C. A. Jan. 20.

Admission - fees, registering and checking; indicating at a distance electrically.—Checks are issued from the tube *b*, which is hinged above, by pressing the finger-plate *e* as shown. A slot in the tube allows it to pass over the knife blade *f*, which ejects a check *c*

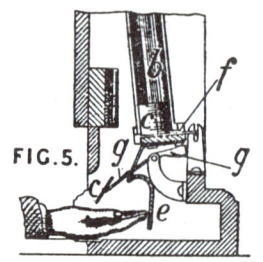

FIG. 5.

through a front opening. The check, in falling, oscillates the trip lever *g*, which closes the circuit of an electric counter in the manager's office. The check-taker places the checks one by one in a tube through a hopper fitted with slides like a powder flask. The bottom slide is bevelled, so that the check deflects it when passing, thereby closing the upper slide. The oscillations of the lever joining the two slides close the circuit of a second recording-instrument in the manager's room. Both tubes are graduated and slotted or glazed, so that the number of checks they contain may be read off at any moment.

643. Welch, E. J. C. March 4. [*Provisional protection only.*]

Oxyhydrogen lamps.—Lime-light apparatus for theatrical representations &c. is arranged so that it may all be operated by one man. An ordinary lime-light apparatus is placed on a frame or stand, supported by brackets fastened to the wall. The stand is formed of an upper and a lower part mounted respectively on a vertical and a horizontal axis so that the light can be turned in any direction by means of arms &c. connected by rods &c. to hand-levers. Different coloured glasses are carried by a circular plate which is fastened to an axle and can be rotated, to bring any one of the glasses in front of the light, by making a circular rack gearing with a pinion. A rod &c. is carried from the circular rack to a hand-lever.

673. Newton, W. E., [*Du Fay, A. S.*]. March 7. *Drawings to Specification.*

Air, cooling and moistening.—The air of hospitals, theatres, and other buildings is cooled by a spray formed by a special spray producer, and the excess moisture is absorbed by quicklime, calcium chloride, &c.

1467. Silber, A. M., and **White, F.** May 20.

Lighting buildings, streets, railway trains, ships, &c., systems of; oil-lamp pendants.—Relates to a method of and apparatus for lighting houses, churches, theatres, streets, railway trains, ships, or

other buildings &c. by means of mineral oil or other combustible liquids. Fig. 1 shows the apparatus applied to a house. A main supply cistern A, placed outside the building and filled from the

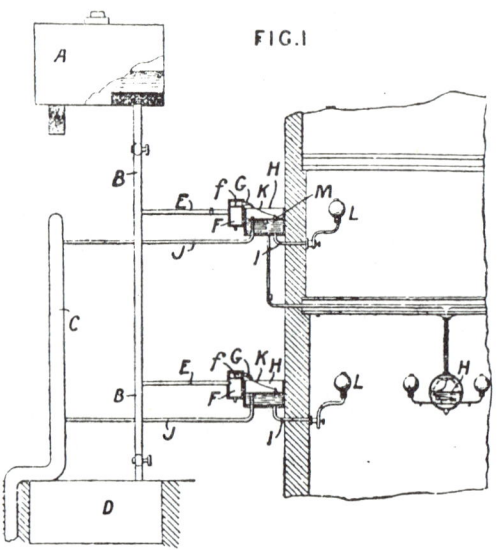

FIG. 1

town's supply or in any other manner, supplies oil through branch pipes B, E to supply cisterns F, H fitted with float valves G, M. From these cisterns the oil is supplied through pipes I to bracket or pendant lamps L as shown. The oil enters each supply cistern H through a box F fitted with a filter *f* and cock G. The cocks G are controlled by china or porcelain floats M attached to the cocks by levers K. Overflow pipes J connected to the house waste pipe C are provided. The pendant lamps may have spherical enlargements to contain a supply cistern, as shown. The pipe B communicates with a cistern D or with the drain C, so that the cistern A may be readily emptied in case of fire &c. The burners employed are each formed of two concentric tubes containing the wick. In some cases the oil is passed into an inner vessel, whence it flows into an outer vessel when it reaches a certain level.

1572. Farini, W. May 30.

Gymnastic apparatus; trapezes.—A form of spring apparatus for projecting a gymnast or any object into the air is shown in Fig. 1. The frame *a* and guide-frame *c* are secured to a firm foundation *b*. A stationary platform *e*, which may be coated underneath with india-rubber or other elastic substance, is mounted at the top of the frame *a*. A movable platform *f*, fitted with india-rubber or other elastic impact surfaces, carries hooks or equivalents *h* to receive the ends of springs *i*, the upper ends of which fasten upon hooks &c. on the platform *e* or frame *a*. The gymnast's platform *k* is mounted on a long stem *l*, preferably made of steel having two notches, the lower one to receive the detent *m*, Fig. 5, moving on a pivot *n*, and the

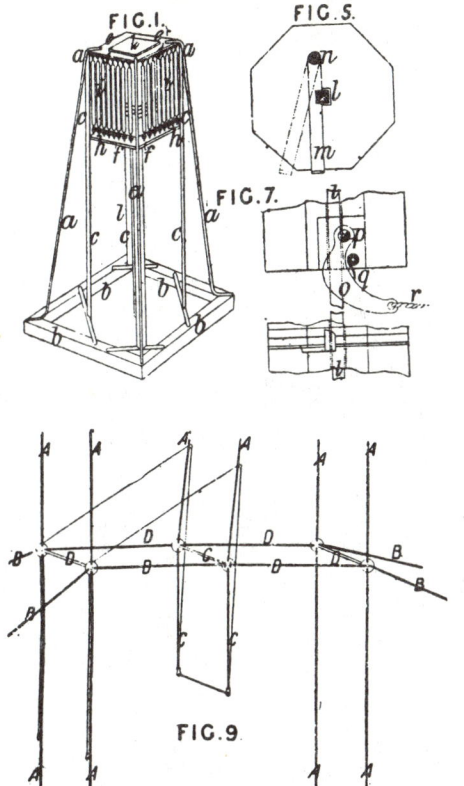

the latter, and attached one by one after the detents are adjusted in the notches in the stem *l*. Fig. 9 shows apparatus for performing gymnastic feats in connection or not with the projecting-apparatus above described. Parallel bars D, suspended by ropes or wires A and secured by guys B, carry a trapeze C and a platform E formed of boards tied together and strengthened by transverse rods *e*[1], the ends of which are supported hinge-like by bolts and clips.

1584 - *see following page*

1584 - *see following page*

2202. Lacomme, J. M. A. Aug. 8.

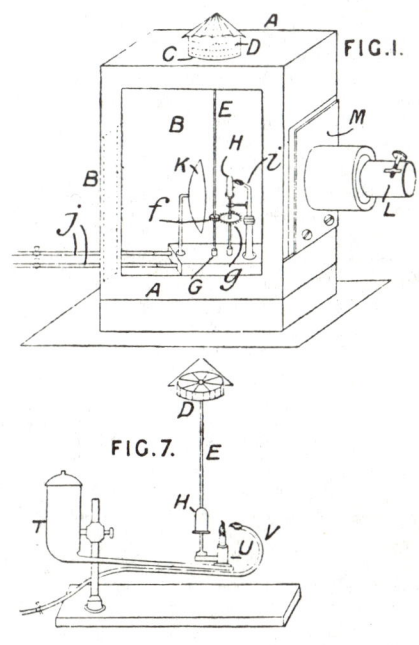

upper one to receive the trigger detent *o*, Fig. 7, turning on a centre *p* and held within the notch by a spring *q*. The springs *i* may be of spiral metal or other material, but are preferably formed of india-rubber as shown. The platform *f*, and with it the stem *l* and platform *k*, are drawn down against the force of the springs *i*, and secured by fixing the detents in the notches in the stem *l*. The gymnast stands upon the platform *k*, and an attendant pulls the cord *r*, Fig. 7, or the artist himself depresses a foot-lever, thus releasing the trigger detent *o* and allowing the parts *k*, *l*, and *f* to be rapidly drawn up by the springs *i*, so as to project the gymnast into the air. When the platform *f* strikes the platform *e*, the detent *m* comes against the detent *o*, and is thus withdrawn from the stem *l*, allowing the latter to descend by its own weight, or aided by springs, carrying the platform *k* out of sight. A hole in the lower end of the stem *l* receives a pin to prevent the stem from being carried through the platform *e*. The platform *k* is fitted underneath with india-rubber &c. to deaden sound when it falls. The springs *i* may be detached from *e* or *f* to facilitate lowering

Oxyhydrogen and like lamps for use in projecting apparatus for the exhibition of advertisements or photographic views, portraits, or pictures by night. A box A, Fig. 1, with doors B has an opening C, with an internal ventilator D which is mounted on an axis E pivoted at G and is rotated by the escape of heated gases at C. A cylinder L mounted in a frame M contains the necessary lens apparatus, the pictures or advertisements being transparent slides which are inserted between the frame M and the box. The illumination may be by the oxyhydrogen flame, the lime cylinder H being rotated by the wheels *f*, *g*, from the rod E, and the gases entering by the pipes *j* leading to the burner *i* which prevents mixture of the gases before ignition; K is a reflector. For using an oxycalcium light, the oxygen is brought, by the flexible tube V, Fig. 7, to bear on the flame from the burner U in which is a wick burning pyroligneous ether or methylated spirit contained in the vessel T.

1584. Hunt, B., [*Finger, L.*]. May 31.

Panoramas.—A band for a moving panorama or like exhibiting - apparatus is actuated by a motor consisting of a series of fixed electro-magnets 6 and two pairs of electromagnets 9 rotating with a shaft 10. Motion is transmitted from the shaft 10 to spindles c, c^1 by screws b, b^1 and worm - wheels. Either of the drums D, D¹, on which the band is rolled, may be locked to its spindle by rods k, which pass through the drums and are adapted to engage teeth on clutches secured to the shafts. The rods k are actuated by a lever M carrying armatures o, o^1 opposite electromagnets N, N¹, having forked ends engaging sliding collars K, K¹. When

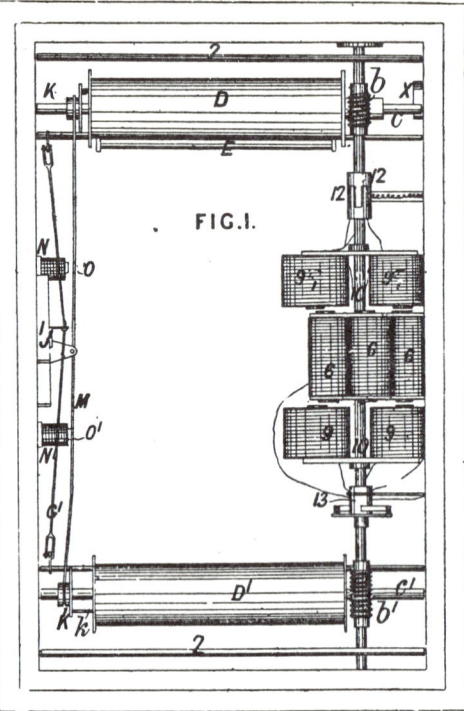

FIG.I.

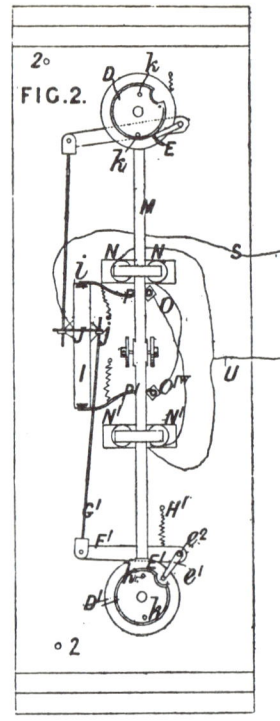

FIG.2.

the band, which passes over rollers 2, is wound on to the drum D, a roller E¹, supported by a spring H¹, falls into a recess in the drum D¹, and through levers e^1 and F¹, pivoted at e^2, and a rod G¹, with collar j, actuates a transverse strip J on a metal strip I so as to free a spring-actuated strip P from an insulating-strip i, and bring a similar strip P¹ into engagement with a similar insulating-strip. The circuit between the battery wires U, S is now completed through the magnet N¹, which attracts its armature o^1, thus freeing the drum D and locking the drum D¹ to its spindle. The band is now wound on to the drum D¹, until a roller E drops into a recess in the drum D and the motion is again reversed. If it is required to run the apparatus for a limited time only, a rubber or other insulating-disc X, with a metal segment and driven by clockwork, is interposed in the motor battery circuit. In a modification, the plate I, the strips P, P¹, &c. are dispensed with, and the rollers E and E¹ are connected by wires to the coils of the magnets N¹ and N respectively, while the drums are connected together and to one pole of the battery, the armatures o, o^1 being connected to the other pole.

2726. Gooding, R. A. Oct. 15. [*Provisional protection only.*]

Fares and admission - fees, checking ; counting-apparatus. — Checks or tickets, consecutively numbered, are delivered to persons entering places of amusement, riding in public vehicles, &c., where checks are required to detect fraud, by an apparatus which severs and delivers intermittently blank tickets &c. from a continuous roll of paper or simultaneously prints or endorses subject-matter, in conjunction with consecutive numbers upon the tickets as they are delivered. A straight or curved grid guide contained by a box or case receives a continuous strip of paper, which passes over a platform at the back entrance of the guide. Between the spaces formed by the guide guide perforators or knives which, when in their lowest position, lie clear of the paper and are connected by hinges to one end of a bell-crank lever connected at the opposite end by a rod with a treadle which, when pressed down, causes the paper to be perforated and carried along towards the exit of the guide. The length of paper withdrawn is retained by the action of a vertical printing-presser, which is made to rise and fall through levers projecting from their junction with the presser at the back to the front of the grid, where they are acted upon by the forward action of the expelling perforators in such a manner as to press the consecutive number and the printing-block forcibly upon the portion of the paper then over the platform, thus forcibly retaining the paper withdrawn, "already printed upon and "between the guide grid ready for the next "delivery." During the action of printing, the ticket in front of the perforators is by their continued action severed from the roll or length, and expelled from the box. The return of the perforators relieves the presser or retaining printing-block, and allows the paper to be withdrawn with the next forward action of the perforators, the rise and fall thus given to the printing-block effecting the rotation of the numerals for consecutively printing the numerals in conjunction with the subject matter upon the tickets &c. An indicator which registers the number of tickets delivered is connected with the cutters or perforators, or the levers actuating the printing-block. In an electric apparatus, for indicating at any distance the number of tickets delivered, a projection of the movable knives or perforators acts as a detent to a magnet connected with a galvanic battery ; the to-and-fro action connects and disconnects the poles of the battery, thus breaking the current with each ticket delivered and causing the fingers of the dials to move. The tickets as delivered are placed in the check-taker's box, and fall on to platforms which are arranged to enclose at intervals of time those already received. The platforms are constructed similarly to internal lids at different heights in the box, and are retained in their open position by means of catches acted upon by vertical wires, the upward sliding motion of which is obtained through an electrically-actuated rack, so arranged that, when any stated number of tickets have been received by the box, the rack and catch will be raised so as to relieve one of the lids, thus checking at intervals of time the consecutive numbers placed in each compartment, and preventing an advanced number from being placed among the lower ones.

2750. Dallmeyer, J. H. Oct. 19. *Drawings to Specification.*

Telescopes and opera and field glasses. — To correct spherical and chromatic aberration and curvature of the field, the object glass is formed of two lenses cemented together, the denser refracting medium, as the flint glass, occupying the external position. The radii of curvature of the external surfaces are preferably as 1 : 12, and the refractive indices of the lenses 1 : 62 and 1 : 51. The concave eye lens has a focal length about one-fifth that of the object glass.

2933. Maitland, W. H., and Maitland, W. L. Nov. 7. [*Provisional protection only.*]

Turnstiles.—Relates to turnstiles for use in theatres &c. by which the number of persons leaving, as well as those entering, is registered by the same turnstile, so that the difficulty of checking the number of persons re-admitted by pass-out checks is obviated. The turnstile is free to turn in either direction, but bars are arranged at one side so that persons going in or out must pass on one side only. Two counters are connected with the turnstile, one for entrances and one for exits, which may be arranged by fitting to the apparatus two wheel trains acting in opposite directions. Before the end of the performance &c. the turnstile is removed to admit of free exit, when reference to the counters will show the total admissions and also the persons leaving who, it is presumed, re-entered the building. To prevent the money taker from turning the turnstile back,

a yielding floor plate is depressed by the weight of the person leaving. The plate may be caused to act upon electrical counting-apparatus, or made to act as a stop to the turnstile until depressed.

3228. Wise, W. L., [*Klinkerfues, W.*]. Dec. 8.

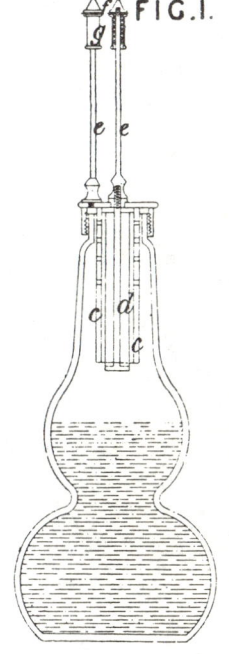

FIG.I.

Lighting and extinguishing gas. — Relates to a mode of and apparatus for igniting gas in which the catalytic action of platinum in igniting gas that impinges upon it is assisted by the passage of a galvanic current, the platinum being used in the form of fine wire but the heat imparted to the wire by galvanism being short of a red heat. Fig. 1 shows one form of apparatus in which a glass vessel, containing a mixture of bichromate of potash and dilute sulphuric acid, is fitted with a cover supporting a zinc plate c and a carbon d. The zinc and carbon are connected to electrodes e fitted at their upper ends with special spring jaws g for holding a platinum wire f. To light the gas the wire f is placed close to the gas jet and the vessel is inclined to bring the liquid into contact with the zinc and carbon. The carbon d may be cylindrical and the zinc c tubular and perforated. In a modification for lighting gas jets in high positions, a long vessel is used, the lower part of which is flexible so that it may be compressed, by a thumb piece and plate, to force the liquid upwards and so bring it into contact with the zinc and carbon plates. A second plate and screw are also provided for adjusting the level of the liquid. The electrodes are each formed of two parts, arranged to work on a common hinge pin, to facilitate getting the platinum wire in close proximity to the burner. The lower parts of the electrodes pass through insulating tubes fixed to a cap which closes the vessel and carries, or fixes in position, the carbon or zinc. For simultaneously lighting and extinguishing a number of street lamps each lamp is fitted with an apparatus as shown in Fig. 7 in which the exciting liquid is brought into contact with the zinc and carbon by an increase in the pressure of the gas. A hermetically closed vessel a contains the exciting liquid and is fitted with a cylinder l enlarged at l^1. The zinc c and carbon d are made in the form of rings and are each carried by two rods or wires e^4, e^3 respectively, passing through the cover b, and making contact with the electrodes e which support a twisted platinum wire above the burner m^1. The pipe m leading to the burner is fixed to the cover b within the cylinder e and gas is introduced into

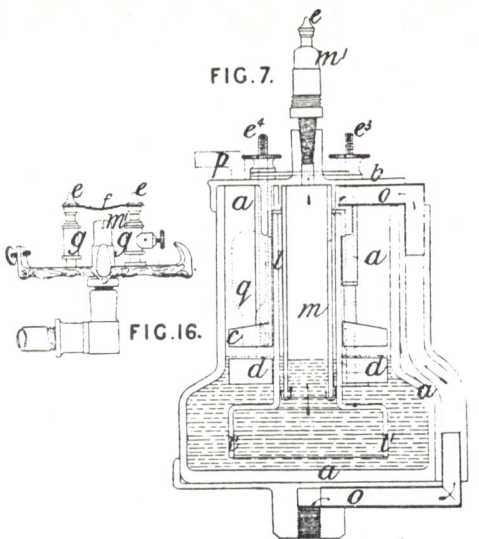

FIG.7.

FIG.16.

the annular space between the pipe and cylinder through the pipe *o*. When the gas is at its lowest pressure the pipe *m* is sealed as shown ; but when the pressure is increased the pipe is unsealed and

the gas passes ; by a still further increase, for a short time only, the liquid is raised to cover the zinc *c* and so start the current and ignite the gas. When the pressure is reduced the gas is extinguished. In some cases a pipe *p* is provided so that suction may be used, either alone or in conjunction with varying pressures, to alter the level of the exciting liquid. A reservoir *q* may be provided to make good any liquid lost by evaporation. In a modification, the gas pipe passes up through the centre of the vessel *a* and is sealed by a bell. In another modification by which one or more gas lamps or jets or whole gasaliers may be lighted simultaneously, the zinc may be depressed into the exciting liquid by pressing on a spring knob, or the liquid may be raised by the gas pressure. The battery is made separate from the gas jets and is connected with them by wires. The supply pipe to each gas jet is fitted with a seal consisting of a bell dipping into glycerine or mercury, or of two concentric pipes as shown in Fig. 7. Fig. 16 shows an arrangement, for use in connection with a separate battery, for igniting the gas jets of gasaliers &c. The apparatus may be used for lighting railway signals, street and other lamps, gas jets in mills, workshops, warehouses, stations, hotels, theatres, &c., and gas lights for illuminating clocks.

1871

604. Wrench, J. H.   March 7.   *Drawings to Specification.*

Magic-lanterns, mechanical slides for. The circular glasses of rotating slides are mounted in metal rings which are formed with holes or recesses in lieu of rack teeth, with which gear the pins of a pinion-wheel turned by a handle. Two glasses may be arranged to turn in opposite directions, one being placed on each side of the pinion.

621. Wright, E.   March 8.   [*Provisional protection only.*]

Fares and admission-fees, registering and checking ; counting-apparatus.—Apparatus for registering the number of passengers carried during each stage of a public conveyance and the fares paid, or the number of persons or parcels passing into theatres, railway stations, &c. where various amounts have to be paid, consists of a box containing ratchet-wheels carrying pointers moving over dials, a separate

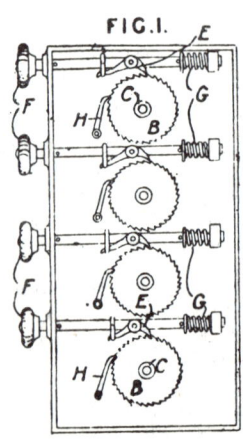

FIG.I.

dial being used for each fare or each amount to be paid. In the form shown, four dials are used, their pointers being carried by the spindles C of the ratchets B, which are operated (when a fare is paid) by pressing one of the knobs F. The teeth of the ratchets C correspond to the divisions on the dials, so that the pointers are moved one division forward each time the knobs are depressed. The ratchets are moved by the pawls E and prevented from turning back by pawls H, the knobs being returned by springs G. At the end of a stage or journey the pointers are returned to zero by an authorized person.

1234. Oliver, G.   May 6.

Acrobatic apparatus ; jumping &c., appliances for aiding.—Apparatus is arranged for enabling a performer to ascend to or descend from a considerable height above a stage. Fig. 2 shows a form of apparatus designed for lifting a performer to a height above the stage. A number of springs *b*, preferably india-rubber "accumulator" springs, are suspended from a joist or beam *a* in the roof by means of hooks *c*. A block *d* is suspended on a rope *e* just above a platform erected across the upper part of the stage, and is fitted with a double-eyed bolt *g*, to one eye of which is attached a wire *h* passing through the platform and almost down to the stage. A trigger bolt *i* working in staples *i¹* on the platform passes through the other eye of the bolt *g*, so as to hold the block *d* down while the lower ends of the springs *b* are secured to hooks *j* thereon. The lower end of the wire *h* is attached to the performer by a suitable harness, such as a belt *k* with straps *l* and *m*, arranged as shown in Fig. 3 and connected with a strong cross strap *o*, to which the wire is secured at *n* by staples and a spring bolt. The performer may readily disengage himself from the wire by drawing the spring bolt. The trigger *i* is released by pulling a rope *i²*, whereupon the springs *b* raise the block *d* to the position shown by dotted lines, Fig. 2, thereby raising the performer, who may alight upon a fixed bar or staging, to which vertical wires may be secured by which he may steady himself. The springs *b* detach themselves from the hooks *j*, and the block *d* falls back the length of the rope *e*. Fig. 6 shows a form of apparatus for making repeated leaps. A wooden tube or trough *s* is hung by iron straps from the eye of a bolt in the beam *a*, and suspended within it from a rope *u* passing over a sheave are india-rubber springs *t*, the lower ends of which are secured to a ring *v* supporting the wire *h*. If preferred, two wires *h* may be used, with handles for the performer to hold. The rope *u*, which is fitted with a stop *u²*, may be alternately pulled and slackened to aid the performer. Check springs *w* may be attached to

the lower end of the tube *s* and to the ring *v*, to prevent the too violent recoil of the springs *t* when the performer is detached from the apparatus. The wire *h* may be attached to different parts of the harness, for imitating flying &c. For descending head first, the point of attachment of the wire may be at *x*, Fig. 3, and a rope network is provided below the stage, or otherwise concealed from the audience, to receive the performer.

2776. Calvert, C. A. Oct. 18. [*Provisional protection only.*]

Admission-fees, registering and checking.—The money taken for admissions to public entertainments &c. is registered and checked by apparatus consisting of a combination of a modification of the apparatus for measuring liquids described in Specification No. 3351, A.D. 1870, with the apparatus for checking money described in Specification No. 178, A.D. 1870, by which the electric apparatus is dispensed with. Connected with the money-taker's apparatus is a barrel or cylinder working liquid-tight between end plates, and provided with two or more tubes to contain a certain quantity of water to be drawn off. This barrel communicates by pipes with a vertical chamber containing water and situated in the manager's or other office where the check is desired to be seen. This chamber is graduated from the top. For every stroke or movement of the money-taker's apparatus the barrel is turned a portion of a revolution, by means of connecting-rods, levers, &c., and discharges a tube of water. A counter may be attached to the barrel to indicate the number of tubes full that have passed through. The check-taker's apparatus is also provided with a similar barrel, to discharge a tube of water into another vertical chamber each time a check is passed through.

3352. Davis, A. Dec. 11. [*Provisional protection only.*]

Theatrical and like wearing-apparel; body armour.—Stage armour is made of coloured, silvered, or gilded beads, preferably tube beads with the colouring &c. inside. The beads are strung on twine or wire and meshed or linked together to resemble chain armour. The strung beads may be made up in patterns and applied to other theatrical and fancy costumes.

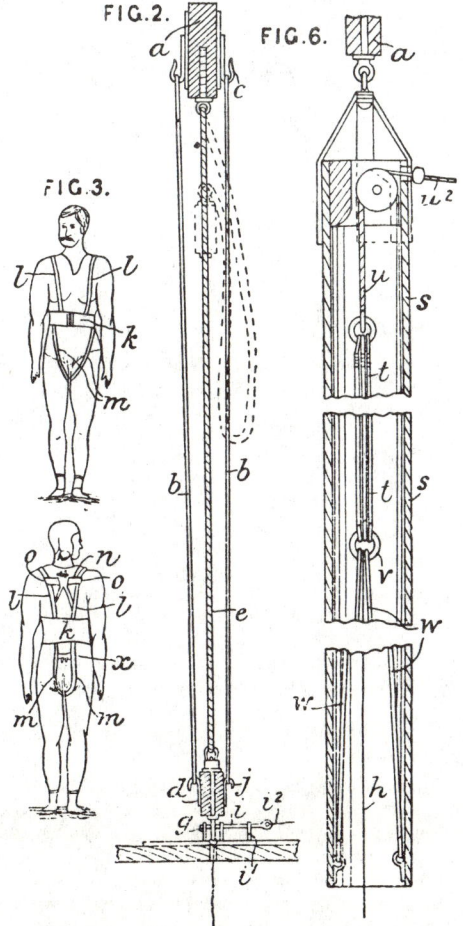

FIG.2. FIG.6.

FIG.3.

1872

498. Racey, G., and **Young, J.** Feb. 16.
[*Provisional protection only.*]

Theatres.—Fireproof drop curtains are made of small overlapping pieces of mica or talc connected by copper rivets and applied crosswise to the curtain, or of pieces of woven asbestos connected together. The curtain is bound at the edges with leather &c. to enable it to be wound on a roller.

999. Warbrick, J. F., and **Clegg, J.**
April 4. [*Provisional protection only.*]

Fares and admission-fees, registering and check-ing.—For registering the number of persons entering a vehicle, theatre, &c., a step, platform, or plank is arranged so that each person entering steps upon and depresses it ; the step, platform, &c. is carried by three levers working in a box of which the step forms the lid ; the two outer rods are coupled together by a pin working in slots ; the outer end of the third lever extends through one end of the box and communicates motion to any counting or registering apparatus. The entrance is so made that one person only can pass at a time, the step &c. being returned to its original position by means of a spring or springs.

1186. Davies, G., [*Busby, A. G.,* and *Woodbury, W. B.*]. April 20. [*Provisional protection only.*]

Lime-light apparatus.—Two or more sets of burners and lenses are placed directly over one another, and are separated by double horizontal partitions, the heat from each set of the lower burners being led away up a side chimney. A rectangular casing contains the sets of burners, and blocks carrying the condensing lenses are hinged to the front of the casing, the front lenses being arranged on adjustable arms, pro-jecting from the blocks, for focussing all the sets of lenses on the same points. When lime light is used, a "dissolving" cock is fixed on the oxygen and hydrogen supply pipes, by means of which these gases are admitted to one set of burners as they are shut off at the other, thus producing a dissolving view effect. The lime pencils are adjusted in the act of putting in or taking out the slides or by turning the dissolving cock. The pencils may be operated by the slides, in which case a wire extends across the slide space, and the insertion of a slide depresses the wire, which is arranged to drive a ratchet. The ratchet is connected to a plate mounted on a spindle, which also carries a cog-wheel gearing with a wheel on a screwed rod, carrying the pencil of lime. The screwed rod can slide through the wheel but not rotate relatively to it, and the lime is gradually fed up until it is all consumed. This mechanism may also be actuated

by hand. In a modified lime-feeding mechanism, an arm is fixed on the spindle, and the ends of the arm strikes and turns a pin-wheel on the lime pencil holder. This holder carries a pin which traverses a spiral slot cut in a surrounding tube, and feeds up the lime. To operate from the dissolving cock, rods are passed through the ends of a vertical bar carrying a rack which is moved by a pinion fixed on one end of the dis-solving cock spindle. In another arrangement, the whole movement is mounted on a single stem and fixed by a set-screw, for easy detach-ment. A spring is fastened to one of the pipes of the burners instead of the base so that the burner may be easily removed. A simple pawl and ratchet movement may be used for raising the pencil. The blowpipe nozzle has a tapered end fitting a similar opening in the burner.

1192 - *see opposite page*

1411. Trotman, F. May 8. [*Provisional protection only.*]

Footlights ; reflectors ; lighting theatres, buildings, &c., systems of.—A continuous reflector is placed against a row of, preferably, flat flame gas burners to reflect the light on to the stage. This reflector may be curved or straight in plan and concave or convex in section ; it may be formed in one piece, or built up of sections. A second continuous re-flector is placed on an incline formed on the stage side of the footlights to reflect the light upwards and outwards towards the audience. Similar con-tinuous reflectors are applied to bottom or top lights and to side or wing lights, and conical reflec-tors are applied to rings or other clusters of burners. The surfaces of the reflectors may be fluted, reeded, or otherwise formed.

1570. Thomas, R. May 22. *Drawings to Specification.*

Lenses ; spectacles and eyeglasses ; telescopes and opera and field glasses.—Lenses, especially lenses for spectacles, eyeglasses, telescopes, opera glasses, and field glasses, are tinted uniformly by build-ing up the lens of two pieces or lenses ground to fit and cemented together by a tinted cement, preferably Canada balsam tinted with Prussian blue.

1192. Thelwall, W. B. April 20.

Theatrical appliances.—Relates to the construction and method of actuating colossal and other figures of men, monsters, and animals for stage purposes. A skeleton of the required figure is made, having attachments for fixing to the operator, and a model or frame of the figure, made of cane, wire, or elastic open basketwork and allowing the requisite movement of the joints, is attached to the skeleton. The basketwork frame is covered with a skin of vulcanized india-rubber or the like, which may be inflated with air, and painted, stained, or dressed as required. The skeleton of the figure derives its movements from the operator's similar movements which are transmitted through rods in such a manner as to retain the proportionate and natural actions. Fig. 1 shows the construction and mode of actuating a giant. The operator is mounted on stilts A. The lower parts of the stilts carry foot-rests and are pivoted to the upper parts at the point B and are capable of movement round the pivot. A spring A^4 is fixed at the lower end of the stilts, and rods A^1 and A^{11} are hinged to the foot-rest and the spring making the foot-rest stable, and relieving the operator's foot of stress by means of the spring A^4. The position of the foot-rests corresponds with the knees of the figure. To allow the figure to kneel, arrangement is made so that the operator may reach the ground in an erect position on his feet. For this purpose a disc of metal at the pivot B, is made so that one quadrant C is attached to the upper part of the stilt, and the remainder to the lower part. When the joint bends, the two parts of the disc slide upon one another, and a bolt kept in place by the india-rubber band E, secures the joint rigid, this bolt being withdrawn at the will of the operator. An india-rubber or metal spring D assists the return of the joint to the

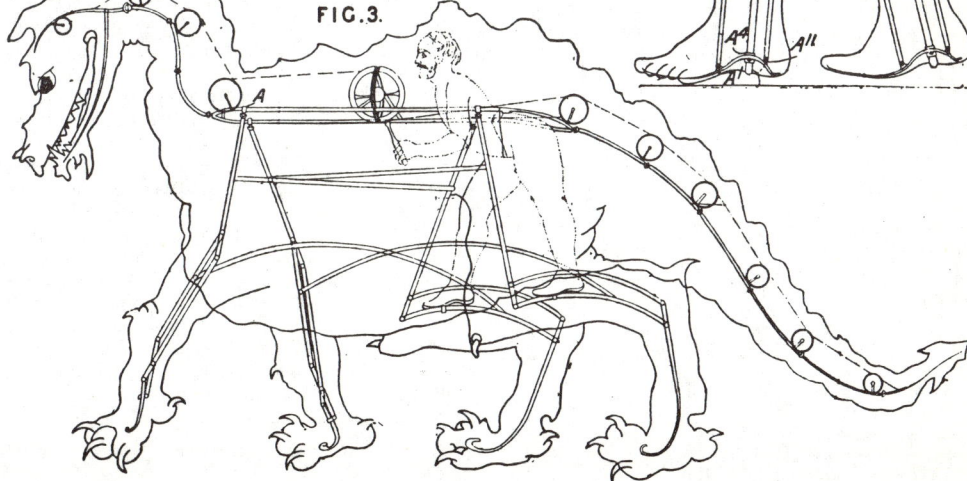

FIG.1.

FIG.3.

locking position, and may also lock it, the disc and band E being dispensed with. The skeleton i[8] now adjusted to the elevated operator whose waist coincides with the waist of the figure. A lined metal band P fits round the operator, and rods having a stiff pivot joint O, a ball-and-socket joint N, a hinged joint K, and a pivot joint I, connect the waist band with the lower part of the stilts and form the hip joints N and knee joints K. Springs H break the force of striking the ground, and assist the operator in rising from the ground, and are placed between a fulcrum h and the point in the knee of the figure which would first touch the ground. Standards P^1 and P^{11} rise from the band P to the extended collar U, and serve to support the shoulder-piece from which suitable branches stand out. The arm rods of the skeleton extend from the shoulder-piece Q to the joints R and R^1. One of these joints is a ball-and-socket joint forming the elbow of the figure; a rod connects this joint with a wrist-piece V, which is fixed on the operator's forearm, and contains an air cylinder or a metal spring to reduce shock in case of a fall. A glove x is attached to the wrist-piece and threads pass from the fingers of the glove to the fingers of the figure, so that any movement of the operator's hand in the glove is reproduced in that of the figure. The hand of the figure is constructed of thin metal plate fitted with pivots to the wrist joints X, on each side of the wrist, and the fingers are pivoted to the hand plate. A casing X connects the hand plate with the wrist-piece. The head of the figure is carried by standards from the collar U, meeting in a cup-and-ball joint n on which the head moves freely. A curved rod n, t forms the skeleton of the head; a support q^1, q passes from this rod and is attached to a skull cap fitting on the operator's head, so that any motion of the operator's head is given to the figure. The jaw of the figure is supported on a rod k hinged at j to the head frame, and the point j is so chosen that the motion of the operator's head has little effect on the motion of the figure's jaw. The jaw is operated by means of the chin-piece f fixed to the operator, and the wire g, i. A speaking trumpet S^2 passes from the operator's mouth to the mouth of the figure. The eyes which consist of thin metal painted and glazed, move in sockets upon universal joints. The eyelids consist of coloured india-rubber, and are actuated on the scissors principle, from the eyebrow of the operator or by other means. The motion of the eye may be taken from the shoulder joints, which are so arranged that when the arm is lifted to the front, the ball-and-socket joint alone acts, but when the elevation of the arm is lateral both joints act. A cord transmits motion to the eyes when the arm is raised to the front, and the eyes drop by their own weight when the hand is extended. The body of the skeleton in front of the operator's eyes is made of copper gauze, coloured tarlatan, or other translucent material. In the construction of an animal or monster the operator is supported in a sling carried by the framework A, Fig. 3. The skeleton of the animal's leg is pivoted to rods jointed to other rods suspended from the framework A. The operator causes the animal to walk by pressing on the intermediate rods with his feet alternately. The front and back legs of the animal may be connected across diagonally, or the operator may work the front legs independently with his hands. The frame A is carried or supported by the legs of the animal, and requires that the operator shall be in position, for the animal to stand. When the legs are connected diagonally the operator's hands are free to operate wings, head, or tail. Other parts of the animal &c. may be similar to those described for the giant.

2053. Lake, W. R., [*Chèradame, A. L.,* *Le Dreux, A. E.,* and *Oursel, V. C. J.*]. July 6. *Drawings to Specification.* [*Provisional protection only.*]

Furniture combined with fans.—A screw fan, driven by clockwork or a weight motor or by a steam or water jet motor, is combined with various articles of furniture. Thus, it may be adapted to music and foot stools, theatre and easy chairs, and seats generally, to desks, and to music stands.

2112. Sutcliffe, W. S. July 13.

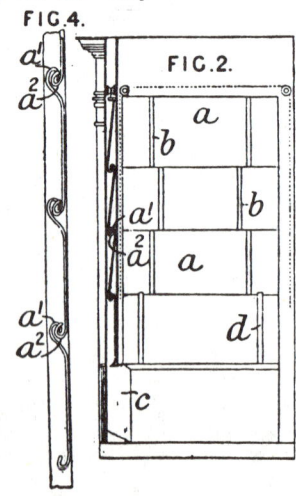

Window-shutters; doors; windows; theatres. — Relates to the construction and guiding of metal or wood shutters, theatre curtains, curtains or blinds for windows, doors, &c., which are stated to be also applicable as sashes and doors. Shutters are built up of a number of metal laths a, Fig. 2, having metal strips b passing through holes or slots in their folds a^1, a^2 and clenched or otherwise secured to the folds so that one lath slides upon the strips of the lath above it when the shutter is lowered into the window recess c. For winding upon rollers the guide-strips are shortened to form connectors of the laths; or the edge of one fold protrudes through or over a notch in the adjacent fold and is there clenched. The shutter, instead of being wound on a roller, may slide in grooves fixed in overhead bearers. A flat surface may be formed if necessary as shown in Fig. 4, and the ends of the slats are carried in grooves. The winding rollers of a roof blind or shutter are contained in a recess or ventilator on the ridge of the hot-house or other roof, and the blinds or shutters slide in metal grooves fixed to the rafters. Operating lines or chains pass over pulleys or rollers and are connected to strips d, Fig. 2, on the bottom lath. When raised into a recess in the top of the window, the bottom ends of the strips d are bent to catch up the upper laths. Shutters &c. formed on the above principle are stated to be a safeguard against fire.

2723. Walker, H. A. Sept. 13.

checking the money receipts from persons entering theatres &c. consists of one or more vertical tubes containing checks &c. which may be withdrawn one

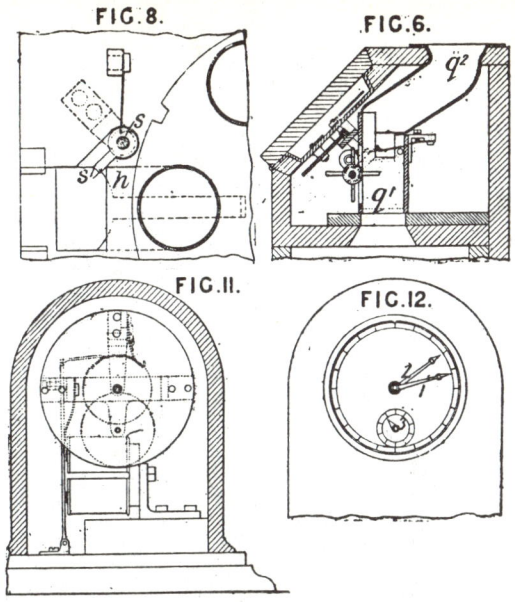

FIG.8. FIG.6.

FIG.II. FIG.12.

Checks and tokens, issuing and collecting ; counting-apparatus. — An apparatus for registering and

by one ; the checks are dropped into another apparatus, and a counter or indicator, placed at a distance from either of the above apparatus, is actuated electrically by the checks as they are delivered and received. Fig. 1 shows a sectional elevation, and Fig. 3 a sectional plan of a check delivering machine ; a modification of this apparatus is shown in Fig. 8. Fig. 6 shows a sectional elevation of the receiving machine, and Figs. 11 and 12 show the electrically-actuated indicator for checking the above machines. In Figs. 1 and 3 six tubes a are shown, containing checks or tokens b which may be round or square flat plates, or balls &c. The tubes, when filled, are locked at the top and are supported by a base-plate c revolving on the pivot f ; a plate e fixed to the frame g prevents the checks from falling out of the tubes except by a slotted opening h. In this opening works a slide i which is actuated by the pull or grip k ; mounted on the back of the pull k is a spring catch m, the upper inclined edge of which projects slightly above the surface of the slide i. On pulling the slide to the left by means of the grip k, the catch m delivers the bottom check ; the next check falls, but on the return stroke due to the action of the spring b, the catch m is depressed until it clears the check. When one tube is emptied, the knob c^4 is pressed in, thus releasing the catch c^1, and the revolving frame is turned by the square stud d^1 at the top. A counting-mechanism consists of a vertical shaft n carrying a number of arms n^1 which successively project partially or wholly across the opening h ; as each check is delivered, the arms are turned and an index hand is moved on a dial n^4 through worm gearing n^3. Precise movements are given to the arms by the spring-detent o^2, Fig. 3. The modification shown in Fig. 8 consists in the method of actuating the counting-apparatus. A vertical shaft s is provided with an arm s^1 projecting partially across the opening h ; as each check is delivered, the arm is deflected and the motion of the shaft s is transmitted to the index-arbor by a pawl and ratchet-wheel mechanism. The checks are received in the apparatus shown in Fig. 6 ; the receiving-passage q^2 leads to the vertical passage q^1, in which is arranged a counting-mechanism of the same form and actuated in the same manner as that in the delivering-machine ; the checks fall in a chamber below the opening q^1. This chamber may be extended and continued downwards, and back to a plate from which the tubes of the delivering-apparatus may be supplied, a limited number of checks being required in this case. The counting-apparatus shown in Figs. 11 and 12 is for use in the office of the proprietor or manager of a theatre &c. to indicate the money taken ; it consists of two electromagnets, one behind the other, the circuit of one being completed by each check as it is delivered, and that of the other by each check as it is received. Each magnet attracts a separate armature, the upper end of which is provided with a pawl gearing with a ratchet-wheel. Two index hands, 1 and 2, Fig. 12, are thus actuated, and when the last check has been received, the hands should coincide ; the index hand 3 registers hundreds.

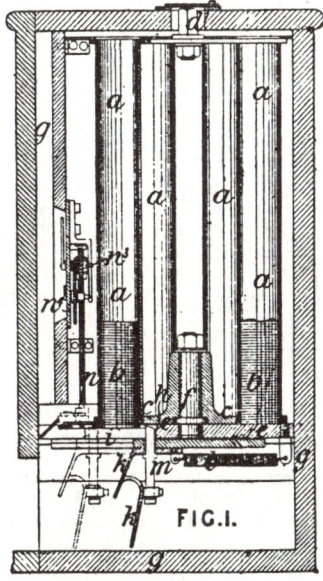

FIG.I.

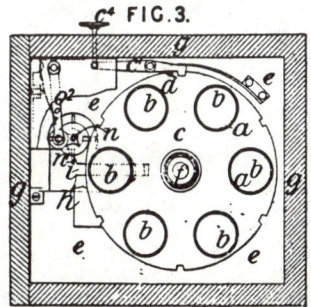

c^4 FIG.3.

2810. Wappenstein, R. Sept. 23.

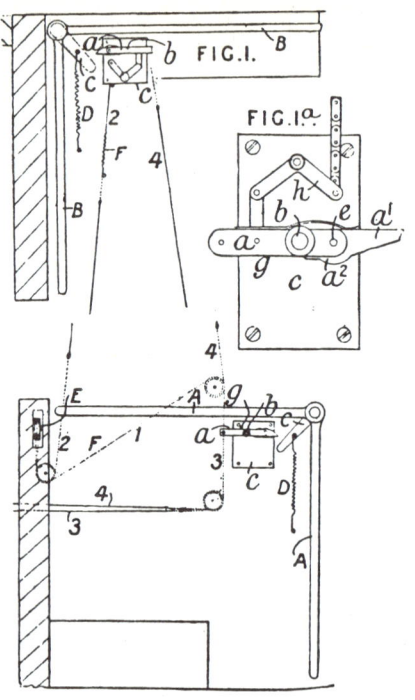

Fares and admission-fees, registering. — The entrance and exit doors of omnibuses, tramcars, steamboats, theatres, &c. consist of two partitions or bars set at right-angles. Each movement of the door permits of the passage of one person, and is registered by automatic mechanism. The system is shown arranged for a tramcar. A lever C, Fig. 1, attached to the door first engages with a spring lever catch a when the door is pushed open. The lever catch is made of two parts pivoted to a plate c and jointed together by a pin e, Fig. 1a. One part a^1 has a shoulder a^2 which engages with the lever part a when the catch is pressed in one direction, so that the lever catch then turns about the main pivot b. A stop g, Fig. 1, prevents the catch from being turned back by the spring F, Fig. 1, out of gear with the lever C. Chains 1, 2, 3 and 4 transmit the motion of the lever catches to any convenient registering mechanism E. When one such mechanism is used with several doors A, B the motion of the catch may be transmitted to the chain 2 by a bell-crank lever h. The doors are brought to their initial positions by springs D. An entrance or exit or combined entrance and exit turnstile may be fitted with this system. The catches are in pairs arranged so that one is operated by a person entering, while the other is operated on exit. One indicator may be operated by several doors.

1873

294. Grieve, T. W. Jan. 25.

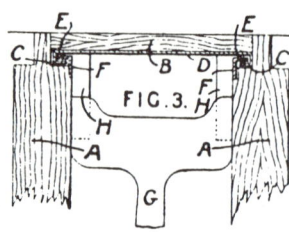

Theatrical appliances ; doors.—The object is to lock the joists of a theatre stage automatically on the closing of a "slider" or trapdoor. The slider B, Fig. 3, runs in grooves C formed in the joists A, and has cramping-irons D on its underside provided with antifriction rollers E which work against guides F. Pivoted rods H and a lever G hold up the slider. The grooves C are extended and inclined to allow the slider to pass under the fixed flooring. The clamps may be on the joists and the grooves or guides on the slider.

692. Watts, T. H. Feb. 24. [*Provisional protection only.*]

Louvred and baffle-plate apparatus.—Longitudinal or other suitable openings are made in ventilating-shafts for theatres, concert rooms, smoking-saloons, &c., and in the interior of the shaft immediately beneath the openings sloping partitions or louvres are placed inclining upwards from either side so as to overlap at the inner edges. Side winds are directed up the shaft and promote an upward draught.

1200. Anderson, W. April 1. [*Provisional protection not allowed.*]

Tickets, issuing.—To check the money received by the conductors or collectors of tramway cars, omnibuses, steamboats, theatres, &c. tickets are issued bearing a number and the amount paid. Counterfoils are retained in a book or otherwise. The backs of the tickets are utilized for advertising purposes. Prizes are awarded periodically to a certain percentage of tickets issued, such prizes being allocated by the usual method of drawing from the counterfoils.

1802. Rae, A. May 17.

Concert-halls ; theatres &c.—Relates to a floating swimming-bath stated to be convertible into a music hall, concert-room, theatre, ball-room, &c., by raising the central "float" to the level of the decks of the hulls or pontoons and decking it over. The saloons may be provided with propellers worked by steam or other power. Twin barges, pontoons, or tubular hulls, of light draught are decked and fitted with cabins, dressing rooms,

&c., and are separated sufficiently to admit between them a central "float" or water casing in which bathing takes place. The "float" has elevating and depressing gear, such as cogged or racked shafts and telescopic guides. Water is admitted through lattice-work at the sides, ends, and bottom, or the bottom may be formed as a filtering-bed and the sides and ends made hollow. The structure is kept end on to the sea, and access is gained from the shore by forming an overhanging bridge or platform which is fitted with a swinging gangway &c. Waves &c. are prevented from passing out of the "float" by a deep shield or false bow fitted between the ends or bows of the hulls. The frame of the "saloon" may be decked over and fitted to form a lounge and promenade. Warm, shower, and other baths, refreshment rooms, &c. may also be provided. Propellers worked by steam &c. power may also be fitted.

2163. Morris, J. M. June 20.

Theatrical appliances.—Relates to apparatus for producing mechanical illusions in theatrical exhibitions, and consists in arrangements for moving and holding a performer, or a weight, in the air without sufficient visible means of support. A tubular wand or stick a, on which the arm or elbow of the performer rests, is mounted in a socket in a platform p carried on four feet r ; it supports a socket b formed on a horizontal arm c. Jointed to the arm c is a cradle or frame e, to which the performer

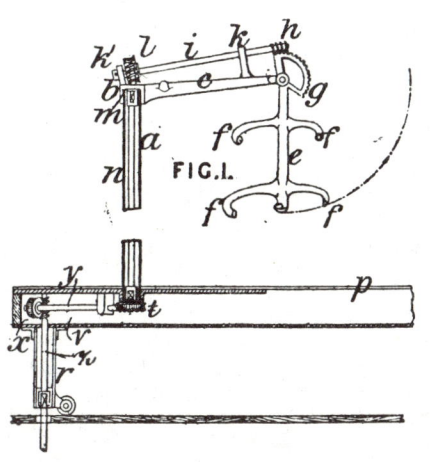

is secured by straps fastened to the ribs f, f or by other means. Fixed to the frame e is a tangent toothed wheel or segment g, which is operated, to raise or lower the frame, by an endless screw h on a shaft i revolved in bearings k, k^1 by means of worm gearing l, m, t, x, and spindles n, y, z. The platform p is placed so that the hollow leg r, in which the spindle z is fitted, is exactly over a hole in the floor, so that the spindle can be turned by inserting a key from below, thus causing the performer &c. to move up and down without visible assistance. A catch or detent may be provided, to cause the tube a to revolve with the spindle n so as to move the performer horizontally as well as vertically. The key being withdrawn, the platform p may be moved about while the performer remains suspended. The segment g and worm h may be replaced by a nut and screw and bevel gearing, or pulleys and cords, chains, or wires may be used instead of the endless screws and tangent-wheels. The worm m and wheel t are connected to the spindle n by means of squared ends and sockets so that the parts may be readily put together and taken apart.

2648. Nolan, P. W. Aug. 7.

Seats for theatres and other public buildings are folded by pushing forward the back D, Fig. 3, which turns on the pivot d until the pins d^1, d^2 reach the slots b^1, b^2 respectively. The back D then descends by its own weight or is forced down, and the pin d^2, in descending, causes the link F to draw the arm E downward, and the strap C^1 to turn up the seat C on the pivot c. The standards B, of which only one is shown completely in Fig. 3, are fitted with guards G to shield the points of the arms c^1. In another form, shown in Fig. 6, two seats B are mounted on a central standard A. When the seat B is folded up, the eccentric slot b^1 moves the pin c^1 which causes the pivoted back C to move into the upright position, and, if not upheld by the eccentric b^1 on the other seat, the arm D drops. The back C and arm D are pivoted to the lug A^1 on the standard A. The seats &c. may be folded up by lifting the seat. The base-plate may be extended so as to support several

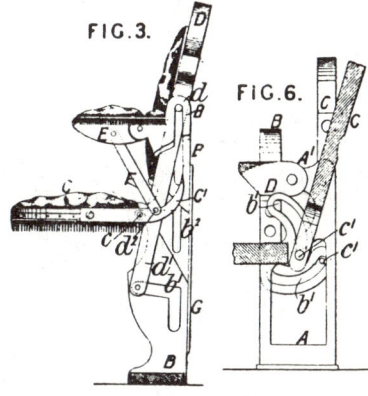

standards. The base-plates are preferably secured to the floor, and, where placed in rows, the adjacent sides of adjoining seats may be connected by a single intervening standard of slightly increased thickness.

2881. Robertson, J. Sept. 2. [*Provisional protection only.*]

Fares and admission-fees, registering and checking.—The number of persons who enter and leave tramcars, omnibuses, public halls, steamboats, &c. is indicated and registered by apparatus actuated by a movable step upon which all person entering or leaving the tramcar &c. must tread. A connecting link, pawl, or equivalent device is attached to the step, and, being connected to or bearing upon an indicator, moves one or more pointers at each depression of the step. A spring or counterweight restores the step to its original position after each depression.

2888. Edwards, E. Sept. 2. [*Provisional protection only.*]

Illusions, producing.— Relates to apparatus for producing optical and mechanical illusions in theatrical exhibitions. A vertical mirror extends from one of the front legs of a table, parallel with the stage front to the opposite back leg. A side scene reflected by the mirror appears to the spectators to be at the back of the table. A bottle, cage, or receptacle having a portion of its back removed to admit an article, or preferably a living child, is placed in front of the scene. At a given signal a second similar child, or article, is projected up through an opening in the table top and the first child, or article, disappears from the bottle, so that a child, or article. appears to leap out of the bottle on to the table. Fire, water, or smoke passing up from the said opening appears to escape from the bottle. A fountain placed where the bottle stands would appear to be under the table. In a second illusion, a bottomless vase, box, or other vessel is placed over an opening in the table top, so that the exhibitor can take articles out of the vessel as they are handed to him by a confederate concealed under the table behind the mirror. In a third illusion, for causing the sudden appearance or disappearance of a performer &c., the performer stands in a vertical recess open in front, but is concealed from the spectators by a vertical hinged mirror which is inclined at an angle of 45° with the stage front. The eyes of the spectators are dazzled, preferably, by the ignition of gun-cotton in front of the recess, while the performer throws back the mirror to reveal himself. The mirror folds against a side of the recess. Two hinged mirrors may be used.

1874

2286. Maas, J. July 1. [*Provisional protection only.*]

Fares and admission-fees, registering and checking; receipts, checking and recording.—An apparatus for counting the money received by the attendants on public vehicles or at places of entertainment or refreshment bars is arranged to show the total sum in pounds, shillings, and pence. A central shaft, rotated by a handle, carries a wheel with twelve teeth, and an index or dial. The wheel gears with two pawls, one of which carries the hammer of a gong, the other preventing the wheel from being turned in the wrong direction. A pinion on the central shaft drives a second shaft carrying a dial or index which indicates shillings. The second shaft drives a third shaft which carries a dial or index indicating pounds. Behind the wheel gearing, and in the same case, is a roll of paper divided transversely into lengths, each representing a penny. The paper is drawn out from the case by rollers pressed together by springs and rotated by toothed gearing, and lengths corresponding to the fares paid are torn off and issued to the passenger or purchaser, and the movement of the wheel gearing adds up the sums received. In refreshment bars &c., a duplicated apparatus is used, one part for indicating the pence and another for indicating the shillings. The two parts are connected to a third apparatus which adds the totals of the two other parts. The paper roll &c. is omitted from the third apparatus.

2334. Morris, J. July 3.

Theatrical and like wearing-apparel; trimmings.— Articles of dress for stage wear are made in portions united together by pins which are attached to strings or cords, so that, by pulling the strings &c., the pins are withdrawn, thus allowing the portions to fall apart and disclose

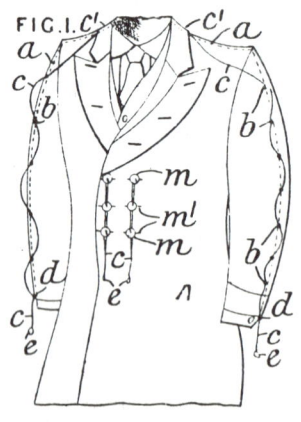

other garments worn beneath. By these means, a person giving character sketches may come upon the stage in ordinary evening dress and, while talking to the audience, may imperceptibly change his dress to that of an old man, and then to that of a lady, and so on, the various costumes being arranged one under another in their required order. Fig. 1 shows the invention applied to a coat A opening along the line *a* outside the sleeves and at the shoulders, and secured by pins *b* attached to cords *c*. The cords are permanently attached to the collar at *c¹* and are passed through loops *d* and provided with tassels *e*. By pulling the cords, the coat is caused to fall below the waist, when a portion of the next garment, such as the skirt of a lady's dress, falls over it and thus conceals it. Buttons *m*, with faces of two different colours, &c., are mounted on wires *m¹* acting as pivots, and are attached to strings *c* by which they are reversed at will. Epaulettes and other like articles may be similarly made reversible. Gaiters or stockings made according to this invention may be so formed that they can be worn over Balmoral boots, to give the appearance of low shoes, and may, on pulling a cord and loosening the pins, be drawn up to the waist, so as to disappear and leave the boots in view. In all cases, the cords *c*, pins *b*, and divisions *a* are preferably concealed from the audience by flaps or other means. Small metal eyes or loops may be attached to the under part of the flaps, to pass through the garments and through these eyes the pins *b* may be passed, to cause the flaps to set flat.

2410. Waterhouse, B. July 9. [*Provisional protection only.*]

Fares and admission-fees, registering.—An apparatus for registering the numbers of persons carried by omnibuses or tramcars, or entering and leaving theatres, concert-halls, public gardens, &c., consists of a step or platform actuating suitable counting-apparatus. The outer end of one of the levers which support the step is connected by a rod to a lower lever with a tooth for revolving a star-wheel. On the same shaft as the star-wheel is a ratchet-wheel with the same number of teeth. A pawl, acting on the teeth of the ratchet-wheel, is carried by a lever pivoted on the shaft; and the other end of the lever carries a pin which projects between two studs on the rod connected to the step. The platform is supported by springs, which are regulated so that a person of full weight, both on entering and leaving, presses down the platform to the full extent and causes the pawl to pass two teeth of the ratchet-wheel; the weight of a child causes one tooth to be taken up. The catch acting in the star-wheel brings the indicator to the exact mark, and a spring brings the pawl into position for actuating the ratchet.

2864. Carter, J. H., and **Carter, J. H.** Aug. 20. [*Provisional protection only.*]

Checks and tokens, collecting; fares, collecting.—As an additional check to boxes used for collecting fares, checks, or tickets in public conveyances, theatres, &c., a glass hopper having an opening at the bottom is fixed above the table of the box upon which the money &c. is placed, so that the money &c. passes down upon the table and may be examined or counted while it is enclosed by the hopper, before it is precipitated into the box in the usual manner.

3228. Lynn, H. S., [*Tobin, T. W.*]. Sept. 21. [*Provisional protection only.*]

Illusions, producing.—A recess is arranged in the edge of each of two mirrors, which are set more or less at right-angles in such a manner that portions of a living figure may be exposed or concealed from view. By substituting and removing dummy limbs or parts for the real ones, and by exposing or concealing the real parts, varied effects are produced. Two curtains extend in curves from the inner edges of the mirrors in such a manner that the exposed figure appears isolated from its surroundings.

3604. Edwards, E. Oct. 20.

Optical illusions, producing. — Comprises an arrangement of mirrors for producing illusions in theatrical and other entertainments, the object being to produce the illusion of a human being or other body being apparently taken to pieces or put together again. Two sets of glass mirrors are fitted vertically or otherwise, one set on each side of a rod or standard; each set of mirrors is composed of two or more glasses superposed, the lower ones sliding into a groove in the floor, the upper ones sliding up or down, and when up resting upon the lower ones. The entire sets are arranged at right-angles to each other and within a recess the front of which is open and facing the audience. The rod is made in as many pieces as there are mirrors. The whole is lighted from the front and adjuncts are used to heighten the effect. A performer is placed inside the recess behind the mirrors and by advancing and retiring, or moving objects toward or away from the mirrors, while they are operated by an exhibitor, causes reflections to appear in or vanish from the mirrors as required. In a modification, the mirrors are each in one piece and the vertical rod is made to resemble a spear; a part of the spear is removed and an opening made in each plate through which the performer's head is thrust, when it appears to be impaled on the spear.

3669. Hall, T. Oct. 24. [*Provisional protection only.*]

Fares and admission-fees, checking.—Tramway and omnibus &c. fares, and admission-fees to theatres, are dropped into openings in a box provided with a glass front and back. The conductor or attendant on seeing that the correct amount has been inserted actuates a spindle connected with spring flaps, upon which the money rests in the bottom of the box, and the money then falls through the open bottom into a sealed bag. Separate openings for silver and copper &c. may be provided, the glass back and front being then inclined so that the coins must fall upon the flaps. In some cases the box may be constructed to contain the money so that the bag is not necessary. In the case of change being required, the full change is given to the passenger and only the proper fare dropped into the box.

4479. Bradley, H., and **Bull, W.** Dec. 31. [*Provisional protection only.*]

Fares and admission-fees, registering and checking. —Relates to an apparatus for issuing and cancelling tickets and registering the sums paid in tramcars, omnibuses, offices, theatres, &c. The tickets, which may be numbered consecutively, are drawn from the apparatus, the price being indicated by a registering-apparatus, and a gong being struck at the same time. In a modification, the tickets are not necessarily numbered, but have the fare or fee printed upon them in duplicate. The attendant inserts into the apparatus a corner of the ticket bearing the amount of the fare &c., which is then obliterated or severed, falling into a receptacle. The withdrawal of the ticket actuates a registering-apparatus, and also impels an arm or escapement-wheel, which causes a bell to be rung and a record of the ticket to be taken. Counting-wheels show the total number of tickets used. In a modification, the inner side of the aperture is fitted with two pressure clips forced together by springs. The clips are opened by the insertion of a ticket, which is torn in withdrawing it. The arm which carries the clips is thus moved, actuating the indicating-apparatus and ringing the bell. The clips may be provided with sharp cutting-edges to separate the tickets from the counterfoil. The moving arm, in severing the tickets, springs back-wards, projecting the counterfoil into a receptacle at the back of the case. Flat surfaces on the clips, inked by the insertion of the ticket, may be made to close on it. The ticket is held lightly, during its withdrawal, by the two flat surfaces, which draw a coloured band over part of its surface.

1875

959. Wirth, F., [*Kreittmayr, J.*]. March 15.

Fireproof compositions.—Relates to a method of fireproofing wood, also applicable to the decorations of theatres, linen, and dresses. The wood is coated, first with dilute potassium silicate until it is saturated, and then, when air dry, with a more concentrated solution, then with pure potassium silicate, and finally with dilute hydrofluoric acid If the wood is to be painted, fluorspar and glass powder are mixed with the colours, and the mixture is treated with concentrated potassium silicate.

1253. Bain, L. April 7. [*Provisional protection only.*]

Omnibus, theatre, and like tickets.—The tickets used in checking the receipts of money on omnibuses &c. and at theatres &c. are bound up in a book, each leaf of which is divided into three portions. Of these, the two outer are handed to the person paying the money, while the foil is retained in the book. The outer portion is, at theatres &c., handed to the check collector, while the middle portion serves as a pass.

1597. Wappenstein, R. April 30. [*Provisional protection only.*]

Fares and admission-fees, registering and checking. —In apparatus used for registering the number of persons entering and leaving omnibuses, theatres, &c., an upper and a lower box are separated by a perforated plate, the holes in which are controlled by slides actuated by hand or from a turnstile. Pins, discs, counters, &c. fall from the upper box through the holes in the plate into the lower box at each entry or exit. The pins &c. may be coloured to denote the fare or admission-fee. When, as in the case of omnibuses, several different fares are charged, the boxes are divided into a corresponding number of compartments.

1804. Maskelyne, J. N., and **Clarke, J. A.** May 14. [*Provisional protection only.*]

Theatrical appliances.—Relates to means for actuating automaton mechanism by an invisible agency, so as to imitate more closely the movements of human &c. figures. Compressed air or gas is employed to set in motion clockwork mechanism, or trains of wheelwork actuated by weights or springs, &c. A piston working in a cylinder connected with a compressed air or gas receiver, or with an air pump or bellows, is fitted with a rod which strikes a locking-lever gearing with a ratchet-wheel on the motive-power axle,

thus releasing the axle and setting in motion the mechanism. When the piston is required to actuate two sets of gearing, the piston-rod carries a tappet arranged to operate a second locking-lever. To accelerate or retard the motion of the mechanism, the levers may be connected by means of wires with valves arranged in the air or gas chamber, or communicating with an exhaust, and acting in connection with a fan wheel forming part of the clockwork &c. The return motion of the piston is effected by a coiled spring or by weights. The compressed air or gas may be stored in a pedestal and discharged in pulsations by means of a valve operated by an electrical or other connection worked from a treadle &c. A similar pedestal &c. may be used for the inflation of bellows within an automaton figure, and for actuating rotating fans and wheels, without the aid of spring gearing.

1874. Davis, H. T. May 21.

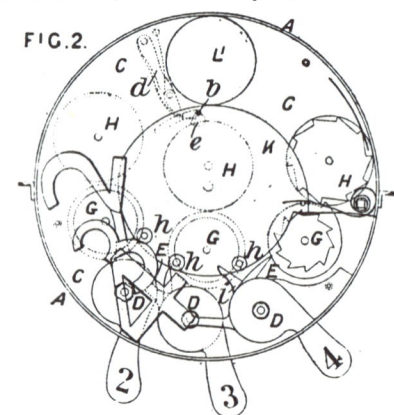

FIG. 2.

Fares and admission-fees, registering; receipts, checking.—In an apparatus used for registering the fares paid to omnibus &c. conductors and in checking the receipts in theatres, shops, &c., a cylindrical case A is covered in by two plates, the upper of which has a central aperture covered with glass and is slotted, as shown, for the passage of levers 2, 3, 4, which, when moved, operate registers intended for different amounts. The levers are mounted on pins D on a central partition or plate C, and, when moved, display the figure 2, 3, or 4, &c., denoting the fare &c. paid, under the central glass cover. At the same time, a spring catch E turns the ratchet-wheel G through the space corresponding to one tooth. A projecting tooth on the wheel G engages with the wheel

H at each revolution and moves it through one tooth-space, so that the whole number of fares indicated by the two wheels G, H is displayed under two apertures in the bottom cover ; the various other kinds of fares are similarly registered on their particular registers. A plate K, pivoted centrally on the plate C, is turned slightly at each movement of any of the levers 2, 3, 4, by the engagement of pins *h* and catches *i*, &c. and moves a pin *b* in a slot in the plate C so that the spring catch *d* and hammer *e* of a bell are forced back, finally being released and springing back so as to strike the bell. Springs are provided for returning the plate K and levers 2, 3, 4 to their original positions, and for preventing the wheels G, H from moving backwards. The bell is secured to the upper plate, which is perforated in order that the sound may issue, and projects under the central plate C through a hole L¹ in it. The bottom plate may be hinged and fastened by a lock, or may be fixed and be provided with a locked slide which may be withdrawn for the inspection of the registers. The internal figures displayed in the central openings may be transparencies on coloured or dark discs, or otherwise. In a modification of the apparatus, a lamp is fixed inside the case or may be otherwise applied, so that the figures are displayed in front of the light. The apparatus may be carried on a strap or fixed to a vehicle &c., wires being attached so that it may be actuated when at the further end inside by the conductor outside.

2120. Mueller, G. June 9.

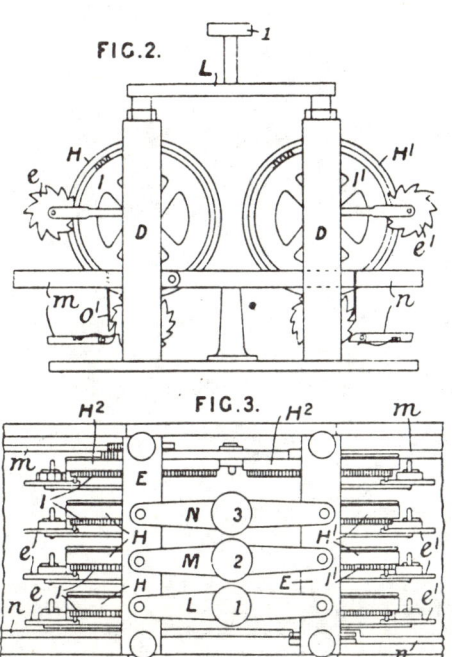

FIG.2.

FIG.3.

Fares and admission-fees, registering and checking ; counting-apparatus. — In an apparatus used for registering the number of persons who enter

and leave tramway cars &c. and places of amusement, registers are set in motion by the action of projections on the vertical shafts of two turnstiles upon pivoted pawl levers *m, n*, Figs. 2 and 3,

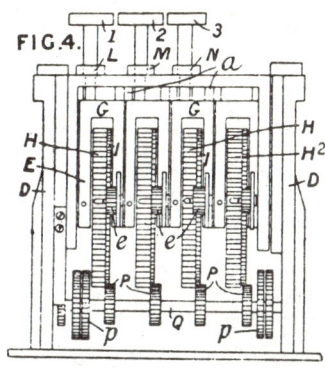

FIG.4.

in a case over the door. In this case are placed four standards D, between which are placed movable frames E carrying the register-wheels H, H¹ on axles in forked metal pieces G ; these pieces slide on rectangular guide bars *a*, Fig. 4, in the frame E. In the apparatus shown the register H² is intended to check the total numbers of entries and exits, while the three registers H, H¹ are put in and taken out of gear in order to register the number of entries and exits respectively during the different stages of the journey of a tramway car &c. Each wheel H &c. is attached to a toothed wheel I which carries a pin for the purpose of moving the other register wheels *e* at each complete revolution. At the beginning of a journey all the knobs 1, 2, 3 on the cross-bars L, M, N are pushed in so that all the wheels I, I¹ are in gear with the pinions P on the lower shaft Q in the case ; after the first stage is finished the knob 1 is pulled out, and so on throughout the journey. When a person enters the car, the shaft of the entry turnstile actuates the lever *m* so that the pawl *o*¹ turns the ratchet-wheel *p*, shaft Q, pinions P, and such of the wheels I as may be in gear with the pinions P, in order to register the entry on the wheels H. After a wheel H has turned through a complete revolution, the corresponding wheel *e* is moved through one tooth space. Exits are recorded on the wheels H¹, *e*¹. The case in which the apparatus is mounted is locked so that the register may be withdrawn and inspected only by the proper person.

2683. Hughes, W. C. July 29.

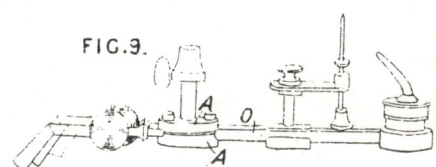

FIG.9.

Limelight apparatus. — The jets of dissolving-view lanterns, are constructed as shown in Fig. 9, no soldering being required. The clamps A are tightened on the supply pipes O by screws. The casing is of metal with separate linings or a jacket, the exterior body being perforated to allow air to enter.

3024. Tee, H. Aug. 27.

Tickets, issuing.—The tickets issued upon public vehicles and at places of entertainment &c. are carried in a roll 1, Figs. 1 and 4, on a flanged drum, and are led between friction rollers 6, 7 within the apparatus shown to an outlet or slot 15. A hand-lever 11 projecting through the top of the case drives a wheel 9 on a spindle 10 by means of a ratchet-wheel 12 and a pawl. A pinion 8 and the roller 7 are thus driven and force a fixed length of ticket through the slot 15 so that it may be then torn off. Pins 16 on the face of the roller 7 engage with and lift the end 17 of a bent lever or bell-hammer 18, which is thrown back, by the action of a spring 22 on a pinion 23 on the axle 19, in order to strike a bell 24 when a pin 16 slips past the lever. The bell is mounted on an arm 25. Units, tens, and hundreds registering-wheels 38, each numbered from zero to nine, indicate through openings 37 the number of tickets issued. These wheels are driven one from the other in the usual manner, the units wheel being mounted on the spindle 10. The roll 1 of tickets may be renewed by slacking the nuts and removing the drum. The lever 11 may also be used to actuate a punch or other cancelling-device. In a modification, the lever 11 is replaced by a sliding stud which causes a pivoted pawl to engage with pins on the face of

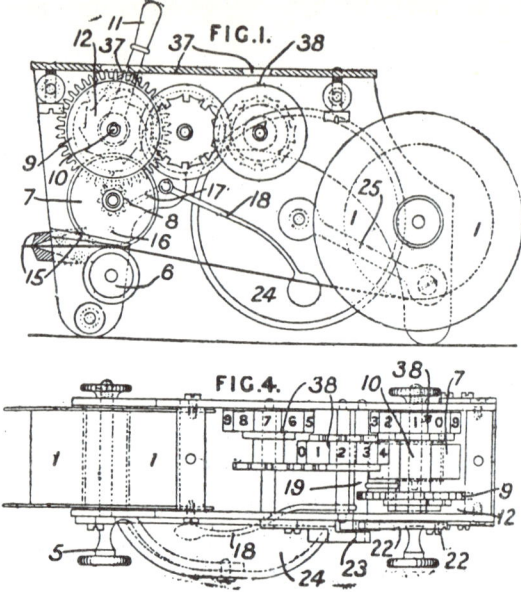

the wheel 9 in order to turn it. These pins act on the bell-hammer in the manner already described. A stop attached to the pawl engages with another pin on the wheel 9 and so prevents this wheel from being turned through too much at any movement of the sliding stud. The stud is returned after each movement by a spring.

3067. Dando, W. P. Sept. 1.

Gymnastic apparatus.— Relates to apparatus of the kind described in Specifications No. 1234, A.D. 1871, and No. 3366, A.D. 1875, for raising a performer suddenly into the air, in imitation of an extraordinary jump, and then sustaining him in mid air. Multiplying gear is applied to the springs, so as to lessen their length or increase the height of the " jump," and a stop is provided to sustain the performer in mid air to enable him to imitate a bird &c. The multiplying gear shown at Fig. 1 consists of a drum mounted in standards *i* on a platform *e*, suspended beneath the stage roof, and having a large part *h* around which the wire *l* supporting the performer is wound, and a smaller part *g* around which passes the strap *k* connected with the springs *a*. The springs *a* are attached at one end to a fixed disc *b* and at the other to a disc *c* sliding on guide-rods *f*. They may be all distended at once by means of a winch handle *o* on a pinion *p* gearing with a ring of teeth *q* on the drum *h*, and they are kept distended by a bolt *m* taking into a hole in the drum *h*. The device for sustaining the performer in mid air, after he has been raised by the release of the springs *a*, consists of an india-

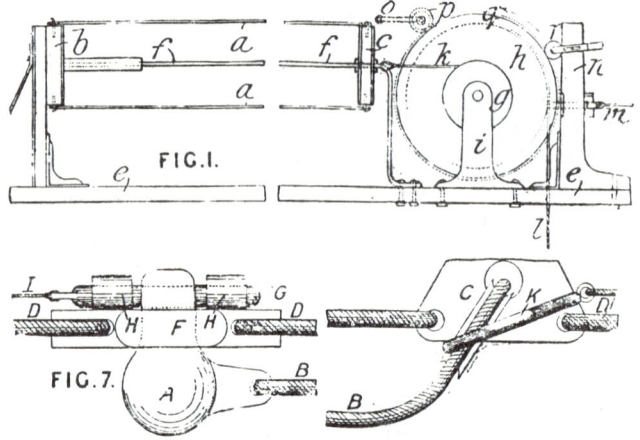

rubber roller *r* mounted on a forked lever between the standard *n* and drum *h*, which acts as a grip to prevent the wire *l* unwinding. In another kind of multiplying gear the wire *l* passes over two pulleys and its end is fastened to a fixed standard. One of the pulleys is mounted in a frame fixed to the movable disc *b*, so that the springs raise the performer twice the distance of their travel. Other arrangements of pulleys or tackle may be used. The apparatus may be constructed with the springs arranged vertically. The Provisional Specification states that the apparatus may be used to represent a monkey jumping from tree to tree or from a considerable height.

Trapezes; horizontal bars.—To enable a trapeze bar to be fixed, when required, for use as a horizontal bar, a frame F, Fig. 7, carrying staples H is arranged at the centre of the stay rope D, and the trapeze bar A is formed with an eye which passes up through the frame F. A bolt G is inserted through this eye, and through the staples H to fix the bar A, which bolt is withdrawn to release the trapeze by means of a cord I. A ring K encircling the trapeze rope B and stay rope D¹ is drawn along by means of a rope to lift the trapeze and assist the performer in swinging. The trapeze bar A is suspended by ropes B from brackets C supported by wire ropes D, D¹ stretched horizontally and vertically.

3215. Bellini, H. L. Sept. 14. [*Provisional protection only.*]

Reflectors.—The reflectors of ceiling lights for theatres, halls, &c. are " partially perforated " for the escape of the heated air from the gas. They are hinged or removable to facilitate cleaning and to allow workmen's " slings " to be lowered.

3366. Oliver, G. Sept. 25.

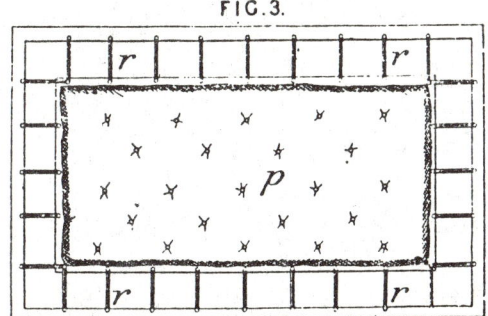

FIG. 3.

Gymnastic apparatus.—To render the " jumping " or weight-raising apparatus, described in Specification No. 1234, A.D. 1871, available for use in buildings which are not very lofty, the springs are arranged horizontally, instead of vertically, as shown at *a*, Fig. 1. They are connected with a stationary crosshead *d* and a sliding crosshead *b* working in guides *c*. The wire or rope *g*, to which the performer &c. is attached, passes over a pulley *h* and is secured to an eye in a bolt *b¹* fixed to the crosshead *b*. The springs may be all distended at once by means of a cord passing round a drum operated by a winch handle and gearing, and connected with the sliding crosshead. They are kept distended by a bolt *i* which passes through the eye in the bolt *b¹* and is operated by a hand-lever *k*. To enable the performer to be raised from different parts of the stage, the apparatus is arranged to turn on a pivot, and a number of pulleys *k* and wires are provided ; both crossheads are made to slide in the guides *c*. The spring apparatus may be placed beneath instead of above the stage and connected with the wire *g* by cords or wires led up over pulleys. The Provisional Specification states that two wires *g* may be used to enable the performer to execute feats in the air. Fig. 3 shows a mattress *p* designed to receive a performer as he descends from a height. It is supported in a frame, by springs *r*, so as to yield under the weight of the performer. It may be provided with a rack and-pawl arrangement *t*, *u*, to prevent its rebound, and thus enable it to be used as a trap, as shown in Fig. 4. The springs *r* may be arranged vertically, and connected with the mattress by cords *s* passing over pulleys, spring boards, and the like. The Provisional Specification states that the mattress may be used as a spring board.

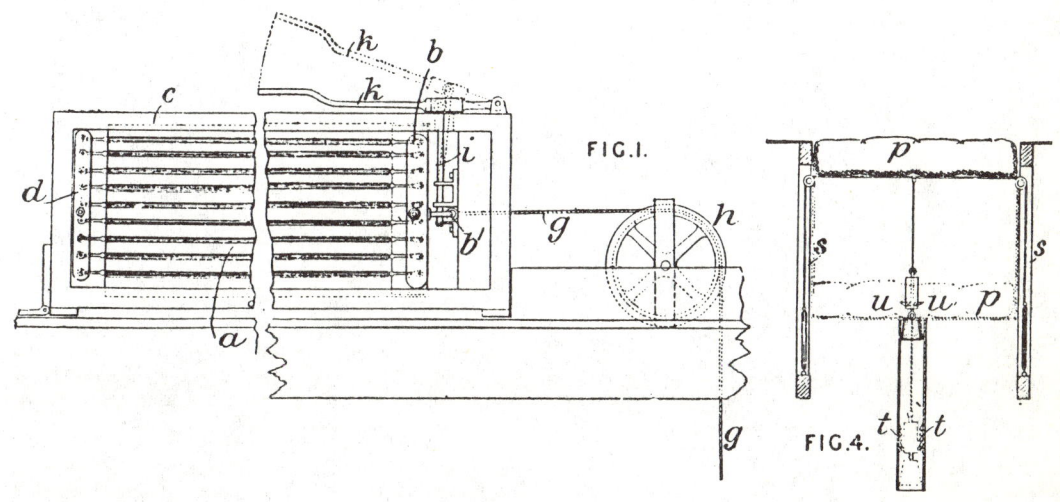

FIG. I.

FIG. 4.

3593. Brown, A. B. Oct. 16.

Theatrical appliances.—Consists in the application of hydraulic power for working stage scenery. A special hydraulic accumulator fed by an automatically-controlled steam pump supplies pressure to hoists for raising the scenes, platforms, &c. and also for forcing water for artificial cascades. The

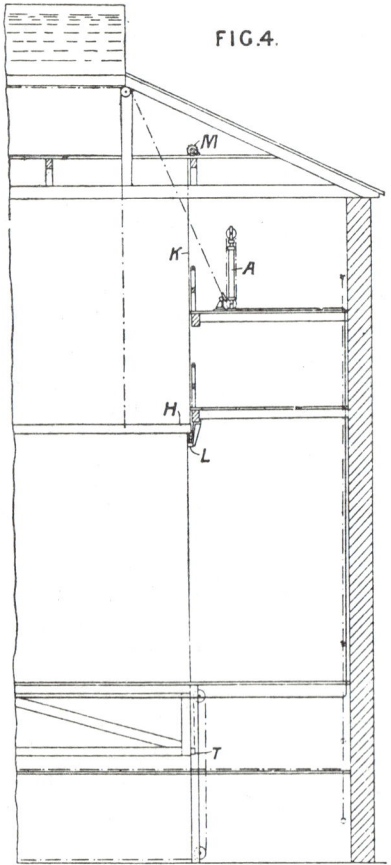

FIG.4.

3602. Bain, L., and Urch, W. H. Oct. 16.
[*Provisional protection only.*]

Fares and admission-fees, checking; receipts, checking.—Relates to apparatus for checking the money taken at restaurants, theatres, and other places of amusement, and on omnibuses and tramway cars &c. The apparatus is also stated to be used for checking the receipt of goods. A number of checks are confined in a vertical pipe and are ejected one by one as required by the money-taker pressing upon a handle connected to suitable mechanism. This part of the apparatus is also connected to indicators at any desired place, so that the proper authorities can see at any time the total number of checks issued. Another indicator placed beside that already mentioned is in connection with a machine into which the check-taker places the checks as they are handed to him by the persons entering the theatre &c. The number of checks so returned to the check-taker is indicated at this second part of the apparatus and also beside the indication of the number issued.

3726. Smith, G. H. Oct. 27.

Seats for theatres and other places are connected to the frame *a* by boxes *d* containing coiled or other springs, which, when an occupant rises, lifts his seat and folds it against the back *b*.

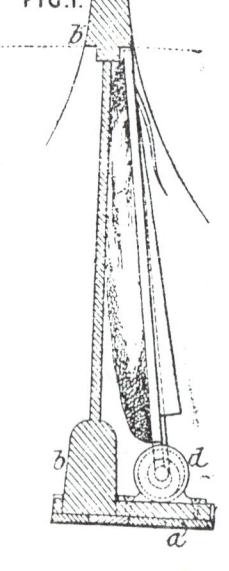

FIG.I.

4068. Scott, J. S., and Poilly, E. de. Nov. 23. [*Provisional protection only.*]

Lighting and extinguishing gas; regulating flame.—Relates to apparatus for the instantaneous lighting of gas burners in towns, theatres, public and private buildings &c. which apparatus is operated by means of the variation of the pressure of the gas in the mains, and may also be used "to gauge the "pressure of supply of gas." The gas on its way to the burner is led under a double bell cap dipping into a liquid, or into a chamber divided by a diaphragm. A gauge or manometer is fitted to the chamber. When the pressure is low, the outlet to the burner is sealed by the liquid and only a small quantity of gas passes to a pilot burner. When the pressure is increased the level of the liquid is lowered and gas passes to the burner, being ignited by the pilot flame. Wire gauze or floats may be used to prevent the flame from flickering as the gas

various scenes are hung from beams H having slotted ends to slide up guides K anchored by springs L and kept taut by ratchet drums M. The beams H are suspended by ropes working noiselessly over the pulleys of hoists A. The ropes are guided by inclined pulleys mounted in blocks which are movable along a slotted casting for adjustment. The platform or bridge T is worked by a hoist similar to that shown at A. The speed of ascent or descent of the scenes &c. can be regulated by adjusting, by means of screw stops. the travel of the hand-levers employed for operating the valves of the hydraulic hoists. The water pressure may be used for fire-extinguishing, for working fans, and for other uses.

bubbles through the liquid. Valves may be used in place of the liquid seal, and sometimes the flow of the gas is regulated by its introduction into a chamber acting in connection with a perforated diaphragm suitably arranged. "These arrange- "ments may be adopted as a gas gauge to keep the "gas burning at a given height or size of flame."

4404. Hunt, W. L. Dec. 18.

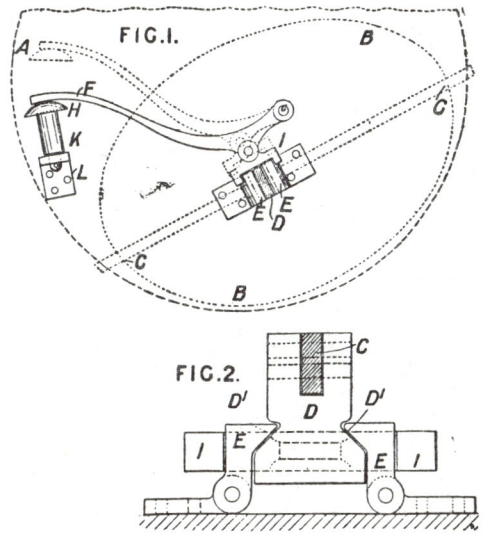

FIG.I.

FIG.2.

Gymnastic and acrobatic apparatus.—Relates to apparatus, to be employed in theatrical and gymnastic performances, for propelling a performer or object from a cannon by means of springs. The actuating springs are retained by a catch or lock, which is released by the explosion of powder &c. within a small tube. Within the cannon, the base or breech plate of which is indicated by the circle A, is a plate B upon which the performer or object rests. This plate is connected by arms C with curved arms, which work in the cannon and are fitted with the actuating india-rubber springs. Secured under the plate B is a lug D having grooves D¹, into which take hinged jaws E. A lever F carries at one end a bifurcated jaw or spanner I, which, when the plate B is drawn back, embraces and holds the jaws E and retains the actuating springs in tension. At the other end of the lever F is a cup H resting on a cylinder K, which is supported in a bracket L and contains gunpowder or other explosive. When the explosive is ignited by means of a match, percussion, or electricity, the lever F is raised, thus releasing the jaws E, and allowing the springs to force forward the plate B, so as to propel the performer or object from the cannon.

4486. Pichler, S. F., and **Gardner, S. V.** Dec. 24. [*Provisional protection only.*]

Theatrical appliances.—Consists of an arrangement of rollers or drums for raising and lowering weights, applicable also for producing illusory effects suitable for public exhibitions. Two rollers or drums are mounted in a box or receptacle and gear together by spur gearing. Separate ropes or chains are attached to, and wound on, each drum, the free end of one rope being passed through an aperture in the upper part of the box and secured at the point to which it is desired the weight should be elevated ; the free end of the other rope is passed through an aperture in the lower side of the box and is secured at the point to which the weight is to descend. The weight is raised by hauling on the lower rope. A differential arrangement of pulleys may be used instead of the two rollers.

1876

97. Pichler, S. F. Jan. 8. [*Provisional protection only.*]

Theatrical appliances.—A walking-figure "for "use in public exhibitions" is constructed like the human form, and the limbs are operated by cams or cranks on the sides of the wheel of a barrow in front of the figure, which move rigid jointed levers connected to the arms, legs, and hips. Stops or other devices are used to stiffen the joints of the limbs when they are not moving. Guides at the upper part of the figure cause the levers to produce lateral motions in the legs and feet. The wheel of the barrow consists of two plates which revolve on opposite sides of a fixed plate. The lower part of the fixed plate is attached to a cylindrical piston in a hollow bar of steel or other material which supports the figure. The bar is corrugated to give it the appearance of a rope, and the upper part is slotted longitudinally. The piston is fixed to a rope or ropes and is drawn through the bar by a winch or other apparatus, thus drawing the figure along the bar. The external plates of the wheel are corrugated to correspond with the corrugations on the bar.

474. Lee, W., [*Pullon, J. T.,* and *Sykes, W.*]. Feb. 5. [*Provisional protection only.*]

Fares and admission-fees, registering and checking.—Relates to apparatus for checking the fares taken on street cars or omnibuses in which the inside fare is double that of the outside or in which both fares are the same, but which is also applicable for registering the number of persons entering public places of entertainment. When the apparatus is applied to a street car, the platform is railed in, leaving a passage for one person only in such a position that a turnstile is turned through a quarter-revolution or a half-revolution according as the person passes to the top or to the inside of the car. The turnstile, by means of a double-acting "capstan" clutch and pawl, drives a counter and a shaft carrying a worm ; spur gearing intervenes also between the turnstile and the counter. A four-toothed ratchet cam and a pawl under the clutch assist the passengers to rotate the turnstile, and prevent the counter from being turned backwards.

Counting-apparatus.—In a counter four loose parallel discs on a central shaft are each numbered with a zero and from one to nine and are provided on one side with ten pins and on the other with one pin. The worm driven from the turnstile engages with the pins on the first disc so that each quarter-revolution of the turnstile registers one fare on this disc. The single pin on this disc engages in each revolution with a hanging tongue, which gears with the pins on the second disc in such a way that, on the change from nine to zero on the first disc, the second disc is advanced from one number to that next in order. The second, third, and fourth discs operate similarly. A worm on a key carried by the inspector may be introduced through a keyhole and turned to set back the discs to zero. This counter may be used in connection with apparatus other than a turnstile.

2180. Krüger, S. D. May 23. [*Provisional protection only.*]

Globes ; revolving lanterns.—The glass cylinders or barrels of large lamps or Chinese lanterns hung or fixed outside shops, theatres, hotels, &c. are made of variously-coloured glass, and are caused to revolve by water motors attached directly to them or connected with them by a band &c. Advertisements may be displayed on the barrels.

2438. Newbold, H. June 13. [*Provisional protection only.*]

Fares and admission-fees, checking.—In order to check the number of persons entering and leaving omnibuses, skating-rinks, theatres, ferries, or other places where a charge is made on all persons entering, a platform of sufficient width to prevent persons stepping over it is connected by levers &c. with ordinary or electric counting-apparatus. The depression of the platform by the passage of each person depresses a spring, rings a gong, and moves

3304. Thomson, E. H. Aug. 23.

Fares and admission-fees, registering and checking; counting-apparatus. — Relates to an apparatus for indicating the number of persons entering or leaving an omnibus, theatre, park, or other place, and for recording on a strip of paper the total number of persons entering &c. during any period of time. A type-wheel *b* is turned by the conductor or attendant each time a person is to be registered, a lever *a* with a pawl *c* being provided for this purpose. A pointer is then moved round a fixed dial to indicate the number of persons which has been registered. In the case shown, separate type-wheels &c. are provided for two different classes of

the register as required. When electrical apparatus is employed, an electric bell, which does not break the circuit when in operation, is placed in the circuit, and an endless band printed or marked with numbers is moved onwards by the movements of the platform in order to register the persons passing.

3231. Peebles, D. B. Aug. 16.

Lighting and extinguishing gas; gas burners. — In the gas governor described in Specification No. 2328, A.D. 1875, [*Abridgment Class* Gas distribution], the weight of the small controlling-governor may be removed and replaced at pleasure by means of an electromagnet. The apparatus is then suitable for controlling the street

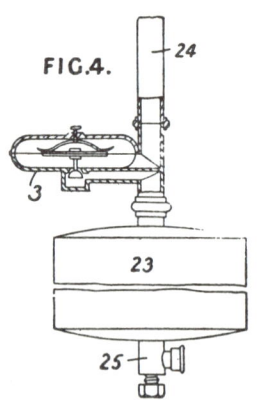

FIG.4.

lamps of a district, single burners, the burners of a theatre, railway station, or factory &c. A gas-torch or lamp-lighter is made by combining a reservoir 23 for compressed gas with a governor 3 such as is described in Specification No. 2446, A.D. 1871, [*Abridgment Class* Gas distribution], the governor being loaded preferably by a spring. The inlet nozzle 25 is fitted with a screw plug and the burner at the end of the pipe 24 may be shielded in the usual way. In the Provisional Specification, a partially self-regulating gas burner is described. A tip of steatite or other substance is fixed in the outer end of the brass shell, and a small block of soft metal, through which a small hole is drilled, is fixed in the inner end of the shell.

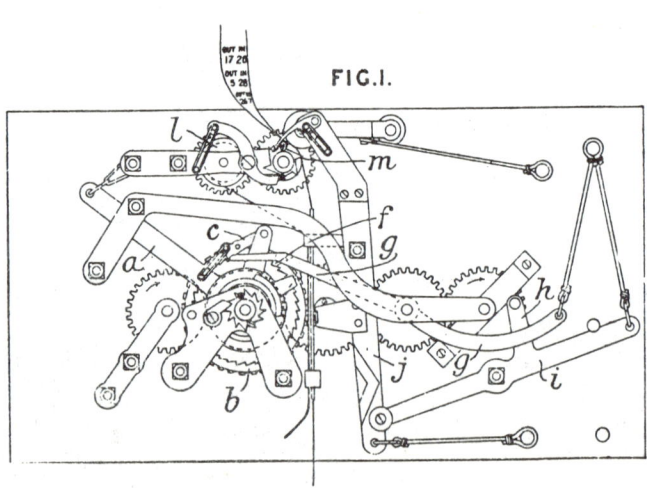

FIG.I.

passengers. At the end of any required period of time, a lever *i* is turned by an inspector and the pawls *f, c* are then lifted by the action of the arm *h* on the lever *g* so that the type-wheels are returned to zero by springs. A platen-lever *j* is also moved by the lever *i* so as to press a strip of paper against the type-wheels and so record the state of the indicating-dials. The lever *j* operates two wheels *l, m*. The wheel *l* moves the carbonized paper by means of which the impression is taken, and the wheel *m* moves forward the record. A bell may be provided to give audible notice of the movement of the indicator and type-wheel. Instead of using carbonized paper for giving the impression, inking-mechanism may be provided for inking the type-wheels.

3867. Woodbury, W. B., [*Wilson, E.*]. Oct. 6. [*Provisional protection only.*]

Limelight apparatus.—The limelight is adapted to a sciopticon magic-lantern "by making the "flame chamber cover movable." The square opening for deflecting the flame is replaced by one which is brought to a point at one end, thus causing the double flames to meet at that end. The oxyhydrogen burner employed consists of a solid block of wood through which the gas pipes pass, and the position of the flame is regulated by means of a brass spring and screw projecting from the instrument.

1877

37. Petit, H. F. E. Jan. 3.

[*Provisional protection only.*]

Advertising.—Pictorial representations of historical scenery or objects, groups of figures, animals, or flowers, fans, cards, or other accessories are appropriately combined upon a drop-scene or curtain with the advertisements it is desired to display. The curtain may have apertures, behind which may pass moving parts, actuated by electricity or by any suitable machinery and bearing advertisements.

147. Webb, H. Jan. 11.

Unicycle for traversing a wire or other rope. — The wheel of the machine is similar to the driving-wheel of a bicycle, and is provided with a grooved felloe to receive the rope as shown. The unicycle is balanced by a trapeze frame M, suspended from the downwardly-projecting ends of the frame D. A single vertical bar may be employed in lieu of the frame N.

Abridged also in Class *Toys &c.*

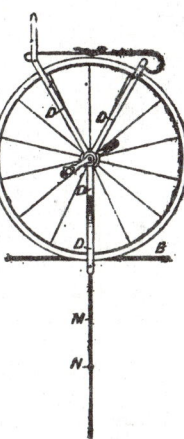

1099. Woodbury, W. B., [*Talbot, R.*]. March 19. [6*d.*]

Relates to apparatus of the kind in which a flame, produced by the combustion of hydrogen or other gas and air, is directed upon lime, platinum, or other suitable substance. The application to magic lanterns and theatres is mentioned.

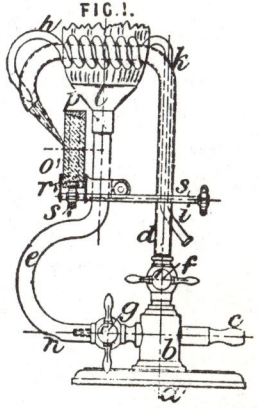

FIG. 1.

Gas and air, mixing and heating.—A stand *a* is provided with a pipe *b*, into which hydrogen is admitted through the junction *c*. The pipe has two branches, *d* and *e*, the supply of gas to either being regulated by the stop cocks *f, g*. Into the branch *d* is inserted at *i* the smaller pipe *h*, which is again brought out at *k*, and, being coiled helically round the pipe *d*, re-enters the latter and ends in a jet concentric with the larger pipe. The hydrogen, entering the pipe *e* through a jet, mixes with air admitted at *n*, the compound being consumed by a "Bunsen" burner at *l*. Compressed air is directed into the pipe *h* at *i*, and, after passing through the coil, where it is heated by the burner, is discharged mixed with gas from the pipe *d* similarly heated, in a jet upon the disc *o*; or the gas may be forced into the pipe *h*, whilst air passes through the pipe *d*. The gas may be either ordinary coal gas, or the vapour of spirit, petroleum, or other suitable vaporizable hydrocarbon; or it may be produced by the action of diluted acid upon iron or zinc. A modification in which four burners are used is also described. Four helical coils pass round separate parts of a tubular ring, to which gas and air are supplied through radial pipes.

Incandescent material ; fitting and adjusting same.—A block of lime, platinum, compressed carbonate of lime, or the latter mixed with asbestos, is fitted into a conical opening in the ring p, which is carried on friction rollers in the frame r, adjusted upon the pipe e. This ring has round it a toothed rack, which gears with a pinion s, by which means different parts of the block may be exposed to the jet. The block and frame can be raised or lowered by a screw clipping it to the pipe e. In the modification mentioned above the incandescent block is carried upon a vertical spindle above the tubular ring.

1957. Newton, F. May 18. [6d.]

Magic-lantern lamps.—The burner is enclosed in a chamber with a glass front, while a reflector replaces the usual glass back, and there are also means for keeping the condensers &c. cool. A hinged reflector f replaces the usual glass back, and f^2 is an eyehole fitted with glass &c. The glass front g is held by clips g^1, g^2, and is fitted with a projecting flange i to prevent the flames striking

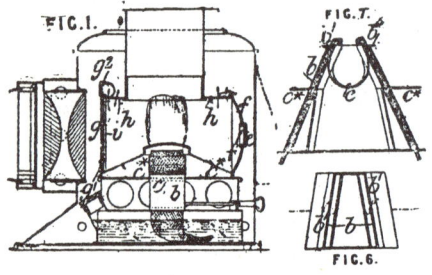

the glass. The wick holder, Figs. 6 and 7, is double, the two wick-tubes being placed at an angle. A flange b^1 protects the flames from air currents. The condenser socket is formed with an annular perforated space round which air circulates. There are side doors when oxyhydrogen light is used. In the Provisional Specification it is stated that, to prevent oxidization of the sheet iron of the lamp, it is coated with copper &c. by electro-deposition.

Abridged also in Classes *Philosophical instruments ; Toys &c.*

2241. Keevil, H. June 8. [4d. *Drawings to Specification.*]

Oxhydrogen lamp for magic lanterns. —The jet is fixed on a pivot, and by a lever the flame is made to play on the lime cylinder opposite either of two condensers. Abridged also in Classes *Philosophical instruments ; Toys &c.*

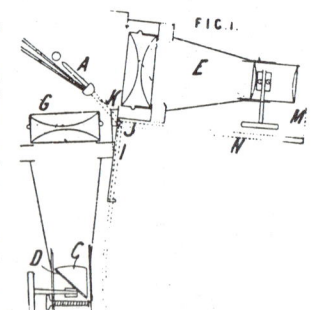

2356. Hamlet, T. June 16.

[*Provisional protection only.*]

Velocipede for tight ropes.—A unicycle is provided

with a seat above the wheels, and with the framework extended downwards past the rope. A small roller is mounted in the frame, on the under side, to keep the machine on the rope, and bars or bars and ropes carrying a second performer are suspended from the frame to maintain the equilibrium.

Abridged also in Class *Toys &c.*

3607. Knott, K. Sept. 26.

[*Provisional protection only.*]

Air for ventilation, treating.—Designed for cooling the air of churches, theatres, and other large buildings, being also applicable for heating purposes. Consists in forcing air from a blower through coils within a tank that is filled with a cooling or heating medium, and then distributing the air for various purposes. If used for cooling, the tank is supplied with a suitable refrigerating-agent or connected to an ice-making machine. For heating purposes it is supplied with hot water from a boiler. The tank is covered with a non-conducting substance, and the coils of pipe can be cleared of any rime that forms in them by the introduction of brine or any other similar agent. For large buildings, the air is distributed by perforated pipes. In those with many rooms, a main pipe from the tank passes around the structure and returns to the blower, perforated branch pipes with stop-cocks distributing the air in each room, the air thus lost being replaced from the atmosphere by a valve in the main inlet pipe of the blower.

Abridged also in Classes *Brewing &c. ; Cooling &c. ; Distilling &c. ; Heating.*

4581. Villiers, R. E. Dec. 4.

Ventilating buildings.—The roof is constructed so that a large aperture in it may be readily uncovered to allow the escape of heated and vitiated air from the building, and to allow ready extinction of fire. In the case of large buildings, the main walls 6. Fig. 1, are connected by two or more girders 2, which again are connected by two, four, or more cross girders 3. The central pair of these

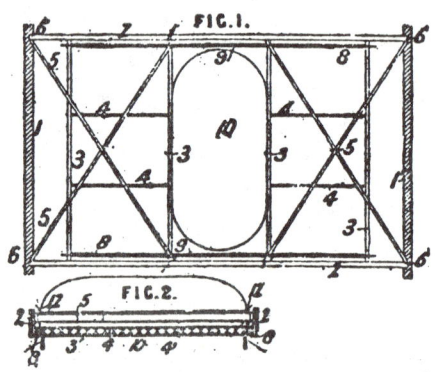

latter are not connected, but the others are joined by girders 4 parallel to the main girders. The whole structure is braced together by diagonal ties 5 and forms part of the roof, the space 10 between the central girders remaining uncovered. Any other suitable way of forming an opening in the roof may, however, be adopted. The opening can be covered when necessary by means of a dome, Fig. 2, which, by means of an arrangement of bevel gearing worked from a suitable point in the building, is moved on wheels 12 along rails 9 carried by girders 8 attached to the framework. The dome may be constructed with sashes which may or may not be glazed. The invention is applied to bath rooms and buildings, billiard rooms, chapels, churches, concert halls, skating rinks, theatres, and other buildings.

Abridged also in Classes *Buildings &c. ; Fish &c.*

4587. Farini, G. A. Dec. 4. [6*d.*]

Theatre stage appliances.—Relates to apparatus by which a performer is projected through the air by the agency of springs, powder, steam, or compressed air. The first part of the invention is an improvement on that described in Specification No. 1572, A.D. 1870.

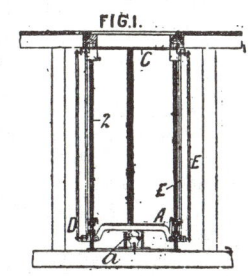

FIG. 1.

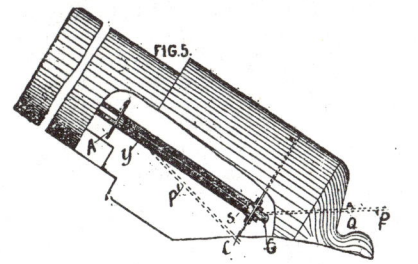

FIG. 5.

The central guiding stem there described is discarded, the bar D, Fig. 1, which supports the platform A on which the performer stands, having rollers working between two guiding pillars 2, one on each side. The bar is connected at its ends to rubber or other springs E attached above to the framework C. The platform is held down by a locking-apparatus at *a*, from which it is released by means of a lever arrangement, and the performer is shot up through the trap &c. B. The second part of the invention relates to improvements on apparatus described in Specification No. 4404, A.D. 1875. In a cannon suspended from the roof is placed mechanism similar to that above, except that the lever of the locking-apparatus is freed by explosion instead of by hand. An arm supporting the lever is in contact with the mouth of a cylinder containing powder, which, when ignited, drives away the arm and releases the lever and platform. The platform may be propelled by powder instead of springs. An outer tube *y*, Fig. 5, is screwed to C, and a second tube telescoping in *y* is fixed to A ; the piston *s* on the end of the inner tube is made tight with packing, and powder is exploded in the space between *s* and the bottom of *y*. Or a tube G is fitted on below C to contain the explosive. Or spiral springs inside *y* are used to propel the piston, which is drawn down to the locking-mechanism by a screw, fitted on to its under side and afterwards detached. Or steam or compressed air may be admitted beneath the piston through a pipe P by opening a cock Q. At the limit of the stroke, a side opening is uncovered, and the steam or air escapes by a pipe P¹, the cock being first closed by hand or by levers from the moving platform. The pipes may serve as guy-rods to the cannon. A pistol &c. fired by electricity or otherwise at the starting of the platform adds effect.

Abridged also in Classes *Toys &c.*

1878

1932. Scantlebury, W. May 14. [*Provisional protection only.*]

Theatrical appliances.—Illuminated effects are produced by vacuum tubes applied to or carried by the performer, or applied to grotesque figures, fairies' wands, glass vessels, or other properties. The current is produced by a special portable battery and induction coil.

2008. Aronson, J. N. May 20.

[*Provisional protection only.*]

Producing scenic effects for theatrical and like purposes.—The scenery is dressed with Geissler or vacuum tubes arranged in any desired design. These tubes are connected with the source of electricity by one line-wire arranged with a series of switches or keys, so that any one, or any number of series of the vacuum tubes may be cut out of circuit or the current through them be reduced, so that at any moment desired they may have the

light shut off or reduced to produce any particular scenic effect ; or the tubes may be arranged in series, and each series have a separate line-wire ; or each tube may have a separate line-wire, as may be required or found desirable. Reflectors may be employed behind the tubes. The dresses of the actors are decorated in a similar manner, in some cases by being connected with a common source of electricity, and in others by means of a portable battery.

Abridged also in Class *Electricity &c., Div. III.*

3862. Bell, H., Bell, J., and **Coleman, J. J.** Oct. 1. *Drawings to Specification.*

Air for ventilation, treating &c.—Relates to cooling and regulating temperature and dryness of air, for purposes of ventilation and refrigeration. Air is compressed by steam pumps and, after a preliminary cooling by water and drying, is cooled to any desired extent by expansion in cylinders the pistons of which are connected to the pump pistons, and is supplied to the places to be cooled or ventilated either directly or through a filter of animal charcoal or other material. The amount supplied may be automatically suited to the temperature of the place by means of a long metallic bar connected to a throttle valve in the steam pipe. Various arrangements of supply pipes are shown. The invention is applied to the ventilation and cooling of ships' holds, cabins, and saloons of railway vehicles, and of various buildings such as hotels, theatres, halls, factories, hospitals, slaughter houses, &c.

Abridged also in Classes *Air and gases, Compressing &c.; Cooling &c.; Drying; Governors &c.; Heating; Railway &c. vehicles; Ships &c., Div. I.; Steam engines.*

4473. Gye, F. Nov. 5. [*Provisional protection only.*]

Arc lamps.—A lamp consists of a carbon stick fixed near a carbon disc which is revolved slowly and is simultaneously moved in a horizontal or vertical straight line so that the face is eaten away in a spiral line. The disc is clamped to a circular plate by means of a coned ring overlapping the edge of the disc, which is also coned. The disc, when worn, may be re-faced in a lathe.

5109. McIlvenna, C. Dec. 13.

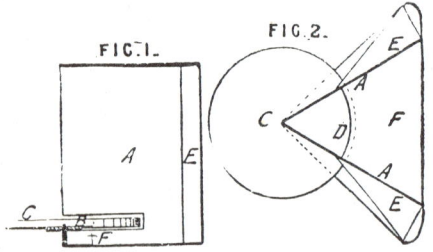

Kaleidoscopic scenic effects.—The images are seen through one or more pairs of vertical mirrors A, A which meet at an angle of 60° and which are attached to a stout framework F, the objects to be reflected being placed upon one or more trays or

discs C the centres of which are in line with the junction of the mirrors and which revolve on the pivot B. This pivot is fixed to the framework F, which forms a stand for the apparatus and is strengthened by the side wings E, these serving also to hide the edges of the trays C. The mirrors are open above and in front, and between each pair a horizontal plate D of glass, tin, &c. is arranged over the trays, so as to give the appearance of a complete circle and conceal the tray edges.

Abridged also in Classes *Philosophical instruments; Toys &c.*

5255. Morgan-Brown, W., [*Peiffer, J., MacCarty, W. F. C.,* and *Périgord de Sagan, Prince T.*]. Dec. 24. *Drawings to Specification.*

Plastic compositions &c.—Relates to the manufacture of light-absorbing powders and their use at night for buoys, sea compasses, barometers, sheet plate signboards, theatrical scenery, pictures, and artificial flowers; also to a special application of electricity, for augmenting the brilliance of the luminous particles. The powders are composed of a carbonate and a phosphate of lime produced by calcining sea shells and adding an equal part of pure lime, with which sulphur is mixed: colouring powders composed of mono-sulphure of calcium, barium, strontium, uranium. magnesium, and aluminium then being added. Powdered phosphorus is also added in some cases. The powders are either mixed with varnish to form a paste, with which the surfaces of metal. wood, and glass are coated and then covered by a transparent glass, or the object is coated with varnish and the powder sprinkled on. Objects made of cellulose, papier mâché, paper paste, artificial ivory, or coralline are whilst damp sprinkled with the powders which are then incorporated into their surfaces. Translucent luminous flexible sheets are also formed by rolling the powders after mixing them with ether and collodion in a close vase; the powders may also be mixed with stearine, paraffin. rectified glue, isinglass, or liquid silex for this purpose.

Abridged also in Classes *Electricity &c., Div. I; Glass; Hydraulic engineering; Ornamenting; Paints &c.; Paper &c.; Signalling &c.*

1879

92. Tongue, J. G., [*Lacomme, J. M. A.*]. Jan. 9.

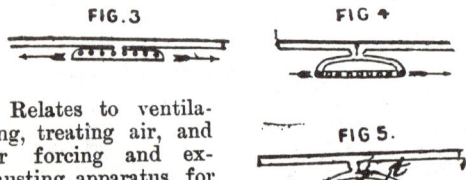

Relates to ventilating, treating air, and air forcing and exhausting apparatus, for mansions, schools, churches, theatres, &c.

Ventilators.—Fig. 3 is an inlet with horizontal apertures; Figs. 4 and 5 bell-shaped with horizontal

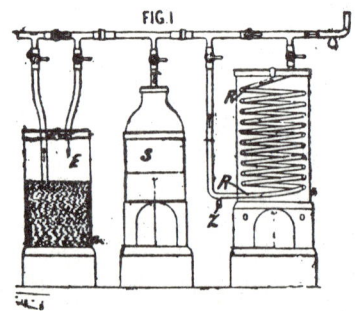

apertures, the latter being provided with a horizontal revolving fan *t*, carried by a spindle *u*, and actuated by the incoming air currents. A perforated pipe may be carried round the ceiling. Similar ventilators for outlet may be placed in lower parts of the room &c.

Apparatus for treating air.—The air is forced through a series of wash-bottles, similar to E, Fig. 1, containing purifying and other materials ; it may be mixed with fumigating &c. vapours from an evaporator *s*, and may be heated or cooled by passing through a coil R surrounded with hot or cold water or ice. Traps *z* serve to retain condensed water.

Abridged also in Classes *Air and gases, Compressing &c. ; Drains &c. ; Medicine &c. ; Rotary engines &c. ; Ships &c., Div. I.*

117. Clark, A. M., [*Martin, A. J.,* and *Tessier, E.*]. Jan. 10.

Fireproof coverings and compositions.—The following substances are employed in admixture in stated proportions for the purposes named. (1.) For fabrics, sulphate of ammonia, carbonate of ammonia, boracic acid, borax, starch, and water. (2.) For theatrical scenery, woodwork, furniture, door and window frames, &c., boracic acid, sal-ammoniac, potassic felspar, gelatine, size, and water. A body is imparted to the mixture by a calcareous substance. (3.) For coarse canvas, sails, cordage, straw, and wood, boracic acid, sal-ammoniac, borax, and water. (4.) For paper, sulphate of ammonia, boracic acid, borax, and water.

Abridged also in Class *Cements &c.*

259. Grieve, T. W. Jan. 22. *Drawings to Specification.*

Theatrical scenic effects.—Lamp shades or glasses are arranged in separately movable portions for use with electric or other lights.

Abridged also in Classes *Electricity &c., Div. IV. ; Lamps &c.*

299. Haddan, H. J., [*Molera, E.,* and *Celrain, J.*]. Jan. 24.

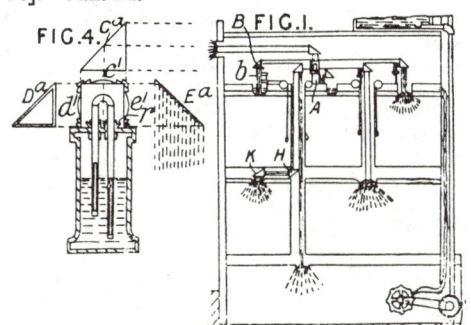

Lighting, systems of.—Relates to a system of and apparatus for illuminating houses and other buildings, streets, mines, theatrical scenes, factories, and the like, whereby the light is transmitted by means of prisms, lenses, and mirrors from a single source to several points in any desired direction. Fig. 1 represents a method of applying the system to illuminate a series of rooms in a building. An electric light A arranged in the uppermost room is enclosed by five Fresnel lenses which concentrate the light into five parallel rays—three of which are shown. These are intersected at different heights by rectangular prisms B, and are deflected into vertical beams *b* which pass through suitable openings to different rooms or to the outside of the building. The prisms can be raised or lowered by pulleys or otherwise to reflect part or the whole of the beam. The vertical beams may be again deflected by other prisms H, K in order to convey them to different rooms in which they are concentrated or diverged by suitable lenses. In combination with the lenses or prisms, suitable substances can be used to enable the light rays to be transmitted without heat, or the heat without light, or to intensify the light, or to give the desired colour, and movable shades may also be employed. The rays of light may be directed by means of prisms through underground pipes for lighting mines, streets, and other places, and the direction of the beams may be charged partly or entirely within the tubes, hollow lamp posts being sometimes employed for carrying beams of light upwards when lighting streets. Cylindrical boxes, having convex or concave glass bottoms and filled with a liquid and with any required substance for modifying the light, are interposed in the path of beams of light for diffusing the light in a room or elsewhere in either convergent or divergent rays. Fig. 4 shows an arrangement of reflectors *r*, lenses c^1, d^1, e^1, and prisms C^a, D^a, E^a round a light.

1245. Pepper, J. H., and Walker, J. J. March 28.

Scenic effects.—Relates to apparatus for producing scenic effects by the aid of mirrors. A vertical mirror *d* is used, mounted in such a manner that it can be moved, either vertically or drawn from a position d^1 into a diagonal position across a chamber *c* behind the stage *a*. When in this

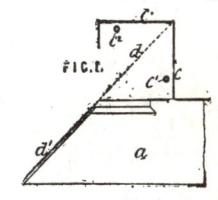

position the mirror hides an object c^2 and substitutes a reflection of an object c^1. The mirror may be either of unsilvered glass, or of graduated opacity. One or more sheets of glass may be used. The advancing edge of the mirror is formed in steps so as to render it practically unobservable. Suitable lights are provided for illuminating the objects &c.

Abridged also in Classes *Philosophical instruments ; Toys &c.*

2970. Bell, J., and Coleman, J. J. July 22.

Cooling buildings and other structures.—Relates to improvements in apparatus of the kind described in Specifications No. 1034, A.D. 1877, and No. 3862, A.D. 1878, for cooling and regulating the temperature of air in the holds, saloons, and cabins of ships, and in railway vehicles, hotels, theatres, halls, factories, hospitals, slaughter-houses, and other interiors, and consists in employing a fan or other blowing-machine for obtaining a supplementary circulation and a uniform temperature. A fan

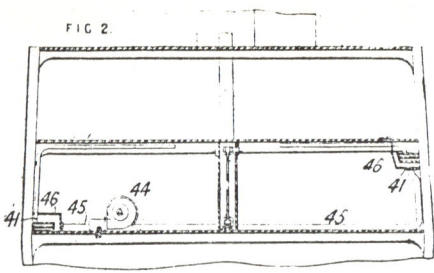

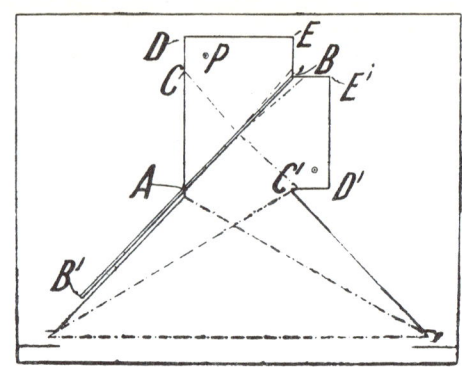

or other blowing-machine 44, Fig. 2, is connected to pipes or passages 45, 46, so as to draw air from one part of the chamber and deliver it at another to cause a circulation beyond that made by the compressing and re-expanding machinery. The passages 45, 46 may be arranged to lie adjacent to, or partially enclose the primary or cold-air passages 41 so as to obtain a practically-uniform temperature throughout the chamber.

Abridged also in Classes *Railway &c. vehicles ; Ships &c., Div. I.*

5185. Denstone, W. H. Dec. 18.

[Provisional protection only.]

Producing scenic effects. — A vertical glass screen A B is placed diagonally across the stage, and is so mounted that it can be readily withdrawn from that position either by raising or lowering, or preferably by running it in grooves and on rollers into the position A B¹ ; the advancing edge of the screen is bevelled off and polished so as to render it practically imperceptible to the spectators. Two scenes or screens are placed at C D, E B and C¹ D¹, E¹ B, one of which is the exact reflected counterpart of the other. A black screen, of velvet or other suitable material, can be passed behind, parallel, and in close proximity to the glass screen, for the purpose of concealing any object at P The edges of this screen are serrated so as to gradually obscure the objects behind it. Illuminating arrangements are provided, and by suitably placing the various screens, a real or reflected object, or both, may be exhibited to the audience.

1880

15. Hawker, T. H. S. Jan. 1.

[Provisional protection only.]

Producing optical illusions. —Scenery or other objects have placed before them a transparent reflector, such as a sheet of glass, inclined at 45 degrees to the mean line of vision of the audience. A second scene is placed out of sight of the audience at an angle and distance relative to the reflector corresponding with the original scene. By arranging the lights on these two scenes they may disappear, or may be transformed from one to the other, either instantly or gradually, or may become more or less transparent and also reappear instantaneously or gradually : or an object may instantaneously appear and then instantaneously disappear.

Abridged also in Class *Toys &c.*

5105. Doubell, E. H. Dec. 7.

[Provisional protection only.]

Magic-lantern slides.—The effect of falling rain is produced on the screen, by the use of an opaque plate with translucent lines, marks, or perforations in combination with a movable semi-transparent screen moving over a pair of rollers, mounted on the slide.

Abridged also in Class *Toys &c.*

1148. Maskelyne, J. N. March 17.

Fares &c., checking : checks, tokens, and tickets, issuing.—The tickets or tokens B are contained in a suitably-shaped box A, and are pressed against the top by a spring G, abutting against the cap A¹, and a plate G¹, at the top. On the top of the box is a fixed plate C, recessed to receive one ticket, which can be pushed through a slot *g*, by the pusher plate D, working in a guide slot and actuated by the lever E on which is a pin which strikes the bell J. A tail *a* operates a counting-train. To prevent old tickets being put in the slot, spring jaws are used which the ticket pushes open, but when it is taken out they fly back and are locked by fingers *h*, attached to the lever E, which is thrown back by the spring E¹. A marking-lever, with an adjustable point on a

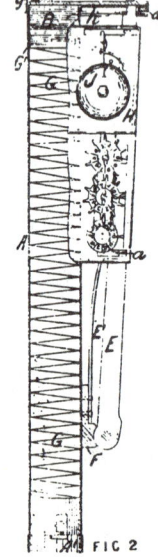

slider, is fitted on the box by which the tickets may be perforated to indicate the stage of the journey during which they are issued.

3416. Frome, C. H., and Gibbs, G. C. Aug. 23.

[Provisional protection only.]

Scenic effects in theatres.—Relates to apparatus for illuminating persons or objects which have to be seen at intervals on different parts of the stage ; and for producing other scenic effects. Across the stage is stretched a wire rope, on which at intervals are arranged plates of metal insulated therefrom, and communicating by wires with batteries or electric machines. On this rope is arranged a carriage, whose wheels are constructed of two outer plates of metal and a central plate of non-conducting material. As the carriage is drawn over the metal plates on the rope, which have also a piece of non-conducting material between them, the electric current will pass on from the carriage on either side down to a lamp fastened on the person or object, thereby producing flashes, or a prolonged light as re-

quired. In lieu of employing a wire rope the plates may be placed at intervals on the stage. The effect of different coloured lights proceeding from a person on the stage, is produced by a cylindrical glass lamp, made in sections of different colours ; on each end of the cylinder are plates journalled in bearings secured to the reflecting-plate, which is again secured to the head or other part of the person. On one end of the journal is fixed a ratchet-wheel with lever and pawl, by means of which, on the performer pulling a wire or string, the cylinder may be rotated ; or coiled springs set in motion by withdrawing a pin or pawl may be employed. Through holes n the journals are placed the carbon points, whose outer ends are connected with battery wires, which are conveniently placed about the body of the person, so that they may be brought out at the hands, or passed to the ends of the wands or properties. On the performers joining hands, or the properties, a current of electricity passes through the wires to the lamps and produces a bright effective light. The lamp may also be secured to the ends of wands or to other objects as required.
Abridged also in Class *Electricity &c., Dir. IV.*

1881

1196. Dade, D. H. March 18.

Non-conducting coverings and composition for walls &c.—Silicate cotton is treated by being mixed in layers in a heated glutinous decoction of Irish moss and starch &c. which renders it soft, elastic, and porous in the interior, leaving a hard but elastic outer skin, which may be rendered harder by a painted or tarred casing of calico or paper. Asbestos, vegetable fibre, paper, felt, hair, &c. are treated in the same way, and for the glutinous materials may be used silicate of potash, silicate of soda, gum arabic, isinglass, &c. It is rendered fire-proof and prevented from charring by the addition of a solution of "trass." It is rendered proof against fermentation, the emission of sulphuretted hydrogen, rot, mildew, and vermin by adding tannic extract obtained from tanyard refuse or by boiling in tannic solution. When partly dry the composition may be moulded into boards of flat, curved, or other forms and provided with canvas or paper backing ; thin sheets of tin or zinc over-lapping the boards and covering the joints are also used. Sheeting is formed with layers of the composition with loose silicate cotton, paper, felt, &c. in between. Wire or wire netting is used to keep the boards, sheets, &c. in position, and tar, paint, &c. may be applied outside. The composition and covering as above are used for stage scenery, lathing, walls, partitions, ceilings, doors, roofs, temporary buildings, barracks, &c. to resist heat, fire, damp, mildew, frost, sound, vermin, rot, putrefaction, &c.
Abridged also in Classes *Cements &c.; Fire, Extinction &c. of ; Heating ; Paints &c. ; Stoves &c.*

1769. Morgan, W., and Morgan, J. April 23.

Forced ventilation ; shafts for ventilation.—The invention is described as applied to mines, but is also applicable to theatres &c. A pipe passing down the shaft has branches passing to the galleries, old workings, &c., and carrying pipes which are open to the top or bottom of such

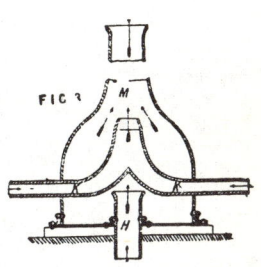

galleries &c. to remove the light or heavy gases therein. The stone pillars in the galleries may be hollow and open above or below and be connected with the branch pipes. Where necessary, the main pipe H opens into a chamber M, through pipes K, in which steam is passed to exhaust the air in the pipe H.
Abridged also in Class *Mining &c.*

2022. Harrison, T., and Garthwaite, C. W. May 9.

[Provisional protection only.]

Chairs.—Relates to opera &c. chairs in which the seat is hinged and turns back. An opening is made in the sides to hold the back part of the seat when it is thus turned up. A hat rail is provided beneath the seat.

2358. Murcott, H. J. May 28.

[*Provisional protection only.*]

Theatres &c. ; arrangement of orchestra.—The orchestra is arranged as usual along the front and below the level of the front edge of the stage, but in gallery form with the highest row in front. An opening of about three feet is arranged between the front edge of the stage and the footlights, which may be mounted along the front edge of a perforated surface screening the orchestra from the auditorium.

3725. Cogswell, H. D. Aug. 26.

Air for ventilation, moistening, perfuming, &c.—Relates to cooling-apparatus applicable to fountains, casks, &c., safes, screens for hospital beds &c., and for cooling theatres, halls, ho pitals, ships, railway vehicles, &c., directly or by cooling air. The air may be moistened, disinfected, medicated, or perfumed by the apparatus. The arrangements may be employed for heating air. Water from a main or other supply is run under pressure through a coil or series of connected pipes at the bottom of a box filled with ice. The cooled water may be passed through a coil or series of pipes in a chamber through which air is driven by a blower &c. into a trumpet-mouthed pipe having branches with cocks leading to the rooms &c. to be cooled. The water may pass through porous pipes or panels in order to evaporate and moisten the air. The trumpet-mouthed pipe may contain materials for disinfecting, medicating, or perfuming the air. The cooled water may be passed through pipes in connection with theatre, hall, church, and like seats. For cooling hospital and like beds, the cooled water is passed through pipes contained in a three-sided screen around the beds. The screen may have porous pottery or like panels traversed by the water which thus evaporates and moistens the air.

Abridged also in Classes *Air and gases, Compressing &c. ; Brewing &c. ; Cooling &c. ; Heating : Hydraulic machinery &c. ; Medicine &c. ; Railway &c. vehicles ; Ships &c., Div. I. ; Toilet &c.*

4267. Lake, W. R., [*Jones, S. L.*]. Oct. 1.

Theatres &c.—Relates to apparatus for exhibiting the libretto of a performance simultaneously with its delivery. The apparatus (one of which is placed at each side of the proscenium) consists of a transparent flexible medium on which the words are printed and which is attached to the

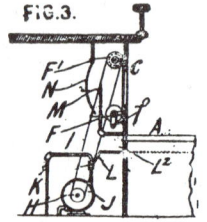

FIG.3.

rollers F, F¹ and by their action passes behind the opening C. The roller F¹ is driven by a motor J which is brake-fitted to regulate the speed. By operating the lever L connected with the stop valve K the rate of speed is controlled either by a person at hand or, by means of levers and cords fitted to each machine, by an operator in front. The transparency is illuminated by means of the gas jets at M and has words for each character arranged upon it either in the same language or a translation. The Specification also describes a portable form of the invention.

4343. Dutton, J. Oct. 6.

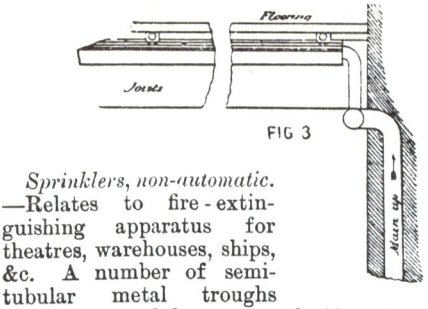

FIG 3

Sprinklers, non-automatic.—Relates to fire-extinguishing apparatus for theatres, warehouses, ships, &c. A number of semi-tubular metal troughs having a curved flange on each side and so covered with metal plates as to leave a space between the latter and the flanges, are secured between the joists of the roof or ceilings by means of metal straps with dependent arms. The troughs are closed at one end, while at the other each is connected by a nozzle with a conduit running along one side of the ceiling of each floor. Each conduit communicates with a vertical pipe carried down the front of the building to the ground floor, where it is connected on the outside with a union or junction, which can at once be connected with the water main, and is fitted with a throttle valve and tap. On making connection with the water main and turning the proper tap, the water passes into the troughs on the floor to be operated upon and issues therefrom in sheets. Where a tank or reservoir is placed on the roof it is preferred to carry an outlet pipe from the same to where the taps and valves are fitted on the vertical pipes, and thus an instantaneous supply is available before connecting with the main.

5663. Lake, W. R., [*Maxim, H. S.*]. Dec. 24.

[*Provisional protection only.*]

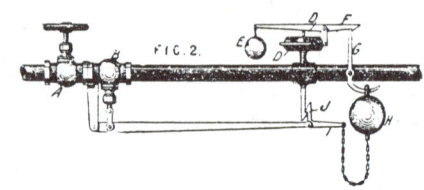

FIG. 2.

Fire-extinguishing in theatres &c. A series of pipes connected to the main water pipe are arranged throughout the building, and perforated pipes are placed above the stage &c. The valves of the perforated pipes are kept closed by the tension of a cotton cord or a wire, consisting of soldered sections, which also maintains in position a weight. When the cord burns or the solder melts, the weight drops on to a wedge and opens the valve, thus liberating the air contained in the pipe placed between such valve and the valve B, Fig. 2, of the supply pipe. The decrease of air pressure in the pipe affects a diaphragm contained in the box D. D permitting the balls E and H to descend and open the valve B which admits water to the distributing-pipes. In a modification, the fire ignites guncotton placed inside a cap of soft metal, which is blown off the pipe and so allows the escape of air necessary for operating the diaphragm. If the apparatus is

used in combination with a steam pump, the diminu-
tion of air pressure in the pipes is utilized for
opening the steam pipes ; if in combination with
an extincteur, the escape of the air and fall of the
weight effect the breakage of the acid bottle.

1882

63. Jensen, P., [*Saillot. H. S.*, and *David, H.*]. Jan. 5.

Fireproof compositions. — Relates to rendering
fabrics, theatrical scenery, &c. uninflammable by
impregnating them with a solution of salts having
incombustible properties.   These salts are either
borates, phosphates, or tungstates, together with
gluco-saccharine or molasses, or they may be su-
crates, glucates, and melanates of potash, soda,
ammonia, magnesia, or alumina.   The lime salts of
the above are preferred.   The salts are dissolved
in a hot saccharine solution to form an uncrystal-
lizable compound and the fabrics are steeped in it
when hot or painted with it when cold.
A bridged also in Class *Cements &c.*

206. Wirth, F., [*Pickhardt, G.*].   Jan. 14.

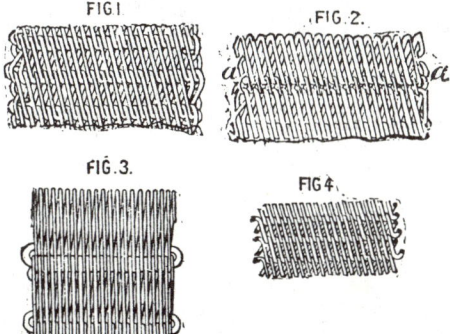

Wirework shutters.—Cross-bars, with a hook at
each end, are inserted within wire spirals the ends
of which are bent inwards, or two half-round bars
with their respective ends bent in opposite directions may be employed when strong link pins are
required.   At *a*, Fig. 2, the free ends are joined
by one, two, or three spirals twisted to suit the
inclination of the fabric.   Fig. 3 shows the network formed from single spirals, and in Fig. 4 is
shown net-work produced from single or double
cylindrical spirals by screwing out and interlinking
corresponding coils.
   Abridged also in Classes *Cements &c.; Fastenings, Lock &c.; Fencing &c.; Fire, Extinction &c.
of; Lifting &c.; Mechanism &c.; Ropes &c.;
Shop &c. accessories.*

305. Aronson, J. N.   Jan. 21.

Incandescent lamps.—The bulbs are made so as to
reflect or refract the light in any desired direction
The reflecting-surfaces may be produced by silver-
ing, painting, gilding, or enamelling, or by shaping
the bulbs so as to form catadioptric lenses or
prisms.   The upper part of a bulb may be made
reflecting, or the bulb may have a body A, Fig. 2,

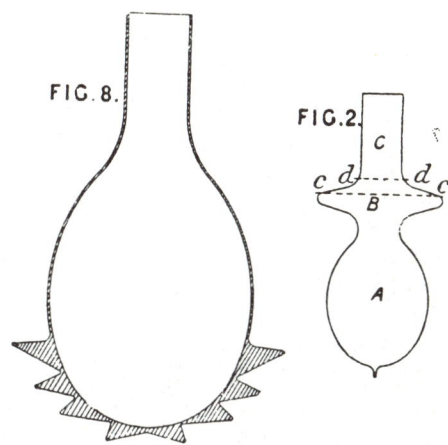

a throat or neck C, and a corrugated part B,
silvered or gilded between *c* and *d*.   The part B
may consist of a number of inverted conical frusta,
silvered on their flat annular surfaces.   Bulbs for
theatre footlights may be plain or corrugated on
one side and silvered &c. on the other.   A bulb
for refracting the rays of light is shown in Fig. 8,
but the rays may be first refracted and then
reflected.

394. Bennett, H. M.   Jan. 26.

[*Provisional protection only.*]

Theatre curtains.—A perforated pipe connected
to the water supply is so arranged that, on lowering
the act drop and turning a cock, a running sheet of
water spreads over one or both sides of the curtain,
which is hung by chains &c. from metallic supports.
The water may be projected on to the curtain from
any convenient source.
A bridged also in Class *Fire, Extinction &c. of.*

413. Thomson, B. L.   Jan. 27.

Covering roofs, walls, &c.—Enamelled or vitrified
plates of iron or tin are fastened by cement, glue,
nails, screws, or other fastenings, and are formed
with a bevel or turn-down edge.   Cloth, paper, or
other fabric saturated with prepared india-rubber,
gutta-percha, tar, asphalt, or ozokerit, or vitrified
iron plates may intervene between the outside
plates and the surface to be covered to prevent
corrosion.   Where nails, screws, or similar fastenings are employed, the holes are slotted, and
rubber, felt, or similar substance placed underneath
to allow expansion and contraction.   For roofs and
similar surfaces the joints are filled in with cement,
glue, or other adhesive materials.   It is further
applied to cover partitions or divisions on the stage

of theatres and for similar purposes requiring protection from fire.

Abridged also in Class *Ships &c., Div. I.*

437. Imray, J., [*Pfaff, C.*]. Jan. 28.

[Provisional protection only.]

Theatre curtains.—The curtain may be arranged to be raised above or be lowered below the stage, or to slide in and out from the side. It consists of horizontal strips of sheet iron or steel bent to a curved or trough shape, the hollow side being presented to the proscenium. Each strip has flanges at its edges by which it is riveted to vertical strips or bands suspended from a rail at the top. The curved form of the strips protects the supporting-bands from fire on the stage side, and distance-pieces may also be inserted between the curtain and the supporting-bands. A flat rail at each side, to which the curved strips are riveted by angle irons, slides up and down in a fixed metal guide. The curtain is secured to a horizontal framed bearer at the top, to which is attached the suspending-bolts, and an overhanging lip or lips rests on a horizontal supporting rail or rails when the curtain is lowered. The rails are trough-shaped and contain sand for the lips of the curtain to dip into and form a gas-tight joint. The frame is preferably inclined so that the curtain bears against one edge of the grooves in which it runs. The slides are fixed to hollow columns, and the framed bearer at the top rests on a hollow cross-beam. Water circulates through this frame and escape openings may be provided and closed by fusible plugs when the supply is constant. The curtain may be operated by a vertical cylinder and ram fitted with pulleys for wire suspension ropes. To cause the movement of the ram and curtain to commence and terminate gradually, the ports are provided with throttle valves worked by an arm carrying a roller working in a cam groove in a plate partaking of the motion of the ram. The escape throttle valve fits loosely to allow the escape of steam from the cylinder when heated. The slide valve may be worked by a rod connected to a piston in a small cylinder fitted with cushioning-arrangements and situated at some distance from the curtain.

753. Keith, C. H. Feb. 16.

Circuses—A travelling circus building is constructed of convertible vehicles placed in a circle with a roof formed by erecting a pole in the centre, which supports a cover secured by ropes to rings fitted to the roofs of the vehicles. The inner side B of each vehicle is hinged

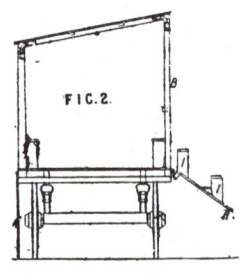

FIG. 2.

and seats I are formed on it to fall down into the circus, as shown. The ends are also made removable and, when the triangular spaces formed between the vehicles are floored and roofed over, a continuous promenade is formed. Shutters are dropped to close the opening under the vehicles, and the triangular spaces before-mentioned are made good with movable seats, shutters, &c. Spaces are left in the circus for the entrance and exit of horses &c., and a portico with pay office and also other movable buildings may be fitted.

Abridged also in Class *Road vehicles.*

858. McLennan, K., McLennan, J., and **Owen, R.** Feb. 22.

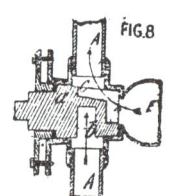

FIG. 8.

Sprinklers, non-automatic &c.—The gas pipes of a building are used for distributing water &c. turned on to them from the water pipe. In an arrangement specially applicable to the stage of a theatre, vertical pipes for supplying water or chemical fluid have horizontal branches above and below the stage flooring and capable of connection with the gas pipes by junction cocks, which are connected by rods and links, and worked from inside or outside; and the main gas pipe and a water pipe join a main junction cock worked by a lever acted on by a pull line either from inside or outside, from the bottom of which passes an outlet pipe leading to the gas apparatus. The said cocks are described below. A gas pipe for supplying lights not connected with the water supply is connected to the main near the main junction cock. The gas batten is supplied with gas through a flexible pipe convertible into a water pipe as above; the suspending rope is connected to a rod movable on a fixed vertical rod, a stop on which prevents the batten from falling on the stage. Water may be supplied to the batten by means of a telescopic joint. A localizing partition may be used at any part of the building, consisting of a woollen &c. curtain immersed in a tank of water &c., and caused by a weight to pass over a roller and unfold itself when the lines suspending the weight burn. The plug *a*, Fig. 8, is made with a groove *c* by which the water pipe E is connected to the gas pipe A, and a groove *b* extending half round the plug, by reversing which the water pipe is cut off and the gas passes unobstructed through the pipe A. Main junction cocks are made with a conical plug hollow at its lower part, with two openings, an outlet at the bottom and an inlet at the sides, so situated that by giving the plug a quarter turn the gas inlet and water inlet connected to the casing at the sides are respectively closed and opened.

902. Haddan, H. J., [*Trivier, T.*]. Feb. 24.

Theatre curtains.—A fireproof fabric for these is woven of threads made by surrounding a core of metal wire, linen, hemp, silk, wool, cotton, or any similar twisted or untwisted material with asbestos or other suitable substance. Or several metallic or textile threads may be twisted together with asbestos threads.

Abridged also in Classes *Electricity &c., Div. II.; Filtering &c.; Fire-arms &c., Div. II.; Fire, Extinction &c. of; Pipes &c.; Ropes &c.; Spinning; Steam engines; Wearing &c.*

1355. Lowe, A. H. March 21.

[Provisional protection not allowed.]

Theatrical appliances.—Consists of a collapsable kitchen dresser the parts of which are hinged so as to form a packing-case during transport. It is furnished with movable shelves which form the plate rack. By pulling a cord, the framework collapses so as to produce a pantomimic effect.

Abridged also in Class *Boxes &c.*

1468. Abel, C. D., *[Nagel, J.].* March 27.

Roofing plates ; theatre curtains.—The plates can be used as a covering for more inflammable materials, such as woodwork, or they may be employed separately for decorations, coverings, curtains, or other purposes, and for covering roofs. Amianthus or asbestos is reduced to small pieces and is mixed with oxide of zinc ; the mixture, either in a dry or moist state, is pressed, by rollers or otherwise, on a net of metallic wire or between two or more such nets. The plate is then impregnated with a solution of chloride of zinc or chloride of iron or manganese and again rolled or pressed. If desired, the plate may be powdered with coloured sand or any coloured fireproof material. The plate is then dried and polished by rolling. If the plates are to be exposed to the weather they may be painted with waterproof paints or they are impregnated with silicate-of-potash solution dried and then impregnated with skimmed milk.

Abridged also in Classes *Cements &c.; Fire, Extinction &c. of.*

2066. Wilkins, S. B. May 2.

[Provisional protection only.]

Fireproof doors.—The door is constructed of iron or steel framing with buckled plates for panels so that a hollow space constituting a tank is formed. A water cistern is placed above the door and connected to it at the top and bottom by flow and return pipes, which may be connected through the hinges or pivots on which the door is hung.

Shutters or screens.—For large openings such as exist in theatres and other large buildings, the shutter is constructed by one of the following methods :—Where the height will admit of it, the shutter or screen may be made in one piece so as to constitute a tank for holding water and worked by hydraulic power, counterpoise weights, or otherwise. It may also be constructed in two parts hung over pulleys so as to balance each other, the upper part sliding upwards and the lower downwards. They are made with plates welded or riveted to iron or steel framing ; and tapered tubes on the upper half slide into openings in the lower half, so that, when the shutter is closed, it forms a tank which can be filled with water from a cistern placed above it. The water may overflow at the top so as to keep the whole cool, and a discharge cock may be fitted at the bottom.

Protecting iron beams.—Where beams support a cistern they may be enclosed by a water-tight casing connected to the cistern by holes through the bottom.

Abridged also in Class *Fastenings, Lock &c.*

2107. Jensen, P., *[Haviland, R. J. L.].* May 4.

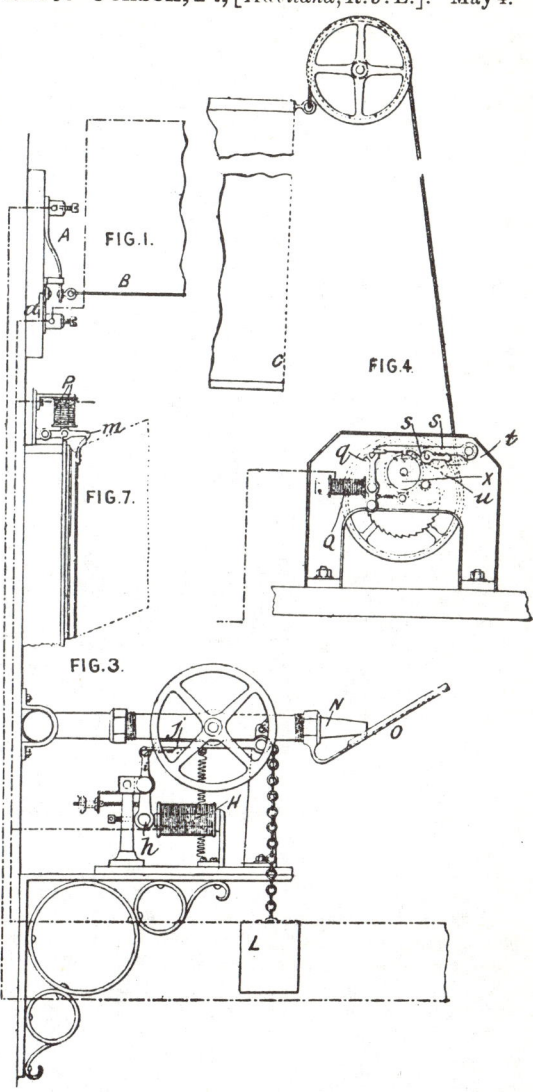

Sprinklers, automatic ; alarms, fire &c.—Comprises automatic and other apparatus for supplying a stream or jet of water in case of fire in a theatre, warehouse, &c., and for causing doors, trap-doors, shutters, &c. to open and the curtain to drop. When the fire burns a weighted cord B stretched through the desired parts of the building, a spring A touches a contact *a,* so that an electric circuit is completed. The passage of the current causes a catch to release a door, Fig. 7, which opens by its own weight. It also turns a cock, so that a nozzle N supplies a jet of water to extinguish the fire, and by traversing an electromagnet, causes a catch on the armature of the same to release a hinged trap-door or shutter, which then falls open and allows the combustion products from the fire to escape. The current also releases clockwork, Fig. 4, which then causes the theatre curtain to descend. The apparatus may work automatically, or two contacts may be provided, so arranged that the closure of one shall lower the curtain only, while the operation of the other shall operate all the above arrangements. The clockwork which draws the curtain is released when an electromagnet Q attracts an armature q supporting a lever S. This lever then drops, and by pressing on a peg on a stop hook lever s, raises the hook end of the same out of a groove in the stop wheel X of the clock-work, and causes a projection t on the lever to move a pawl lever u out of gear with the pawl wheel. The nozzle supplying water for extinguish-ing the fire has an adjustable guide O for directing the stream. It has a cock which is opened by a weight L when a magnet H attracts a keeper h. The movement of the latter permits the descent of a lever j, a projection on which thus passes from under a peg on the chain pulley and permits the descent of the weight. The door, Fig. 7, and

also the trap-door, are so arranged as to open by their own weight when the current causes a magnet to attract a catch m.

Abridged also in Classes *Buildings &c.; Chim-neys &c.; Fastenings, Lock &c.: Hinges &c.*

2780. Morgan, W. T., and Kidd, R. L. June 13.

[*Provisional protection only.*]

Magic-lantern slides.—The pictures are printed &c. on concave films which are transferred to curved glasses, to improve the definition at the edges of the enlarged picture.

Abridged also in Classes *Buildings &c.; Orna-menting; Photography; Printing other than letter-press &c.; Toys &c.*

2889. Abel, C. D., [*Gwinner, R., Kautsky, J., Dengg, C., and Roth, F.*]. June 19.

Theatres.—Relates to the arrangement of the stage and to hydraulic and other apparatus for work-ing the same and also the scenery and fireproof curtains. The stage is divided into four sections parallel with the proscenium, each supported in cup-shaped sockets on columns carried by the rams of hy-draulic cylinders B, C, D. Each section consists of three or

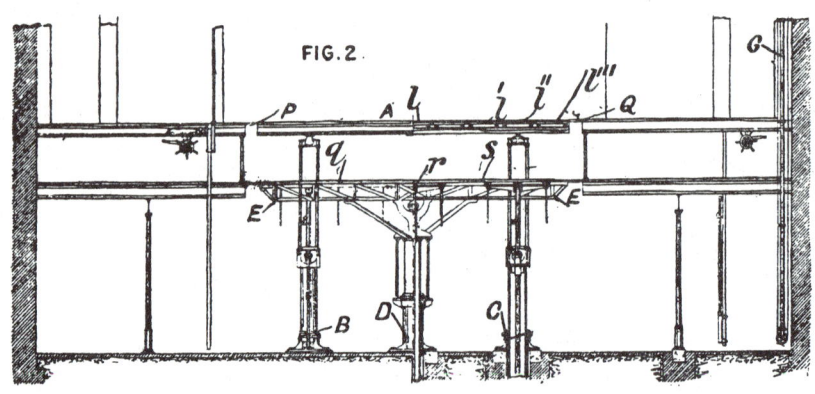

FIG. 2.

more iron bearers for the reception of the scene carriages, of a hinged trap, and of two other bearers for the recep-tion of the trap slides l. The stage has also two long-tudinal traps P and Q, so that, by suitably operating the rams of the cylinders B and C, a rocking motion can be imparted to it. The large trap bearer E is carried by a hydraulic ram and its platform is formed of three parts q, r, s carried respectively by the rams of the cylinders B, D, and C. The trap slides l and scene carriages are arranged as follows :—The trap slides run on angle irons fixed to suitable bearers A, Fig. 7, and may be carried across the openings E by turning the shaft B, whereby the rail D is thrown forward by the link c to bridge the opening and the hinged rail F drops into it so that the trap slides can pass freely under the fixed part of the floor. The iron frame B, Fig. 4, runs with three rollers a, b, c formed of pressed leather, paper, or other material upon a rail d, fixed below the stage A, while other rollers h, i take bearings at the top. A socket k is

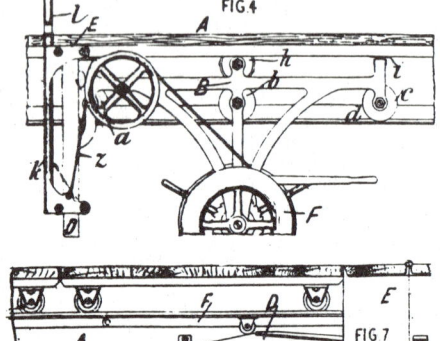

FIG 4

FIG 7

carried by a slide E on the vertical rail D, so that the support l for the scene may be raised or lowered by a hand-wheel F provided with a drum on which the rope z is coiled and with a ratchet-wheel and pawl. A modification has the socket k fixed to the frame and its vertical motion dispensed with. The fly scenes, hanging from the fly-loft, are actuated by a hydraulic ram G, Fig. 2. They are connected to it by three or more ropes joining a single chain or rope passing over the ram. For flying apparatus, the parallel beams of the pulley floor are fitted with carriages running on wheels, from the axles of which two columns, connected at the bottom by a bridge, are suspended. By a suitable arrangement of ropes passing to windlasses, the flying box has three motions. From one rope it receives a horizontal, from a second a curvilinear, and from a third a vertical motion.

Fireproof curtain, operating.—A vertical hydraulic cylinder has a hollow ram through which the water pressure is admitted from above when it is required to raise the curtain. For lowering the curtain the water is discharged by cocks or valves placed at different parts of the theatre. The descent is retarded by the curtain being caused to turn a cock when nearly closed. It at the same time opens an aperture in the roof for the escape of smoke and gases.

2935. Clark, A. June 20.

[Provisional protection only.]

Fireproof proscenium screens.—By the first arrangement the screen is constructed of iron or steel plates and angle irons, and arranged to slide up and down in guides. It is preferably constructed double with the intervening space filled with air or water, or packed with a non-conductor of heat or with a fire-extinguishing compound. It is attached to a transverse girder at the upper part, whose ends project at the sides and rest on the rams of hydraulic lifts, and may also be counterbalanced by suitable weights. By another arrangement the screen may be made in two parts which partly counterbalance each other, one rising as the other descends.

3932. Astrop, W., and **Ridgway, R.** Aug. 17.

Fireproof liquid compound.—A saturated aqueous solution of alum is treated with ammonia or other precipitant to throw down a gelatinous precipitate of hydrate of alumina. The precipitate is collected by filtering, and washed on the filter, then dried, pulverized, and gradually mixed in a mill with an alkaline silicate, such as that of soda or potash, which is by chemical decomposition formed into a basic silicate of alumina. The compound may be diluted with water to suit the article to be treated, and may be used alone or mixed with colour to form a paint or varnish. In some cases it is preferable to use the alkaline silicate and hydrate of alumina separately. The compound may be used as a plaster, but ordinarily it may be applied to woodwork with a brush. Fabrics may be dipped into the liquid then dried and ironed. Oil paintings and old theatrical scenery may be coated on the back, but the canvas for new work should be primed with the compound.

Abridged also in Classes *Cements &c. ; Paints &c.*

4073. Justice, P. M., [*Vankeerberghen, V.*]. Aug. 25. *Drawings to Specification.*

Theatres.—A fireproof screen is liberated by the action of an electric current completed by means of a special thermostat, in case of fire.

Abridged also in Classes *Bells &c.; Electricity &c., Div. III. ; Fire, Extinction &c. of; Philosophical instruments; Registering &c.; Signalling &c.*

1883

501. Sanderson, J. G. Jan. 30. [*Provisional protection only.*]

Incandescent lamps.—Bouquets or other devices carried by dancers in a Maypole or similar dance are provided with lamps which are connected to plates near the lower ends of the bouquet holders. Each of these holders is inserted in an outer holder which is formed with internal contact-plates in connection with conducting-wires in the streamers. The lamp circuit is completed by depressing a pivoted spring lever on the outer holder and so bringing the second pair of contacts together, the first pair being brought into contact when the holders are put together.

941. Clark, A. M., [*Meyer, G.*]. Feb. 20.

Paper hangings : stage scenery.—Relates to a process and to products resulting therefrom for rendering uninflammable and incombustible, paper hangings, stage scenery, and ornamental moulded objects &c. The pulp is prepared of a composition into which enters asbestos fibre or other similar material. The raw fibre is first ground, and afterwards carded, the carded material being first placed in a vat, and moistened with water, while a quantity of sodium chloride or potassium chloride, is added to purify the asbestos. Mica, talc, plaster, &c., pulverized to a fine powder, is also added. For the manufacture of cardboard, or paper of inferior quality, ochreous clay, mineral colours, or artificial ultramarine, according to the colour desired, may be substituted for the talc and plaster. The pulp thus prepared receives a first sizing of gelatine and a second fireproof composition of liquid silicate. The manufacture of the paper is conducted in the ordinary way of making laid or watermark paper either by hand or machine. The papers are afterwards ornamented by the application of an incombustible ink, which may be made of any colour.

Abridged also in Classes *Acids &c., Div. I.; Cements &c.; Electricity &c., Div. II. ; Fire, Extinction &c. of; Moulding &c.; Paper &c.; Writing-instruments &c.*

1078. Wirth, F., [*Pickhardt, G.*]. Feb. 27.

Fireproof screens for theatres.—The form shown in Fig. 7 consists of thick spiral springs *f* directly screwed into each other to form bands of any required width, which may be rolled flat.

Door and window guards.—When made wide, strips of fabric of this nature are stated to be specially applicable for " closing doors " and windows."

Abridged also in Classes

FIG.7.

Beverages ;   Fencing &c. ;
Furniture &c. ; Harness &c. ;
Lifting &c. ; Mechanism &c. ; Ships &c., Div. 1.

2601. Clark, A. May 24.

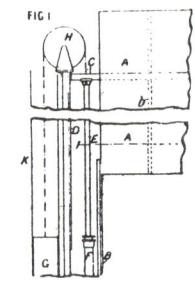

Fireproof screen for theatres. The screen or curtain A is formed with iron or steel plates riveted to the opposite sides of a framing of channel irons at the edges, and upright bars of T iron *b*, forming a double skin with an air space between. This intervening space may be filled with water or packed with fire-resisting or non-conducting material. The curtain works up and down in the wrought-iron channels B affixed to the proscenium wall K. Near the top of the curtain two channel irons are riveted to the plates and united by through bolts to form the girder C, the ends of which project at the sides, work in the guides D. and rest on the heads of the hydraulic rams E which work in the cylinders F and are operated by suitable apparatus. The curtain is counterbalanced by the weights G which act by means of chains over the sheaves H. By another arrangement the rams act as counterbalances without using separate weights, by inverting the cylinders and passing the chains over sheaves mounted on the tops of the cylinders and under sheaves attached to the lower ends of the rams. The Provisional Specification states that the screen may be made in two parts working in opposite directions and so geared as to more or less counterbalance each other.

3010. Lake, W. R., [*Knell, J. W.*]. June 16.

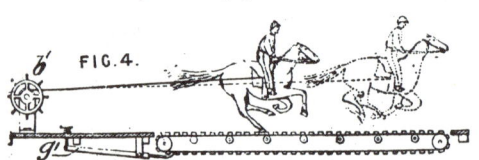

Theatrical appliances. — Illusory effects are produced, whereby horses, vehicles, &c., while remaining stationary, appear to be travelling along a road of considerable length. A horse and vehicle are placed on an endless path fitted in or on the stage and are kept from moving forward by means of a stay cord or chain. When the horse is started, instead of going forward he will move the endless path, thereby rotating the wheels of the vehicle and causing a panoramic scene in the background to move upon rollers in the opposite direction, thus producing the effect desired. The rolls are concealed behind trees &c. which rotate as the scene moves. To aid the effect currents of air from a blower or fan may be turned upon the occupant of the vehicle so as to produce a fluttering of dress &c. Fig. 4 shows the method of representing races, hunts, &c. The horse is attached by a wire to the windlass *b¹*, by means of which it may be allowed to gain or lose ground as desired. Each horse has a separate endless path, the motion of which is controlled by depressing the outer end of a pivoted lever *g¹*, whose inner end bears on the periphery of the roll.

5221. Seyde, F. N. Nov. 2.

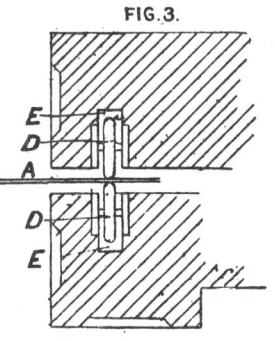

Fireproof curtains and drop-scenes for theatres are constructed of wire gauze, used either alone or attached to, or concealed between thicknesses of other suitable material. To prevent the possibility of flames communicating with the auditorium through the side grooves in which the curtain slides, flaps of wire gauze are attached to the jambs of the proscenium opening, so as to securely clip the side edges of the said curtain. The foot of the curtain or screen is received into a groove formed in the stage floor, and closed by a falling trap when not in use. To prevent twisting when being wound up, the edges of the curtain A are held between a series of pairs of friction rollers D mounted in their frames in cross-grooves E formed in the jambs of the proscenium.

Abridged also in Class *Fire, Extinction &c. of.*

5307. Jensen, P., [*Mac Kaye Manufacturing Co.*]. Nov. 9.

[Provisional protection only.]

Theatre and like chairs.—Composed of "a "swinging bracket, supported on a columnar stand, "which bracket carries a pivotted back and a "folding seat provided with a folding leg : folding "arms being also applied." Two such chairs are preferably hung on one stand. On folding the seat the arms and legs also fold and the whole may be swung back on the stand to form with other similar chairs an exit arch or passage. The folding is preferably effected automatically by prings. Each chair is provided with a hat, coat, and umbrella stand.

Abridged also in Class *Buildings &c.*

1884

934. Duncan, W. H. Jan. 8.

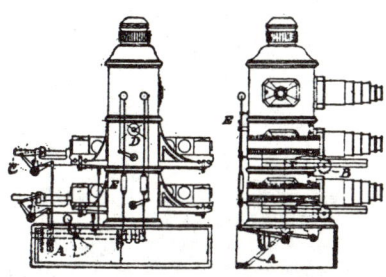

Dissolving-view apparatus.—The slides are carried in racks on each side of the lantern, and are moved forward by the action of a pedal A and ratchet-wheel B. On arriving at the end of the rack, the slide is pushed sideways in front of the lens by the levers &c. C, and after exhibition are moved back again in the rack on the other side of the lantern. The action of the pedals at the same time turns the gas-cock D by means of the rods &c. E, and also shifts the lime cylinder to present a fresh surface to the gas flame each time.

1378. Duncan, W. H. Jan. 14.

Advertising in connection with dissolving-view apparatus. A dissolving-view entertainment is given, and at its close there are thrown upon the screen photographs of the goods it is desired to advertise or images of models in motion and other opaque objects to be exhibited.

1597. Duncan, W. H. Jan. 17.

Portable buildings. — The building shown in Figs. 1 and 2 is composed of a number of separate structures *a, b, c, d*, each standing on its own set of wheels, arranged to be connected together to form a complete room for exhibitions or other entertainments. The windows are fitted with shutters *f, f* sliding on friction rollers and connected together by rods so that they may by a handle, conveniently placed, be simultaneously closed for the purpose of showing dissolving views.

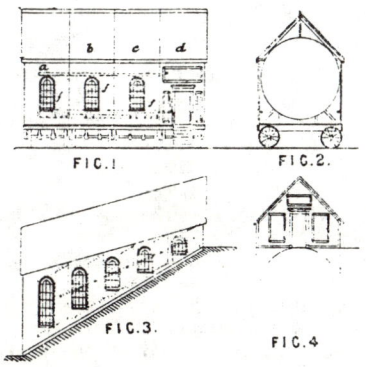

For standing on sloping banks the sections forming the building are without wheels and are dowelled into a slanting base frame, as shown in elevation in Figs. 3 and 4.

2154. Nagel, J. Jan. 25.

Theatres.—Consists of an improvement upon the fireproof and waterproof plates described in Specification No. 1468, A.D. 1882, which plates are made by pressing a mixture of asbestos and zinc oxide on to nets of metallic wire, and treating with zinc chloride and other substances. As an addition to or substitute for the zinc oxide, magnesia, gypsum, or lime is used, or a mixture of two or more of these bodies, and in place of the zinc chloride some other metallic chloride or chlorides or aluminium sulphate may be employed. The wire net or like material is coated with the asbestos mixture and passed between rollers carrying an endless band saturated with the chloride or other solution used. The plates may be coated with varnish or otherwise treated to render them fireproof and waterproof. They may be applied directly to form stage decorations, curtains, and the like, as well as roof-coverings and protective coverings for woodwork and other inflammable materials.

5157. Clark, A. M., [*Trouvé, G.*]. March 19.

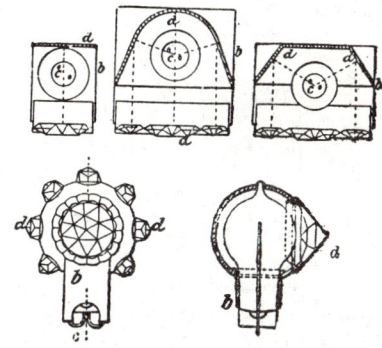

Theatres. — The invention is described with regard to electric jewellery, sceptres, &c., but, by increasing the dimensions, is stated to be applicable for lighting up theatrical scenery and illuminations for stage effects. The luminous rays emitted by a small incandescent lamp or lamps are intercepted either by means of lenses, faceted or not, or by coloured artificial gems or stones. The lamp *c* is mounted in a suitable holder *b*, and the gems *d* are variously arranged with respect to it, as shown. In some cases the effect may be increased by employing mirrors or reflectors placed at an angle of 45° on either side of the gems. In order that the luminous effect may be produced at any moment a small contact-maker is employed which consists of an iron tube upon the outside of which are flexible strips to which the battery wires are attached, preferably by means of varnished thread. Similar strips are placed in the interior of the cylinder and secured by a wedge of insulating material. The circuit is closed by establishing contact between the outer and inner strips by sliding an ivory ring along the tube.

6097. Wood, J. P. April 8.

Conjuring-apparatus.—Relates to cabinets with invisible cupboards. Mirrors are so arranged in the cabinets as to enclose a space and at the same time to reflect the square ends or other parts of the cabinet, to make it appear empty. Articles may be concealed in the enclosed space.

6598. Allison, H. J., [*Sherman, J. W.*]. April 21.

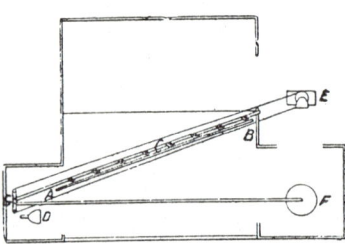

Theatrical appliances for illusionary effects. The improvements relate to apparatus for producing effects by reflection from a sheet of glass. A, B is a vertical sheet of glass placed obliquely across the stage in front of the actors. Above this sheet and parallel to it is a row of gas-jets on the pipe C. D and E are lime or electric lights, D being fixed and E rotating. F is a powerful gas-light placed above the objects of which the images are to be thrown on the glass and which stand in the compartment in which the light is situated, out of view of the audience. Two taps at G are connected together so that the opening of one supplying the pipe C closes the other supplying the light F, and at the same time the light E is turned away from the objects to be reflected by means of wires moved by the mechanism actuating the taps. The light D, which also illuminates the objects to be reflected, can be turned down independently by the operator at the same time.

Shutting off the gas from the pipe C causes the light E to be directed upon the objects, which are then made visible to the audience by reflection. Small branch pipes are provided to prevent the entire extinction of one set of gas-jets while the other is being used.

9200. Abel, C. D., [*Franquin, P.*]. June 19.

Fireproof buildings, factories, &c.; theatres.— The walls are built of hollow bricks A forming continuous passages for air-circulation, with the object of keeping them cool in case of fire. The iron floor joists are enclosed in fireclay casings B leaving air-passages between the casing and the joists. Openings are made in the roof to be opened in case of fire, in order to localize it.

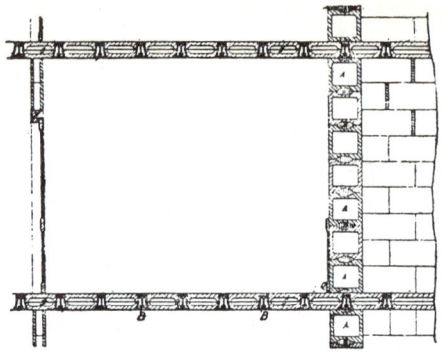

The doors and all other woodwork are encased in iron, and the window-shutters are made of movable metal bars like venetian-blind laths. In theatres, the openings in the partition walls round the stage may be provided with double curtains composed of beams of wood encased in iron and sliding in iron grooves coated with fireclay.

9604. Gibson, J. H., and **Glazier, W.** July 1.

Theatres. — The curtain-stretching apparatus described below is stated to be applicable for supporting scenery. The Figure shows a side elevation of a portion of two of the four bars A, B. The bars are jointed at the corners by screwed pegs and nuts, or screwed pegs J and screwed holes, a double-flanged metal shoe K being placed between, so as to grasp the bars and hold them at right angles to one another. A central hole through the shoe permits the passage of the pin. A flanged plate F embracing the edges of the frame slides on a pin G over the hinge C to prevent bending. H is a stop screw. The hinges are fastened to the bars by screws and nuts. The curtains are attached to the frame in the usual manner by pins N.

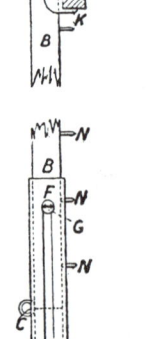

10,358. Jensen, P., [*Steene, L. van, and Cattreut, L.*]. July 19.

Chairs.—Relates to folding armchairs for use in theatres &c. The chair is made so that the arms and seat automatically rise when not in use, occupying the least possible space, which is especially important in theatres &c. The seat *a* and arms *b* are pivoted by pins D^1 to a framework B consisting of the back and legs and strengthened by a cross-stay *e*. The seat is counterbalanced by a weight A and is connected by links F to prolongations of the arms beyond their pivots, the pins connecting the links to the seat *a* working in curved slots in the frame. When the occupant vacates the seat, it, as well as the arms, folds automatically. The footboard *d* is pivoted and counterbalanced. Springs may be used instead of,

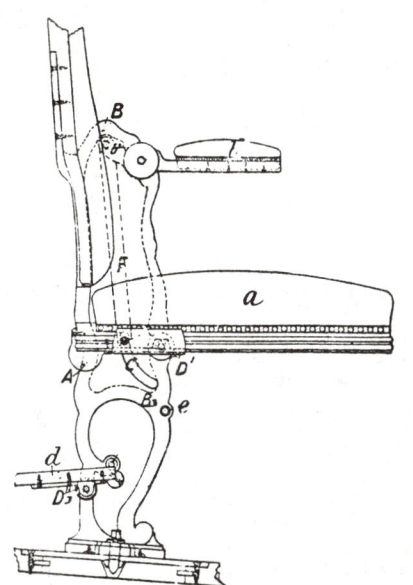

or to assist, the counterweights, and india-rubber buffers may be provided to deaden the noise.

12,382. Boehle, H. Sept. 13.

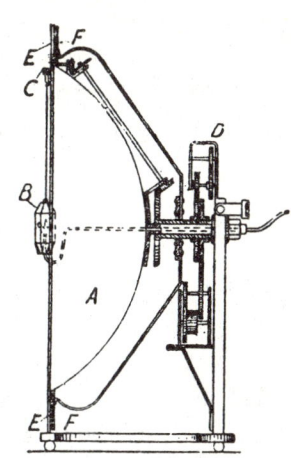

Reflectors. — The object is to obtain brilliantly-coloured effects, somewhat resembling fireworks, by means of an ordinary gaslight, lamp, or the like. A convenient form of the instrument is shown, though the details admit of considerable modification. The reflector A is made of a great number of small reflecting-surfaces turned in various directions; at its focus is the light B, which is surrounded by a transparent casing, formed of differently-coloured panes of glass. The case is suspended by a wire from a bevel-wheel C which is connected with a motor D, and so caused to revolve. The same motor rotates a ring F, placed behind a stationary ring E, and, the edges of both rings being cut into a pattern, the reflector itself appears to be rotating, while the revolution of the case causes constantly-changing coloured light to be thrown in all directions from the surfaces of the reflector.

1885

1173. Gillett, W. F., and **Moreton, H. B.** Jan. 27.

Shafts for the ventilation of public buildings, theatres, dwelling-houses, &c. The shafts D and F are arranged as shown, with the concentric pipes A and G of a revolving cowl mounted upon them. An up-draught is created in the shaft F, while fresh air passes down the shaft D.

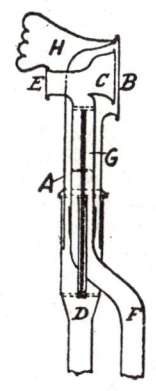

1373. Spencer, J. R., and **Chantler, H.** Jan. 31.

Theatres, scenes for. A longitudinal hole, circular or dovetailed in cross-section as shown at A, B, is made through a wooden roller. A cord or rod in a hem of the scene is put endwise into the hole, the scene C hanging out through a slit.

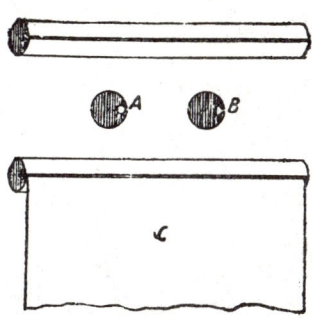

8727. Justice, P. M., [*Heysinger, I. W.,* and *Pusey, J.*]. July 20. *Drawings to Specification.*

Theatres; churches and schoolrooms.—Relates to the application of electric lamps to theatres, churches, altar pieces, and schools, the lamps serving the double purpose of illuminating and of displaying words, letters, numerals, or other designs. The filaments of the lamps are formed in the shapes of the said designs.

14,949. Ransome, T. Dec. 5.

Coated fabrics, fireproof. The fabric is formed by coating wire gauze, wire cloth, or wire netting on one or both sides with suitable fibrous or other material, such as woven or felted fabrics, paper, paper pulp, asbestos, &c. The material is first rendered fireproof by treating with tungstate or phosphate of soda or other suitable substance, and is then coated on one side with silicate of soda, and while moist applied, with the coated side upwards, to the wire gauze &c., to which it is attached by weaving, twisting, knitting, or felting. The fabric thus formed is used for coverings of walls, floors, doors, shutters, and ceilings, for curtains, screens, floorcloths, and scenery, and for covers for papers, goods, and other substances, &c.

1886

3920. Oller, J. March 20.

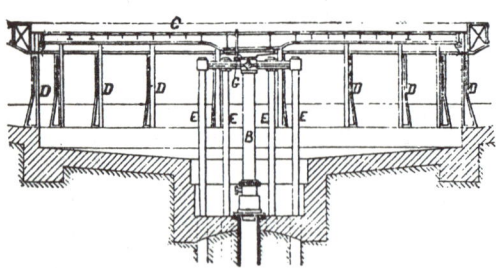

Circuses.—The arena may be lowered when required for aquatic performances or wild beast exhibitions. The floor C of the arena is attached to the hydraulic ram B carrying guide-posts E, and is formed with projections at its circumference guided by the fixed iron columns D. When the floor is required in its ordinary position, it is rotated slightly by a pinion G to allow the guides D, E to act as supports.

6154. Noakes, D. W. May 6.

Limelight apparatus.—The Figure shows a triple dissolving lantern. The jet slides A are adjusted by racks and pinions B, or their equivalents, operated by external milled heads C, C and then

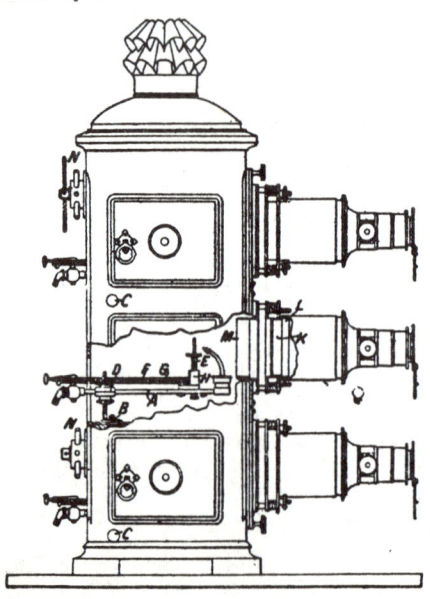

clamped in position by a double lock-nut device D. The lime-cylinder is carried by a column E around and along which grooves and flutes are cut engaged respectively by a worm-wheel and worm on parallel spindles F (one only being shown); by turning these spindles the lime-cylinder is raised and revolved, while it may be moved to or from the jet by means of the rod G fixed to the sliding supporting-block H. Two dissolving-cocks N, N are provided each with six branch pipes; the upper one is connected by two of its pipes with the main gas supplies and by two others with a jet; the remaining two lead to the second dissolver, the other four pipes of which pass to the lower jets. Bye-passes from the main pipes are also arranged for sending a slight supply of gas to the jets after the service from the dissolving-cocks has ceased.

10,500. Jones, G. W. Aug. 16. *Drawings to Specification.*

Theatres.—For the purpose of changing the scenery a sheet of glass is placed at an angle of 45° in front of a scene visible directly, and from this a second scene may be reflected and become visible when the lights illuminating the first are lowered, and those illuminating the second are raised. The valves controlling the supply pipes for each set are so connected by links that they may be operated from one hand-lever. There is a bye-pass to maintain both sets constantly alight.

16,388. Buatier, J. Dec. 14.

Optical illusions, producing.—Relates to a method of producing an illusive effect at theatres and other places, whereby a person is able to appear or disappear from the view of an audience. The illusion is brought about by employing, to line the walls, ceiling, and floor, a material having a light-absorbing surface, such as black velvet. The Figure shows the method of producing the illusion. A, B, B are the back and sides of the stage &c., and C, C[1] are hinged doors, all covered with, say,

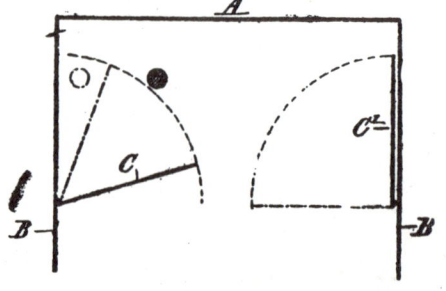

black velvet. Any person, as represented by a small circle, standing behind one of these doors would be invisible to the audience, but by shutting the door suddenly to the position as at C¹, the person would be exposed, without the audience discerning that anything had moved, although a strong light may be all the time thrown on to the stage. The same effect can be produced by having the back A movable, so as to approach to or recede from the front, and containing a trap door with a screen behind.

16,389. Buatier, J.   Dec. 14.

Theatrical appliances for producing illusionary effects. Consists of apparatus by which an apparent transforming of one object into another is effected before the full view of spectators. As an example, an enlarged picture of a caterpillar may be transformed first into a representation of a cocoon, and then into the full butterfly. A framework A is covered with paper and on it is drawn, previously or at the time, a representation of a caterpillar. A visible cord E is drawn

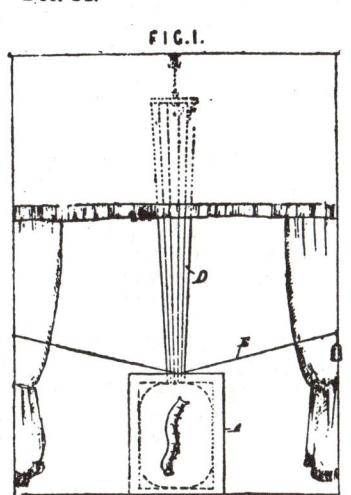
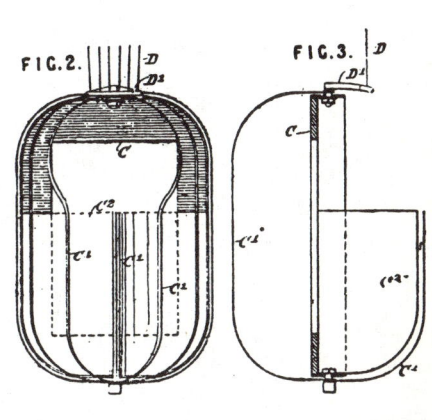

down to be apparently attached to this frame, this action being intended as a blind ; while invisible steel wires &c. D connected by a cord passing over pulleys to a counterpoise behind the stage, are attached to a plate D¹, Figs. 2 and 3, carrying the receptacle C². This is composed of a number of ribs C¹, say 12, covered with yellow silk to imitate a cocoon, and contains a person dressed to represent a full butterfly. The suspended apparatus is drawn up through a trap in the floor unseen by the spectators, and with the ribs shut up close together. On a given instant, the person within causes the ribs by means of a spring to suddenly open out, break the paper on the frame, and form the cocoon, and later on he emerges from the framework and exposes himself to full view.

1887

1667. McMullin, M.   Feb. 2.

Theatrical appliances.—Consists in the application of electric bells or incandescent lamps to portable articles such as wands, brushes, head - gear, flagstaffs, banners, staves, crosses, &c. The Figure shows a wand provided with a self - contained battery *b* and wires led to a lamp. The circuit may be closed and broken at intervals by switch buttons operated by the actor's hand, or the making and breaking of contact may be controlled by clockwork. In the application to brushes, conducting - wires are substituted for bristles, so that sparks pass when an attempt is made to use the brush.

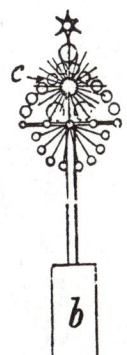

1906. Farini, G. A.   Feb. 7.

Chairs ; hat hooks ; coat stands ; brackets.—Relates to chairs for theatres &c. The chairs are arranged in pairs, their adjacent sides being supported by a fixed or removable standard A with slide bars *a, a*. The front legs E, *e, e* are hinged to the seat D, and the seat to the rod C¹, which is carried by the brackets C, C². The arm F and its support *f*¹ are both jointed. The leg G is jointed to a lug *g* on the bracket C². In folding, the seat D is turned up and then one chair is pushed back on its slide *a* and turned down behind the others as shown. Hat hooks *h, h* are arranged on the standard, a sliding tumbler, glass, or umbrella holder *j, j* on the arm, and a rod for holding a coat on the back of each chair.

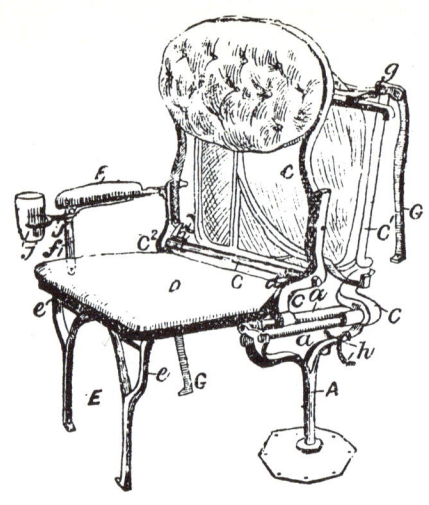

2315. Lake, H. H., [*Holbrook, B.,* and *Mann, H. N.*]. Feb. 14.

Forced ventilation.— Relates to the ventilation of rooms, schoolrooms, churches, theatres, halls, &c. The hot gases from a stove F, gas jet, or lamp are passed along a chamber W communicating with the flue, and connected at I with a side chamber S opening into the room at E. The port E may be connected by a pipe with any part from which foul gases are required to be drawn, and two of these ventilators may be enclosed in a casing opening at the top into a flue, and provided at the front with a suitable sliding door or draught regulator.

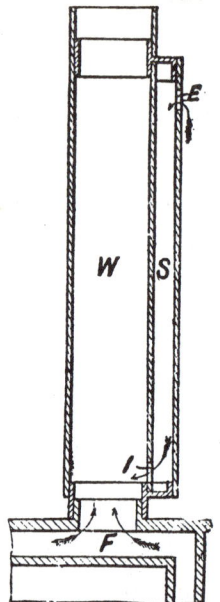

5202. Fairfax, J. S. April 7. *Amended.*

Theatrical appliances; targets.—Relates to the representation of animals, birds, ships, clouds, soldiers, targets, &c., the requisite motion being obtained by projections on an endless rotating band, or series of bands, which are hidden by theatrical scenery. The

objects are usually mounted on wheels running on guides alongside the endless bands, motion being transmitted to the various parts of the object by cams, cranks, lazy-tongs motion, pendulum rods, link-work, &c. The Figure is an elevation showing two roadways with objects on them, which are moved by endless bands A at different speeds. The endless wires B may run across the stage in the form of telegraph wires, and are used for moving clouds, rotating windmills, water-wheels, &c. The bands may be driven by a small engine or by hand. The roadway or guides may be curved to represent wave motion, motion of a ship, &c. When birds, animals, &c. are used for targets, they are hinged so as to fall back when struck, and are replaced automatically by coming in contact with inclined surfaces. By using "Morris's tubes" and small charges of ammunition, rifle practice may be obtained in a limited space. Small targets, painted to different scales to represent different distances, may be exposed intermittently by a moving slide which is actuated by an eccentric on the pulley shaft.

6882. Emerson, J. E., and **Midgley, T.** May 10.

Theatres, curtains for. Helical coils of wire A, A are woven together by screwing one into the other, the edging being formed by longitudinal coils B. The material is then flattened by passing through special rolls, after which it may be coated with or embedded in rubber, canvas, &c. The coils may be kept from spreading laterally by cross-rods. The material may be used for fireproof theatre curtains.

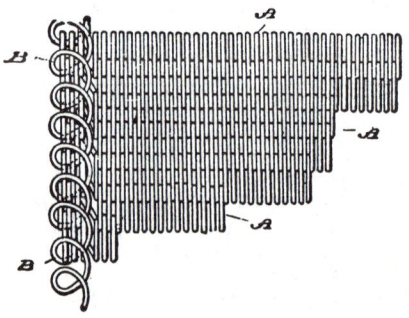

8627.   Vaughan, T. W., and **Brown, J.** June 15.

Extinguishing gas. —Relates to the water-joint apparatus in use for controlling the supply of gas for lighting theatrical scenery. The coupling-pipe H has annular teeth H[1] gearing with the pivoted toothed sector G, which is connected by the levers F[1], E[1] with the gas cock E. When the pipe H occupies the position shown by the full lines the gas is on. By raising the coupling-pipe to the position indicated by the dotted lines the teeth H[1] gear with the sector G,

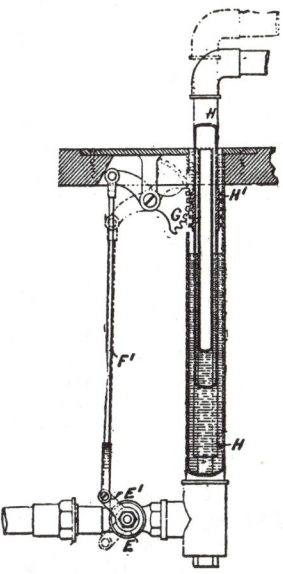

which, operating the levers, depresses the lever E[1] and cuts off the gas supply.

9798.   Buatier, J.   July 12.

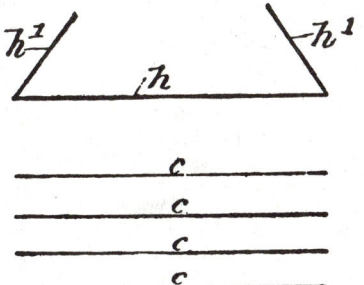

Theatrical appliances for illusionary effects. The object is to produce the appearance on, and disappearance from, the stage of a person or object. The Figure is a diagrammatic view of an arrangement of screens by which a ghost is made to appear gradually in full view of the audience without change of light. c, c, c are a series of screens, preferably of fine vertical wire threads, supported by flexible strips at top and bottom, which are attached by fine wires to cross-bars. When tension is put on these screens in a vertical direction they collapse horizontally, so that the wires come close together and form a practically opaque screen, which is made to take roughly the form of the person who represents the ghost. When the tension is relaxed the screens expand and, by reason of the fineness of the wires, become invisible. The action is as follows:—The screens c, c are drawn up through the stage in their expanded

condition, and tension put on so as to collapse them; the person is then raised behind, concealed by an opaque screen h, with side flaps h[1], h[1]. This opaque screen is then lowered and the wire screens again expanded, leaving the ghost exposed to full view. The disappearance is performed in a similar manner.

10,402.   Boult, A. J., [*Shaffer, W. C.*]. July 26.

Theatres.—Relates to automatic means for operating fireproof curtains. Some easily-fusible solid is confined in the case A in which the piston B fits; on heating, the piston rises and may be made to disengage a pawl from a ratchel-wheel on the roller of the curtain.

11,646.   O'Sullivan, D. R.   Aug. 27. *Drawings to Specification.*

Theatre and like tickets or tokens for a special form of admission-checking apparatus. The tickets are circular and of greater diameter than any coin in circulation, to prevent them from being returned to the issuer through the money shoots. They are perforated in the middle and bevelled at the edge.

12,197.   Petter, J. B.   Sept. 9.

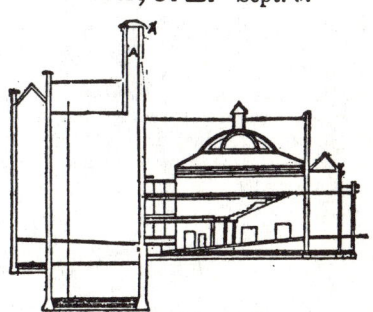

Theatres.—One or more shafts or chimneys A are arranged over the stage or platform, and are mechanically or automatically opened in case of fire so as to carry off the products of combustion and facilitate escape of the audience. Fresh air is drawn in through the exit passages from all parts of the building.

12,304. Heath, W. E., and Geddes, W. Sept. 10. *Amended.*

Theatres, fireproof curtains for. The screen or curtain, of some absorbent fabric with or without a layer of asbestos, is wound upon a roller A situated either below the stage or above the opening of the proscenium. In the former case a light lattice girder B is attached to its free edge, from which chains or ropes C extend upwards and are connected with counterweights sufficiently heavy to draw up the curtain as soon as released. In the latter case a heavy stiffening-bar is affixed along its free edge of sufficient weight to draw it down. The counterweights and stiffening-bar are normally supported by catches, releasable by

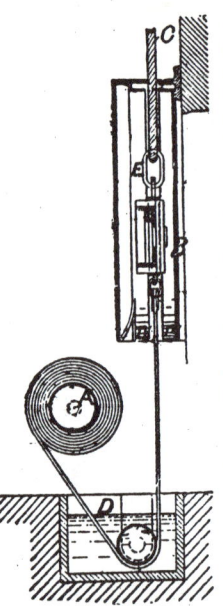

means of wire or equivalent connections from some certain point or from various points about the building. The curtain may be used dry, or, on the other hand, a trough D, containing a solution of tungstate of soda or other fireproofing-substance may be provided for the curtain to pass through while being unrolled. This, when below the stage, is at a slightly lower level than the roller, and itself contains an additional roller round which the curtain passes, first dipping down before beginning its upward movement. When the roller is above the proscenium the curtain may be contained within the trough. For the purpose of keeping the curtain wet, after it has been unrolled, a perforated pipe may be fitted up near the top, connected by a valve either with the trough or a water-main. The valve may be automatically opened on the descent of the curtain by the striking of the girder B against a projecting lever. In order to keep the side edges of the curtain close against the proscenium opening friction-wheels are attached to it, which run in vertical guides E. Otherwise the same end may be attained by means of vertical rods, one on each side of the proscenium, which carry wings capable, by a slight rotation of the rods, of being made to press the curtain against the proscenium walls.

12,328. Melville, A. Sept. 12.

Theatres and the like, fireproof curtains for. Slagwool is interwoven with wire gauze, netting, lattice-work, or other perforated metal framework.

12,603. Baird, W. Sept. 17.

Fastenings, emergency-exit. — The fastening is arranged so that a theatre &c. door opens automatically in case of panic. A pair of bolts B, B, connected by a link C, are fitted with a helical or other spring D, which withdraws them when the catch E, entering a slot or notch F in one of them, is released. The catch E is pressed forward by a spring and is operated to release the bolt by pressure on a

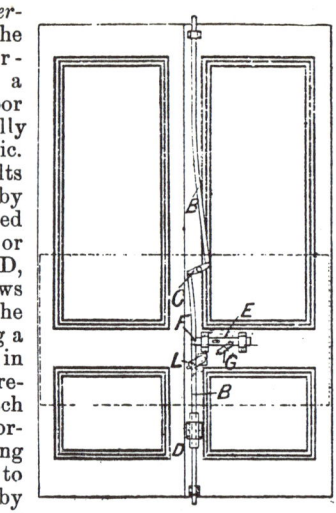

board hinged in front of the door, acting by means of a bell-crank lever or otherwise. The bolts are shot by a portable handle operating the pivoted link L.

12,640. Barnett, F. Sept. 17. *Drawings to Specification.*

Theatres and the like, fireproof curtains for. The curtain is divided horizontally, the halves being attached on opposite sides to endless chains so that they approach one another when the chains are moved in one direction, and recede into recesses above and below the proscenium when the chains are rotated in a reverse direction. The upper part is heavier than the lower part of the curtain, the difference in weight causing the two parts to approach and lock at the centre on being released. A winch is provided to work the chains and withdraw the curtain into the recesses, a suitable brake preventing the return.

Window-shutters; doors.—The same arrangement may be used for door and window shutters; or the shutter may be divided vertically and the halves slide horizontally into recesses.

12,817. Clarke, M. W. H. Sept. 21.

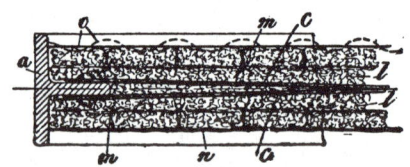

Theatres and the like, fireproof curtains for. A rectangular angle-iron or ⊤-iron frame *a* is strengthened by horizontal, vertical, and diagonal stays *c*, which cross one another to form lattice-work. On each side of the lattice-work, layers *l* of slagwool, asbestos, or other mineral fibre are secured by means of barbed wires *m*, transverse bolts, staples, wire network *n*, or sheet metal *o*, either flat or corrugated. The sides of the frame are fitted with T or angle-iron strips, which slide in grooved bars or guides built into the masonry. The curtain is balanced by weights connected by wire ropes passing over pulleys. The curtain may be raised by a winch, or by vertical hydraulic rams. Electric devices may be used for releasing the curtain, suitable brake devices preventing too rapid a descent.

13,025. Fisher, J. A., and Booth, L. Sept. 26.

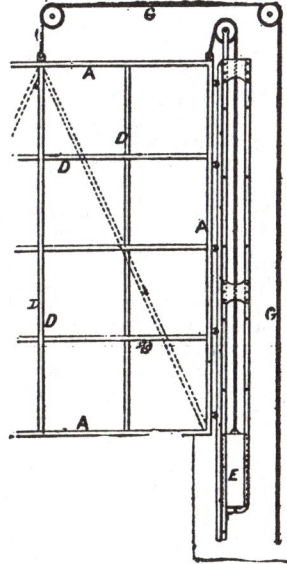

Theatres and the like, fireproof curtains for. The curtain or screen is formed of an iron frame A covered on one or both sides with asbestos fabric which is secured by hoops D placed over the fabric and bolted to the frame. Counterweights E partly balance the curtain, which is raised by a cord G of combustible material. In the event of a fire, the cord G is burnt, and the curtain automatically descends. The curtain may be divided horizontally so that the parts can slide over one another.

13,193. Stanley, J. M., and Stanley, T. B. Sept. 29.

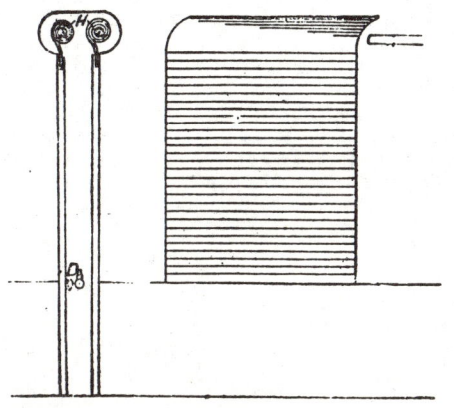

Theatres. — Relates to means for arresting the spread of fires in theatres, by preventing free admission of air. With this view shutters or curtains of non-combustible materials are fitted on all doors and windows, or between the auditorium and stage. The arrangement in the Figure con-

sists of two curtains, which are wound round axes H for raising and lowering, and have a nozzle or perforation in a pipe D in the space between for delivering steam or water.

13,258. Dutton, W. H. Sept. 30.

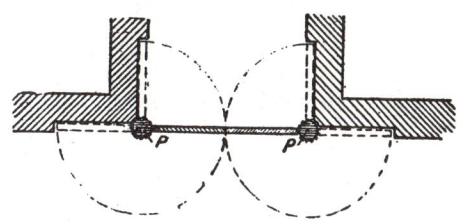

Doors, staircases, &c. — The door-posts P of theatres and other buildings are made to rotate on spindles, and so facilitate the ingress and egress of people. The extreme positions of the door when open are shown in dotted lines in the plan. The invention may be applied to posts fixed to corridors, passages, newels of staircases, or any place of ingress or egress.

13,588. Walker, L. A. Oct. 7.

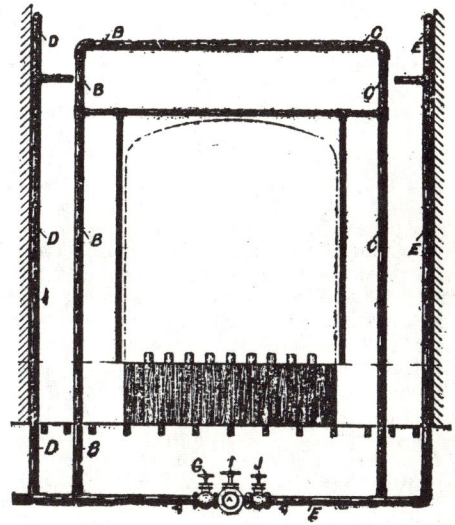

Sprinkling-apparatus, non-automatic. — Relates to sprinkling-apparatus to be fitted more especially in large buildings, such as theatres, mills, &c. The apparatus consists of a series of perforated pipes B, C, D, E carried round the side walls and across ceilings, and connected to the mains. Separate valves G, I, and J may be used for each branch, or a single four-way valve may be used, by means of which all the pipes may be controlled. In theatres pipes may be arranged to form a curtain of water in front of each tier or circle. Pipes with open gratings or other suitable contrivances are constructed to carry off the water.

13,740. Duplany, C. M. Oct. 11.

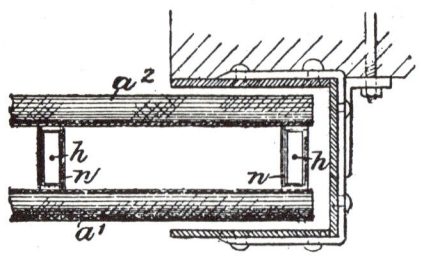

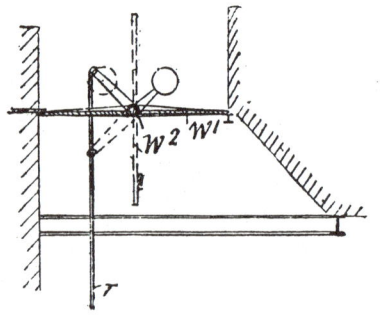

Theatres and the like, fireproof curtains and smoke shafts for. The curtain is made of two sheets a^1, a^2 of woven asbestos or other flexible fireproof material arranged a short distance apart, and connected by rings n which are secured by strips of asbestos at regular intervals. These sheets are secured at the top and bottom edges to light girders, and fold evenly when drawn up by a rope or wire attached to the bottom bar or girder. The lifting-rope passes up through the centre of the curtain and over pulleys to a crab. The bottom bar is partly balanced by weights at the ends of cords h passing up through the rings n and over suitable pulleys. The curtain is supported in its raised position by bell-crank levers under the ends of the bottom bar. These lever bolts can be withdrawn to release the curtain by means of rods, links, and wires passing to the prompt corner, flies, or other part of the house. A strip of hinged flooring through which the curtain passes is simultaneously released, and the lower bar descends to the floor below the stage. The bar is padded with asbestos to form a buffer. A chimney is built at the back of the stage as shown in the lower Figure, for carrying away heated air and smoke in case of a fire on the stage. The counterweighted door or flap w^1 turns on a central pivot w^2 and is actuated by a rod r connected with the releasing-mechanism of the curtain.

14,101. Gardner, C. Oct. 18.

Theatres and the like, fireproof partitions and screens for. The partitions are formed of double sheets of metal secured together at the edges, the space between being filled in with water. In the Figure, the screen D is connected by a chain m with a lifting-crab H, and is partly balanced by a counterweight n. The screen is kept in its raised position by a brake acting on a pulley on the shaft h, the pressure being regulated by an eccentric J. In case of a fire breaking out, the brake is released, and the curtain descends between guides in metal side columns, which support the girder F. The lower edge of the curtain is open and fits in a groove g in the sill G, through which water from the main K is supplied to fill the curtain. The proscenium walls are fitted with hollow partitions, which are also filled with water from the main K when the valve is opened. Vertical pipes from the main K are fitted with hose pipes, which play on the outside of the roof and on the stage. The curtain may be divided horizontally into several parts which are connected to drums of the crab of different diameters by separate chains. The valves may be opened and the curtain released automatically by the burning of cords.

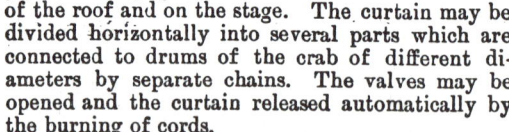

14,543. Tepper, E. Oct. 25.

Theatres, scenery and curtains for. The scenery is composed of wire gauze, preferably woven galvanized iron, stretched on light iron frames and covered with fireproof paint. Large backgrounds and curtains for rolling may be made of a fabric having a galvanized iron warp and wool yarn weft, the latter being impregnated with the paint. The composition of the paint may vary, but 78 parts of white cheese (curds), 8 of slaked lime, $5\frac{1}{2}$ of phenol, and $8\frac{1}{2}$ of alum is preferred.

14,556. Stones, J. Oct. 26.

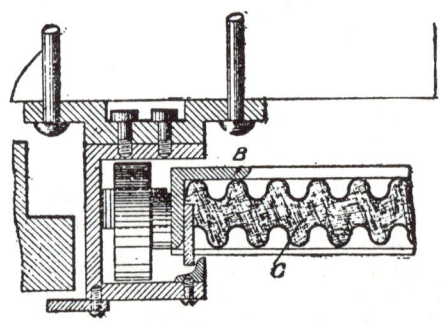

Theatres and the like, fireproof curtains or screens for. An angle-iron framework B is covered on both sides with plain or corrugated sheet iron or steel, the space between the sheets being filled in with silicate cotton or other fireproof material C. The frame is strengthened by vertical, horizontal, and diagonal pieces of T or angle iron. The curtain is counterbalanced, and is raised by a winch in any suitable manner. The curtain may be divided horizontally, the upper part lifting the lower one by means of projecting strips which interlock.

16,722. **Aird, A.** Dec. 5.

Theatres; concert halls; doors. — Relates to a folding turnstile combined with a panel gate, or door, for use in the exits of theatres, concert halls, &c. The turnstile is shown in the Figure. The arms A, of which there are four, are pivoted to a collar T sliding on the spindle B, and are linked by rods D to arms C attached to fixed pivots. Links E connect the arms C to a second sliding collar F. The upper part of the spindle B is hollow, and allows spring catches G, attached to the collar F, to slide within it. The catches engage with the top of the spindle B, excepting when forced together, by pressing down a cap H. The weight of the arms and rods then forces down the collars F and T and the turnstile collapses. The frame R, on which it is mounted, swings on a hinge S, and may be turned so as to lie close to the wall. The cap H, which releases the catches G, is guided vertically and actuated by a plate I operated by a chain J from any convenient part of the building. A bolt, which holds the frame R in position when the turnstile is in use, is connected to the plate I and is actuated by the collapsing-mechanism. An electric register is employed to check the number of entrances. The turnstile

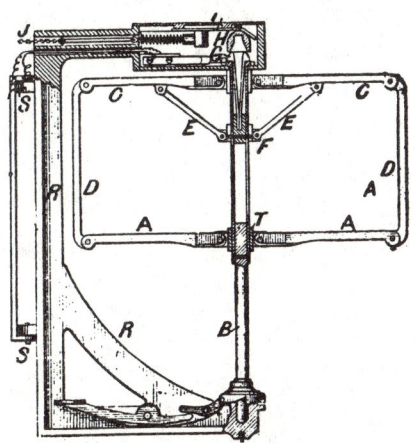

may be used in combination with a gate hinged to the wall opposite it and which may be opened at the same time that the turnstile is folded, thus allowing many persons to pass out at once. The gate, which may be folding, is held in its place by a bolt in the floor, also actuated by the chain J.

16,744. **Ober, W. Y.** Dec. 6.

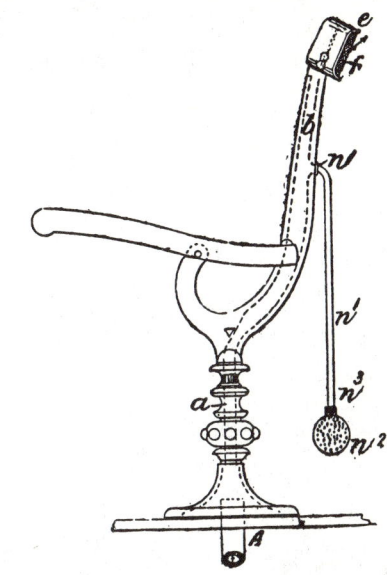

Chairs; seats.—Relates to chairs and seats for theatres, combined with ventilating-apparatus. The standard a and back b of the chair &c. are made hollow to form an air passage from supply pipes A, preferably below the floor, to a distributing-chamber e with perforated back f and suitable valves. A flexible tube n, n^1 with a perforated ball n^2 and cock n^3 is connected to the air passage in the back. When the seat and back are both pivoted, instead of forming a passage through the standard and back a flexible connection is used and the distributing-chamber is modified.

17,107. **Cardwell, W. A.** Dec. 12.

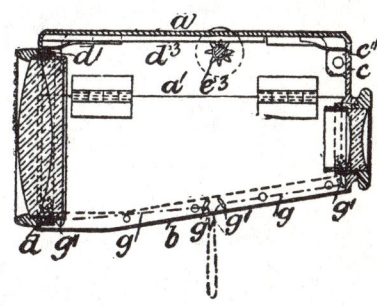

Opera, field, and marine glasses.—The framework is constructed so as to fold up when not in use, and occupy less space. The Figure shows the arrangement in section. The top a is rigid, and has side flanges a^1. The end c, carrying the eye-pieces, is hinged to the top in such a manner that it will be firmly held both in its vertical and horizontal position. The end d carrying the object glasses is similarly hinged to a focussing-slide, which is traversed in the top a by a rack d^3 and pinion e^3. The sides are formed by flaps hinged to the flange a^1, and the bottom is formed by a piece of flexible material *b*. The whole can thus be folded into a flat form, having the thickness of the flanges a^1. When required for use (after opening out the flaps) the lenses are turned into position by pulling a cord *g*, which is led through eyes g^1 on one flap and out through the flexible bottom *b*. Modifications are obtained by making the sides flexible, and having the bottom *b* either flexible or rigid.

1888

77. Wiles, J. F. Jan. 3.

Advertising on theatre screens. Fires are confined to one part of the theatre by a screen or sheet of water which falls from a water pipe A placed in front of the stage or otherwise, through perforations or a slit B in the underside of the pipe. The water falls through an opening C in the floor into a trough D, whence it is carried off by the pipe G. Advertisements may be thrown upon the screen, or it may be illuminated by coloured lights for producing scenic effects in theatres.

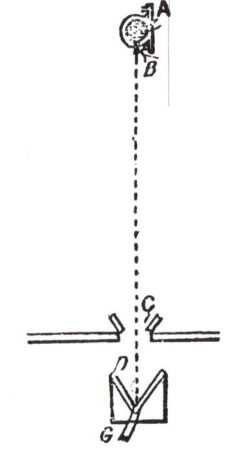

246. Lane, J. Jan. 6.

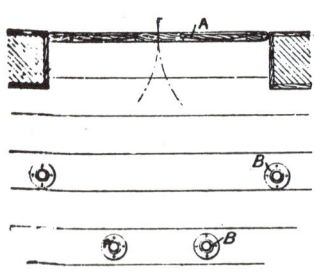

Crushing in doorways and the like, preventing.— In theatres, churches, &c., vertical pillars B, erected between the floor and ceiling in front of the doors A, serve to divide the crowd and prevent extreme crushing in the doorway. The flanges are secured to the columns by a nut and screw arrangement which allows for adjustment or removal, and are provided with spikes or projections, which are forced into the floor or ceiling.

356. Hart, F. W., and Bishop, W. Jan. 9.

Theatrical appliances for producing scenic effects. Relates to a lamp for burning flashing powders. The powder is dropped through a funnel *e* into a receiver which is contained inside the reservoir A. When air is forced into A by means of a pump consisting of a flexible ball *h* and a valve chamber *g*, the powder is forced up through the pipe *a* and discharged between two pairs of flames *w. w* of a gas lamp or spirit lamp B. A chamber plug may be used for dropping the measured quantity of powder into the receiver, or an ordinary lifting conical plug. An apparatus is described for distributing compressed air or gas to any required number of lamps.

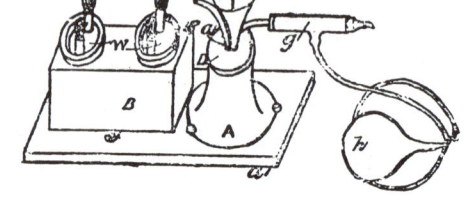

1302. Campbell, S. Jan. 28. *Drawings to Specification.*

Fire-escapes; pipes and tubes, supporting; buildings modified for fire-extinguishing.—Means of descent from the galleries and upper boxes of theatres and other public buildings are provided by an endless web carrying seats and extending down an oblique passage. The rate of descent is regulated by brakes on the rollers. A parallel stairway, separated from the web by a low partition, affords ingress for firemen and contains hose pipes. At the top are shelves for hand grenades.

2192. Braham, P. Feb. 14.

Chairs; seats; school seats. —The improvement is applicable to existing chairs and to seats and chairs for schools, churches, theatres, ships, libraries, &c. An adjustable frame or back B, either plain or stuffed, is connected to the uprights of the chair or seat frame by hinges, ball-and-socket joints, springs, elastic material, or screws so as to support the sitter at the shoulders and above the hips and to enable him to alter the inclination of the back to suit himself. The backs can be taken off to be sent away for re-stuffing, and re-fixed without skilled labour.

2730. James, A. Feb. 23.

Lamps, actinic. Relates to magnesium lamps for photographic purposes. The magnesium powder is placed in a funnel-shaped reservoir O, and blown through curved pipes a, a^1 into the centre of argand or similar burners b^1, b^2, by means of an air pipe c. In the apparatus shown, three burners are supported on a pedestal B, to the bottom of which the gas pipe f is connected. A reflector R is fixed on rods r attached to the gas-supply pipes.

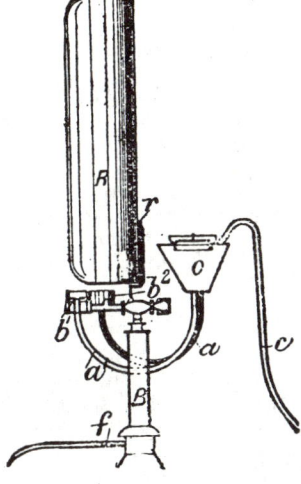

3708. Lee, R. B. March 10.

Ceilings; floors; partitions; roofs; doors; columns; girders; theatres.— Asbestos fibre is mixed with concrete or cement to which may be added finely-broken slag, coke, firebrick, &c. Slabs, blocks, &c. are formed of this composition, and may, if desired, be strengthened by an internal metallic skeleton, as described in Specification No. 14,726, A.D. 1885. The construction of a fireproof curtain for a theatre is shown in the Figure. A metal frame is divided into a number of small squares or panels by lattice bars, these panels being filled in with the slabs of cement and asbestos as shown in the squares 1, 2, and 3. Internal skeletons of metal bars and wire netting are shown in the squares 4 and 5. The outer surface is coated with fireproof material, and painted to represent an act drop. The curtain is overbalanced by hollow weights containing water which escapes when the weights reach the ground. The curtain is held in any position by a bolt or brake.

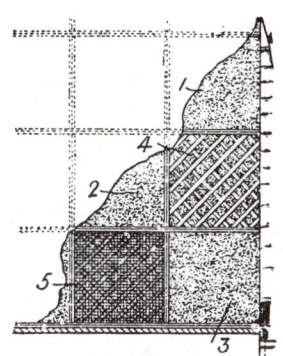

3795. Coninck, F. de. March 12.

Fireproof paints.—Two and a quarter parts of sifted asbestos are mixed with one of zinc oxide, and combined with a solution of 30 parts of chloride of zinc (56° Bé.), 50 parts of borate of ammonia (3° Bé.), and 20 parts of solution of gelatine containing 25 per cent. of dry glue. Or the first mixture may be added to any oil paint. The paints thus obtained are suitable for application to cloths in general, theatrical scenery, carpets, wall-paper, wood, furniture, &c.

5247. Pennefather, De F., and Dinsmore, J. H. R. April 9.

Air, drawing-off and supplying, methods of.—Air is supplied to rooms &c. or to ejectors for exhausting foul air by means of a cowl A, which may, when necessary, be assisted by a water spray h. In the form shown air is led down the pipe B, at the bottom of which water is led away. The air then passes up to the distributing-pipes C by the ascending pipe B^1. Foul air passes away by the pipes Q, P. In another form ejectors are placed on the pipes C, or pipes may lead from the rooms to an ejector. The pipes may be inside or outside the building &c. or may be built into the walls. The apparatus is applicable to theatres, &c.

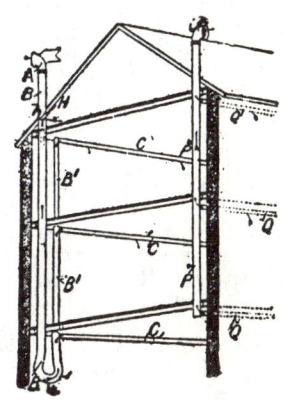

5254. Castan, L., and Castan, G., [*trading as* Gebrüder Castan]. April 9.

Theatrical appliances.—Relates to optical illusion apparatus by means of which a human being or other object appears to float free in the air. The object is placed on a horizontal circular glass disc A, which may be rotated by the crank c, bevel-wheels e, drum d, and strap b passing round the drum and the frame B of the glass disc. Antifriction rollers a are provided to assist the rotation. The person &c. is reflected in a vertical position towards the spectators by a mirror E, held at an angle of 45° in the frame D carried by the framework C, and by a suitable arrangement of the light &c., the framework and mechanism being invisible by the spectators.

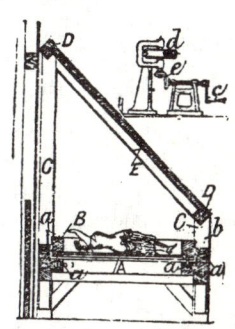

7067. Fuhrmann, A. May 12.

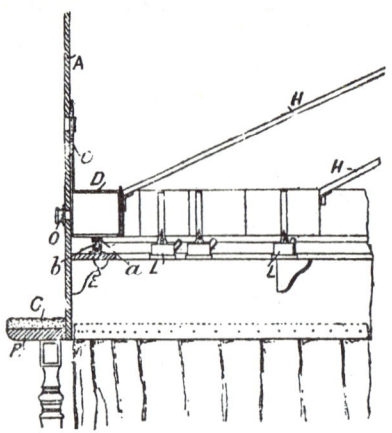

Panoramas.—The spectators sit round the outside of a circular casing A provided with eye-pieces O. Inside the casing a ring of stereoscope boxes D, connected by a circular rail *a*, travels round over rollers *b* on a circular shelf E. All the views thus pass before each spectator. The motion is intermittent, so that time is given for inspection. The boxes are connected by rods H to a sleeve on a central pillar, where the actuating-mechanism is placed. Behind the boxes lamps L are placed to illuminate the transparencies. The names of the views appear on boards *c* through slots in the casing A.

7498. Kilham, J. T. May 22.

Theatres, scenery for. The apparatus is intended for rapidly changing the scenes without lowering the gas or the drop scene. The scenes are painted upon a series of slats *c*, c^1, c^2 having extensions *a* pivoted at *c* to uprights A, D, E. Each set of uprights is connected by cross-pieces to form a frame, the frame composed of the uprights A

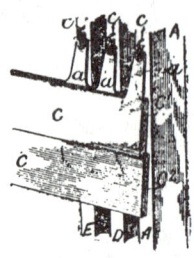

and cross-pieces being fixed, but the others movable by handles behind. When it is desired to change the scene, the frame carrying either the slats c^1 or c^2 is slid so that these slats cover up the slats *c*. Scenes may be painted on both sides of the slats, and the parts can be reversed so as to show either side,

7732. Lancaster, F. J., and Nixon, E. May 26.

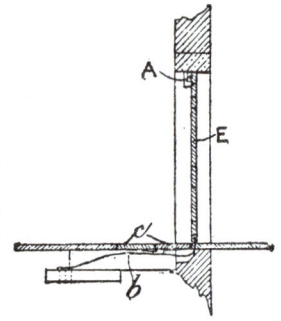

Door-opening apparatus.—Relates to emergency-exit apparatus. A spring bolt *b* is withdrawn from the bottom of the door E by the depression of hinged flooring *c* when stood upon, the door being thrown open by a spring A.

7962. Stead, T. W. May 31. *Drawings to Specification.*

Theatres, fireproof screens for. The metal screen is divided horizontally, the two halves being connected by wire ropes passing over pulleys in such a manner that they approach and recede simultaneously. The lower half, which is lighter than the upper half, is fitted with a cistern. On filling the cistern with water, the bottom part overbalances the top, thus keeping them apart. When it is required to close the proscenium opening to prevent spread of fire, a valve in the cistern is opened, the water escapes, and the upper half of the screen descends, drawing up the lower half until they meet.

11,158. Smith, A. L. Aug. 1.

Fireproof coverings.—Relates to a fabric especially applicable for making scenes and side wings for theatres, concert halls, &c. Coarse flannel or woollen woven fabrics, felts, or union materials, which may be made in specially-wide widths, are coated on both sides with whiting, white lead, or other white pigment, coloured or not, and mixed with size and water.

13,105. Harradine, W. N. Sept. 11.

Ventriloquial apparatus.—A series of portraits or pictures are arranged in a frame, and are made to change by rolling one picture away, by flaps, or by revealing another behind. An aperture is cut in the lower jaw of each portrait, and a mechanical movable mouth is inserted. This mouth answers for any number of pictures.

13,361. Schlosser, E. Sept. 15.

Chairs for use in theatres and the like. The back and seat of the chair are hinged so as to fold and leave a free passage for exit. The Figure shows a plan of two chairs, side by side, one open, the other folded up. The part a^1 of the seat is carried by a horizontal shaft, and the part b^1 by a vertical shaft in a side standard A. The two shafts are geared together by equal bevel-wheels,

and helical springs surrounding the vertical shaft tend to fold a^1 and b^1 into the plane of the standard A. Spring hinges *g*, *h* connect and tend to fold the parts *a*, *b* on the parts a^1, b^1, the back and seat proper being held when open by snapping-devices, which can be released by pressing a knob *k*. A locking-bar prevents any one from releasing the catches when the seat is in use. *i* is a catch for fixing the parts when folded up. Each side

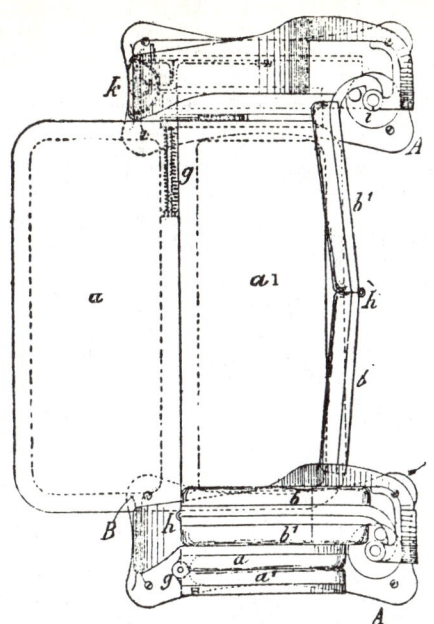

standard carries a folding seat and back, and is provided with a ledge or support B for the adjoining seat

14,171. Potter, E. T.   Oct. 2.

Magic-lanterns.—Instead of a series of slides, a continuous band D, on which are painted the scenes, or from which are stamped the letters of an address &c., is drawn by clockwork H or otherwise from a spool K to a spool F between the lens

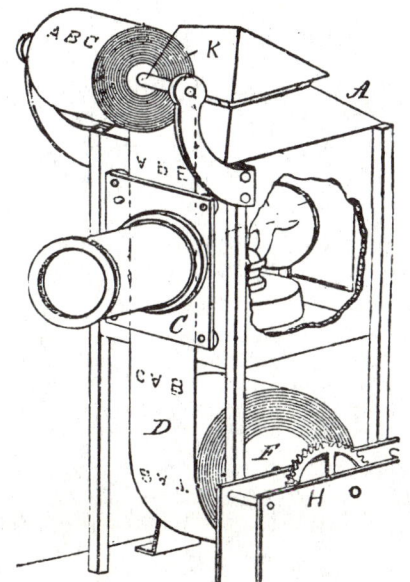

plate C and the body A.   An opaque material may be employed for the strip D, where the words or

parts of the scenes can be represented by simply stamping out the material of the slide so as to let the light shine direct on the screen ; otherwise translucent material, such as prepared paper, collodion, &c., must be used.

17,005. Cockman, A. E., and Melven, G. de.   Nov. 22.

Optical illusions, producing.—Relates to an apparatus for causing the upper part of a living person to appear as though supported upon a pedestal resting on a suspended platform, or as floating above the platform, the illusion being brought about by a trick platform, and by covering the cavity, in which the lower part of the body is hidden, the top of the platform, and the whole of the background with black velvet.   The suspended platform A is painted white on its edges, and has the cavity B beneath it covered with black velvet.   Around the body is a raised flange *a* covered with black velvet, outside which

is a frame D, D¹ constructed in two parts, and painted so as to represent a white pedestal.   The person may be revolved in view of the audience by the mechanism shown.   Arrangements are described for allowing the person to get into or out of the apparatus without being seen by the spectators, and for taking away the framework D in such a manner that it appears to be a solid pedestal, leaving the person apparently floating above the platform.

17,559. Villiers-Stead, F., and Hedgman, E. R.   Dec. 1.

Hiring opera glasses. — A receptacle is provided having a spring lid and an internal compartment for the opera glass, which, when the lid is opened, is pushed up to a convenient position by a spring false bottom.   The lid is normally locked by catches which can be freed by a coin or by a key.   A door is

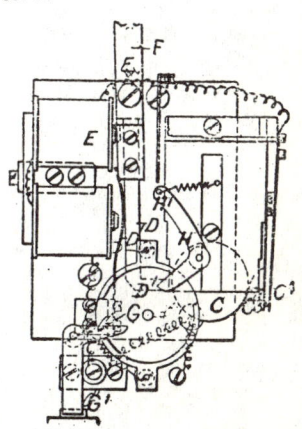

provided at the side of the case which is locked by the bell crank G, G¹. The key can be inserted in the lock either way up; in one case on being turned it engages the bell crank G, G¹ and unlocks the door; in the other it engages the bell crank H, H¹ and pressing on the tail of the pivoted lever F moves it so as to unlock the lid or, if the lid be open, to allow of its being closed. The key is of course in the possession of an authorized person. Where electricity is available the coin C is brought to rest between the end D¹ of the lever F and a shoulder C³ on one of two contact-springs C⁴, thereby pressing the latter together. Circuit is thus completed for an electro-magnet E, which attracting the armature D on the

lever F frees the lid. The part D¹ moving with the lever F allows the coin to fall to the till. A modified form of this arrangement is described in which a second pair of contacts is provided. If the coin happens to stick, a vibration is set up which ultimately shakes it off into the till. Where electricity is not used a push-piece is provided, the coin shoot being carried by the lever F. When a coin is in place, the push strikes it and moves the lever so as to disengage the lid; on releasing the push a spring returns the parts and jerks the coin off its support.

Fraud, preventing.—The form of the catches prevents the lid from being closed until the key is employed.

19,024. Day, St. J. V., [*Stanton, W.*]. Dec. 31.

Theatrical appliances.—Relates to bird and animal models for theatrical and like entertainments. A suitable framework A is fitted with bands or belts D for securing the bird &c. to the operator within, and is covered with canvas or other material to which the feathers are sewn. The beak, eyelids, wings, and tail of the bird are worked by cords within reach of the occupant. A piece of gauze G in the neck provides a means for breathing and talking. A tube P from the beak to the mouth of the operator affords means for drinking from a vessel. An elastic bag, which can be inflated by a pair of bellows, may be fitted within the bird at any part. The plumage is built up of feathers, the smaller of which are sewn on the inside, and the larger on the outside. The feet are enclosed in leather or other covering, and slipped into the feet of the bird.

1889

540. Hobson, C. W. Jan. 11.

Opera and field glasses.—Consists in forming the lenses A, A oblong, oval, or square in field, marine, opera, and other glasses, thereby allowing of a flat-sided frame, and

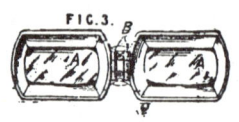

securing lightness. The lenses may be secured in various ways, but preferably they are hinged at B, B.

934. Wilson, R., [*known as* Robert Romah]. Jan. 18.

Gymnastic and acrobatic apparatus.—Adjustably suspended by cords C from the roof of a building are bearings B which support lengths of rails or tracks A, the ends of which form fishplates for securing the

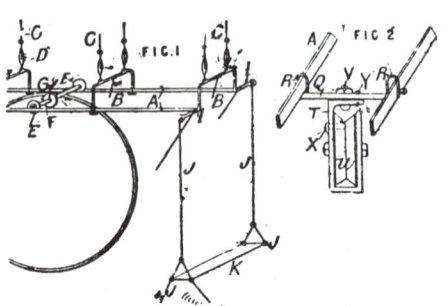

lengths together. The last of the supports at each end has arms I from which the stand K for the gymnast is secured by chains &c. J. Running on the rails are rollers E on a spindle F having a central grooved wheel G from which a large hoop, made of any suitable material, and of one length or of several pieces joined together, is suspended. It is on or in this hoop, thus capable of traversing

along the rails, that the acrobat performs. By fixing the hoop on a pulley u, Fig. 2, carried in a frame T suspended by a pivot V from a cross-beam Q carried by hooks R fixed to the rails by screws &c., several modifications in the performance may be introduced; for example, the grooved wheel u may be fixed to the frame T or free thereon by means of the pin X, and the frame T may revolve or be fixed by the pin Y. Several modifications of the apparatus may be made. In one, a single track of wire &c. may be inclined, and the hoop caused to travel upwards and downwards thereon, while a model engine may run simultaneously above the wire.

1419. Plessy, G. Jan. 25.

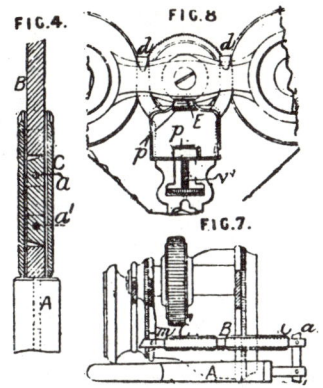

Opera and field glasses ; eyeglasses.—Relates to handles for opera glasses, eyeglasses, binoculars, quizzing glasses, and like articles. The handle is made in two parts A and B, Fig. 4, connected by a double joint a, a^1, which is made rigid when required by sliding over it the piece C. When the opera glass &c. is specially constructed to receive the handle, the part B is connected to a projecting piece on the side of the glasses by a compass-like hinge with stops to limit the play. When out of use, the handle, in addition to being folded at the joint a, a^1, can be turned up in front of the object glasses. Fig. 7 shows another arrangement, in which the part B has a single hinge at m and is fixed to the frame between the barrels. A second sliding piece is employed to make the joint m rigid. To apply these handles to existing glasses, a clamp E, Fig. 8, is provided. Hooks d, d are formed at the end of the forked arms of the clamp to grasp an upper edge of the frame, while a sliding plate p, worked by a screw v^1, brings the jaw p^1 under the corresponding lower edge.

1570. Hughes, W. C. Jan 29.

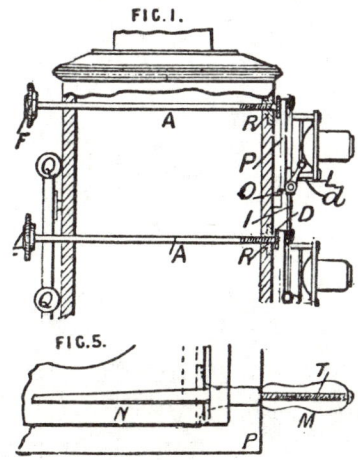

Dissolving-view apparatus.—In triple and like lanterns, the pictures can be made to register on the screen from behind by means of the rods A,

Fig. 1, with milled head F. The end of each rod is screwed and passes through a nut R, and beyond it is clamped to the part P, pivoted at O, in such a way as not to interfere with its rotation. By turning the head F the picture can be raised or lowered on the screen. The perforated diaphragm is raised by turning a crank handle L having a long toothed spindle gearing with a rack I at both sides of the diaphragm. The shutters, for closing the lanterns, slide in grooves in the diaphragm, and rest upon horizontal arms N, Fig. 5, which can be moved vertically by hand and clamped in any required position ; for the latter purpose the handle M is fitted upon a screw spindle T, and can be tightened upon the part P by rotating it. The slide-stage is carried by a piece fixed to the part d, Fig. 1, of the lantern, and it is vertically adjustable by racks and pinions, clamping-nuts being provided to fix it as desired. At the joints of the gas distributer hollow spheres Q, Q are formed to make the pressure more even.

1784. Stirton, J. A. Feb. 1.

Advertising. — Advertisements are put on the borders of programmes, circulars, bills, trade lists, &c.

2727. Rastrick, R. J. H. Feb. 16.

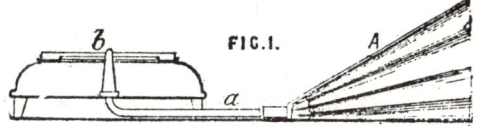

Theatrical appliances for producing scenic effects. Relates to magnesium-light apparatus which may be used to represent lightning for theatrical purposes. Means for feeding the pulverulent or strip magnesium to the flame, and also ensuring better combustion of the metal, are described. In the apparatus shown in the Figure, which is adapted to give flash light, the powder is ejected from a bellows &c. receptacle or blower A through a tube a and nozzle b to a spirit &c. lamp flame. For continuous magnesium light the receptacle A is replaced by another in which works a fan, a blower being used in conjunction to aid combustion. The strip magnesium is fed forward from a roll by clockwork &c.

3279. Hart, F. W. Feb. 23.

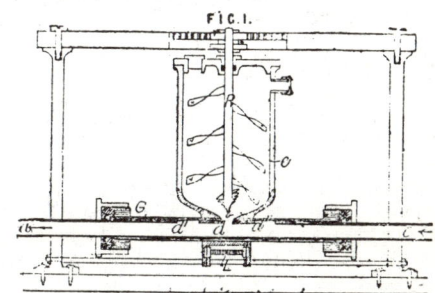

Theatrical appliances for producing scenic effects. Relates to means for producing continuous or flash lights, for long or short intervals and according to desired codes, for photographic, scenic, signal, and other purposes, being an improvement on the invention described in Specification No. 356, A.D. 1888. The magnesium or other powder is put in a hopper *e* in which works a spindle R, having vanes for feeding the powder through the opening to the tube or container *a*, *c*, through which it is ejected in the direction of the arrows to the lamps by a pneumatic arrangement. The hopper is mounted on a sleeve G surrounding and sliding on the tube *a*, *c*, which latter has graduated port openings *d*, *d*¹, *d*¹¹, so that by sliding the sleeve and hopper by a pivoted hand-lever L, so as to bring the opening over one or other of the ports, flashes of longer or shorter duration can be obtained. The vane spindle R is geared so as to be rotated continuously in the same direction by such sliding movement, or it may be worked by hand. A modification is described in which the powder is supplied by a rotating hopper. The lamps or burners, which may be spirit &c. or gas, are arranged in pairs in a line, and so disposed in the case of burners that the flames have a certain position in relation to the ejected powder. Also, when gas is employed, the burners are disposed on an adjustable frame carrying the flashing-apparatus to enable the light to be directed at any angle.

3839. Hughes, W. C. March 5.

Limelight apparatus.—The object is to allow of the accurate lateral and vertical adjustment of the burner to the focus of the lantern. The foundation plate A, which slides in grooves in the bottom of the lantern, carries cross-pieces or brackets B, J,

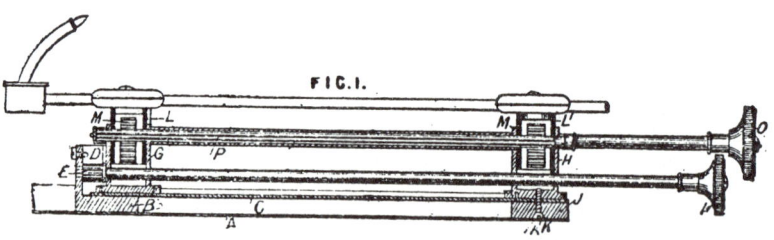

FIG. 1.

on which rides a radial arm C carrying tubular pillars G, H. The arm C and pillar H are pivoted to the piece J by a screw K. The burner can be adjusted laterally by means of the rack D and pinion E, upon operating the thumb-button I. The vertical adjustment is obtained by operating the thumb-button O, which causes the serrated spindle P to engage with racks M on the tubes L, L¹, the latter sliding vertically in the pillars G, H. A worm, supported in bearings affixed to the lantern, engages with a rack on the plate A and allows of its being moved to and fro.

4931. Short, A. J. March 21. *Drawings to Specification.*

Theatrical appliances for producing scenic effects. To represent an explosion in a house or building, the windows, doors, &c. are provided with rubber or other opening-springs, and bolts or fastenings controlled by levers. When the explosion takes place, a lever is pulled, the spring bolts are released and withdrawn, and the doors, windows, &c., fly open under the force of the springs.

5218. Pocock, C. S. March 26.

Opera and field glasses.—Consists in substituting a flexible body A, A for the usual telescopic body. The field-glass frame C is connected to the bridge B by hinged or slotted links E, E. The hinges K may be provided with springs which tend to open the links E, E, while, when the glasses are closed, a spring catch L engages a socket in the barrel M of the focussing-adjustment. The details may be somewhat varied.

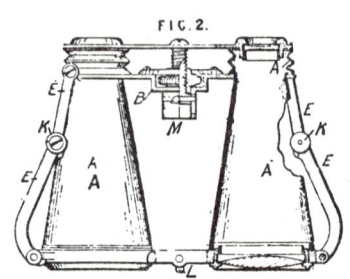

FIG. 2.

5287. Levi, S. J., and Carré, E. March 27.

Opera and field glasses.—Relates to means for rapidly focussing field, marine, or opera glasses. The central guide-tube B of the spindle A is slotted on each side, and a pin *a* passing through the spindle projects into radial slots *e* on two wheels D mounted on an axis *d*, and turned by the thumbs. In modified forms, the pin *a* may be connected with crank-pins on the wheels D by links ; the wheels may be replaced by levers or segments ; or other variations in detail may be introduced.

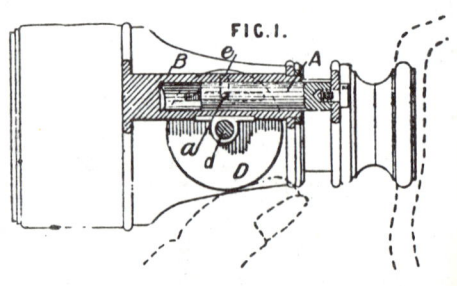

FIG. 1.

6474. Weil, I. April 16.

Opera glasses.—The inner tube A of the adjusting - mechanism is made larger than usual and closed at the bottom so as to form or contain a receptacle for salts, scent, &c. The stopper *a* is covered by a cap B.

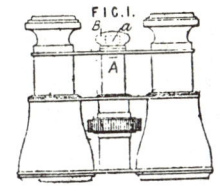

6999. Gray, C., and **Kemp, H.** April 26.

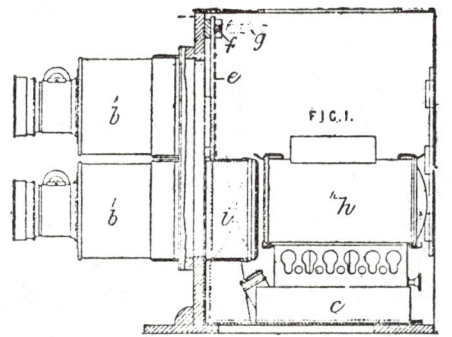

Dissolving-view apparatus.—Consists in making the illuminating-apparatus, with or without the condensers, movable so as to come opposite either objective. In the Figure, an oil lamp *h* is carried on a platform *c*, and worked up and down by the rack *e* and pinion *f* on turning the crank handle *g*. The condensers *i* move with the lamp and come opposite either of the objectives *b*, *b*.

7241. Wilson, J. May 1.

Sheet - metal buildings and parts of buildings and structures. — Relates to constructions, in corrugated or other sheet metal, of buildings, walls, warehouses, sheds, fortifications, batteries, theatres, partitions, balconies, doors, ceilings, floors, columns, and other structures. Two or more corrugated sheets A are

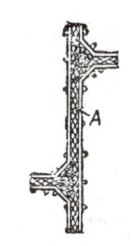

arranged with the ridges touching one another, or opposite to one another, so as to form a series of tubular spaces. The structure may be lined with wood, the spaces between the lining and sheet metal being filled in with wood or any suitable material or liquid. The tubular spaces may be used for cooling by liquid or air, heating by liquid, steam, or air, ventilating, as a means for extinguishing fire, or as passages for wires, rods, pipes, and the like. The spaces between the sheets may be filled in with concrete, asphalt, cork, sawdust, sand, or other suitable packing. The sheets may be built up of strips riveted together. The structure is strengthened by angle iron or wooden frames, tubes, metal strips, and the like. In one

arrangement, a single corrugated sheet is used, the spaces on each side being filled in with wood strips. Parallel plates may be secured at a distance apart by bolts or rivets, the intermediate spaces being filled in with concrete &c. Instead of the corrugated sheets, plain parallel sheets with intermediate tubes may be used.

Columns; theatres, fireproof screens for. The screen is made of corrugated sheet metal with the corrugations arranged vertically or horizontally. In one arrangement, the screen slides between two hollow columns filled with water, and is counterbalanced by a weight attached to the operating-cord. The curtain may be released by the cutting or burning of the cord in case of fire. The curtain on descending opens a valve between the column and curtain and allows water to pass to the latter. The corrugated sheets are perforated so that water is sprinkled over the stage &c. in the event of a fire. The curtain may be divided horizontally, one half sliding upwards and the other downwards below the stage. In another arrangement, the curtain is divided vertically, the halves being mounted on inclined guides or rollers.

8772. Le Mesurier, H. B. May 27.

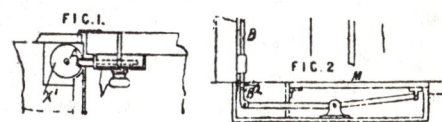

Fastenings, emergency-exit; sash and like fastenings.—The fastening is for emergency exits for theatres and other buildings and for windows and like purposes. Fig. 1 shows the arrangement adopted for single doors. The latch bolt V, which may be operated by a handle in the ordinary manner engages the slotted drum X^1 on the spindle A. A second slotted drum on the spindle A is situated below the floor, and is locked by a lever held up by a spring or weight. When one or more persons are standing on a treadle in front of the door, the lever is depressed and the spindle A set free, so that pressure on the door will open it. When the invention is applied to double doors, one of them is provided with a double bolt, the lower part of which B, Fig. 2, is released from its socket by the bolt B^2, which is raised to a level with the floor by the weight of a person on the treadle M. The bolt B is connected with the upper bolt, and also with a sliding bolt which locks a pair of drums with which the latch on the second door engages. Pressure on the treadle M thus withdraws the bolts on one door, and simultaneously releases the other door. When the device is applied to windows, the drum is arranged to revolve on a horizontal spindle on the lower sash, and is engaged by a spring catch on the upper sash, and by a spring locking-bolt on the lower sash. Exit doors may be opened by electricity by means of electromagnets placed below the treadles.

9068. Lake, H. H., [*Knell, J. W.*]. May 31.

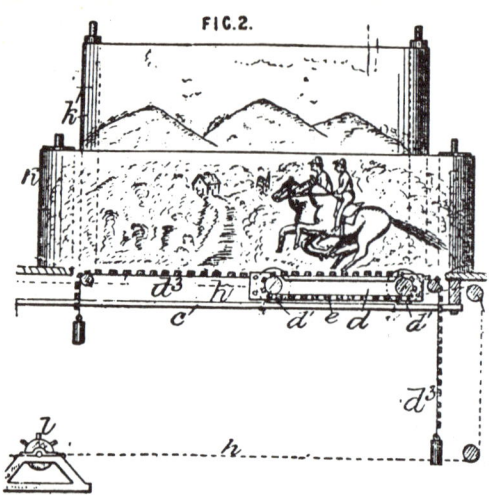

FIG.2.

Panoramas; theatrical appliances for producing scenic effects. To represent horse-racing &c., an endless track *e* is mounted in a frame *d* supported on wheels d^1, which run on rails *c*. The animal is suspended by a standard from the frame, *d*, in such a manner that free motion is permitted. A movable track d^3 is secured at each end of the frame *d* so as to fill up the gap in the stage. Two or more carriages *d* are arranged side by side, and carry animals in active motion so as to produce the semblance of a race. The carriages are drawn along the rails by chains or ropes *h* connected to a windlass *l*. The apparatus may be arranged to represent a boat race or other contest. The background k^1 is arranged behind the foreground *k*, and moves at a different speed.

9955. Colby, E. J. June 18.

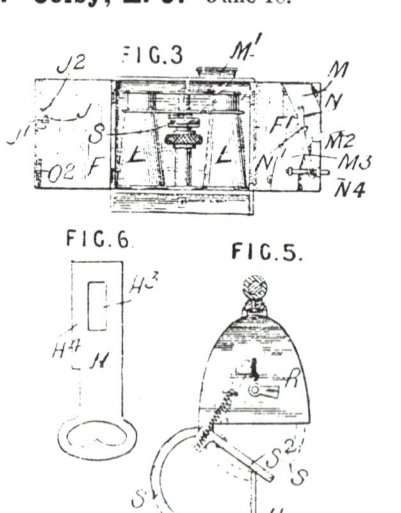

FIG.3.

FIG.6.   FIG.5.

Hiring opera glasses.—The opera glasses L, L,

Fig. 3, are placed in a case having folding doors F, F¹ fixed to the back of the seat in front of that occupied by the user: the doors F, F¹ carry the coin lock, and, when closed, the spring bolt N⁴ engages a catch O² and secures them. A key H, Fig. 6, is attached by a chain to the user's chair.

Coin action.—When the glasses are required for use a coin is inserted at M¹, and falling down the shoot M rests between the lug M² and the friction roller N¹ on the lever N. The key H is now inserted through the slot J¹, in a swivelled part J which must be vertical in order that J¹ and J² may register and admit the part H⁴ of the key. On turning the key the coin thrusts back the lever N and slides back the bolt N⁴, when the doors fly open under the influence of spring hinges, the key passing through the edge of the slot J¹.

Fraud, preventing.—To prevent the glasses from being taken away, a padlock R, Fig. 5, is attached to them and stands out horizontally. As the key H is inserted it comes in contact with the bell-crank S², and the shackle S in shutting passes through the hole H³ in the key and is locked by a spring, securing the glasses to the chain; they cannot be released until the padlock is unlocked by a separate key.

Coin-discharging mechanism.—After the key has been turned the coin falls down the shoot M³ to the money box.

10,285. Harris, H. I. June 24.

Door-opening apparatus.—Relates to fastening and opening mechanism for emergency-exit doors for theatres and for doors in general. The Figure shows the application of the apparatus to one of a pair of sliding doors, but hinged doors may be fitted with it. When the door A is closed the bolt H is raised behind it by the springs L, L. On sending an electric current through the magnet N the bar J is attracted and the bolt released, after which the spring M of india-rubber &c. opens the door. A number of doors may be placed on one circuit so as to be opened simultaneously, and a number of switches may be provided, any one of which will close the circuit. The fastening may be fitted with a rod Q and lever handle R, or with other mechanism operated by hand or by the foot, by which it may be released independently of the electric apparatus.

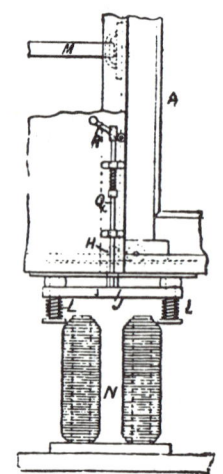

10,884. Jones, E. C., and **Gleason, W. J.** July 5.

Hiring opera glasses; sale apparatus; fastenings for lids; actuating-mechanism.—Relates to the sale and hire of articles, but especially to the hire of opera glasses in theatres. The glass is placed in a case A, the lower half of which is closed by a

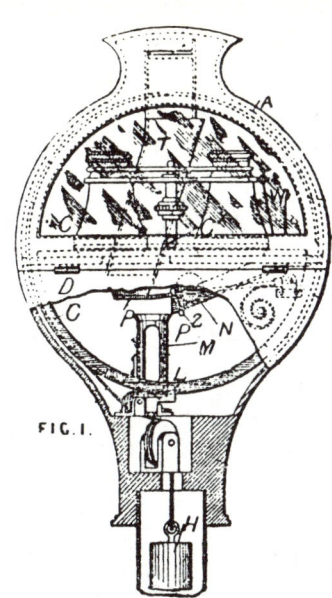

FIG. 1.

tions of horse &c. races. Each competitor is set on a separate track made of jointed strips B mounted on rollers. It is stated that the tracks revolve in proportion to the power exerted upon them by the horses, so that no actual progress is made by the competitors. To produce the appearance of a race, each frame E carrying a track is moved gradually to the footlights A by a separate operator below the stage by means of a winch and ropes. The space in which the frame E moves is covered at the ends by jointed tracks e^1 moving in guides.

12,547. Schleicher, W. Aug. 8.

Chairs for theatres or public buildings. The seat A is pivoted at b to one standard B, and rests on a ledge c on the other. The back supports D, D^1 are pivoted at d, d^1, and are connected by a rod e to the seat so that as the seat folds upwards they fold down The outer ends of D, D^1 bear against flanges on the standard C.

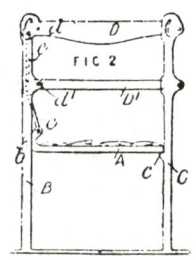

The seat may be arranged to fold downwards, and may be made automatic by weights or springs. When the chairs are folded avenues are formed at right-angles to the rows.

locked door D, while the upper part is cut away. A shutter C, of glass or other material, having a corresponding aperture in one part, is pivoted on a central axis C×, and normally is turned so that the aperture in the glass is closed, being held in this position by a pivoted latch L. The shutter tends to turn under the influence of a spring or weight H so as to bring its aperture into coincidence with that in the case and allow the opera glass to be removed. Where the glass is only for hire it is attached to the case by a chain W.

Coin action.—The coin passed down the shoot T falls upon the lever P, and tilts it so as to lower a catch P^2 from in front of a ball N. The ball so freed falls down a shoot M, and striking the latch L disengages it, whereupon the shutter rotates and the opera glasses are exposed for use.

11,738. Scott, J., and **Smith, H. D.** July 23. *Drawings to Specification.*

Theatrical appliances for producing colour effects. A row of gas or electric lights is mounted in a cylinder fitted with coloured glass. By rotating the cylinder through toothed gearing, strips of glass of the required colour are interposed between the lights and the stage. The light carrier is suspended from hollow bearings, through which the gas pipes or wires are conducted.

12,230. Williams, E. A. Aug. 1.

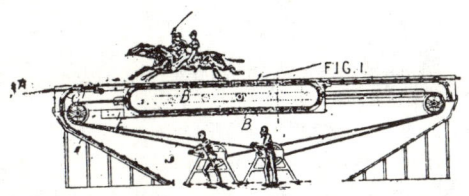

FIG. 1.

Theatrical appliances for producing representa-

12,847. Hillman, W. Aug. 14.

Gas and oil lamps; pianoforte lamps; footlights; reflectors.—Relates to lamps and reflectors for lighting musical instruments, stages, shop fronts, pulpits, and the like. The invention may be applied in connection with oil lamps, gas burners, and candles. The Figure shows an oil

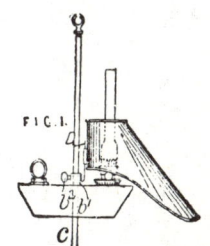

FIG. 1.

lamp which may be secured to the supporting-rod c by a screw clip b^1, b^2, or by a spring or other device. The reflector D is shaped as shown, and is fluted or corrugated to concentrate or distribute the light as required. For lighting pianofortes by oil, the lamp and bracket may be so arranged that the reservoir is inside the instrument. Various modified arrangements, adapting the invention to the various purposes mentioned, are described and illustrated in the Specification.

12,860. Wrench, A. Aug. 14.

Magic-lanterns. — The objects are to provide means for exhibiting both mounted and unmounted slides ; to automatically register the latter, and to conceal the change of the slides by an arrangement which gives the effect of a falling curtain. Behind the rear-plate of the ordinary stage for exhibiting

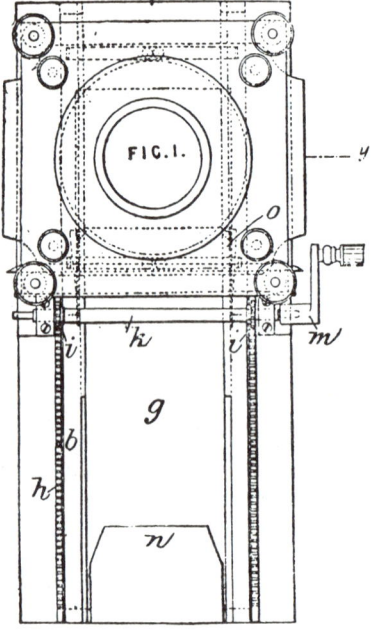

mounted slides are a pair of vertical grooved guides *b*, connected to the body of the lantern by packing-pieces so as to leave narrow spaces between in which slide the edges of the plate *g*. The grooved guides *b* are cut away at their lower ends so that unmounted slides can be placed on the block *n*, fixed to the lower end of the plate *g*, in alignment with the grooves ; the plate is then raised by turning the handle *m* on the spindle *k* the pinions *i, i* on which gear with racks *h* on the plate. In the grooves of the guides *b* are spring catches *o*, which yield as the unmounted slide moves upwards, but spring forward and support it in position in front of the lens as soon as it has passed ; the carrier *g* can then be lowered for a fresh slide, which in rising pushes up the last so that it can be removed at the top. The plate *g*, shutting off the light as it rises, produces the effect of a curtain falling over the picture. In a modification, the mounted slides may be worked vertically and automatically registered in the manner before described, the carrier actuating the screen or shutter.

12,913. Newton, H. C. Aug. 15.

Magic-lanterns. — The invention is to enable objects which can only be placed in a horizontal position to be exhibited without interfering with rapidity of working. Two ordinary dissolving view lanterns A, A[1], with lime light or electric lamps, are employed, the upper being hinged to the lower so that it can be tipped back as seen in the

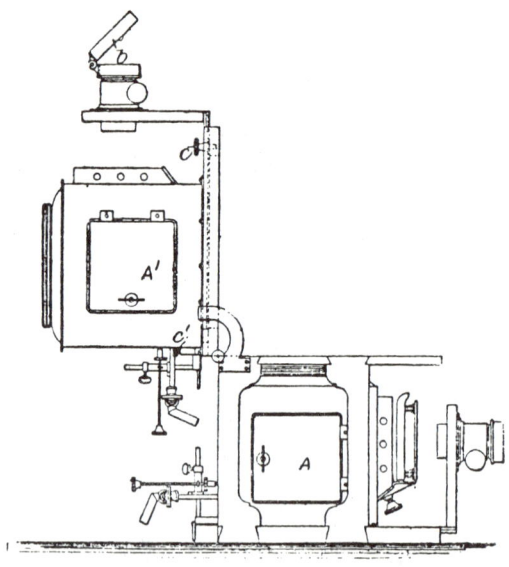

Figure ; a mirror *b* pivoted to the front can then be adjusted so as to reflect the rays of light on to the ordinary screen. *c, c*[1] are set-screws for clamping the focal adjustment slide and lamp tray. When the lantern A[1] is turned down and the mirror *b* turned back, the lanterns may be used in the ordinary way.

12,972. Steward, J. H. Aug. 16.

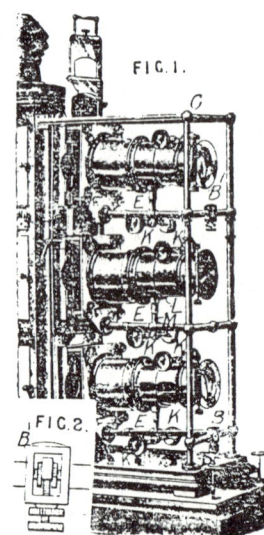

Magic-lanterns and dissolving-view apparatus. — The Figure shows a telescopic front for a triple lantern, the arrangement of the adjusting-details being somewhat varied where the front is not telescopic or the lantern single. A skeleton framework C supports racked bars E, E, E which may be attached as at A to the frame, or adjustable vertically and horizontally as at B, B[1] (see also Fig. 2). Means are thus provided for exactly superposing the discs of light on the screen. The telescopic fronts are drawn out by a slide piece moved along the rack E by a pinion turned by the milled heads K ; with this slide piece the front is connected by a bar and crutch L, M.

13,153. Barnett, F. Aug. 21.

Air, supplying and drawing-off, methods of ; shafts. — The system of ventilating sewers described

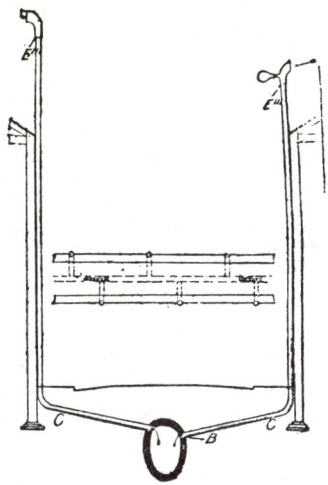

below is stated to be applicable for churches, theatres, music halls, factories, &c. Two pipes C, C are let into the crown B of the sewer, and carried up to a point above the house tops on opposite sides of the road. The inlet is fitted with a cowl E^{1111}, which always faces the wind, and the outlet with a cowl turned in the reverse direction. A through-current is produced in the direction of the arrows.

14,515. Paris, A. J. Sept. 14.

Fireproof coverings.—Fireproof blocks are formed of plaster enclosed within a covering of burlap or other fibrous material, and are suitable for covering walls, ceilings, partitions, and the like, and for making fireproof curtains and screens for theatres. The plaster employed is formed of quicklime, plaster of Paris, sand, pulverized coke, and glue, to which hair may be added. The blocks are formed by placing a covering of burlap over a mould 1, Fig. 5, then introducing the plaster 8, and covering the same with the burlap, the ends and sides of which are folded over to enclose the plaster entirely ; pressure is applied by the plate 2 and a lever or screw press. The piece of burlap for enclosing the plaster may be made of similar shape to an ordinary letter envelope blank. The blocks 11 are secured by nails 12 to the partition studs 9 and joists 13 of the walls &c., as shown

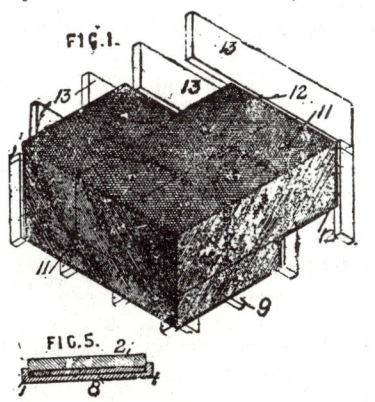

in Fig. 1, and are arranged to break joint, alternate blocks round the corners being scored across the centre and bent at right-angles. A finishing-coat of plaster is applied to the blocks after they are secured in position.

14,671. Lake, W. R., [*Colt, J. B.*]. Sept. 17.

Reflectors for magic-lanterns. A parabolic reflector B is employed with a hood C in front having a glass window *c*. The burner of the lamp is passed into the chamber thus formed through the burner case *e*, and a flue *d* is situated above; the ordinary glass chimney is dispensed with.

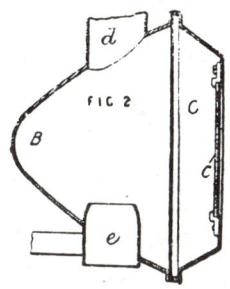

15,168. Cornelius, E. F. J. Sept. 26.

Theatres.—The front of the theatre is constructed of four glazed colonnades or balconies arranged one over the other. Each balcony communicates with a floor or part of the theatre by means of a number of doors, and has a separate series of steps leading down into the street. Refreshment rooms, cloak rooms, water-closets, &c. are arranged in the balconies, the ticket boxes being provided at the entrances on the ground floor. The rooms for the performers and workmen are arranged at the back of the stage, and communicate with a colonnade or balcony at the back of the theatre. Water cisterns on an iron fretwork roof over the stage are fitted with plugs which can be readily withdrawn.

15,496. Granger, L. E. Oct. 2.

Chairs ; hat pegs. — The chair, for use in theatres &c., is shown in the Figure in its folded position. The seat B and back C, each in three parts, are hinged respectively to projections at the back and front of the standard A. The seat at its back end has a projection carrying anti-friction rollers, which run upon the curved bar D. This bar is fixed to the lower end of the back, and projects beyond the standards A in front, to form a hat peg. Rubber seats are made on the standard at b^3, and on the bar D to prevent noise &c. when the seat B is opened out. The hind legs F of the standards A are made adjustable by screws h^1 in slots.

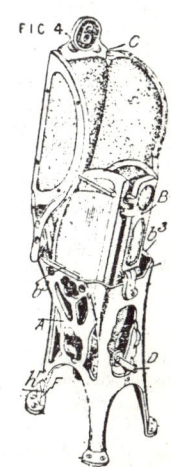

17,378. Scott, A. W. Nov. 2.

*Limelight appa-
ratus.*—Relates to
apparatus for satu-
rating coal gas, air,
or other gas with
hydrocarbon v a-
pours for use in
limelight and
other apparatus.
The carburetting-
chamber A, which
contains a per-
forated tube B, is
tightly packed with
a porous material,
and is charged
with hydrocarbon
through the tube L.
Flexible tubing
being fitted to the

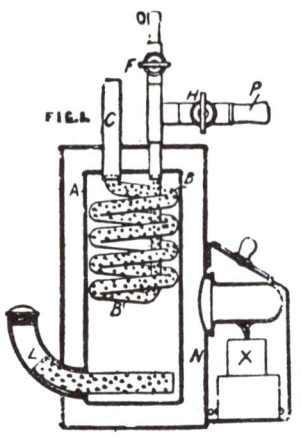

nozzles C, O, P, the oxygen or other gas to be
carburetted traverses the nozzle P, cock H, and
tubes B, C to the hydrogen jet of the burner, pure
oxygen going direct to the burner through the
cock F and nozzle O. The efficiency of the
carburetter is increased by enclosing it in a
vessel N containing air or water, which is heated
by a burner X.

18,583. Hughes, A. Nov. 20.

Magic-lanterns and dissolving-view apparatus.—
Relates more especially to multiplex lanterns for
producing dissolving views. The bodies of the
lanterns are preferably made mostly of aluminium,
the fronts M being collapsable leather bellows
instead of brass tubes as usual. The bodies are
carried on brackets swivelled to sockets s^1 which
slide on the uprights B and may be clamped in any
required position by screws s. By the above
arrangement and by connecting the lanterns or the
lowest lantern and the baseboard A by adjustable

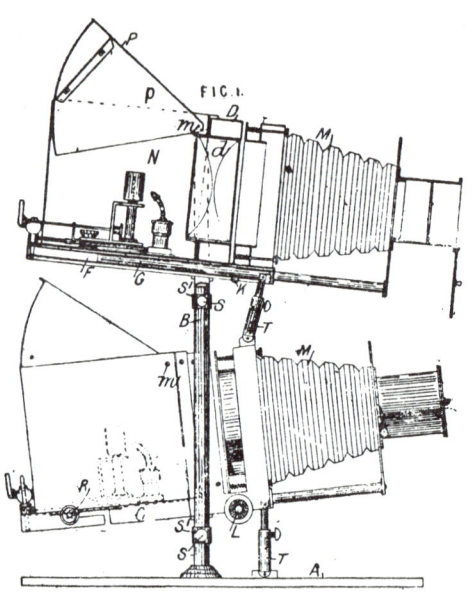

telescopic tie-rods T, the whole lantern bodies may
be moved in order to bring them into position for
registering on the screen, and consequently the
objectives are not thrown out of the optical axis.
The fronts are opened out by means of rods G
sliding in tubes F and racked so as to be operated
by pinions K on arbors L. The condensers d are
mounted in a frame D fixed upon the bottom
frame C, and the body of the lantern N with the
lamp rigidly attached slides on the frame C and
may be fixed in any required position relatively to
the condensers by screws R. The lid of the
lantern is shaped as shown and hinged at m, a
baffle-plate p preventing the light from passing out
and directing the hot air &c. through holes at P.

19,926. Bond, H. Dec. 11.

*Magic - lantern oil
lamps.*—Relates to
dissolving view ap-
paratus so arranged
that the operator can
work at the back in
full view of the screen,
the images being pro-
jected on the screen
by means of reflectors
at each side of the
lantern. The lamp A,
which has glazed sides,
may be removed by
raising a spring catch
and sliding it back-
wards in guides, the
curved flanges h^1 of
the condenser tubes H
being pivoted so that

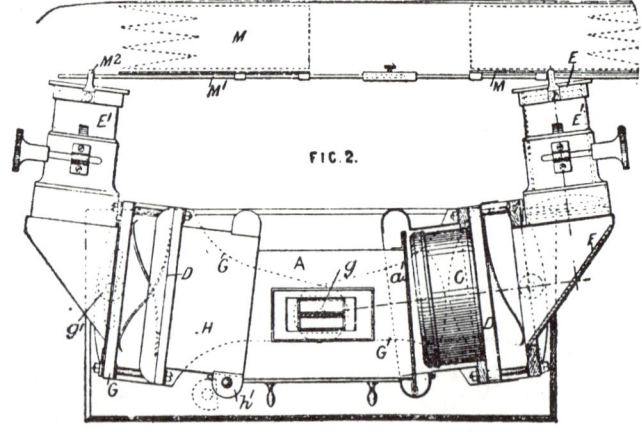

they can be moved out of the way. Means for viewing the flame are provided at the back, and the wick-
adjusting mechanism is also operated from behind, the buttons being connected by means of bevel-wheel
gearing with the raising-pinions.

1890

401. Redwood, T. H. Jan. 9.

Theatrical appliances.—Relates to flash lights for stage effects &c. The flame from the lamp *b* is spread out by impinging on a metallic sheet or screen C on to which is ejected the magnesium &c. powder by a deflector or diffuser d^3 on the powder nozzle d^2. The lamp may be provided with a hinged cone or hood b^3, a grating b^2, and a damper b^5; any lamp or a gas jet may be used.

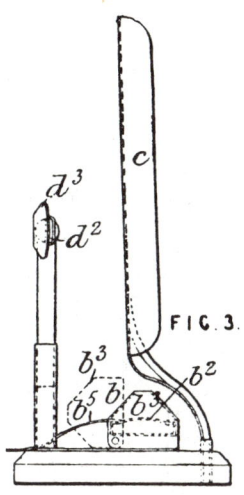

611. Hughes, W. C. Jan. 13.

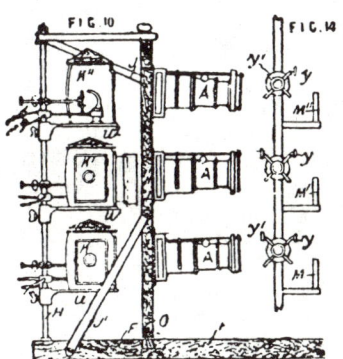

Lime-light apparatus for dissolving-view apparatus. The lighting-apparatus is carried upon the platforms *v*, u^1, u^{11} on the pillar H or the pins M, M^1, M^{11} mounted thereon, and the dissolving valves or taps are adjustable on the pillar H; these taps may be of the form shown in Fig. 10, or may be fitted with T junctions *y*, y^1, Fig. 14, so as to be connected by flexible tubes which will not interfere with the vertical adjustment.

1884. Jensen, P., [*Underwood, H. G.*]. Feb. 4.

Pyrotechnics.—To produce powders such as "red fire" and "green fire" in the form of a cake, the ingredients are mixed with alcohol in a water bath at a temperature of 200° F., and the pasty mass is then run into moulds for cooling and hardening.

1959. Held, H. Feb. 5.

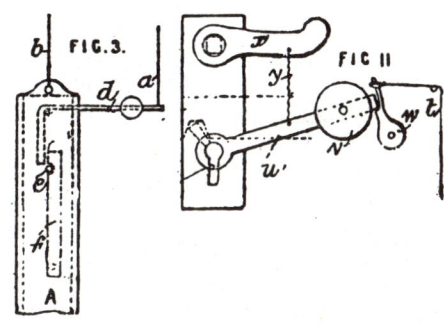

Door-opening apparatus.—Relates to apparatus for releasing and opening the doors of a theatre &c. in case of fire. Throughout the building wire ropes *a* are carried, which, when pulled, release a central weight A. The central weight falling pulls ropes *b*, which release secondary weights. The secondary weights release the locks and fastenings, and open the doors. Fig. 3 shows means for releasing the main weight A. The weight is suspended from the stud *e* by the pivoted catch *f*. A pull on the rope *a* moves the lever *d*, and releases the catch. The secondary weights are similarly suspended by catches released by sliding blocks secured on the rope *b*. The secondary weights are connected with sliding blocks or carriers working in guides above or underneath the door. These carriers act on pins in the doors. A special form of carrier is described for enabling a swing door to be opened in either direction by hand without affecting the mechanism. Instead of wire ropes being employed throughout the building, hemp &c. ropes may be employed, which are consumed in case of fire, and release the weights automatically. The weights may be released when solder &c. is melted by heat. Wires from the secondary weights may be arranged to release the locks and fastenings for the doors. A device for this purpose is shown in Fig. 11. The wire *t*, when pulled, draws back the catch *w*, and allows the weight *v* to descend. The weight *v* turns the arm u^1 connected with the key, and also operates the latch handle *x*, which is connected with the arm u^1 by the wire *y*.

3150. Gudgeon, R. H. Feb. 27.

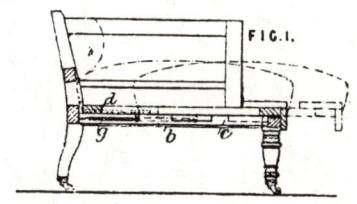

Chairs; seats.—Relates to sliding seats or bottoms for chairs and seats of all kinds, such as theatre chairs &c. The frame *d* of the seat is supported and guided on flanges *c* on the side bars of the frame *b*. It is normally held back by the spring *g*.

3847. Lake, H. H., [*Knell, J. W.*]. March 11.

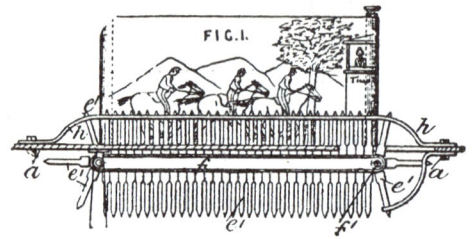

Theatrical appliances for producing scenic effects. To increase the scenic effect of races between moving objects on the stage, a series of slats *e¹* are mounted on an endless travelling belt *f* in front of the stage so as to represent a moving wall or fence. These slats or palings pass through an opening in the stage floor *a*, and are retained in a vertical position by guides *h*. The endless band is driven in a direction opposite to that of the competitors by a pulley *f¹*, which is rotated by suitable mechanism below the stage. The moving objects or competitors are preferably mounted on an endless path, the background scenery being operated in the usual manner.

4215. Westaway, J., and Treliving, J. March 18.

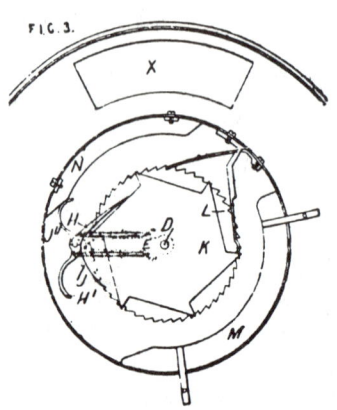

Fares and admission-fees, registering and checking. —A spindle D carries a pointer travelling over a dial indicating the number of passengers in the vehicle &c. When turned in one direction a pawl J on an arm E turns a ratchet-wheel L geared to a counter. When the spindle is turned from zero in the opposite direction a pawl H advances a ratchet-wheel K, carrying forward a station-indicating disc behind an aperture X. Each pawl is lifted out of contact while the other acts by means of ridges M, N in the paths of the tails H¹, J¹ of the pawls. Another pointer may indicate the number of journeys made.

4364. Bissmire, C. E. March 20.

Theatrical appliances for producing scenic effects. To facilitate the change of position of living figures or other objects without the fall of the drop curtain, sheets or blinds of gauze are interposed so as to cause a gradual disappearance or dissolution, these blinds being withdrawn again after the change is made. Several blinds of varying thickness may be used as shown in the Figure, a single sheet being first interposed, and afterwards the sheets of double and treble thickness. In a modification one pair of rollers are used, a continuous sheet of gauze of varying thickness being unwound from one roller and rolled up on the other roller. The rollers are fitted with operating cords or springs.

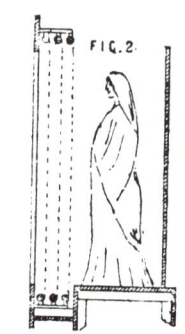

5474. Lyon, H., and Leslie, H. J. April 10.

Resistances, adjustable. A jar A is fitted at the bottom with a fixed conical metallic plate B; a second plate B¹ is carried by a screwed spindle F fitted with a hand-wheel F¹. The jar contains acidulated water or other liquid, and the resistance is adjusted by turning the wheel F and so raising or lowering the plate B¹.

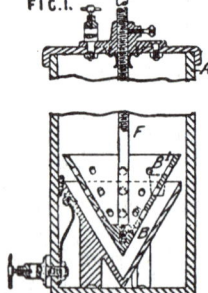

5771. Cawdery, J. W. April 16.

Theatrical appliances.—Instead of supporting the wings vertically by stays bolted to the stage, the upper edge *i* is adapted to run between rollers *h* or *h¹* carried by a frame *g*. This frame *g* is hinged to a ladder *e*, which is capable of sliding in guides *a* fixed to the fly floor. Stay rods *j*, pivoted to the frame *g* and to sliding blocks *l*, support the frame or platform *g* when it is turned on its hinges *e¹* into a horizontal position, spring catches being provided to lock the blocks *l* in either position.

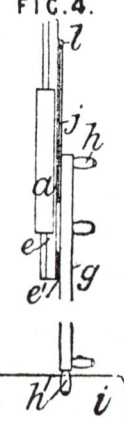

7448 Green, J. May 13.

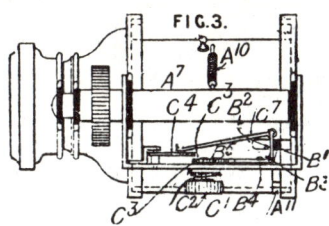

FIG.3.

Opera and field glasses ; reflectors.—Relates to an attachment for lorgnettes or opera glasses and like instruments, such as those described in Specification No. 5333, A.D. 1890, designed to permit the user to see behind him, or at either side. Two reflecting - mirrors are carried in front of the objectives by a cross-bar B^1 which slides in a slot A^{11}. The reflectors can be adjusted at any required horizontal angle by turning the thumb-piece C^1 carrying a toothed wheel C^3 gearing with a sector B^5, which forms part of a supporting-plate for the bar B^1, and is pivoted at B^4. The adjustment for vertical angles is performed by the same thumb-piece and toothed wheel, which are pressed inwards against a spring C^2 until the wheel C^3 gears with a toothed sector C^4. The latter is connected by a rod C^7 with a crank B^2 turning the bar B^1 about a hinge B^3. By turning the thumb-piece sufficiently far, the reflectors may be brought quite out of the line of vision, and the opera glasses used in the ordinary way. In this case, the apertures in the cylindrical casing containing the reflectors, through which rays are received upon the reflectors, are closed by a sliding spring shutter A^7, but upon returning the reflectors to position for use, the shutters are released, and returned by springs A^{10}.

7479. Tubini, T. May 14.

Panoramas.—A number of magic lanterns are arranged side by side round a common centre on a platform so as to project sections of a scene or picture side by side on a circular wall or screen to produce a complete picture. The platform and foreground are lighted by separate lanterns which prevent radiation on the screen.

7636. Resuche, R., and **Vailly, A.** May 16.

Theatres ; balconies ; partitions ; stairs.—Relates to emergency exits for theatres &c. Balconies *a* are constructed outside the building on a level with the floors, and are provided with spiral or inclined staircases *c* which lead down to the ground. Apertures or doorways in the wall are closed by sliding partitions, which are operated by springs or gravity, and are controlled by spring catches, balance weights, and winding-winches. In one arrangement, the partitions are pivoted to the balcony so as to turn outwards level with the floor.

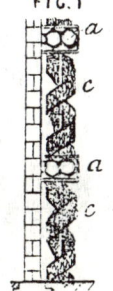

FIG.1

In another form, a large partition or screen is constructed of two sheets of iron, having a space between them packed with cork, wood, or light material. This screen is partly balanced, and on being released descends into a recess in the ground.

9047. Hengler, A. H. June 11. *Drawings to Specification.*

Circuses ; theatres.—Relates to the production of aquatic scenes in circus arenas, theatres, and the like. The arena is covered by a waterproof sheet, which is drawn over the side of the enclosing fence so as to make it water-tight. Water is supplied to the arena by two large flexible pipes, which are connected with supply tanks fitted with valves for turning on the water at a given signal. The water is pumped back to the tanks after the performance by pulsometer or other pumps.

9752. Nicholls, T. June 24.

Seats. — Relates to turn-up seats for theatres &c. The seat D is hinged to the back rail E of a pair of parallel rails carried by the standards. These rails are spaced as shown so as to support the seat when turned down.

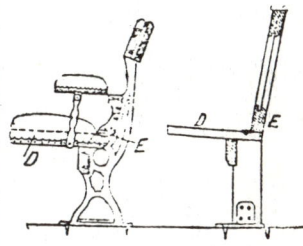

A spring is attached under the back rail so as to turn the seat up when the occupant rises. The arms may also be pivoted and connected to the seat so as to fold with it. The standard and its rails are formed so that the seat is out of the way when turned up. These seats can be adapted to any required position.

9834. Keller, J. June 25.

Theatre and like tickets are provided with coupons, numbered, and made up into series corresponding to the rows or sections of contiguous seats in the theatre, the various series being conveniently arranged for inspection so as to constitute a diagram of all the seats which remain to be disposed of. The tickets are separated from one another and from their coupons by perforations, and at each of the junctions of the rows of perforations a rectangular aperture D is punched. These apertures

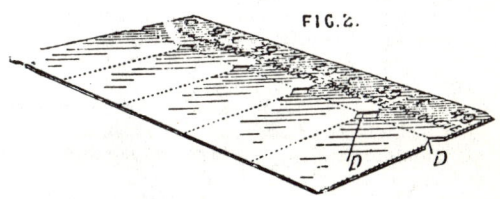

FIG.2.

facilitate the severance of the tickets, and also serve to regulate the feeding of rolls of tickets to a dating-machine.

9934. Stocks, W. June 26.

*Magic - lantern &c. oil lamps; reflectors.—*Relates to lamps and reflectors for optical a n d other lanterns. The burner chamber B is hinged to one of the supports *b*, and has projecting pieces *e*, which form a burner cone and allow suffi-cient air to pass be-tween the flames and the sides of the chamber to keep the latter cool. The glass panes at the front and back of the chamber B are placed in grooves b°, and are made practically airtight at their upper ends by hinged pieces b^2. The flue, which is tele-

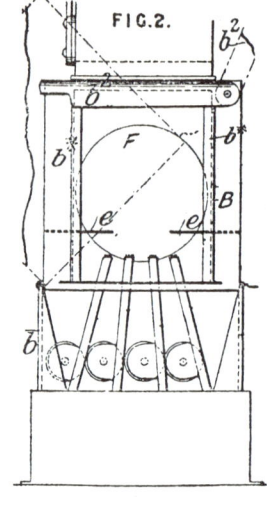

FIG.2.

scopic, can be adjusted by a rack and pinion to regulate the quantity of air entering through the gauze baffles at the lower part of the burner. An adjustable reflector F is provided.

11,784. Schirm, J. W. C. C. July 28.

Magnesium and like lamps.—To effectually diffuse the magnesium, zinc, or alu-minium powder throughout the flame, it is placed in a hopper *r*, whence it falls into the pipe *a* and is carried by the gaseous pressure to the

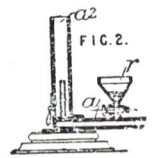

FIG.2.

" Bunsen burner " a^2. For flash lights the powder and gas are discharged by compressing an india-rubber ball working in connection with suitable valves, and the mixture is ignited by a pilot jet. A similar arrangement is described in which benzene, or alcohol or the like, is used instead of gas.

12,230. Christy, T. Aug. 5.

*Fireproof coverings and compositions.—*Relates to the manufacture of the waterproof or impermeable material described in Specification No. 13,917, A.D. 1888, and its application as a substitute for gutta-percha, rubber, leather, oiled silk, and the like, or for use as a greaseproof impermeable paper ; and also to the treatment of the material whereby it is rendered uninflammable or fireproof. For making a thin material, a fibrous fabric, such as unsized paper, or a woven fabric is saturated with a solution of glue or agar-agar, to which has been added glycerine, and a solution of a chromium salt, such as bichromate of ammonia or potash, to which liquid ammonia has been added. The material is then hung up to dry and bleach, being then ready for use. To obviate the necessity for bleaching by exposing to light, reducing-agents, such as ammonium sulphite, may be added to the chromium compounds, either before or after admixture with

the glue ; or the chromium salt may be partially reduced by previously heating. The paper &c. may be replaced by a woven or felted fabric joined to paper by the composition, felt, lint, carpet felts, asbestos materials, wood pulp, &c. Various substances may be added to the composition, such as resins, fats, disinfectants, farinaceous substances, oils, and dyes. The material thus treated is un-inflammable, but to make it still more fireproof it may be treated with a solution of silica before it is saturated with the glue composition. A fire-proof fabric or material is thus produced which is especially applicable for theatrical decorations, ballet skirts and dress linings, &c.

12,762. Wieland, H. W. Aug. 14.

*Theatrical appliances; glass houses; rooms with optical-illusion effects.—*Consists in making a room, conservatory, or the like of an equilateral tri-angular shape, and lining the walls completely with mirrors. The entrance and exit are through the floor or ceiling. By this arrangement the room will appear limitless, and everything therein multi-plied infinitely. The invention may be applied to places of public amusement as well as to fitting rooms for tailors, costumiers, &c.

12,845. Motte, H. Aug. 15.

*Panoramas; theatrical appliances.—*The object is to produce the optical effect obtained by travellers in vessels, balloons, railway carriages, road car-riages, or other vehicles when looking out at the country. For this purpose pictures of the scenery are painted on transparent materials, or are cut out or otherwise produced on panels F which are mounted concentrically on rotating rings. In the arrangement shown in the Figure the spectators are seated in vehicles B with openings *a* for limit-ing the view to the portion of landscape displayed. The carriages are set in motion on a circular track C, and the outer panels F are rotated in a reverse direction by belt or other suitable gearing. The inner panels representing distant objects are rotated more slowly, or in the same direction as the carriages. In a modification the spectators

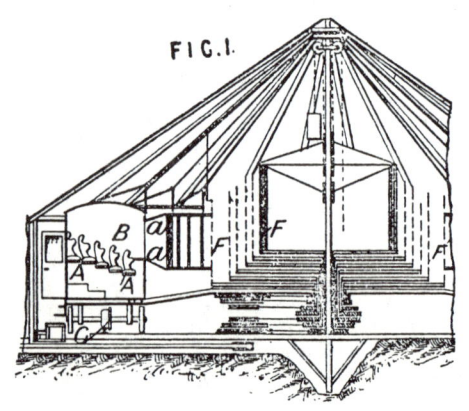

FIG.1.

are seated in the centre and the outer concentric objects or pictorial representations are rotated at different speeds, the inner objects being moved more rapidly than the outer. Objects such as trees, houses, &c., may be mounted on radial arms and be brought into the field of view in succession by means of a ratchet-wheel and pawl arrangement. In another form, the background is painted on a long sheet of canvas or cloth which is unrolled from one cylinder on to another. The principle of the invention may also be used for producing theatrical effects.

13,056. McLennan, K. Aug. 20.

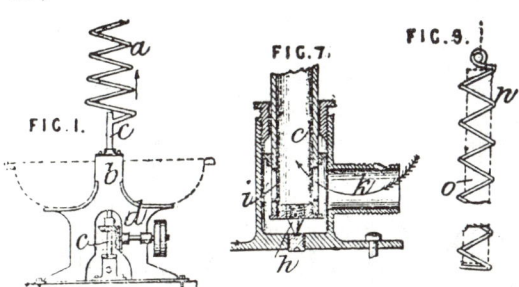

Theatrical appliances.—The object is to produce brilliant spectacular effects by the aid of rotary or stationary spiral tubes and metallic coils, which are preferably perforated for the emission of jets of water, steam, or illuminating-gas. In Fig. 1 the spiral tube a is mounted on a vertical tubular spindle c, which is rotated by gearing d driven by a winch handle or by other power. Water or gas is supplied to the hollow spindle c by a tube k, Fig. 7, through holes i in the spindle, or by means of a tube which forms a continuation of the spindle. The spindle c is mounted on ball bearings in a stuffing-box, or on a steel pivot h. A basin may be fitted on the stand b, and the spindle c may be driven by a turbine which is worked by water supplied by the basin or a separate pipe. A conical core decorated with tin foil, glass, or the like may be arranged within the coil a. Wire coils n, Fig. 9, arranged about ornamental cores or wax lights o, may be suspended in rows, clusters, or be mounted diagonally, and may be combined with mirrors, gauze, or transparent screens.

13,201. Chapman, F. M. Jan. 23, [*date claimed under Section 103 of Patents &c. Act, A.D. 1883*].

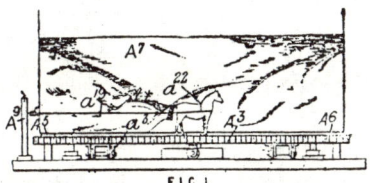

Theatrical appliances ; panoramas.—A turntable A^3 mounted on trucks a^3 and on a central spindle passing through the stage floor, is rotated by one or more horses a^{22} on the stage which are connected to a fixed post A^9 by wires A^{19}. An endless panorama A^7, mounted on vertical rollers A^5, A^6, is driven by teeth formed on the periphery of the turntable. The horses are drawn back or allowed to move forwards by tightening or slackening the wires a^{19}, the turntable being driven after the manner of a tread-mill.

15,024. Morgenstern, L. Sept. 23.

Optical illusions, producing.—Relates to apparatus for enabling a performer to be apparently suspended in mid air, and to move from side to side, upwards or downwards, or even to turn somersaults, without any visible means of support ; and consists of a black velvet-covered framework, having black velvet curtains which move automatically upwards and downwards,

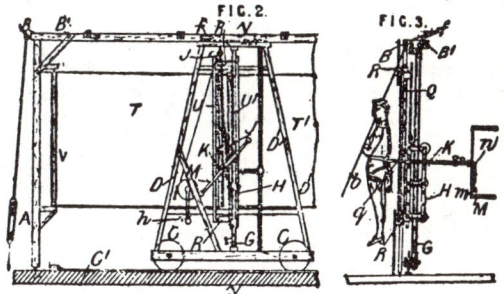

or from side to side, as the supporting-bar, which passes horizontally backwards from the body, is moved. The movements are obtained by two travelling frames, one capable of horizontal and the other of vertical movement, and by a crank capable of revolving the horizontal supporting-bar. Fig. 2 shows a back elevation of the whole apparatus, and Fig. 3 a cross vertical section on the line y y. A is the main frame, secured by guy ropes b, and joined above by two bars B, B¹, between which run rollers f, connected to the frame D, D¹, capable of side-to-side motion on wheels C, C running on the track C¹. The vertically-movable frame is shown at H, having rollers running on the vertical tube G carried by the framing D, D¹. To raise or lower this frame cords pass therefrom round pulley-blocks J to a drum I having a crank handle h. The performer wears a special corset, not claimed in this Specification, connected to the shaft K by means of an internal rod n screwing into the belt of the corset. As the crank handle M is turned, the performer turns also over and over, while by releasing the catch m and unscrewing n, the person is easily released and may walk away from the apparatus. The curtain Q which rolls on and off the spring rollers R as required has a hole q therein, through which the highly polished shaft K passes. To hide the horizontal movement, two curtains T, T¹ are provided, which wind or unwind as required on the vertical spring rollers V, U, U¹.

15,025. Morgenstern, L. Sept. 23.

Optical illusions, producing.—Relates to a metallic corset for holding a person in mid air without any apparent means of support, to be used in connection with the apparatus described in Specification No. 15,024, A.D. 1890, for giving different movements to such a person. The essential parts are two bands A and B surrounding the performer. To the band A a tubular bar I (connected to

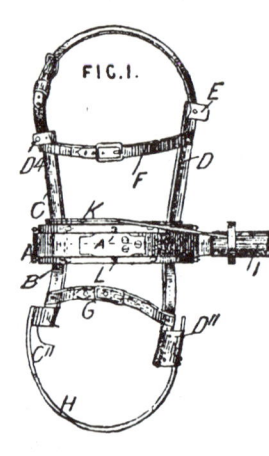

the operating-mechanism described in the former Specification) is removably attached, while the band B firmly holds the actor and is capable of easy revolution within the outer band, suitable friction rollers L being supplied. Two pairs of ribs or stays C, D are attached to the inner band, and are connected by cross-pieces D⁴, C¹¹, E, D¹¹, while shoulder straps F, hip straps G, and a saddle strap H are also attached thereto to support the person in any position. A cord K enables the operator to rotate the actor. All the portions of the metallic corset and the cord K are hidden by the dress of the actor.

15,292. Stroud, W., and Rendell, J. R. Sept. 27.

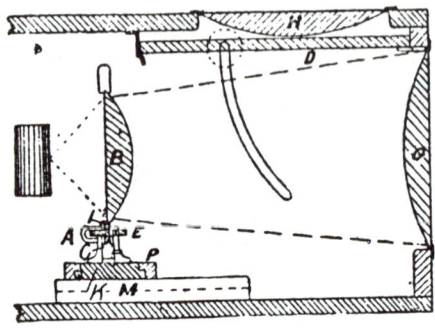

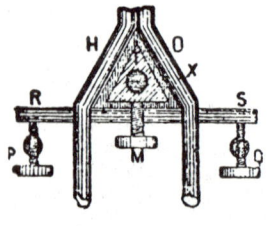

Magic-lanterns.—The front of the lantern is formed into a box having the condenser B and two objectives G and H, a mirror D being arranged to turn down when desired, so as to reflect the light vertically through the latter, and so allow of a slide being placed horizontally. A second mirror and objective (not shown) turn the beam again into a horizontal direction. The lens B may be adjustable vertically by a spring and screw arrangement A, C, I, E, and horizontally by slides K, M working at right-angles to each other. The oxyhydrogen burner is adjustable in the following manner. The gas pipes H, O are attached to a triangular tube X working on a triangular rod T, and secured at the correct vertical height by a screw M ; the rod T can rotate on a central pillar. R, S is a rod also secured to the tube X, and horizontal adjustment is effected by screws P, Q at either end, passing through standards fixed to the base-plate.

16,699. Dando, W. P. Oct. 20.

Theatrical appliances.— Wire ropes attached to the scenery battens pass over central and side guide-pulleys, and are secured to rods carrying counterweights. By raising or lowering the

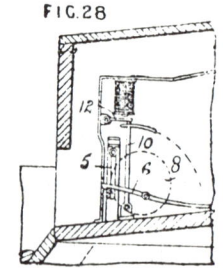

counterweights by ropes from the flies, the back scene and set scenes can be operated simultaneously. The weights are slotted to allow them to be threaded on the rod at a reduced part, rubber buffers being inserted between the weights to prevent rattling. The length of the counterweight boxes may be reduced to one half by suspending the rod by a single purchase pulley. The rise and sink scenes are operated by a crab under the stage, the wire ropes from which pass round guide-pulleys, and are attached to the lower ends of the sliding uprights carrying the scene. The side wings are carried by chariots or wheeled frames below the stage, the slots or openings in the floor being filled in with strips of wood as the wings are withdrawn. These strips are secured by transverse pins which engage with the undercut and slotted flooring. The "carpet cut," or opening for drawing off the carpet or stage cloth, is closed by a hinged flap which is controlled by a lever and cranked shaft. The cloth may be wound on a roller below the flap. Scenery battens or ceiling pieces can be adjusted or suspended at any angle by providing them with a pin and perforated plate attachment, or with a screw and nut arrangement to which the suspending-wires are connected. For producing thunder &c., metal, wood, or other balls or blocks 8 are retained in an inclined box by hinged frames 5 and catches 6, and are released by the fall of a weighted arm 10 which comes in contact with the catch 6. The pivoted arm 10 is held in a raised position by a spring detent 12, which is controlled by an electro-magnet, a cord, or by other devices which can be set in action by the prompter. The balls, when released, roll down a trough, shoot, zig-zag passage, or the like provided with any suitable sound-producing device.

16,903. Hertz, C. Oct. 23.

Conjuring apparatus.—Consists of a suspended platform, on which a person is secured full length,

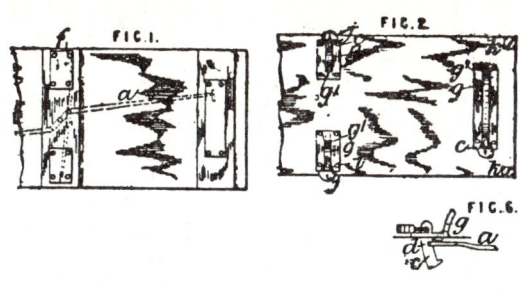

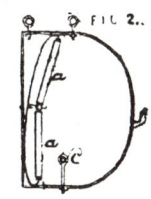

but from which he can easily be released and another take his place. Figs. 1 and 2 show a portion of the bottom and top of the platform respectively, suspended by hooks *k*. On it are collars *g*, hinged at *g¹*, for the neck, wrists, and feet, secured by locks *j* to hasps *c*. Beneath the platform, but hidden by boards underneath, is an arrangement of levers *a*, operated by a dummy bolt *i¹*, which causes the

ends of the levers to withdraw from slots *d* in the hasps *c*, whereby the hasps may be raised and the person released.

18,265. Schroeder, F., and Sloman, B. Nov. 13.

Footlights; shop - front and like lamps; reflectors.— The jets or burners *c* of "batten foot" and side lights" for stage use, shop fronts, and the like are arranged about a foot apart on the gas-supply pipe, and are backed by a reflector formed in two sections *a, a,* of which the lower one reflects in a forward, and the upper one in a downward, direction. The surfaces of the reflectors *a, a* are prism-shaped or corrugated. A wire network may be placed in front of the burners as a protection against fire.

18,369. Thompson, G. S. Nov. 14.

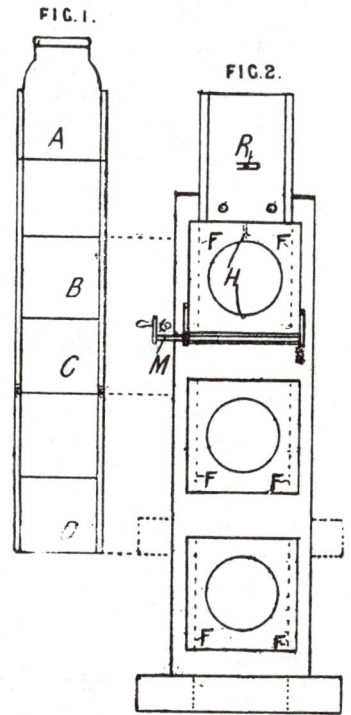

panel B is prevented from descending over the middle lens by a slot H in the framework of the top projector and a pin at the back of the panel. The panel A can also be suspended on a hook R.

19,402. Scott, A. W. Nov. 28.

Magic-lanterns and magic-lantern apparatus.— Relates to the production of magic-lantern slides, and to lanterns for throwing these images or the like on to a screen, either in a "single colour, light and shade, or in their true colours," or in a combination of colours. In the arrangement described, four photographic images are obtained, simultaneously on one plate, or successively in the case of small objects. For this purpose four sets of lenses are used, and four differently-coloured screens are

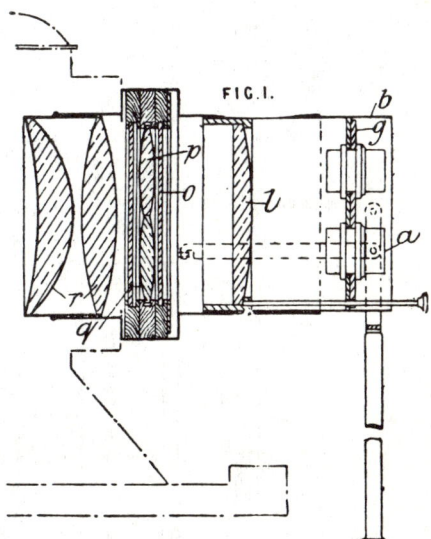

Magic-lanterns, shutters for. The Figures show the arrangement for a triple lantern, but the shutter may be adapted to biunial lanterns. The shutter, Fig. 1, consists of side pieces holding four panels A, B, C, D, the first two of which are not fixed but slide in grooves. It is raised and lowered between guides F by a rack and pinion with a handle M. The travel is sufficient to bring the panels C, D from above the middle and lowest lenses to a position below them or *vice versâ*. The

placed in front of the sensitive plate to cut off the correspondingly-coloured rays. The colours of the screens are produced in a specified manner, and the lenses are provided with stops corresponding with the sensitiveness of the colours. The positive or slide O obtained from the negative, as before described, or otherwise, is placed in position in the lantern, Fig. 1. Behind are placed condensing-lenses p, and a coloured screen q corresponding with that used in obtaining the negative. The lenses r are the ordinary lantern condensers. In front of the slide is a registering-lens l by which the several images are made to overlap and register on the screen, and also the lenses a corresponding with those used in obtaining the photograph. By covering one or more of the coloured screens various effects will be produced. In a modification, the condenser l is dispensed with. In this case the lenses a are hinged to the carrying-plate g, and are adjusted by a cam. Arrangements are also provided for sliding the tube b and the lens l or its equivalent.

19,642. Crowe, W. J., Phillips, H. T., and Betts, W. J. Dec. 2.

Strands. — The strands are formed with a core of twisted asbestos fibres b, round which wires c are spun spirally, and over these are twisted strands of manilla, hemp, or other fibre d which

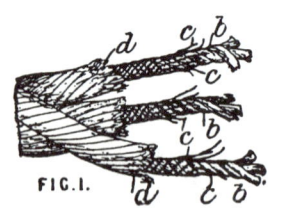

FIG. I.

may be dipped in a fireproofing-solution. Where incombustibility is not an object, a core of india-rubber may replace the asbestos.

19,808. Vaughan, T. W. Dec. 4.

Sun burners. — The enamelled dome A has a flue a situated above an adjustable damper b, which also serves as a reflector. The gas jets d, d project from an annular chamber c^2 to minimize the shadow, and the

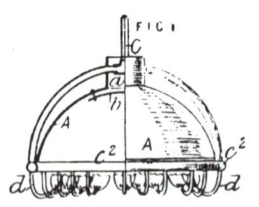

FIG. I

gas supply is heated by placing the gas pipe C in the flue. By arranging the gas jets in proximity to the dome A, and by adjusting the damper b, the combustion is rendered more complete, and foul air is drawn off.

20,392. Morgenstern, L. Dec. 13.

FIG. I

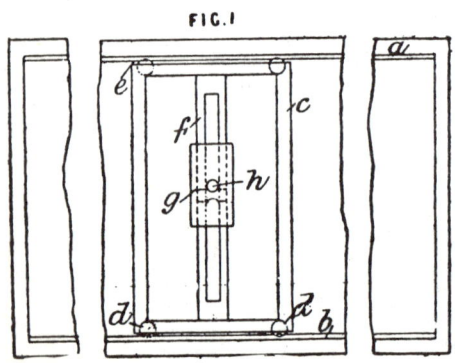

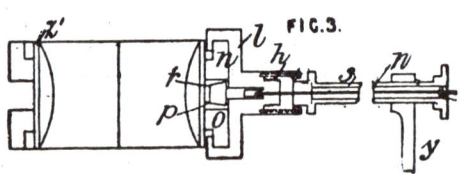

FIG. 3.

Optical illusions, producing. — Relates to apparatus for supporting and moving a person in mid-air without visible means of support. A main frame a has rails b, e, on which runs a second frame c on rollers d. In the centre of the latter frame are uprights f on which a truck g may be raised or lowered by a pulley or the like, and which carries a spindle h. The whole of the framework is covered with black velvet, a slit only being left for the spindle, and this is hidden by black curtains so that nothing is visible from the front. The spindle h carries a cup-shaped end which screws into a boss l, the latter supporting the belt surrounding the performer. The belt consists of two similar parallel steel bands n, o, each made in two parts which can be joined together, while the two bands are connected together by a split ring z^1. This arrangement allows the performer to get into or out of the belt as required. The inside face p of one band has teeth cut therein, so as to be operated by a pinion r which revolves as desired by a rod s which is passed through the spindle and secured therein, and provided with a handle at its other end. The spindle is also provided with a handle y for rotating both the spindle and belt together.

20,633. Salomons, Sir D. L. Dec. 17.

Magic-lantern apparatus. — The stage is provided with adjustable runners actuated by set-screws provided with locking-nuts so as to regulate the position of the abutments for slides which have stops, or for ordinary slides.

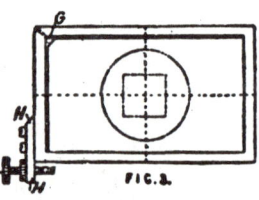

FIG. 2.

In order to ensure the registration of the images from two or more lanterns, standard slides are provided according to which the lanterns are set. The standard slides have some geometrical design traced upon them as shown in Fig. 3, or they may consist of perforated metal or the like, and one being placed in each lantern the images of the designs upon them are made to register. The standard slides may be wholly of one material, the edges being carefully trued, or, as shown, may consist of a glass plate placed in a metal frame and held by a peg or ring G of ivory or the like to prevent breakage from expansion or contraction. The frame has a bracket H having a set-screw acting as an adjustable stop.

20,976. Lake, H. H., [*Burgess, N.*]. Dec. 23.

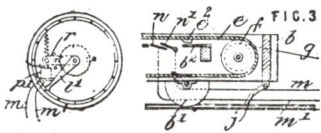

Theatrical appliances.—Relates to apparatus for representing horse or other races. An endless travelling track *e*, mounted in a carriage *b* on wheels b^1, is fitted with slides or rollers which run on guides b^2 fixed to the carriage. The carriage is moved slowly along the stage at a rate proportional to the speed of the track by a rope *g*, which is fixed at one end and wound on a drum *f* mounted on the axle carrying the track. A spring motor, electromotor, or the like acting on the driving-axle may assist in propelling the carriage. Or the carriage may be driven by a weight connected by a cord to the fore part of the carriage ; an anchoring or holding cord is then wound on a drum at the rear of the carriage, and is released and locked alternately by tappets on the endless track acting through a pawl and ratchet arrangement. To prevent recoil or backward motion, a pawl *j* underneath the carriage engages with a rack or the wooden floor. Two or more horses or other racers are mounted on, and secured to, separate carriages, and, on running, set the endless tracks in motion, the distances being recorded on dials in view of the audience. For this purpose, a tappet e^2 fixed to the endless moving path strikes a spring arm n^1 and completes an electric circuit through wires *m*, m^1, and a coil p^1, the circuit being broken again as the tappet passes the spring. An arm *r* carrying the armature is retracted by a spring, and carries a spring pawl which gives motion to a ratchet-wheel and indicator hand l^1.

1891

1016. Aitchison, J., and Bradley, T. Jan. 20. *Amended.*

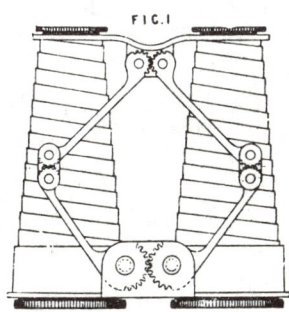

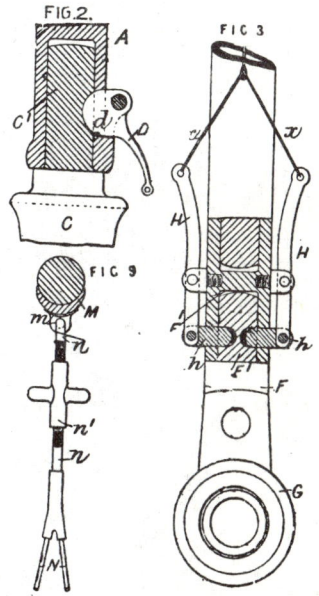

Telescopes and opera and field glasses ; stereoscopes.—The barrels or tubes of opera, field, or marine glasses, telescopes, or stereoscopes are made of tapering spirals of flat steel, as shown, and are extended or compressed by diamond linkage with geared joints. The handles of the instruments are constructed in a similar way. The cells holding the tubes may be formed of aluminium lined with brass.

2041. Kaufmann, N. E. Feb. 4.

Bicycles adapted for use by gymnasts.—Direct-action bicycles for trick riding are formed in parts or segments, which may be detached one from the other by the rider seated in the saddle. The back-bone A, Fig. 2, is provided at each end with a socket for receiving a tongue C^1 on the rear fork C, and a tongue on the neck. The sockets and tongues are locked together by cams *d* attached to pivoted levers D. These cams are released by operating the levers through cords &c. The handle-bar stem is clamped in a split socket by a thumb-screw. The bearings G, Fig. 3, of the front wheel are fixed to lugs F having tongues F^1 entering sockets E^1 formed in the fork prongs. The tongues and sockets are locked together by bolts *h* attached to levers H operated through cords *x*. The wheel rim is connected to the hub flanges by four pairs of spokes N, Fig. 9, each pair being connected to a hook *n* taking into an eye *m* formed on the rim M. One of the hooks *n* is divided, and the parts connected by a right and left handed nut n^1. The remainder of the spokes are "dummy" ones passing through holes in the rim and flanges, and held in position by clamping-rings.

2165. Lutticke, G. F.   Feb. 6.

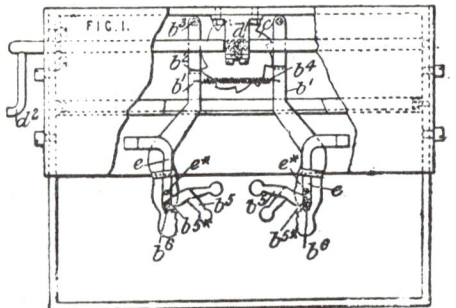

Magic-lanterns, slides for. Jointed figures are operated by levers, cams, &c. in such a way as to represent various movements by the figures. The slide shown, which represents two boxers, is in the inverted position ready for use in the lantern, the plates concealing and enclosing the mechanism being broken away. The lower part b^1 of each body is pin-jointed at b^3 to the frame, the two being connected by a spring b^4. At b^2 is a shoulder against which the teeth of an irregular ratchet wheel *c* press as it is rotated, through worm gear d^1, by the handle d^2. The figures are thus alternately pushed apart by the teeth *c* and suddenly drawn together by the spring b^4, as in the act of boxing. The arms b^5 are jointed at b^{50} to the bodies and have pins b^6 engaging in slots in a counterweighted lever *e* which is jointed to the bodies at e°. The levers are thus jerked at each movement of the bodies, causing the arms to be irregularly thrown about. Various other slides, representing policemen, dancing girls, &c., are shown, which are actuated by one or more push-rods instead of by the wheel *c*.

2399. Jordan, W., and Broadbridge, E. Feb. 10.

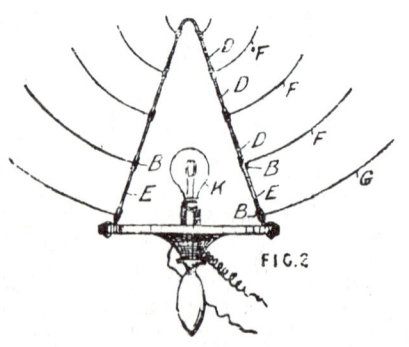

Theatrical appliances.—Relates to the construction of flowers, jewellery, and other devices to produce ornamental effects for theatrical, decorative, and like purposes. In Fig. 2, coloured glasses D, E are supported between rings B connected together by ribs to form a cone. The rings B carry reflectors F, G shaped to resemble petals and leaves. Light from the electric or other source K is coloured by passing through the glasses D, E and, impinging upon the under surfaces of the reflectors, is reflected on to the upper surfaces of the reflectors immediately below, thereby giving the impression of an illuminated flower. The invention may be adapted to fixed or portable articles.

2725. Sanders, W.   Feb. 14.   *Drawings to Specification. Amended.*

Opera and field glasses.—A photographic camera is made in the form of an opera or field glass, one tube containing the sensitized film, lens, and shutter, and the other the finder and focussing-arrangements. The photographic parts are arranged to be easily removable, so that ordinary lenses may be inserted and the apparatus used as an opera &c. glass.

3727. Cheffins, W.   March 2.

Magic-lanterns, slides for. Consists in a variety of transparent jointed figures or puppets, mounted in conjunction with the slide or framework in which they are held while being exhibited, so that they can be caused to move as in the action of walking, running, boxing, fencing, gesticulating, or performing other movements. The figures are supported on slides *a*, *a*, and slender rods *e* are connected to the jointed limbs for the purpose of enabling them to be manipulated from beneath. In the Specification the construction of figures representing dancers, pedestrians, gymnasts, &c. is illustrated : also the detailed construction of the slides *a*, and the frame in which the figures are supported.

4387. Hughes, W. C.   March 11.   *Drawings to Specification.*

Oxyhydrogen lamps.—The oxygen and hydrogen are stored under pressure in metallic bottles or gas bags, and are delivered through cocks to small weighted bags from which they are supplied at a constant pressure to the burner. The movements of the small bags control the cocks on the gas reservoirs. A special form of rotary-disc valve or cock is used.

5106.   Hughes, W. C., and **Woodruff, H.**
March 21.

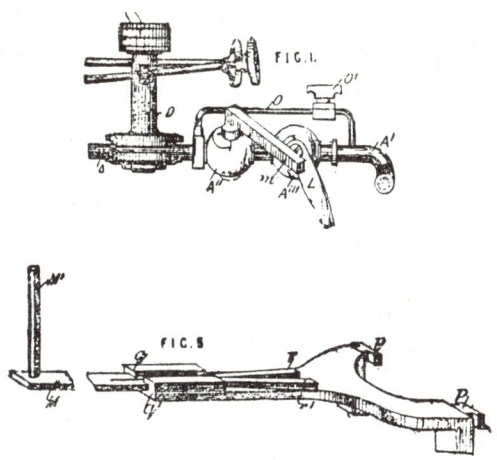

Oxyhydrogen lamps for magic-lanterns.   An ordinary blow-through chamber jet is employed, and
the two gas pipes A, one only of which is shown in
Fig. 1, terminate in extensions A^1, to which flexible
tubing is connected in the usual way.   Two taps
A^{11}, A^{111} are provided in each extension, the taps
A^{11} being operated independently by handles m,
while the taps A^{111} are turned simultaneously by
the common lever L.   It is thus possible to regulate the supply of both gases or either independently.   A bye-pass O, with cock O^1, is provided
in each tube to ensure the jet burning slightly
should the lever L be accidentally turned too far.
D is a hollow standard to receive a plug fixed to an
adjustable bracket on the body of the lantern.
The oxyhydrogen burner is supported on a bracket,
Fig. 5, preferably formed with T-shaped studs p, p,
to engage with slotted plates on the body of the
lantern, and the spindle M^1 for the socket of the
oxyhydrogen apparatus is carried by a spring slide
M working in guides q, q^1 on the bracket and split
at the end ; the two parts r, r^1 tending to open in
the guides hold the slide in the adjusted position
by friction.

5172.   Buatier, J.   March 23.

*Optical illusions, pro-
ducing.*—Relates to thea-
trical illusions.   A person
stands on a platform B
within a cage A ; a veil is
held around the cage for
a short time to hide it
from the spectators, after
which the cage and its
occupant will be seen to
have both disappeared.
The platform, apparently
solid, is in two parts, an
outer rim b, which re-
mains behind, and an
inner portion b^1 which
rests upon a trap C,
through which the inner

portion, the cage, and its occupant all pass during
the short interval during which the veil is held up.
To prevent the descent of the cage &c. moving the
veil, the latter is suspended from a very fine ·and
practically invisible outer cage, which at the last
instant falls to the floor and collapses.

5922.   Pocock, C. S. and **Pocock, A. W.**
April 7.

Opera and field glasses.—The body A, A is of
flexible material spirally corrugated, and having a
spiral wire to extend it which may act as a spring
if desired.   The frames D for holding the eye-
pieces are arranged to be capable of rotation in the
top plate E to allow for the necessary turning
movement as the glasses are expanded, and a rack
H is attached thereto passing into a tube L on the
middle plate R.   With the rack H gears a pinion
F, so that adjustment for focussing is obtained by
turning the milled head I.   The rack H is fixed
to a plate J which can be adjusted by screws K, K^1
passing through slots in the plate E, and so allow
of the accurate collimation of the eye-pieces and
objectives.   An extending frame of levers M, M^1,
M^3 is provided to hold the glasses rigid when expanded, one or more cross-links P being pivoted
say to M^3.   The free end of the link P carries a
pin which is inserted into a hole in the lever M
when the glasses are expanded, but otherwise is
folded along the lever M.   Adjustable screw stops
O, O^1 are placed in position for parts of the
extending frame to abut against and so ensure
rigidity.   The body A may have parallel corrugations
expanded by wire rings.

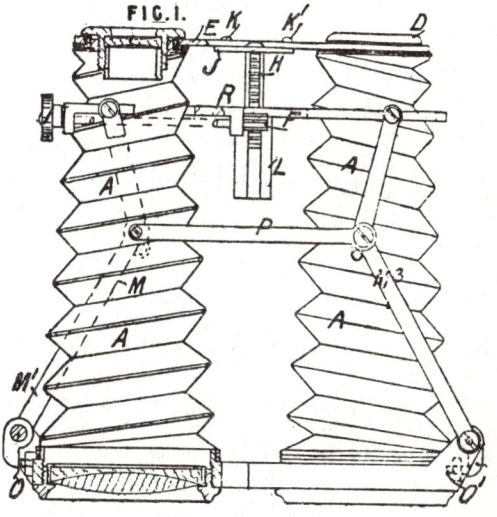

7487.   Haddan, R., [*Engel, F. H. F.*].
April 30.

Magnesium lamps.—By means of the pinion s
and sector v the powder reservoir P can be turned
upon the blowpipe R until it is inverted vertically
over the cavities i, which are then charged by
gravity.   The cavities i communicate through
channels x with the pipe R, so that, on lowering

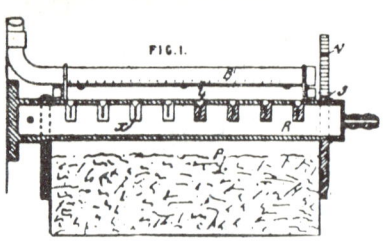

the reservoir P and passing the blast. the powder is projected through the flames from the gas-batten B.

8891. Smith, A. May 26.

Stands.—Relates to a pedestal for supporting acrobats during equilibrium and trick performances. An upright *a* is secured by a screw a^3 or other means to a base a^2, while it is supported on the sides by curved arms *c*, resting on the ground at c^1, and hinged at their upper ends to a collar *b*, adjustable in position on the pole *a*. Hinged struts *d* are also provided. The upright may be made telescopic, the upper portion a^1 being secured in position by pins a^4, or by other means. At the summit is the performing platform *f*, while steps *i* are provided at intervals up the pedestal to allow the performer to mount to the top. Each step is hinged at *h* to an adjustable spring trap *g*, by

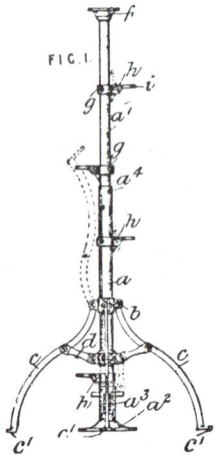

which it is secured to the pole. When not in use the apparatus can fold up for convenience in packing, each step *i* and leg *c* turning up, while each strut *d* turns down.

9221. Vilén, N. June 1.

Chairs for theatres &c. where the rows are close together. The seat E is supported on the side rails D by the rollers F, so that it can be pushed back and hung on to the back of the chair if required. Room is thus allowed for persons passing. A rail G prevents the seat from coming too far forward.

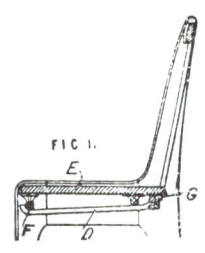

10,482. Forret, J. A., and Todd, F. D. June 20.

Theatrical appliances.—Relates to magnesium flash lamps for producing stage effects &c. The powder, stored in a recess B in the stand A, is ejected by a pneumatic device attached by a clip-controlled tube to the pipe K, through the pipe D terminating in the extension E and fitted with a spherical valve which automatically closes the powder receptacle when the lamp is not in use. Surrounding the exit E is the wick or burner I.

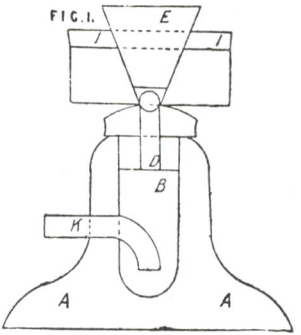

11,520. Anderton, J. July 7.

Magic-lanterns; stereoscopes; polarizers.—The object is to produce stereoscopic effect in magic-lantern pictures. Two stereoscopic slides are approximately superposed upon the screen, but each lantern contains a polarizing-device, preferably a series of glass plates C, C set on a frame A at an angle in the manner indicated in the Figure behind

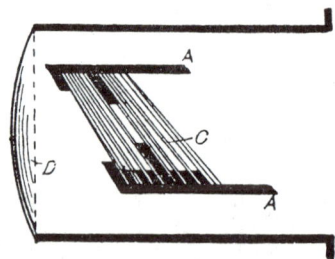

the objective D. The light from the two lanterns is polarized in planes at right-angles to one another, and the observer looks through a pair of analysers with their planes of polarization at right-angles. The result is that one eye sees one picture and the other the other, and stereoscopic effect is produced. The screen is preferably constructed of calico covered with dead silver paper.

13,683. Williams, G., and Berlyn, F. H. P. Aug. 13.

Ornaments a n d ornamental effects. —Glass, porcelain, or other studs or marbles b^1. Fig. 1^a, are inserted in perforated metal or wooden frames or gratings f, and are retained by a parallel perforated back plate or grating f^1. In Fig. 3^a the discs and balls a, m are secured in wooden frames f, f^1, c. The invention may be applied to decorative work for theatres, churches, and other buildings and structures.

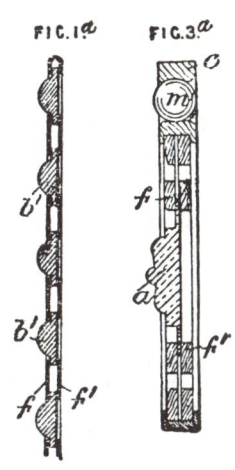

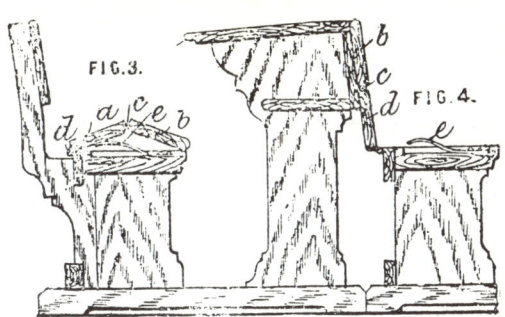

the scholar is to stand for any considerable time the whole seat may be turned up, as shown in Fig. 4.

16,223. Boulter, C. A. Sept. 24.

Opera and field glasses ; telescopes. —Consists in providing opera and field glasses and double telescopes with spectacle sides and nose-piece to support them at the eyes without the necessity of using the hands. Where additional support is necessary it may be attained by cords or rods A secured to head gear, or by others B fixed to some part of the clothing, or by counterweighted rods C passing over the ears.

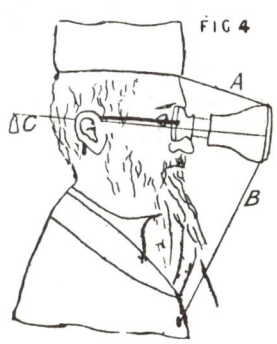

13,765. Lutticke, G. F. Aug. 15.

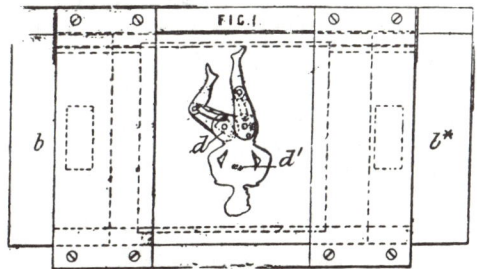

Magic-lanterns, slides for. The object of the invention is to actuate movable figures &c. by means of a slide or slides, usually glass, to which the figures are connected by concealed mechanism. Fig. 1 shows one form. In this case the figure d is loosely connected to a fixed glass slide at d^1, at the front and back of which are movable glass slides b, b^o through holes in which pins connected to parts of the figure are passed. The limbs of the figure are linked together in a special manner and the movement of the slides b, b^o causes the figure to dance. In another form, the figure is made of flexible material and is rolled up on a spring roller behind a screen representing a table. When a spring slide, which is concealed by the table and by the figure as it unrolls, is actuated, the figure appears to rise out of the table. Various other arrangements of linkwork and actuating-mechanisms may be used.

14,423. Ramminger, A., and Stetter, K. Aug. 26.

Seats for schools, theatres, churches, &c. The seat is in two parts a, b, hinged at c and d. Flat springs e cause the seat to take the position shown in Fig. 3 when the occupant stands, giving more room in the case of a school desk, and allowing people to pass in the case of a theatre seat. When

18.598. Edwards, E., [*Lüddeckens, E.*]. Oct. 28.

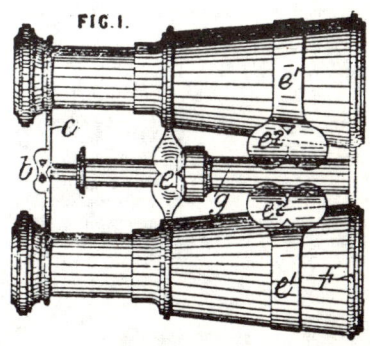

Opera and field glasses.—In the case of opera-glasses nose rests b are fitted to the plate c, and finger rests e and e^1 to the plates c and f respectively. In field glasses the rests e^2 are formed on rings e^1, which can be adjusted so as to bring the rests nearer to or further from the tube g.

20,576. Jordan, W. Nov. 26.

Theatrical appliances.—In illuminating stage scenery &c. the light from a lamp such as J is reflected by the movable mirror G to the scene &c. H through coloured glass panels E carried on a moving band C.

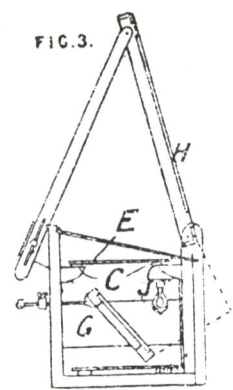
FIG.3.

21,716. Franck-Valery, E., and Franck-Valery, P. Dec. 11.

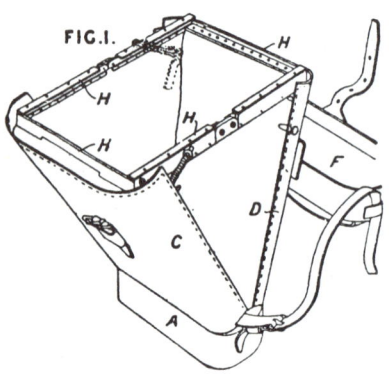
FIG.I.

Opera glasses, cases for. Relates to a photographic camera which, when folded up, may be used as an opera-glass case, and which is strapped for being carried on the back as such. It consists of a frame or front A to which are hinged the sides C, D provided at the ends or back with an articulated spring frame H, shown open, which serves to receive the dark slide. To collapse the camera or case, the frame is pushed inwards.

21,877. Jefferson, C. B., Klaw, M., and **Erlanger, A. L.** Dec. 15.

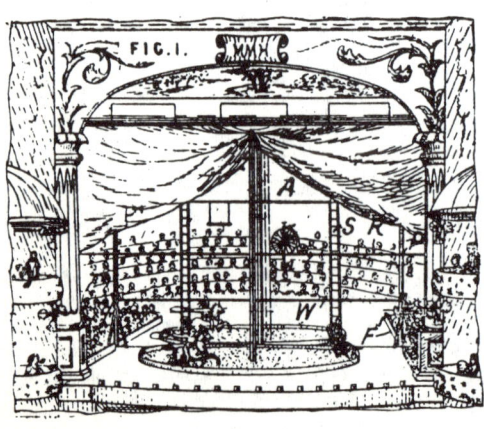
FIG.I.

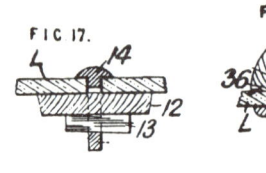
FIC 17.

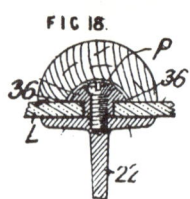
FIC 18.

Theatrical appliances.—In order to produce scenic effects in dramatic representations, the back wall of the stage is lined with mirrors A so that the audience, the scenery, and all that goes on upon the stage will be reflected and produce illusions as to the size of the place, the numbers of performers and people present, &c. The edges of the mirrors are secured in vertical grooved standards, or in braced rectangular frames bolted together and connected to the wall by tie-rods. The joints of the mirrors are concealed by posts P, tight ropes W, R, ladders S, and other scenic devices. Lay figures F¹ arranged in the wings are shown by reflection. The end sections with the mirrors near the wings are hinged and mounted on rollers so that they can be turned back to permit the entrance upon the stage of animals, troops, &c. As shown in Fig. 17, the glass sheets L are secured between a wooden block 12 and the flanged head of a frame 14 by a cottar or key 13. Or, as shown in Fig. 18, the flanged strip 36 is secured to the standard 22 by screws. The post P is secured to the standard by bolts. In modifications, the mirrors are secured between the flanges of a T-beam or standard, and side strips or angle-irons bolted to the web of the standard.

21,887. Millis, F. W. Dec. 15.

Ventriloquial figures.—Fig. 1 shows the method of working the eye and lower jaw of a figure by means of compressed air. A similar method is employed for moving the arm or leg. The lower jaw 2 is fixed to a rod 3, hinged at the back of the head 1, and normally kept closed by a spring 4. The eye is pivoted at its centre, from which projects a short arm 14, while it is kept in its normal position by a coiled spring 4. The head is mounted on a vertical shaft 15 provided with an arm 16. The operator presses a rubber ball which forces air into the bellows 10, the bottom boards 8 of which are free to move, and are provided with hooks 7 from which cords 5 pass to the levers or arms 14, 3, 16, whereby the eyes, lower jaw, and head are moved. In a modification, the whole head is moved; the head may be mounted on a glass tube.

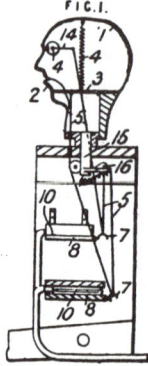
FIC.I.

1892

242. Coulson, R. Jan. 6.

Emergency - exit fastenings. — T h e b o l t u s e d f o r theatre &c. doors resembles an ordinary tower b o l t, but its nose *a* is jointed at *b* to the main part of the bolt and is kept extended by the spring *d*. Ordinary pressure, *e.g.* of one person leaning against the door, fails to overcome the force of the spring, but the pressure exerted by a number of persons causes the spring to yield so that the door opens. In the

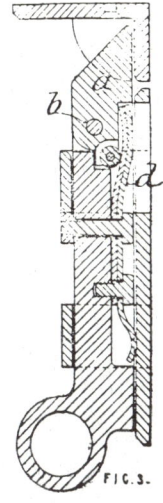

Provisional Specification it is stated that the socket may be jointed.

3209. McDade, J. J. Feb. 18.

Hiring opera-glasses ; fastenings for lids ; coin action.—The case is made with a spring cover which carries the hasp D ; the opera - glass is placed upon a false bottom G and pressed down against the action of springs until the hasp D engages the hooks $d^\times$, $d^\times$ on the levers D^1, D^1 pivoted at d^2, d^2. The spring E draws the levers D^1, D^1 together, and fastens the cover. When a coin is inserted it forces apart the levers D^1, D^1 and sets free the hasp D, whereupon the cover flies open. The coin after it has acted falls down a guide - shoot to the money box.

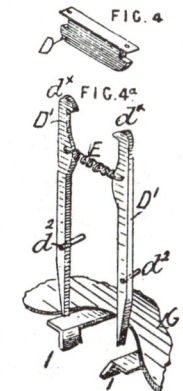

Fraud, preventing.—On removing the opera-glass the bottom G rises and projections I, I come against the tails of the levers D^1, D^1 and prevent them from closing, so that the receptacle cannot be fastened until the opera-glass is replaced.

3942. Boys, C. V., and **Cunynghame, H. H. S.** March 1.

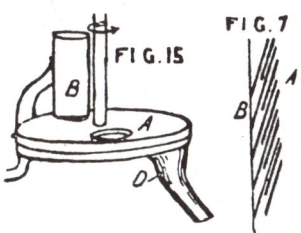

Theatrical appliances. — Diagrams, patterns, pictures, or words for advertisements and scenes in theatres &c. are made up of parts o n s l i d e s or the like &c. so that, on moving the latter, different pictures &c. will be brought to view. In o n e arrangement, a transparent front in part blocked out is b a c k e d by a slotted slide, Fig. 3, and by a background, Fig. 1. In another, a louvre device, Fig. 7, is used, in which the l a t h s B m o v e through the fixed laths A. Pivoted laths, prisms, &c. and bands wound on rollers may be

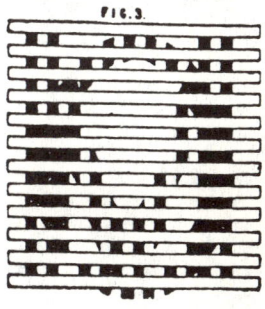

also used. Any motor, such as the movement of a vehicle, may be employed. To induce the public to work the apparatus, a coin or packet is automatically delivered when a certain amount of work is done. An aperture in the revolving disc A, Fig. 15, transfers the coin &c. from the receptacle B to the chute D.

4668. Mason, W. H. March 9.

Magic-lanterns, slides for. Upon unglazed paper or other suitable substance a design or writing is traced with a solution of saltpetre thickened with gum arabic, or with other inflammable chemical substance. This design is mounted as a slide, and after being ignited at one or more places, is brought into the field of the lantern and focussed. As the design burns it gradually appears on the screen in white on a black or coloured back ground, according to the nature of the paper upon which it was produced.

4999. Wenig, E.
March 14.

Theatrical appliances.—
In magnesium lamps for
theatrical purposes, the
powder contained in a
compartment R is forced
by the pneumatic ball G
through the pipe *h* into
the compartment T,
where it is ignited.
Surrounding the lower
part of the tube *h* is a
tube H terminating in a
foot *n* at the lower part
and provided with a flange
p at the upper. This tube
on being raised or lowered
regulates the quantity of
powder injected into the
flame.

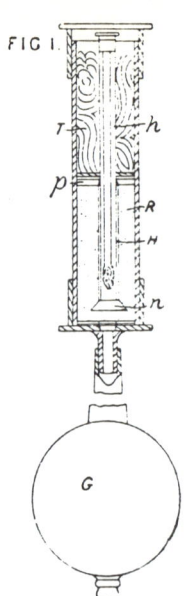

5526. Siemens Bros. & Co. and **Bailey,
F. G.** March 21.

*Theatrical appliances;
exhibitions.*—Relates to
apparatus for producing
brilliant flashes to imitate
lightning in theatres or
exhibitions. The appa-
ratus consists of a fixed
carbon F and a movable
carbon E mounted on a
lever B, which is con-
nected to and operated
by the core C of a series
solenoid, or the armature
of an electromagnet. The
carbons are connected, as
shown, with the terminals
G, H. In operation, the
lever B is raised by a

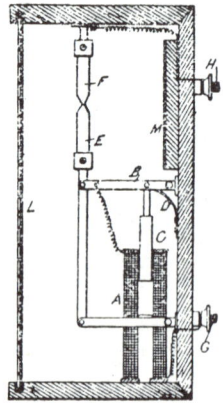

spring D to bring the carbons into contact, but
is pulled down when the current is switched on,
by the solenoid core, thus producing a flash
between the carbons. With the separation of the
carbons the circuit is broken and the solenoid
ceases to act, and consequently the spring D again
brings the carbons into contact. The series of
flashes thus continues as long as the current is
maintained. The apparatus is enclosed in a frame
provided with a mirror M and a glass front L.

5528. Booth, H. S. J., [*Hermann, C.*].
March 21.

Telephone systems, coin-freed. A number of
theatres, concert halls, &c. are connected to a
central station where various hotels &c. can be put
into connection with any required theatre in the
usual manner. Fig. 3 shows the coin mechanism
at the hotel, which may be contained in a portable
box and connected with fixed conductors by a
plug G[1] and a switch G. The coin passes down a
shoot B[2] into a pocket B[3], where it rests upon a

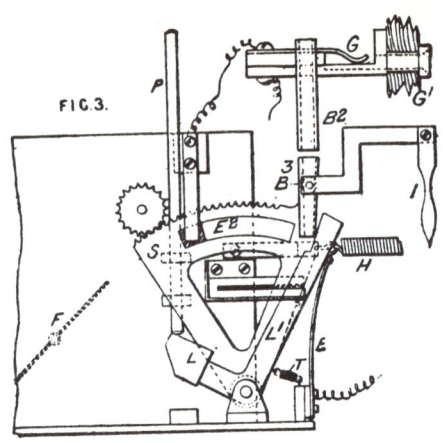

ledge in a bell-crank lever L, L[1]. The pocket B[3] is
carried by a segment S geared, by ratchet and
pawl, with a clock train driving a fly F and controlled by a spring H. On pressing down the push-
rod P the lever L, L[1] is thrown over to the left, and
the coin causes the segment S also to move to the
left. On releasing the push-rod P, L, L[1] is returned
by the spring T and the coin falls out, while S is
slowly returned by the spring H. Circuit is completed for the telephone so long as the spring E is
clear of the insulating-piece E[2]. A pointer I
moving over a scale outside the box indicates the
time that will elapse before circuit is broken. An
indicator, which may be operated by switching-on
the transmitter lines at the central station, shows
the theatre &c. with which the person is in
communication.

5541. Noakes, D. W. March 21.

*Lime - light appa-
ratus.*—Relates to that
type of apparatus in
which the hydrogen
and oxygen gases or
their equivalents are

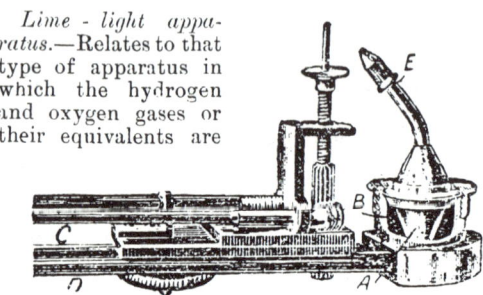

mixed before issuing from the burner. and consists
in the substitution of two or more mixing-chambers
for the single chamber packed with granulated or
similar material which is usually employed. In the
form shown, there are two chambers arranged,
the one within the other, the gases passing from
the supply pipes C, D to an outer chamber B, and
thence through the open bottom of the inner conical
chamber A, thereby completing the admixture of
the gases before they arrive at the burner E.

6924. Terlinden, G.   April 11.

Chairs ; ward-robes ; hat, coat, and umbrella stands.—Relates to a chair with a locked receptacle formed under the seat and at the back for a hat, coat, umbrella, &c., the chair being specially adapted for use at restaurants, theatres, &c. In the form shown, the back *h* is pivoted to the seat *f* and the seat to the front of the chair, or the back may be opened from the rear. The hat is held by a wire loop *x*, the coat on a hook *w*, and the stick &c. in a spring socket which sinks if filled with water. Any locking-device may be used, but a special form is described.

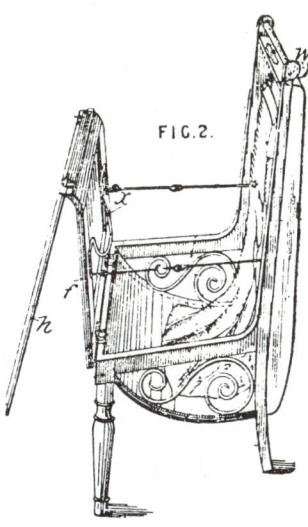

FIG. 2.

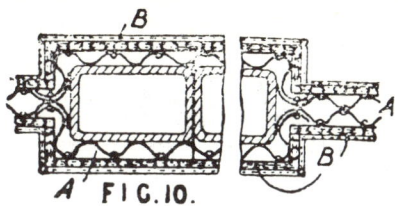

A   FIG. 10.

6940. Hayes, G.   April 11.

Fireproof buildings and structures.—For making walls, partitions, &c., metallic lathing B, preferably consisting of sheets with horizontal corrugations, is riveted or secured to a vertically-corrugated sheet-metal backing A. Fig. 10 shows a horizontal section of a chimney with fireclay flues, the lathing being plastered over. Two, three, or more of the sheets A may be riveted together at their ridges to form a foundation or skeleton structure. Tubes or bars of angle, H, I, or T section may be used in combination with the sheets A, and a central wall or core of firebrick, terra-cotta, asbestos, sheet felt, or plain sheet metal may be interposed between the sheets A. The spaces between the sheets A may be used as ventilating-flues, or as conduits for pipes, electric wires, bell wires, &c., or they may be filled in with concrete, mineral wool, asbestos, or other incombustible material. By this invention walls, shafts in buildings, staircases, roofs, cottages, barns, stations, factories, churches, hospitals, theatres, partitions for buildings and ships, doors, portable buildings, and other structures can be readily erected or constructed.

8185. Simpson, H.
April 30.

Lime-light apparatus.—The lime is rotated by gearing with a ratchet-wheel 62, which is operated by a pawl 63 on the lever 18 of a slide-changing and dissolving apparatus. The ratchet-wheel 62 is supported by a slide 64, adjustable on the lantern in accordance with the position of the lamp, the pawl 63 being correspondingly adjustable on the lever 18

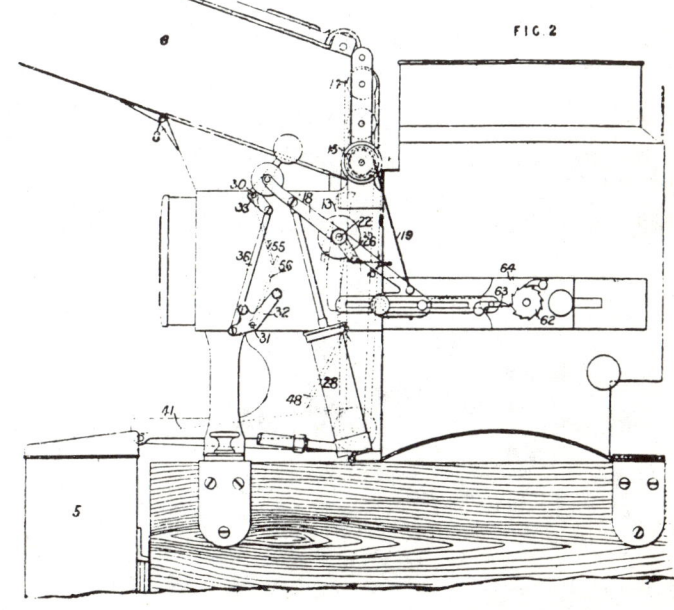

FIG. 2

8708. Latelle, C., and Latelle, R.
May 7.

Bicycles and unicycles adapted for use by gymnasts &c. A bicycle A is adapted to be propelled along a tight-rope, and to rotate a trapeze frame C¹, of hexagonal, square, diamond, or other shape, from cross-bars C³ of which the trapezes H are suspended. A metal framing G is connected to the axle of the bicycle and to a shaft J, to which motion is communicated by

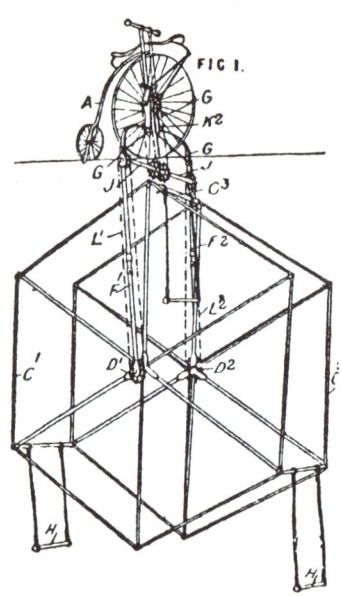

9628. Stern, M. May 20.

Advertising.—Theatre stage curtains are provided with views of streets or figures or other pictorial designs, in which suitable spaces contain advertisements.

chains K². Rods F¹, F² from the shaft J pass to the divided axle D¹, D² of the trapeze frame, and motion is communicated from the shaft J thereto by the chains L¹, L². Instead of a bicycle, a unicycle may be employed; and in places where there is little space, it may be carried stationary by means of suspensions from the roof and guy ropes.

9033. Maskelyne, J. N., and Morritt, C. May 12.

Theatrical appliances for producing illusions.

Consists of a board A having hollow pillars B and shackles D for securing the hands and feet, and, if desired, the neck of the performer. A screen C is passed around the board. The illusion consists in

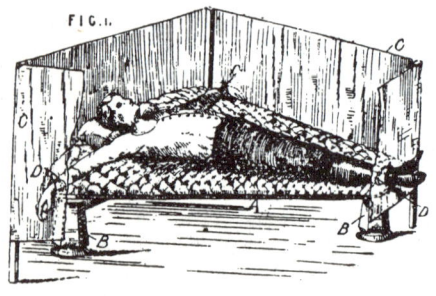

the performer playing musical instruments, or doing other acts, while apparently secured in position on the board with his hands and feet protruding from the screen. The feet, however, are dummies, and the hands those of a confederate or confederates, which have been passed through trap doors in the stage up the hollow pillars and through the openings, after releasing the performer's hands and feet from the shackles.

10,345. Chadwick, T. H., and Chadwick, J. G. May 31.

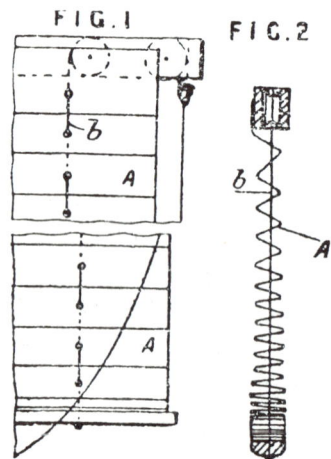

Window blinds; curtains, drawing and suspending.—Window blinds and drop screens for houses, mills, manufactories, workshops, theatres, &c., and for railway and other carriages, are raised and lowered by cords *b* interlaced through openings in the fabric A or through rings attached to the fabric and secured to the bottom bar of the blind &c., which when pulled up is folded in regular pleats.

10,568. Hughes, W. C. June 3.

Lime-light appa-ratus.—The oxygen and hydrogen are conveyed through separate bent tubes *j, k* to the burner N, adjacent to which is the lime cylinder p^1 carried by an adjustable screw-threaded spindle O^1. The oxygen and hydro-gen valves are simultaneously ope-rated from a central hand-piece by con-necting-levers. Bye-pass cocks may be fitted.

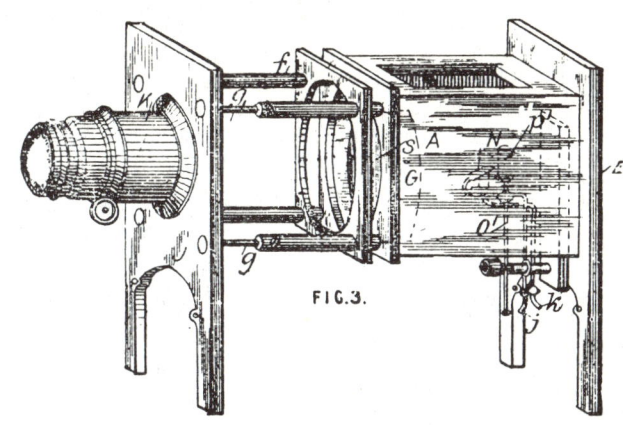

FIG. 3.

11,675. Mulhall, G., [*known as* Testo, G.]. June 22.

Acrobatic apparatus.—Consists of apparatus for resisting the pull of a horse. The acrobat holds between his teeth a pad of the usual description, having a swivel to which is connected one end of a rope *b*, the other end of which is joined to an extension spring *c*, adapted to withstand a pull of between eight and ten hundred-weight, and also attached to the whipple-tree of the traces. The back rope *d* has a loop through which the wrist is

FIG. I.

passed, and is connected at its other end to one pull-rod of a spiral compression spring *e*, capable of withstanding a pull of a ton, the other rod of which is secured to a fixed point.

13,597. Morritt, A. July 26.

Theatrical appliances for producing illusions. Consists of a framework for trick cabinets &c. A perforated framework is made resembling a panelled door, consisting of vertical stiles B and a hori-zontal rail supported by a rectangular frame A, thereby leaving openings C. Behind this frame-work there slides laterally, in grooves in the top and bottom of the frame, a second perforated framework or shutter consisting similarly of vertical stiles E and a horizontal rail, but the stiles are faced with strips of looking-glass F. By this arrangement the spectators may be allowed to look through the openings C without any change in the interior of the chamber being apparent.

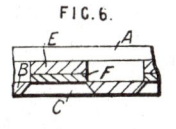

FIG. 6.

14,948. Felbermann, L. Aug. 18.

Advertising.—Relates to programmes for theatres, concerts, races, and the like, and to similar means for advertising. The programme &c. is made in the form of an opening and closing fan, and the face of the fan is ornamented with one or more portraits, or pictures, relating to the event for which the programme &c. is to be used.

16,026. Kershaw, A. Sept. 7.

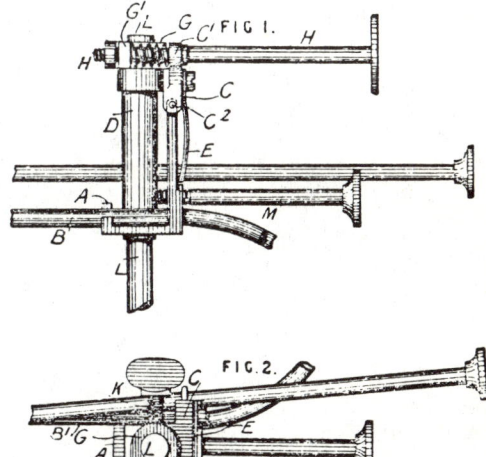

FIG. I.

FIG. 2.

Lime-light apparatus.—Relates to means for adjusting the position of the jets. A bracket C on the tube D is hinged at C^2 to a bracket A mounted between the parallel gas tubes B, B^1, a spring E on the bracket A tending to press for-ward the hinged bracket C. A tube arranged to turn within the tube D has a collar G and a lug G^1 for receiving an adjusting-screw H, which has its bearing in a lug C^1 on the hinged bracket, the tube being clamped to the pillar L by a screw K. The rotation of the screw H effects the lateral adjustment of the burner, while the vertical adjustment is effected by a screw M which rocks the whole burner arrangement upon the hinge C², the opposing pressure of the spring E preventing back-lash. The details may be modified.

16,120. Rodeck, C. G. Sept. 8.

Theatrical and like appliances.—In theatres, circuses, and the like, artificial birds, balloons B, flying figures A, or other objects are suspended from winding-drums mounted on carriages a which are propelled on rails by pedals, cranks, and bevel gearing. The rails may be suspended from the roof, or be secured to a floor b suspended from the roof, and made with slots between the rails for the passage of the suspending-ropes S. The rail track is made up of a number of curves crossing one another, the crossings being provided with switches which are operated by a lever on the carriage a. The winding-drum is driven from the driving-axle by bevel gearing which is thrown into or out of action by a clutch. A barrel spring is wound up when the object is lowered, and assists in raising it again. A band brake is fitted on the spring drum to control the winding-drum. For forming clouds, low-pressure steam, or water atomized by being forced past plug valves under pressure, is supplied by pipes c through nozzles and past hinged or plug valves which are normally closed by springs. A second series of pipes and nozzles d communicate with a blower D which can be made

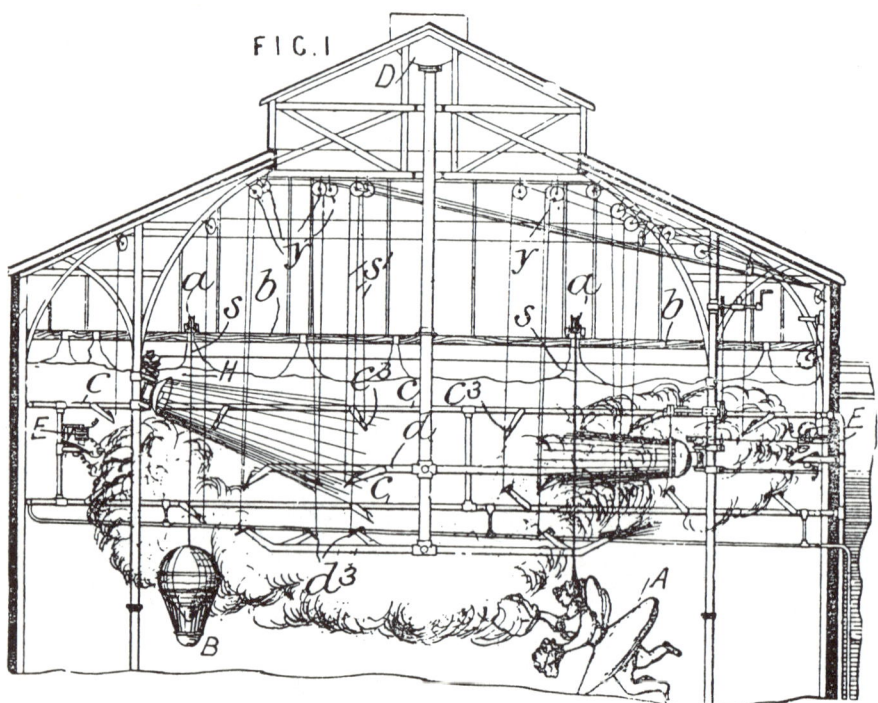

to act in either direction, and either withdraw the clouds or control them by means of compressed-air currents. The valves e^3 may be opened and closed automatically in an oscillatory manner by an electromagnet and circuit E. The circuit is completed through the valve when closed, and is broken when the valve is opened by the electromagnet. When steam is used the pipes c are first warmed by a current of hot air supplied by a tubular coil in the boiler. The valves c^3, d^3 are opened by cords s^1 passing over pulleys y. The lamp or projector H is secured to a spindle which can be swivelled by a crank and hand-cord. The projector can be fixed in any required position by a locking-lever pivoted to the crank engaging with a fixed toothed sector. The light may be tinted by placing a disc with coloured glass in front of the reflector.

16,183. Graydon, J. L. Sept. 9.

Crushing in doorways and the like, preventing.— Wings b, b^1 are hinged together to form a barrier as shown to limit the entrance to a theatre, railway station, racecourse, &c. The wings b are hinged to posts z, and studs or T-shaped projections c fixed to the wings b^1 slide in horizontal guides d. In the event of an outward rush of people, the wings are pressed back against the walls w. Rollers e, running on the floor, assist in supporting the wings.

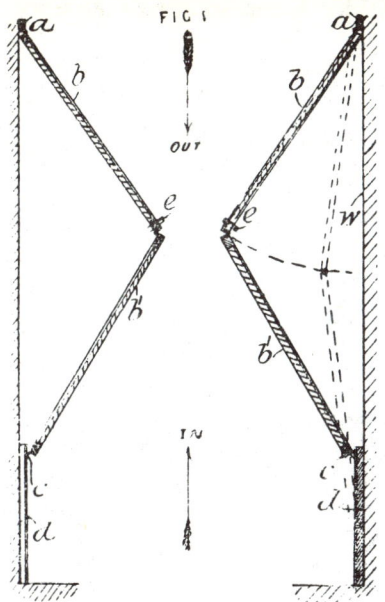

FIG 1

OUT

IN

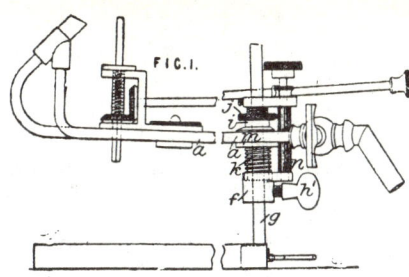

FIG. I.

to the socket which supports the burner upon the usual pillar, the spindle carrying the lime cylinder without affecting the perpendicularity of the spindle. The burner tubes a are fastened to a collar i, which slides upon a socket f secured to the pillar g by a set-screw h^1. A nut j screws upon the socket f, and a spring k bears at one end against an enlargement of this socket, and at the other against the collar i. The latter is thus held in contact with the nut j, so that, by adjusting the nut, the burner will be moved vertically. The lateral motion is obtained by operating a toothed spindle n, which engages with teeth on the rear end of a flange m on the collar i.

16,554.   Beeton, C. J.   Sept. 16.

Checks and tokens, issuing.—The money-takers' box in theatres &c. is closed in by a grille, as shown at E. The checks used are larger than the largest coin of the country, and the opening F is only just large enough for such coin, while the meshes of the grille are not large enough to allow a check to be passed either in or out through the grille. An issuing box C is fitted at one side. The check passes down a curved shoot within this box, and tilts a projecting lever during its passage so as to actuate registering-mechanism.

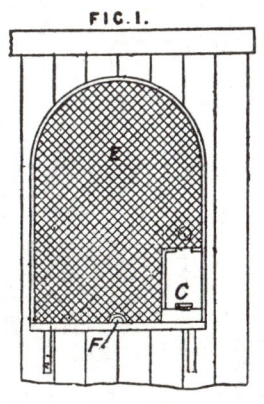

FIG. I.

18,836.   Anderson, J. E., and **Wrench, A.** Oct. 20.

Lime-light apparatus.—Relates to means for adjusting both vertically and laterally, relatively

20,137.   Clark, H. M.   Nov. 8.

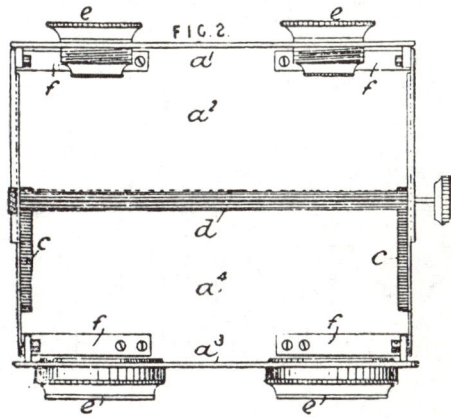

FIG. 2.

Opera and field glasses.—The lenses e, e are mounted in plates a^1, a^3 which can turn down upon the face of plates a^2, a^4 when not in use, and are held in either position by flat springs f, f. The plates a^2, a^4 are adjusted for focussing by racks c, c and a long pinion d.

19,883.   Savage, H. T.   Nov. 4.

Mouldings; ceilings; theatres.—Instead of using gold leaf for decorating mouldings, cornices, theatres, &c., oxidized metal leaf is applied in a similar manner, and produces an illuminated iridescent effect.

21,280. Menotti, O. Nov. 22.

Acrobatic apparatus. —Relates to means for adjusting the wires used by acrobats for "rope" walking and the like, and consists of a vertical bar A, securely held by stays *a* provided with adjusting-couplings *a¹*, having a loose sleeve or collar C to which the wire B is fastened. This sleeve can be raised or lowered, according to the trick to be performed, by means of the cords D, E, the ends of which may be afterwards secured to the floor or other part of the building so as to hold the sleeve firmly, or the latter object may be attained by means of a set-screw *c*.

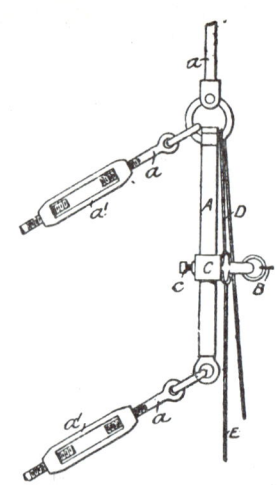

21,673. Johnson, E. Nov. 28.

Handle-bars of cycles or manumotive vehicles are mounted so that they may be readily adjusted without dismounting, machines so fitted being especially adapted for use by ladies, trick riders, and others. The handle-bar F is provided with a central collar I having recesses H, and is mounted in clips or stays fixed to the top of the stem A. The upper end of the stem A contains a tube C pressed upwards by a spring E and carrying a projection G for engaging the recesses H in the collar I. A pin *b*, fixed to the tube C, passes through a slot in the stem A and is secured to a thumb-piece B. The projection G may be disengaged from the recesses H by depressing the thumb-piece B, when the handle-bar may be turned or adjusted into any position. The pin *b* may be acted upon by a lever.

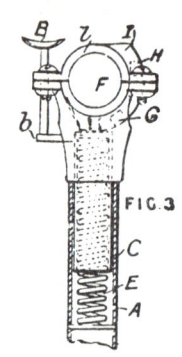

FIG. 3

22,151. Simpson, H. Dec. 3.

Lime-light apparatus for magic-lanterns. Relates to apparatus of the kind described in No. 8185, A.D. 1892. The lime cylinder is rotated by means of the ratchet-wheel 42 and the pawl 43 mounted on the swinging frame 44; the frame is rocked by the cam 40. One rotation at a time is given to the cam 40 by a weight or other motor released electrically, pneumatically, or otherwise by a single operation of the exhibitor.

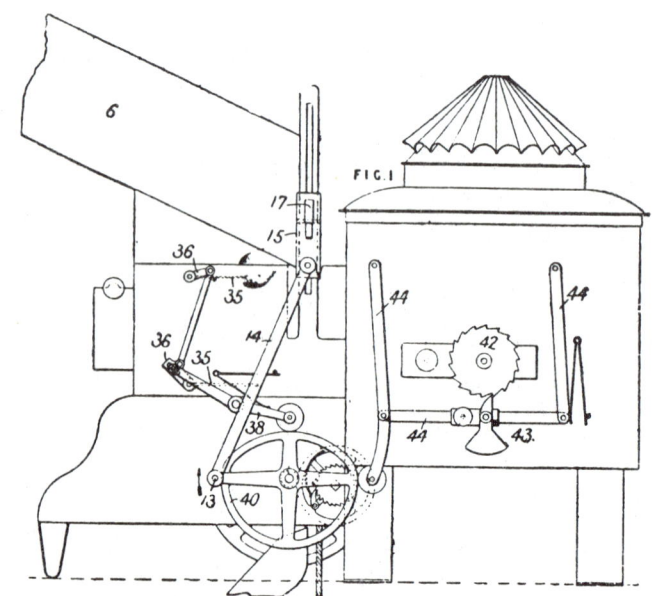

FIG. 1

22,952. Cryer, A. Dec. 13.

Theatrical appliances for producing scenic effects. To produce ghostly and other scenic effects, especially during dark scenes, stage dresses and other properties are coated with luminous paint, and subjected to a strong light immediately before the appearance on the stage. A suitable paint is composed of a mixture of ordinary luminous powder and india-rubber varnish (in the proportions of one of the former to two or three of the latter) reduced to the required consistency by the addition of benzoline, naphtha, or the like.

23,756. Allen, S. W. Dec. 23.

Magic-lanterns and dissolving-view apparatus.—Fig. 7 shows the slide-carrier a adapted to receive two slides c, c^1, the latter being in front of the condenser while the former is being changed. On rotating, the spindle b, c is brought in front of the condenser. A spring-cranked arm e pressing on the rollers d, d^1 ensures the correct position of the slides. In Fig. 9, the means of changing the slide and dissolver is shown. The spindle b carries a ratchet-wheel f^1 which is engaged by the pawl f^2 on the lever f during the stroke from right to left, and so rotated half a revolution. The dissolver is a screen g on a frame g^1 carried by a lever h^3. The lever h^2 pivoted at x^7 is connected to a spring sleeve h^4 on the lever h^3. The dissolver is raised so as to exhibit the view only when the lever f is over to the left, when a friction roller x^8 on that lever lifts the lever h^2, but as soon as the stroke to the right is begun, the dissolver drops, as indicated in dotted lines, and conceals the change of the slide. The door of the lantern is at the side and has folding flaps, so that, when raised slightly, light can fall on the lecturer's book, but is cut off from the front. The form of the dissolver may be modified.

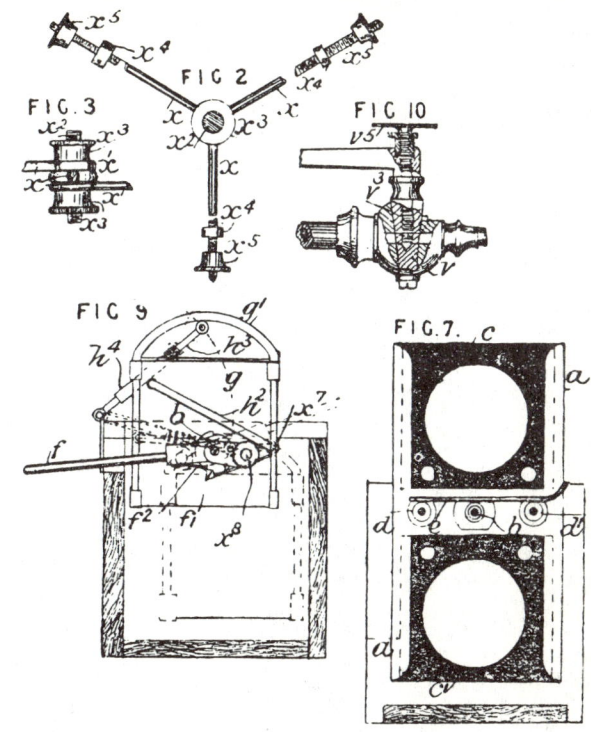

Fig. 10 shows the gas cock which is employed. The plug v has a screw v^3 for regulating the gas passage adjusted as required by the milled head v^5.

Tripod stands.—The legs are steadied by three horizonal tie-rods x, Figs. 2 and 3, having loops x^1 at the end through which a screw x^2 is passed and fixed by nuts x^3. The other extremities of the rods are passed through the legs of the tripod, and held by tightening up the nuts x^4, x^5 on each side

1893

1546. Wise, W. L., [*Spectatoria Co.*]. Jan. 24.

Theatres : scenic effects.—Relates to means for representing historical or other events such as the discovery of America by Columbus, the burning of Rome, or the like, or for producing fog, clouds, rain, wind, water currents and waves, and scenic effects in imitation of natural or other scenery. Fig. 1 is a plan of the stage or scenic part of the exhibition. The size of the proscenium opening B^1 is regulated by means of a vertically-adjustable slide or drop, and two laterally-adjustable slides B^2, all operated simultaneously by winding drums and cords. Stages C on curved tracks D carry the scenic arrangements, machinery, or persons required for the performance, and are moved along the tracks by electric or other motors C^1, winding drums, and cables F. Adjacent stages are coupled by hooked trip levers which are thrown out of action when the stages reach the limit of their rearward movement, thus permitting the uncoupled section to remain stationary while the adjacent section continues its movement. The stages may be mounted on unflanged wheels which can be turned on vertical axes for the purpose of steering in any required direction. Water channels M, M^1 communicate with a reservoir in the centre of the stage, and a floating stage or boat is propelled and manœuvred by wheels bearing against the bottom. Waves are produced by rotating screws R, or pivoted plates P operated by cranks or cams and reciprocating rods. The plates may be pivoted so as to offer no resistance to the water on the return stroke. A sailing vessel may be connected to an anchor block fixed to one of the cables F. Storms are produced by fans S^1 forcing air through tubes N. Rain is produced by horizontal perforated pipes below the fly-gallery, and fog is formed by slaking lime in a perforated box. The scenery is illuminated by lamps and reflectors within rotary drums which are fitted with coloured transparent materials for producing the required tints. Clouds or cloud shadows are formed by causing the rays of light to pass through painted curtains or

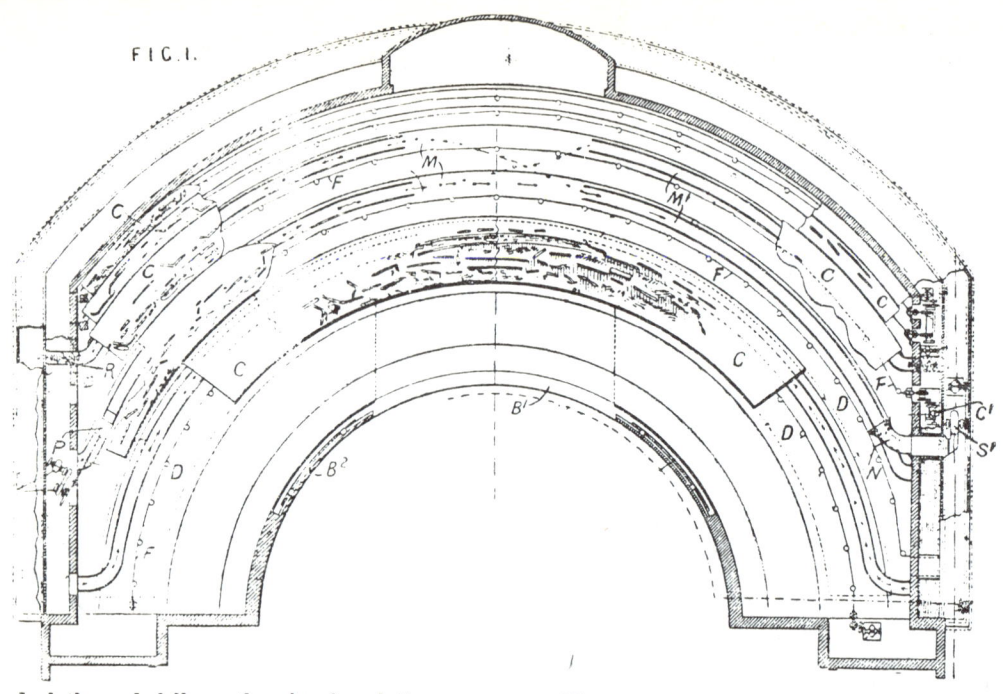

FIG. I.

cloud cloths and fall on the sky foundation or scene. The curtain is mounted on rollers carried by pivoted sliding frames. A star-light night effect may be obtained by arranging lights behind a perforated drop. Electric or other motors may be used as the source of power for moving the various apparatus. The proscenium opening has a border of electric or other lamps set in reflectors so that the reflected rays cross in front of the proscenium and form a screen of light. The drop screen may be dispensed with as the curtain of light prevents the audience seeing anything on the darkened stage.

1547. Wise, W. L., [*Spectatoria Co.*]. Jan. 24.

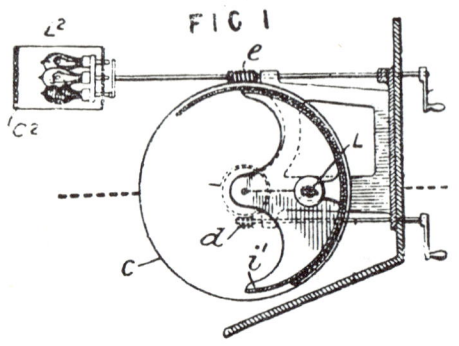

FIG 1

Theatres : illuminating scenery.—Light from electric lamps L, gas jets, or the like is reflected by concave reflectors i^1 through drums C of coloured transparent or translucent material on to the scenery or surface to be illuminated. In order to produce the shades and tints of dawn, sunrise, morning, evening, moonlight, &c. in succession, the drums C are painted with varying tints, and are rotated by worm, bevel, or other suitable gear e. Cloud shadows moving over land and water are produced by painting the clouds on the drums. The reflector consists of two cylindrical segments fitting one within the other so that the aperture between the edges can be widened or narrowed by rotating them relatively to one another by worm gear d.

Auxiliary lamps L^2 within coloured globes, or a coloured drum C^2, may be fitted to the ends of the drum C. Instead of the rotary drums, the colourator may consist of bands or curtains on rollers, or a vertical sliding frame with a suitably coloured transparent covering stretched over it. Masking shields or screens are provided for concealing the machinery in the fly-gallery.

3756. Tupper, E. Du' S. Feb. 20.

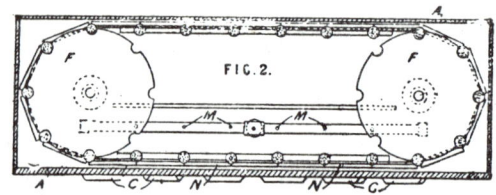

FIG. 2.

Advertising.—Transparent "crystals" or beads C, forming letters &c. in the opaque front of the case A, are illuminated and coloured by a light M in combination with coloured screens N attached to an endless chain mounted on revolving discs F. The device is applied to clocks, bottles, and to illuminating in connection with stage effects.

4644. Simpson, H. March 3. *Drawings to Specification.*

Oxyhydrogen lamps.—The lamp is for a magic-lantern in which it is mounted on a sliding plate.

This plate can be clamped as required to adjust the lime cylinder in focus. The lime spindle is mounted horizontally to save gearing and carries a ratchet-wheel at its end, which is slightly rotated every time a fresh view is exhibited by a pawl on the slide-changing mechanism.

5554. Barton, J. H. March 15.

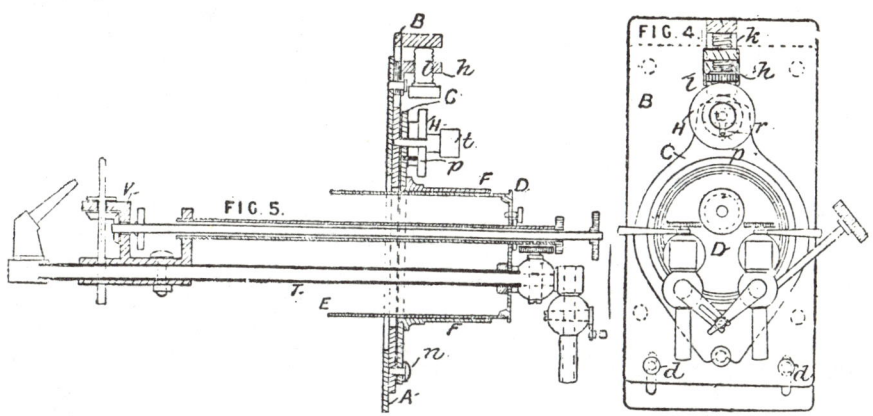

Oxyhydrogen &c. lamps.—To prevent the escape of light from the rear of the lantern, the gas tubes T and the apparatus V for regulating the lime cylinder are carried by a disc D which closes the outer end of a tube E. The latter moves telescopically in a tube F attached to a plate C, which is pivoted at n to a second plate B secured by pins and slots d to a plate A screwed to the back of the lantern. The vertical adjustment of the jet is effected by the screw l and a block h, which is attached to the plate A, and works in a slot k in the plate B. The lateral adjustment is obtained by releasing the screw t and rotating the milled head H, when a pin p thereon engages with a slot r in the pivoted plate C. Slight variations in the above arrangement are described

5936. Hayward, S. K. March 20.

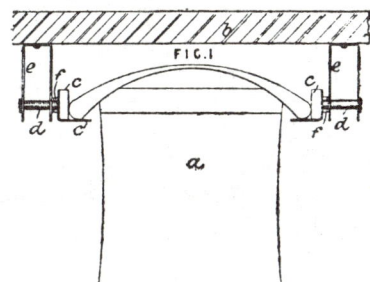

Seats. With hat-holders for theatres, churches, and the like. The hat a is supported on ledges c carrying bolts d which slide in the supporting plates e attached beneath the seat b. The ledges are preferably urged inwards by springs f.

9289. Hargreaves, W. May 9.

Theatres, fireproof screens for.—Horizontal sections I, J are adapted to slide past one another in vertical guides i, and are raised and lowered by a winch and winding drums L, provided with a pawl and ratchet-wheel l^{11} to prevent recoil. A ledge or flange j supports the section I when it is lowered. Spring doors T are fitted in the lower section to facilitate the escape of performers from the stage in case of fire. In a modification, the horizontal sections are operated by drums of different diameters so that they complete their different motions in the same time. A brake band is fitted on a drum on the winding spindle to control the motion of the screen.

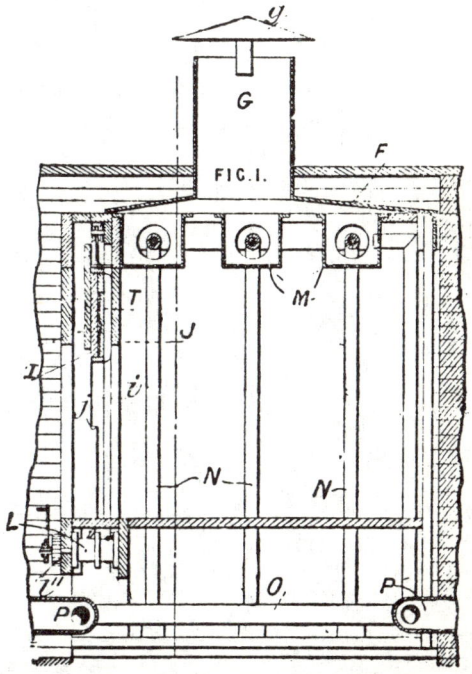

10,221. Boult, A. J., [*Fuller, M. L.*]. May 23.

Theatres; stage illusions.—A series of mirrors or reflectors F are arranged in a circular, parabolic, or curved manner at the back of the stage to produce and multiply images of objects on the stage. An arched ceiling A and an inclined floor B of mirrors project from the back F to the roof and floor of the stage ; and a number of electric incandescent lamps, either white or coloured, are arranged on the border lines of adjacent mirrors.

10,296. Browne, M., [*Fuller, M. L.*]. May 24.

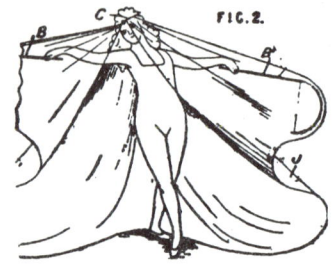

Dress or costume specially adapted for theatrical dancing. It comprises a long skirt J, secured to a circlet C, adjusted to the head of the dancer. Beneath the skirt are secured, so as to be completely concealed, two bent cane or metal rods B, B¹, which are manipulated by the dancer.

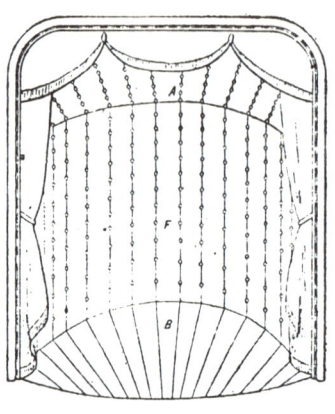

10,238. Matthews, L. May 23.

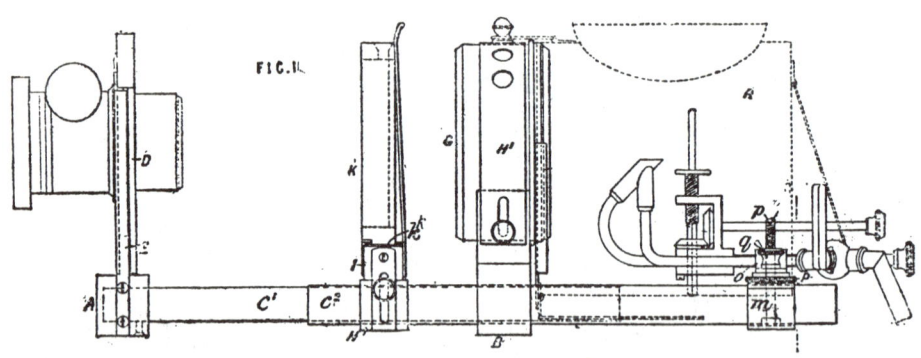

Lime-light apparatus.—On a pair of telescopic tubes c^1, c^2 are mounted the various parts of the lantern. The lime-light burner is fitted on a slotted cross-bar O, adjustable laterally and vertically by screws p and nuts P, q on sockets m.

10,301. Lake, H. H., [*Fuller, M. L.*]. May 24.

Theatres; scenic effects.—Electric lights C are arranged above the ordinary stage A and below a temporary stage B, and the light is reflected upwards through glass plates or lenses in the floor B. One or more platforms M, with glass plates P¹, are mounted on hollow columns H above the reflectors. By darkening the stage, and throwing a light upwards through the plate P¹ on a serpentine dancer or other performer,

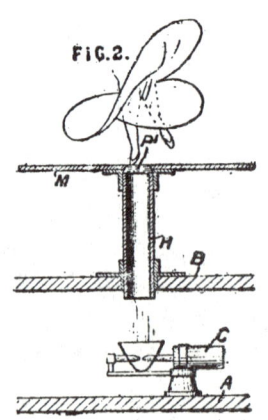

an illusion is produced of the person floating or dancing in air.

14,600. Anton, G. July 29.

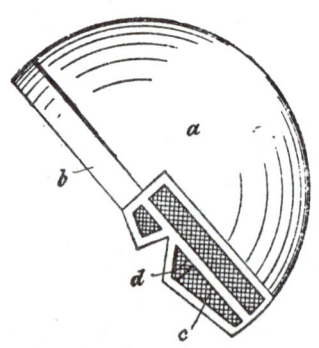

Wigs for theatrical and other purposes. The head form a is of wool or silk web with a rim b

of ribbon and the usual network *c*.   Springs *d*
may be provided in the network *c*.

17,429. **Morritt, G.**, and **Winson, J.** Sept. 16.

Conjuring apparatus.—Relates to apparatus for
the disappearing person trick. Fig. 2 is a sectional
plan of a double cage D, B, one within the other,
fitted with curtains, and mirrors E, F for causing
a performer to disappear. The performer ascends
to a raised platform A by steps, opens the door *d*,
and enters the inner cage. The outer curtains are
then drawn down, the peformer swings back the
hinged mirror F, opens the door *d¹* and, after
closing the door and mirror again, is concealed
between the mirrors E, F. The vertical mirror E
is fixed at an angle of 45°, and reflects the side
bars *b* of the cage so as to make the back of the
cage B appear complete.

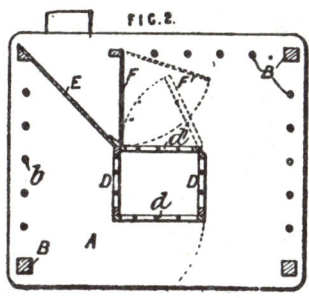

17,701. **Jackson, A. C.**, and **Toms, H. L.** Sept. 20.

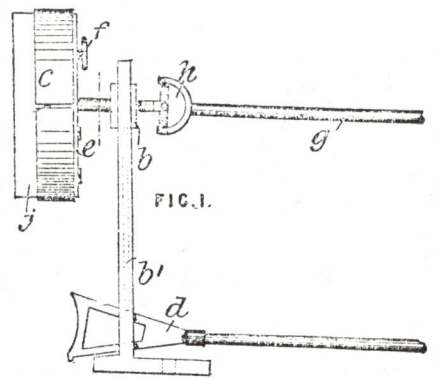

Lime-light apparatus.—The lime cylinder *j* is
grooved to correspond with the holder *c*, which is
made in two parts, secured together by a set-screw
f engaging in a slot in the back plate *e*. As the
lime is consumed it may be rotated by a rod *g*,
which is jointed at *h* to allow of its being worked
at an angle. The block *b* carrying the above
apparatus may be raised or lowered by means of a
wedge-shaped piece *d*, which engages with a rod *b¹*
depending from the block.

18,440. **Newton, F.** Oct. 2.

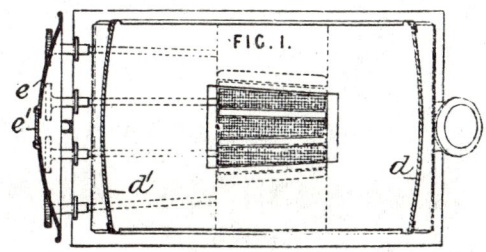

Magic-lantern lamps.—In lieu of the construction
described in Specification No. 1957, A.D. 1877,
the reflector *e* is protected from the injurious

action of the flame by a glass *d¹*, which closes the
rear end of the lantern. Both the front and rear
glasses *d*, *d¹* are curved to minimize the risk of
fracture on expansion and contraction. The reflector

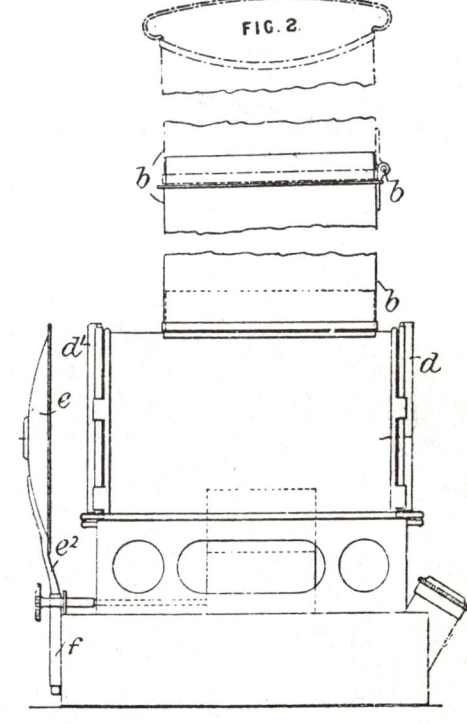

is formed with a central sight hole *e¹*, and has a
stem *e²*, which fits tightly into the socket *f*, to
allow of the reflector remaining in the position in
which it is placed. The flue *b* is made several
inches longer than before, and is hinged or jointed
at *b¹* to permit of the draught being adapted to
suit a small or large flame.

18,623. Cooper, E. S. Oct. 5.

Limelight apparatus.— Consists of an apparatus for operating the coloured glasses in front of lime-lights used for scenic and other effects. In the Figure the part marked e, e^1, e^2 is a series of concentric tubes so arranged that any one of the coloured plates c^1, c^2, c^4 can be rotated so as to come in front of the light, by simply moving the corresponding handle of the series h. In a modification, the axes connecting the plates with their corresponding handles are in the form of parallel rods, instead of concentric tubes as above.

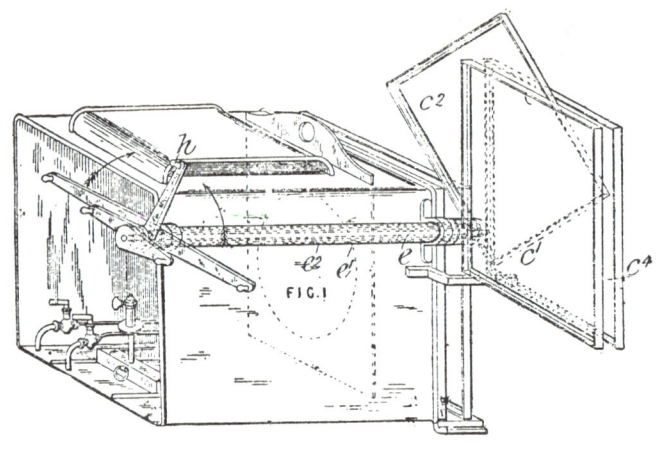

21,960. Johnson, J. Y., [*Bartlett, W. H.,* and *Risley, I.*]. Nov. 16.

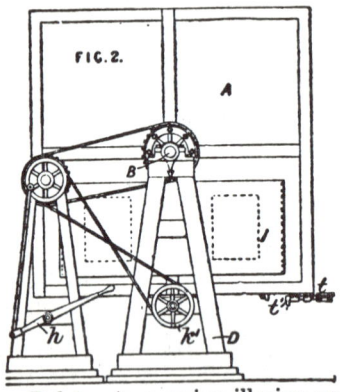

Swings.—Relates to a swing illusion apparatus. A box A is fitted up internally as a room, the furniture &c. therein being secured in position, and is supported on standards D by trunnions B, preferably perforated. Within the box is a transverse shaft carried by the trunnions, either level with them, or elevated therefrom by supports. A wire cage or basket having seats is suspended by cords &c. from the transverse bar, so that it can, if desired, be swung backwards and forwards gently. The whole box is capable of being swung, or even entirely overturned, by the arrangement of gearing shown, either by employing the lever h, or a crank handle on the pulley k^1. The box is entirely enclosed in an apartment, and persons enter and leave the former by means of a bridge t, the box being fixed in position meantime by a bolt t^1. The windows in the box are covered with a hood or screen I. The passengers being seated in the cage, a slight swinging motion may, or may not, be given to the swing itself, and shortly after, the box is set swinging, and if desired, completely overturned; the occupants being under a complete illusion as to their actual motion. A brake arrangement is provided under the control of the attendant within the cage. The box is lighted by electricity or gas.

22,665. Tennent, H. N. Nov. 25. [*Grant of Patent refused.*]

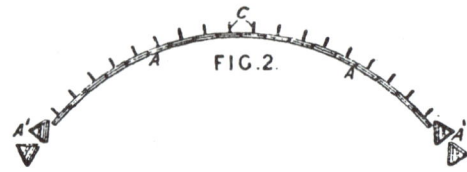

Theatres; scenic effects.—A series of mirrors A are arranged at the back of the stage in a polygonal form so as to reflect a number of images of the performers. Triangular frames A¹, mounted on vertical pivots at the sides of the stage, are each provided with mirrors on two sides, which reflect images on to the other mirrors. Triangular struts C are hinged to the frames so as to fold back out of the way when not in use.

22,866. Rosher, C. H. Nov. 28.

Air, heating and purifying.—Relates to means for purifying and heating air for ventilating and heating theatres, laundries, Turkish baths, dwelling houses, and the like. The air is first passed through a chamber containing a series of cloths of flannel or other fabric arranged on interchangeable frames for purifying the air; afterwards the air is led into the outer chamber C of the furnace B by means of the inlets c, and after circulating round the furnace

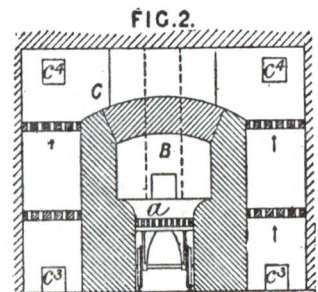

and becoming heated thereby escapes by the outlets c^4 for use in warming and ventilating. Instead of an ordinary firegrate a, receptacles or containers for holding the fuel may be placed on the trolley supporting the firegrate a.

22,954. Friese-Greene, W. Nov. 29.

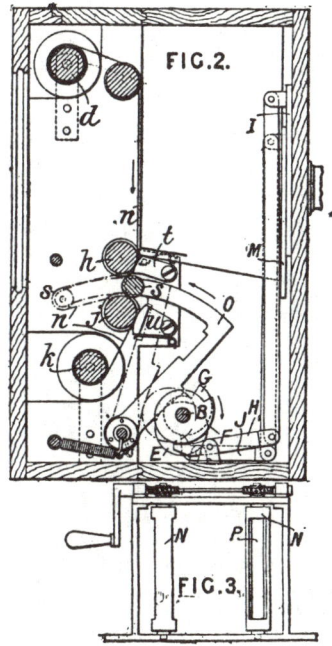

Theatres, scenic effects. The apparatus is for taking a series of photographs on a long band, and it can then be converted, by the addition of a lamp and a dissolving apparatus, into a magic lantern which is more especially used for scenic purposes in theatres. In the latter application, if space is limited, a special arrangement of a prismatic reflector is employed for deflecting the beam of light. Fig. 2 shows the camera. The band n is wound from the roller d to the roller k by turning a handle on the spindle B, which is geared with the spindle of the latter roller. The action is, however, intermittent, for spring arms O carrying a roller s are by the action of eccentrics E thrown rapidly forward between the guide rollers h, j and the spring clamp u preventing the strip being drawn off k, a definite length is pulled off the roller d^1. The slack is then taken up gradually, a spring clip t holding the band above it taut. As soon as the length of the band is in position the cams F, G come into action upon a pair of levers H, J, operating shutters M, in such a way that an instantaneous exposure is given through a common aperture, one shutter falling over the nose of the cam when the other has its aperture in front of the lens. This shutter mechanism and other details of the apparatus may be varied. When the lamp is introduced so as to convert the apparatus into a magic lantern, the views already produced can be exhibited in rapid succession, the shutters being removed. Fig. 3 shows a dissolving apparatus for use with a double lantern, the shutters being formed as slotted cylinders N, P, rotated from one handle, so that when one slot is fully open to the rays of light, the other shuts them off. The slides may be caused to gradually change colour by applying a substance, such as chloride of copper, which alters under the increasing heat due to the proximity of the lamp.

24,039. Cresswell, M. B. Dec. 14.

Theatres, scenic effects. Electric lamps E are arranged between partitions B, underneath a floor of transparent or translucent material D. Reflectors F throw the light upwards through the panes D. The stage may be made up of movable sections mounted on castors C, or the lamps may be fitted in recesses in the stage G, as shown in

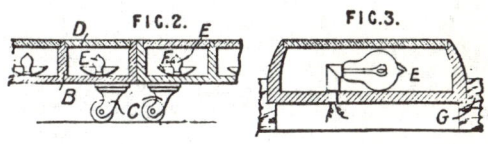

24,064. Dando, W. P. Dec. 14.

Theatres, scenic effects. Relates to apparatus for showing tableaux-vivants, or living pictures. Fig. 4 is a sectional plan of a stage or platform C constructed with four compartments, and mounted on a central pivot D, behind a frame I, fitted with pivoted mounts K, L which are adapted to fold against the frame out of the way when the stage is rotated to bring another living picture into view. The frame A is mounted on wheels, and is fitted with antifriction rollers E on which the stage C runs. Pivoted steadying legs are provided under the platform to prevent vibration, and steps F lead to the platform from the floor or theatre stage. Light ladders N lead to a bridge which carries lighting apparatus &c. The top and bottom mounts L are connected by rods or wires, and are folded simultaneously by a cord M. The sides K may also be connected in a similar manner, and all the sections may be returned into position by springs or weights when the cords M are released.

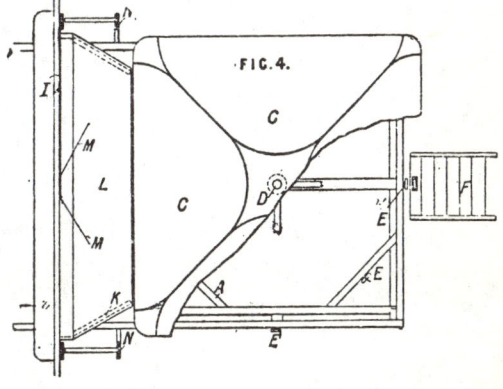

24,135. Simpson, H. Dec. 15.

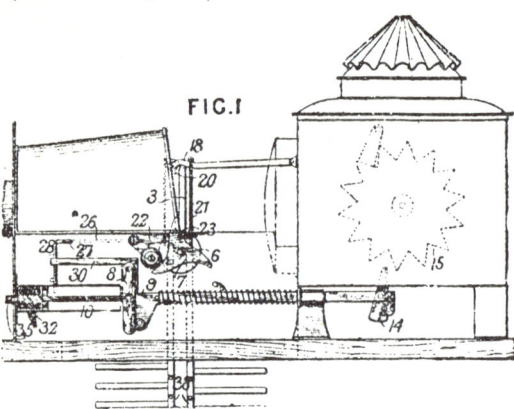

FIG. I

Limelight apparatus.—Improvements are made on the apparatus described in Specification No. 4644, A.D. 1893, in which the slides are carried by an endless chain passing over a square spindle in front of the condenser. The said spindle is rotated, to change the slides, from a distance, preferably pneumatically, the same power being used to operate the dissolving shutter and to rotate the lime cylinder. In the said arrangement, it is necessary before rotating the spindle to move it or the lantern horizontally to allow the slides to clear the condenser of the lantern, and the object of the present invention is to so form the condenser that the spindle may be mounted at such a distance from it as will allow the slides to clear it. The Figure shows an arrangement in which the apparatus is operated by a bellows 32, to which hydraulic or pneumatic power is applied by squeezing a similar bellows at any required point. The movement of the apparatus may, however, be effected by a weight, by clockwork, by gas pressure derived from the bottle supplying the lantern, or by an electric current controlled by the exhibitor. The bellows operates a piston rod 10, an extension 9 of which carries a pawl 14 gearing with a wheel 15 which rotates the lime cylinder. A pawl 8 rotates the spindle 6 carrying the slides, and a hooked bar 30 operates a lever 28 on the dissolving shutter 26.

24,807. Plunkett, H. G. Dec. 23. *Drawings to Specification.*

Theatres, scenic effects. In order to produce the scenic effect of a performer dancing upon water or in space, the floor of the stage is made up of large mirrors laid on a soft bed of felt or the like, and the back, sides, and proscenium opening are lined with black velvet. The interior of the box or stage may be painted to represent clouds and sky, and special reflected effects can be obtained by painting the raised ceiling over the stage. The performer is illuminated from the centre of the auditorium by a powerful light, and lights at the sides shine on the floor or figure. Perforated cards or similar devices may be placed in front of the side lights to produce a wavy effect on the floor, or ordinary magic lantern effects can be produced. The shoes of the dancers are soled with rubber to prevent slipping. Warm air may be blown in, upon, or underneath the drapery of the dancing figure to give a floating effect in space.

24,814. Rimington, A. W. Dec. 23. *Drawings to Specification.*

Theatres, scenic effects. Apparatus is used for producing upon a screen rapidly-changing combinations of colours, which may illustrate the connection between the musical scale and the spectrum, or may be independent of any connection with music, as, for example, it may be used for scenic effects on the stage. The apparatus consists of a series of lamps, electric, oxyhydrogen, or otherwise, adjustable by means of screw fittings behind a condenser so as to throw their light wholly or partly upon one and the same portion of a screen. In place of the usual slides of a magic lantern, systems of coloured diaphragms are arranged, one of which in each system is opaque. The latter, and with it one or more of the former, are thrown back on pressing a particular key of a keyboard, by which the instrument is operated. Additional slides, to vary the intensity of the colours or throw special forms on to the screen, are brought across the cones of rays by a pedal or stops. The keyboard may be that of a harmonium, American organ, or piano, so that the music is produced simultaneously.

1894

37. Challis, J.
Jan. 1.

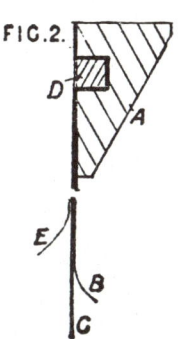

Advertising; displaying. — Show bills, pictures, &c. B are mounted on canvas &c. C, which is then stretched or strained over a frame A, being secured thereto by fillets D or otherwise. Over the canvas is secured a backing E.

243. Martin, W. Jan. 4.

Seats.—The seat *b*, having weighted arms *c*, is pivoted at *d* to a socket *a* clamped by a set screw *i* at any height on the upright or cross bar of a counter, desk, table, &c. Stops *e, g, h* hold the seat in one of its two positions. A special support may be used, in which case the socket *a* is dispensed with. The seat is applicable for use in schools, churches, halls, parks, gardens, theatres, &c. when space is limited.

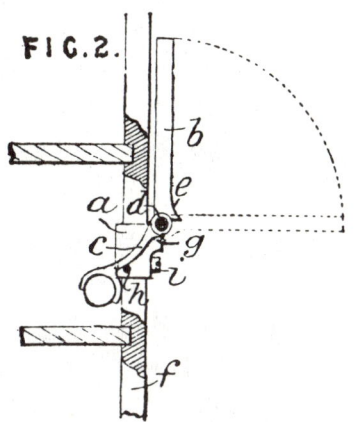

1024. Malden, B. J. Jan. 17.

Limelight apparatus. — Relates to burners in which oxygen gas under high pressure is mixed with low pressure hydrogen, carburetted hydrogen, or common coal gas, before being ignited at the burner nozzle. The oxygen gas issuing from the nozzle C at high pressure sucks the low pressure hydrogen or other gas up through the channels E, F, G[1] into a chamber L. The gases are thence forced by the pressure of the oxygen in the nozzle

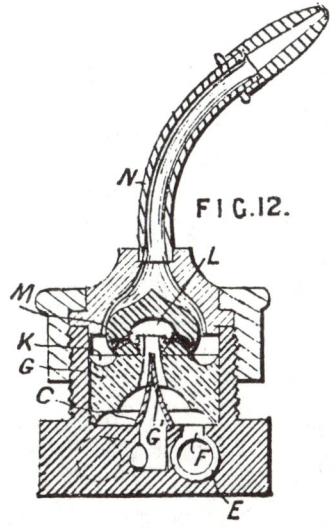

C through a number of apertures M into an annular groove K, whence the mixture ascends the tube N to the burner nozzle. This construction, which may be simplified by omitting the parts G, L, and by prolonging the nozzle C into the lower end of the tube N, prevents the mixed gases from lighting back and causing an explosion.

1433. King, W. F. Jan. 23.

Advertising.—Electric incandescent lamps are so grouped that by switching the current to certain lamps a succession of words may be formed. The arrangement in the Figure is adapted to produce the words " empire " and " palace."

2365. Gwyer, G. W. Feb. 3.

Limelight apparatus.—Fig. 1 shows the saturator in combination with the supply tubes, while Fig. 2 is a plan of the saturator only. The ether &c. is supplied through the opening *g*, and the outlet tube *e*[1] is connected with the tap *d*, through which hydrogen is usually supplied. Oxygen enters from the tubes *r, f*[1], passes along the chambers *x, x*[1] to the buffer chamber *x*[2], and thence through the tubes *e*[1] *h, a* to the nozzle. When the saturator is

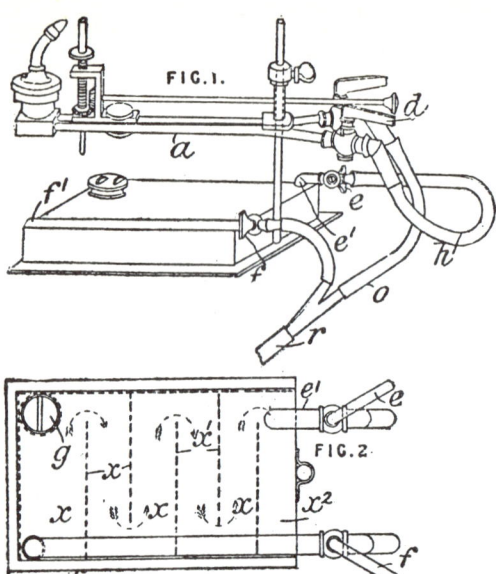

FIG.1.

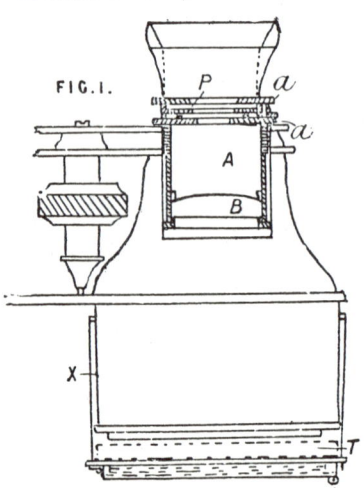

FIG.2.

not in use, oxygen passes up the tubes *r, g, o,* and hydrogen enters through the tap *d,* the valves *f* and *e* being closed and the tube *h* connected with the hydrogen supply. The apparatus can be easily used with a double lantern, and may be arranged to form part of the stand.

3954. Butterworth, R. H. Feb. 24.

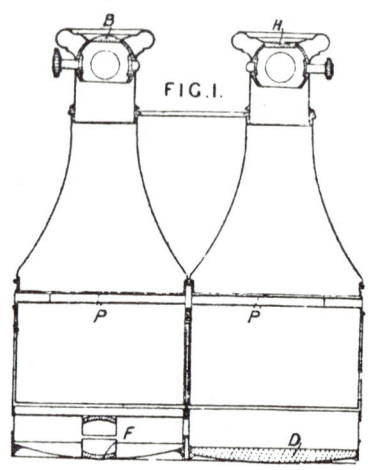

FIG.1.

Opera and field glasses and photographic cameras combined. From one tube of the field glass the eye-piece is removed, and in its place is inserted the tube A with lens B and dark-shutter P, arranged so that on pressing a lever the shutter falls and brings for an instant an aperture therein coincident with the apertures in the plates *a, a.* Means are also provided for holding the shutter in this position when time exposure is desired. At the object glass end of the tube a folding frame is fitted into a rim T, which can be slipped into the hood X or over the casing. This folding frame

receives the plate holder which is covered, until the whole is firmly in position, by a sliding lid.

4407. Dean, A. R. March 2.

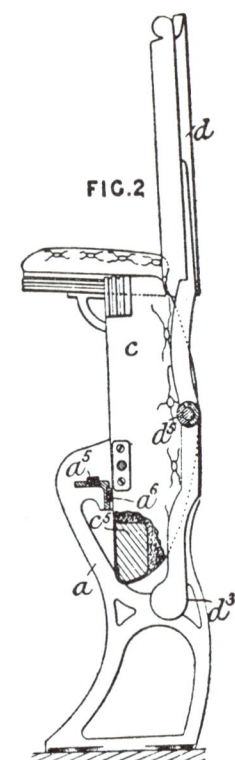

FIG.2.

Chairs. — For theatres &c. The seat *c* and the back *d* are pivoted in the frame *a* and weighted at c^5, d^3 so as to assume a vertical position when the sitter rises. Stops a^5, a^6 and d^5 may limit the motion. The movable parts may be arranged to move together by means of slotted or plain links or by gearing such as a toothed sector on the back and a pinion on the seat, and the counterweight on the back may work both seat and back. The back alone may be movable.

4735. Wood, W. H. March 6.

FIG.1.

Opera and field glasses, stereoscopes, and photographic cameras combined. In the frame of an ordinary opera or field glass, lenses, shutters, and diaphragms may be so interchangeably arranged that the apparatus may be used as an opera or field glass, a detective camera, a stereoscopic camera, or a stereoscope. Thus the ordinary object glasses D may be removed and photographic lenses F with shutters substituted. A dark slide is placed in the diaphragm chamber P of one tube and a ground glass or like screen in the other, the eye lens B being changed for a focussing lens H. as indicated in Fig. 1. Or both tubes may be arranged for photographing, in which case a third tube may be added for focussing purposes. When used as a stereoscope the object glasses are removed and frames with the necessary transparencies placed in the diaphragm chambers.

5155. Lyons, L. N. March 12.

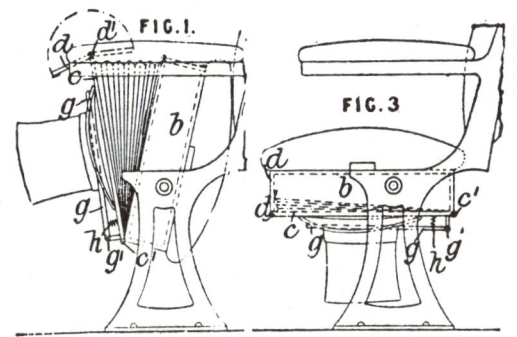

Chairs ; seats.—To the underside of the hinged seat of a theatre chair &c. is fixed a box b, the bottom c being hinged at c^1, and the front d at d^1. The lower edge of b and the bottom c are connected by accordion pleated leather &c. The box may have a partition. The U-shaped hat holder g is hinged at g^1 and is caused to grip the hat brims by means of a spring h.

6834. Cinquevalli, P. B. April 5.

Hats fitted with conjuring apparatus and with pockets for holding small articles.—Relates to attaching pockets to caps, for the purpose of catching balls therein for stage purposes. The pocket B^1, similar to a billiard pocket, has a metal rim b^1, which is carried by a light frame d projecting from the top of a tightly fitting cap D.

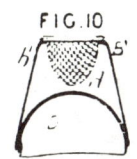

7673. Dickinson, B. April 18.

Magic lantern lamps.—The burner and fittings i of the gas or other illuminant are carried by a bar t^1 pivoted at t^2 to a frame or carrier b. Slots b^1, b^2, b^3 in this frame allow of the bar t^1 with its attachments being moved horizontally to effect the lateral adjustment of the burner ; and the parts may be secured in the required position by means of a set screw c. The vertical adjustment of the burner is effected by moving the frame b in an outer frame a by the screw r and guide pins d and slots s, or by equivalent devices. A shade 1 surrounding the flame at the two sides and at the back and carrying the hinged reflector 2 is mounted on the inner frame or carrier b.

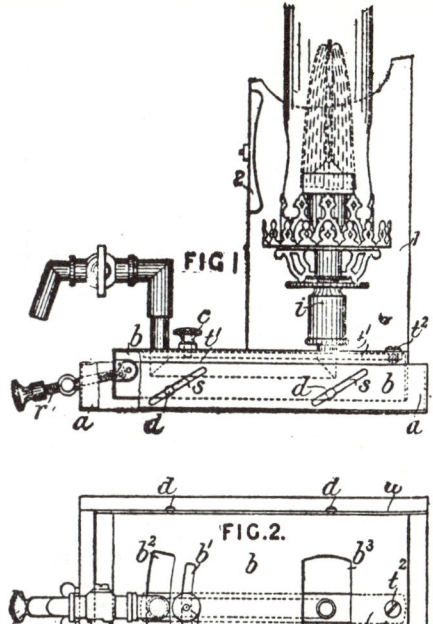

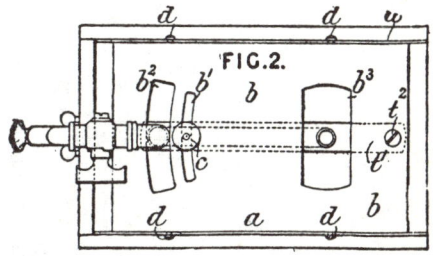

12,213. Aitchison, J. June 23.

Optical instruments ; opera glasses, &c.—The apparatus is for supporting optical instruments in position before the eyes, and it may be assisted by a cap or the like, to which the head band may be attached. The form shown is a simple one for supporting an opera glass, but it may be varied by the addition of adjustment devices, substitution of cheek pads for the nose-pads shown, &c. The head bands 18, 18 are secured to rods 23 pivoted in the flanges of a plate 22. The plate extends forward in front to form a block 26 and bracket 25 in which slides the frame 13, 13, 24 by which

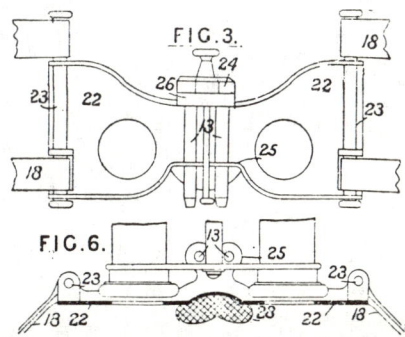

the glasses are secured, as shown in Fig. 6. 28 is the nose-pad.

12,572. Newton, H. C. June 28.

Oxyhydrogen lamps.—Relates to means for centering the jet in optical lanterns. The jet is carried by the sleeve L, which can move on the vertical axis H, lateral adjustment of the jet being effected by the rotation of the worm I, which gears with the wheel H[1]. The piece G, which works on pivots F, has a boss G[1] on its upper surface and a forked piece G[2] on its lower, which is slightly hollowed to receive an internally-threaded ball J, which practically forms a universal joint. Rotation of the rod K, which gears with the ball J, thus produces a rotation about the axles F and gives a vertical adjustment of the jet, shown by the broken lines.

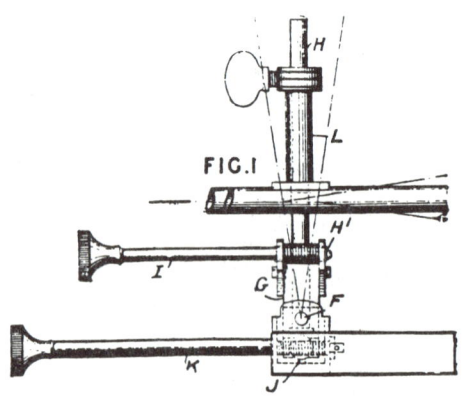

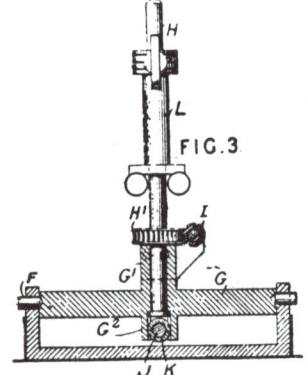

16,326. Train, J. Aug. 27.

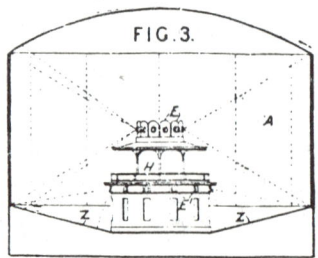

Panoramas. — A series of magic lanterns E, mounted on a stationary or revolving platform, throw the scenes on to a polygonal or curved white screen A ; and auxiliary lanterns E[1], below the platform H carrying the spectators, throw light on the foreground Z. Instead of the screen forming a complete circuit, it may be of a horse-shoe or other incomplete shape, and a representation of a deck-house, ship, or other object, may fill in the broken part of the screen.

16,916. Taylor, H. Sept. 5.

Limelight apparatus. — Means are described by which one or more lights can be manipulated from any part of the theatre or other building. In Fig. 1, which is a view of a theatre proscenium from the rear, is shown an arrangement by which two lights can be operated by an attendant standing on the stage on the prompt side. Each lamp is carried in a frame B which is pivoted at *b* in an outer frame C which can be

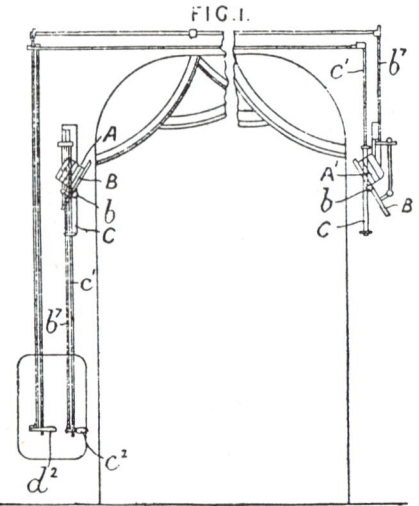

swung about a vertical spindle *c*[1]. The spindle *c*[1] of the lamp A, on the prompt side, extends downwards and, at a convenient height above the stage, is provided with a handle *c*[2] by which it and the outer frame C can be rotated. The handle *c*[2] can be moved up or down on the shaft *c*[1] to operate a rod *b*[7] by which the frame B is rotated through the gear shown behind the lamp A[1] on the "O. P." side. The shafts *c*[1] and *b*[7] of the lamp A[1] are carried upwards and are manipulated by a handle *d*[2] on the prompt side through a suitable arrange-

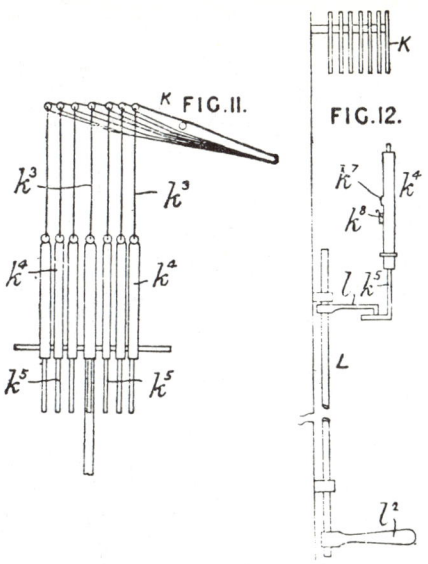

K FIG.II.   FIG.12.

a limelight) may be operated by the attendant from his position on the stage or elsewhere by means of levers, rods, or wires. The rods or wires attached to the various screens &c., which move on guides attached to the outer frame C, are secured to the ends of levers K, Figs. 11 and 12, and from the other ends of these levers depend wires k^3 attached to sliding rods k^4 carrying projecting pieces k^5. By means of a handle l^2 a sliding rod L can be placed in such a position that a projection l on it engages with any of the pieces k^5. By thus depressing the rod L, the required screen &c. is operated and held in position by a stop k^7 on the rod k^4 engaging with a spring-block k^8. When a second screen is drawn up in front of the lamp, the spring-block k^8 is moved aside and the previously operated screen is released and falls into its inoperative position.

17,077. Dando, W. P., and **Gwynne, J. E. A.** Sept. 7.

Lamp lenses.—To avoid throwing rings of light on the stage &c. from an arc-lamp, the peripheral portion w of the lens is obscured by a coating of opaque varnish or by grinding, the obscuration decreasing towards the centre. Both surfaces may be so treated or only the outer. The lens may be tinted or a coloured screen employed to overcome the extreme whiteness of the light from an arc lamp.

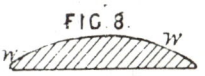

FIG. 8.

ment of bell-cranks and rods. The handles c^2 and d^2 may be coupled so that the two lamps may be operated simultaneously and, instead of being arranged to slide on their shafts the handles may be pivoted to collars on the shaft, so that their movements in a vertical plane may be used to operate the rods b^7. If desired, the coloured screens, the lenses, the shutters, and the burner (in the case of

17,604. Goodwin, T. Sept. 17.

Lime-light apparatus.—The supply pipes M, N for the oxygen, hydrogen, or other gases are controlled by a single conical valve K, which has a bye-pass k^1 in communication with the hydrogen supply pipe N. The gases then traverse a tube A, which is packed with fine wire to prevent the passage of flame, and which carries the curved burner tube E. The vertical and lateral

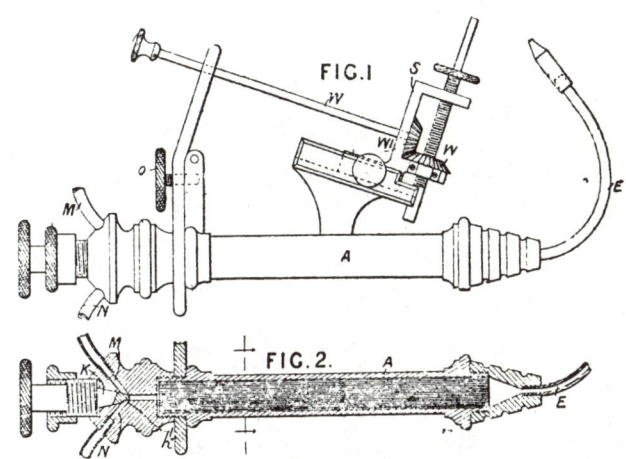

FIG.1.

FIG. 2.

adjustments of the lime cylinder are effected by the sliding bracket S, the bevel gearing W, W[1], and the spindle w.

17,830. Taylor, E. Sept. 19.

FIG.3.

Doors ; theatres, fireproof curtains for. A braced metal frame 10 is covered on both sides with asbestos plates or boards 4, and the internal spaces may be filled in with silicate cotton, asbestos, or other incombustible material. The external faces of the plates may be rendered proof against moisture by means of suitable paint.

18,083. Kiralfy, I. Sept. 22.

Circuses, theatres, &c., movable stages for. Temporary stages are constructed of sections which are mounted on wheels and propelled or moved by travelling ropes or bands so as to cover a circus arena, the water of an aquatic spectacular exhibition, or the like. Fig. 5 shows the sections A, B of two independent stages of different heights mounted on wheels A^4, B^3 running on rails A^6, B^5. The sections B fit within the uprights A^2 of the sections A when drawn back, and hinged sides or flaps B^7 are turned down to complete the stage when it is in use. Carriages or stages E are arranged to run on longitudinal rails E^2 of the sections A, or they may be raised by levers so as to rest on castors F^1. The sections may be moved simultaneously, or individual pulleys on the driving shaft can be thrown out of action so as to produce a stage of the desired shape.

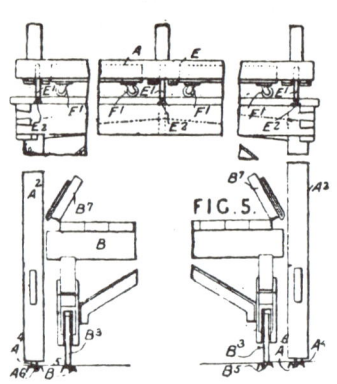

FIG. 5.

19,698. Wulff, E. Oct. 16.

Circuses.—A series of frames A, C, fitted with swing doors B, D automatically closed by springs B^1, are arranged so that a trained horse, or other animal or performer, can thread its way in and out. A clown teases the horse and, to save himself when run after by the horse, climbs a frame E, and holds on to a door F by handles i and foot rests h. The door is mounted centrally on horizontal pivots g, and is rotated by the horse pushing the lower half. The clown then hangs head downwards by his feet, and afterwards runs away, and the same play is repeated.

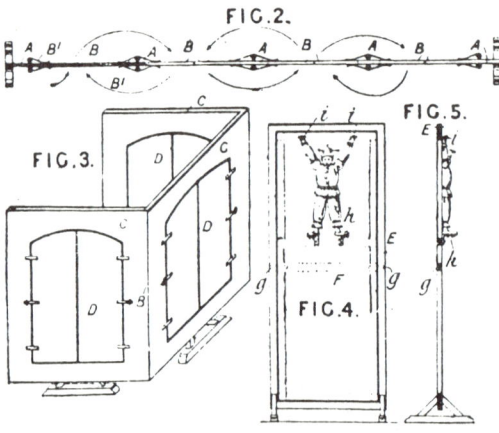

FIG. 2.
FIG. 3.
FIG. 4.
FIG. 5.

20,054. Bloch, E. Oct. 20.

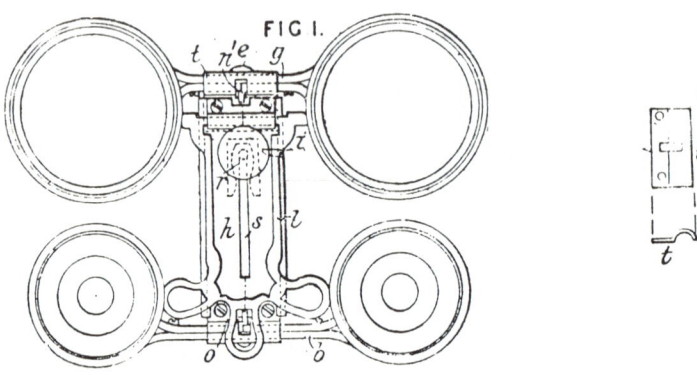

FIG 1.
FIG. 6.

Opera glasses.—Fig. 1 is an underside plan of the instrument folded. The object and eye glass frames g, b are pivoted to a flat sleeve h and to a plate o sliding therein respectively. Thus when the glasses are turned up at right angles they can be moved relatively for focussing. A spring device r, cut from the plate o and controlled by a button i whose shank passes through the slot s, holds the glasses when adjusted, or this may be done by rack and pinion. l is a handle hinged to the sleeve s. The parts t, u of the pivot arrangement employed for the frame g are shown in Fig. 6. They are screwed to opposite sides of the sleeve h so as to form a bearing socket. The middle part of g passing through them is formed with two flat faces at right angles, upon which in the two positions the spring e bears. A slot is cut in the part t and in this works a lug n^1 on the frame g which limits the turning movement of the latter to a right angle. The pivot arrangement for the frame b is similar, but the bearing and spring are formed in one with the plate o.

21,140. Siemens Bros. & Co., [*Siemens & Halske*]. Nov. 3.

Lighting, systems of ; switches.—Relates to apparatus for controlling electric lighting, such as on the stage of a theatre. Fig. 1 shows a side view. A number of parallel bars A B slide within a casing V, and each is fitted with a handle D. Each bar is connected by a cord with one of a set of movable contacts C sliding over resistances. The bars are counterbalanced at E, E. In order that several bars may be moved simultaneously, they are adapted to be gripped, being covered with a strip of caoutchouc, between rollers K and a rotary cylinder G. Springs L tend to cause the bars to be gripped. Cams H, fitted with suitable handles, are arranged to work against the ends of the bars I, and so release the bars when desired. The cylinder G is rotated by the wheel N, and to give a slow movement a pinion Q may be pushed forward to engage with a rack O.

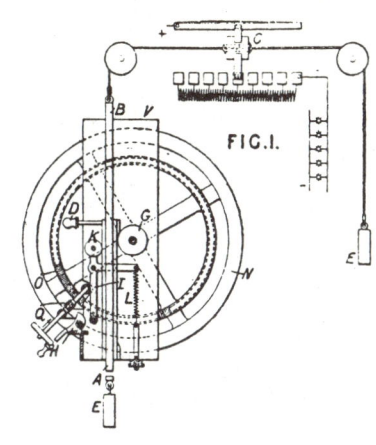

FIG. I.

21,844. Chandler, W. Nov. 12.

Brackets.—The Figure represents a holder for suspending a scissors from the person. The wire frame A is provided with a suspension loop *a* and with a cup *d* to protect the point of the scissors. Projections *b* retain the scissors in place when clipped by the clip B. The frame A may be of wood &c., and may be adapted for suspension on a wall &c. Tools of various kinds, and also fans, opera glasses, umbrellas, walking sticks, &c., may be thus suspended or held.

FIG. I.

22.211. Harvey, W. H. Nov. 16.

Opera and field glasses; reading glasses &c.—The object and eye-glasses are carried by plates *a*, *d*, the former hinged to the main frame *c*, and the latter to a sliding frame *g* which can be extended by screw *k*, the rods *h*, *i* sliding in guides. In this way the lenses may be folded down flat on the main frame in which apertures *l*, *m* are made, the latter to receive short tubes on the eye-glass frames, the former to allow of the folded object glasses being used as a reading glass. *p*, *p* are hinged flaps which serve the purpose of a case when the instrument is folded, and when set, as shown in Fig. 3 (and in full lines, Fig. 1), protect the instrument from rays of light so as to compensate for the absence of tubes. Suitable catches may be fitted to hold the parts rigid.

FIG. I.
FIG. 3.

22,132. Selbini, J. Nov. 15.

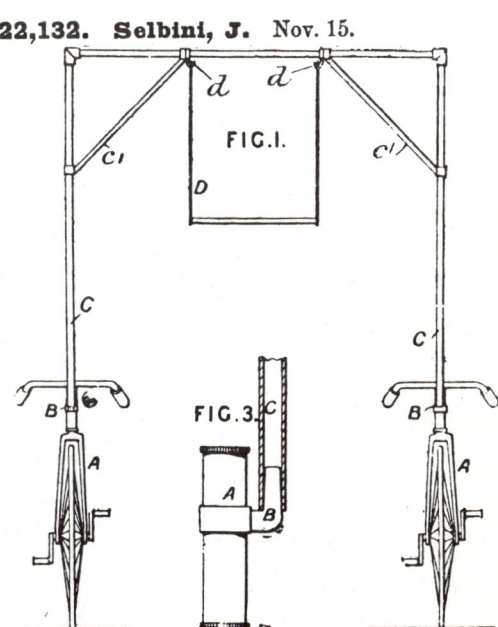

FIG. I.

FIG. 3.

Bicycles adapted for use by gymnasts and acrobats.—Relates to a trapeze carried by two bicycles for use in stage or other public performances. The bicycles A, made extra strong, are each provided with a stout hook or support B serving to carry a rectangular frame C, strengthened by struts *c¹*, and carrying, from hooks *d*, a trapeze D.

22,990. Barber, T. W. Nov. 27.

Panoramas.—The magic lantern apparatus used to produce the pictures has several radial lenses with an electric arc light in the centre for illuminating the slides. Fig. 7 is a sectional elevation of one form of this apparatus; 33 is one of the lenses, 35 a condenser, and 39 a slide carrier. A rectangular diaphragm is placed near the carrier, which is adjustable by micrometer screws to make the adjacent pictures join correctly together. The lantern may be rotated on its stand when required by worm gear. In another form of the apparatus for exhibiting the continuous flexible film, there is only one lens which is revolved at a sufficiently rapid rate to produce a continuous picture. The building in which the magic lantern views are exhibited is shown in section in Fig. 5. The wall on which the pictures are thrown is made slightly concave. The lantern is placed on a stand in the centre, round which are seats for the spectators.

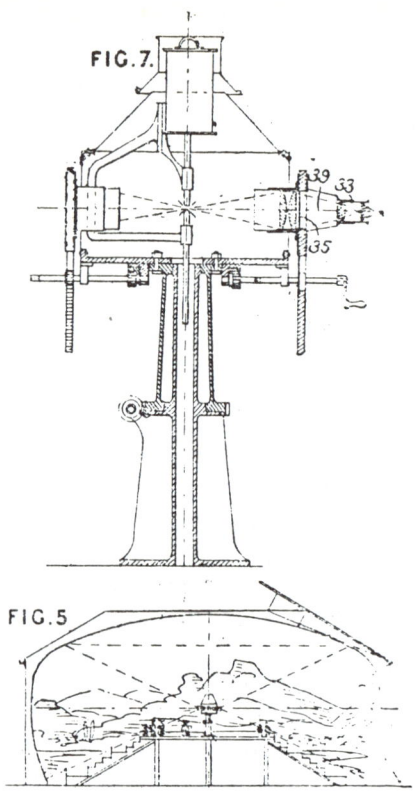

24,655. Alston, F. Dec. 19.

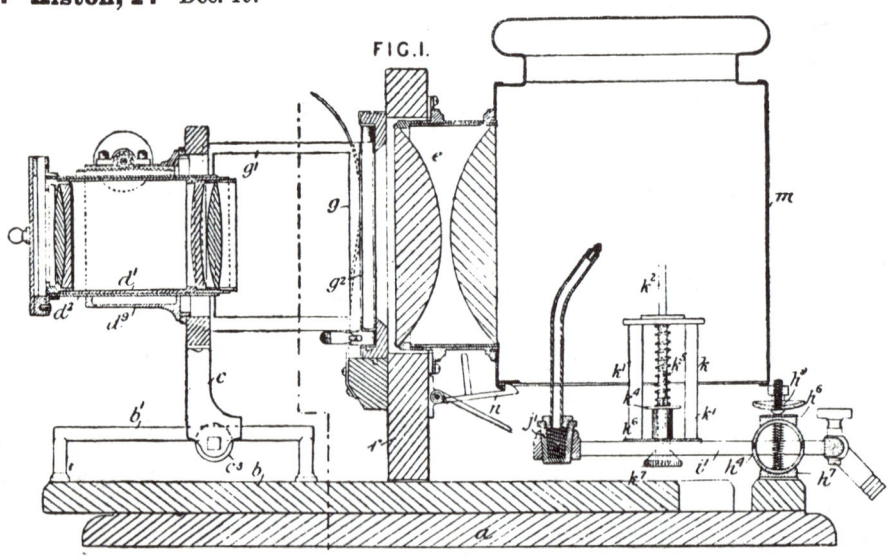

Magic lanterns.—Relates to the type in which an open space is left between the objective and the condenser. The objective is mounted on supports c sliding on rails b^1 attached to the tail board b, adjustable on the base board a; it can be fixed by screws c^3. The loose lens carrier d^1 slides within a sleeve d^3, and the latter can be adjusted in the jacket d^9 by rack and pinion. The upright f supports the stage g and the condenser

tube *e*, while the lantern body *m* is secured to
the latter by flanges entering grooves, and by a
spring fastening *n*. To the stage *g* are hinged two
slide carriers *g¹*, *g²* which alternately fold in front
of the condenser. When one of these *g²* is in
front of the condenser, the other *g¹* is turned back,
as shown, so that the slide can be changed. The
correct mutual action is ensured by forming
cranks on the hinge spindles, and connecting them
by a rod which carries the operating push.

24,821. Grottendieck, W. G. Dec. 20.

Magic lanterns; stereoscopes. — Two or more
lanterns *a, a* throw pictures, from stereoscopic photographic slides, on to a screen *b*, and the result is
viewed through eye-glasses *c, c*. The pictures
from the different lanterns may be tinted by glasses
of preferably complementary colour, and the viewing apparatus *c* may be of glass, gelatine, &c.
correspondingly coloured, and may be arranged in
the wall of a dark room, as shown, or may form
a pair of spectacles.

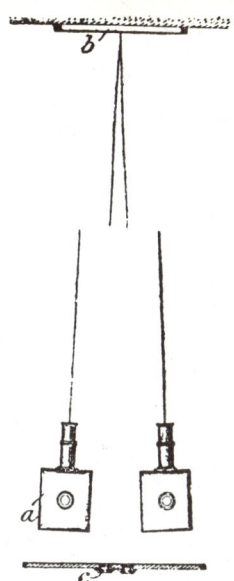

1895

976. Scudamore, F. A. Jan. 15.

Theatres.—An imita-
tion flying machine is
suspended by wires, and
may be raised or lowered
or moved across the
stage. The machine has
a light body A, with a
seat B, and two or more
air-cushions L to obviate
shock on alighting. It
may carry a steam boiler
and engine, or other
motor, the shaft being
geared to drums for
winding down the wires
H, which pass over sup-
porting sheaves *m* and
are attached at their
other ends to the body
A. The sheaves *m* are
carried by a beam M,
which is hung on two
diverging rods N so that
the beam M and sus-
pended machine may be
moved across the stage
by tackle *m⁴*. The ma-
chine may also be
movable backward on
the stage by a third
tackle. The beam may
be otherwise hung by
grooved wheels on hori-
zontally stretched ropes.
The machine carries an

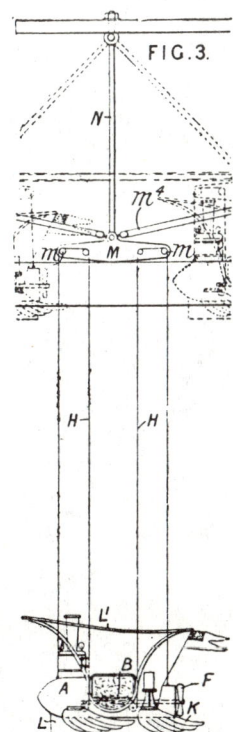

"aëroplane" L¹, wings
K which are flapped by links and cranks geared to
the engine shaft, and a "propeller" F on the
engine-shaft. The boiler is heated by gas-burners.
In a modification, the machine is lifted by a
stationary engine or winding drum, the supporting
wires being passed over guide-sheaves near the
upper ends of the rods N, and under pulleys in the
machine; the wings and propeller are then driven
from these pulleys, no motor being necessary on
the machine.

2195. Houldershaw, W. Jan. 31.

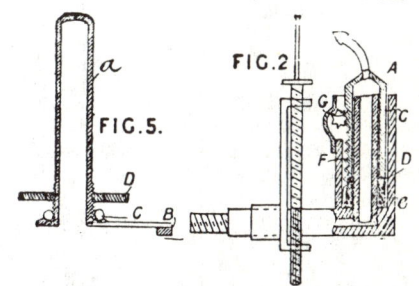

Oxy-carbon and oxy-hydrogen lamps.—
In the lamp shown in sectional elevation
in Fig. 1, compressed oxygen is supplied
to the T-piece A, and, when the valve A¹
is unscrewed, passes into the interior of
a corrugated or fluted chamber B surrounded by a dome C. From this chamber B the gas passes, by the corrugations

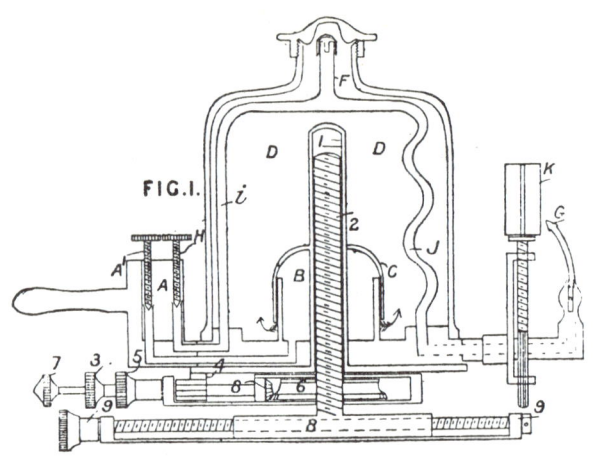

FIG.I.

or flutings, into the outer chamber D, which contains some absorbent material saturated with ether or benzole. The gas bearing ether or benzole vapour passes into the pipe F, and there meets a stream of pure oxygen supplied by the pipe *i* when the valve H is unscrewed. In the sinuous pipe J the gas and vapour are thoroughly mixed before reaching the burner G, the jet from which plays on the lime cylinder K. A close-topped tube 1 in the centre of the saturator D fits over a screwed spindle 2, which projects from a carriage 8, which can be moved to and fro in a slide 9 by means of a screw, as shown, or by a rack and pinion. By rotating the nut 6, by means of a milled-head 7 and bevel-gear 8, the lamp can be raised or lowered and, by means of a milled-head 3 and bevel-pinion gearing with a toothed-quadrant 4 on its base, the lamp may be rotated on the spindle 2. Fig. 2 shows another means of adjusting the height of the flame. The burner chamber A slides in an annular chamber C, a gas-tight joint being made by an asbestos or soft-metal washer D compressed by a screwed sleeve *e*. On the burner chamber is cut a rack F, with which gears a pinion G which is rotated, by a milled-head, to raise or lower the burner. Fig. 5 shows the method of applying the stand, shown in Fig. 1, to ordinary lime-light apparatus. A tube *a* with quadrant B, corresponding to the one in Fig. 1, is placed over the spindle 2 in the said Figure and, by means of a nut D, the gas pipes C, C are held in place. The bracket carrying the lime cylinder slides on a bar of triangular section, and is moved to and fro by a screw and nut while the cylinder is rotated by a worm and wheel.

2432. Stelling, H. Feb. 4.

Wearing apparel for athletic purposes. —Consists of a loose garment A, such as a night gown, shirt, wide coat, or blouse, having a lining D to which straps B, having hooks H at their ends, are attached, and is intended for use by performing gymnasts. The person wearing the garment performs on a bar, and, when desired, slips or is pulled through the garment, leaving the latter hanging therefrom.

FIG.2.

2746. Neale, W. B. B. Feb. 7.

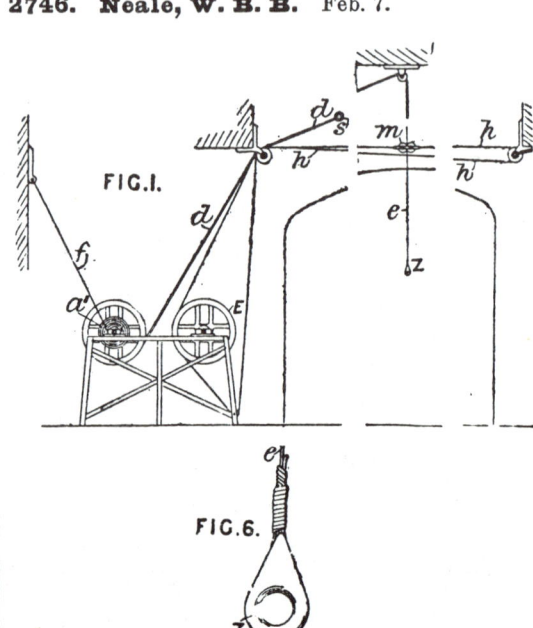

FIG.I.

FIG.6.

Theatres ; suspending apparatus for aërial dancing. The aërial dancer or performer can be raised above the stage by a wire *e* and a rope *d* from a winch, and be moved transversely by an endless rope *h* coiled round a winch barrel E. The wire *e* passes between grooved pulleys *m* mounted between parallel plates attached to the rope *h*, and a portion of one of the plates is hinged to allow for the ready insertion or removal of the wire. The weight of the performer is partly balanced by an accumulator or a rubber or other spring *f* attached to the wall and to a rope wound on a spirally grooved cone a^1 of the winch. In order to allow for the adjustment of the length of the rope *h*, the drum E may be made in two parts which are provided with interlocking teeth so as to move independently when separated, and as one pulley when together. A loop Z, at the end of the wire, is strengthened by a supplementary wire loop, the end of which is twisted round the straight part of the joint and secured by means of solder or the like. Wires from two or more performers may be connected by ropes to a ring *s* at the end of the rope *d* so as to ensure the raising of the said performers simultaneously.

2948. Rodeck, C. G.   Feb. 11.

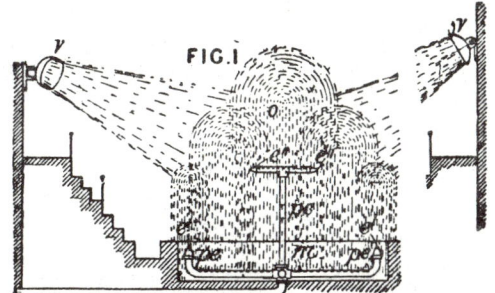

FIG. I.

Circuses ; theatres.—Artificial rainbows are produced by throwing beams of light on spray fountains O in the arena or central basin *m* of the water show. The spray is produced by forcing water through perforated pipes e^1, e^{11}, the latter of which is carried by a fixed or rotary vertical pipe *p e*. Electric lamps and reflectors *v* are arranged above the spectators in the required position. A glass floor for supporting dancers or performers at the water level is made up of radial or concentric sections mounted on screws or other lifting apparatus. Artificial breakers and frothy waves are produced by forcing steam or compressed gas through nozzles in the water.

4807. Cloquet, L.   March 6.

Panoramas, scenic effects. Pictures are drawn in a kind of spherical perspective on one or more spherical or curved shells or wall surfaces so as to represent the interior of buildings, outdoor scenes, &c. to the spectator at the centre O of the shell or shells. Fig. 10 is a vertical section and Fig. 11 is a horizontal section of an arrangement with three surfaces. The inner shell is cut away to represent an arcade A, E, C ; and apertures S, representing windows, are made in the middle shell. The external shell X, Y is painted to represent a view of the country outside the building. The lines on the curved

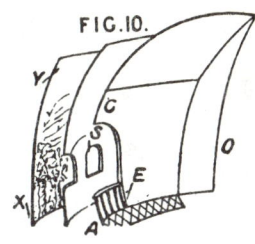

FIG. 10.

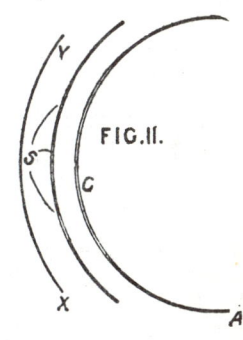

FIG. 11.

surfaces may be obtained by means of shadows cast by discs or strings interposed between the curved surface and a light at the centre. The surfaces may be lighted by suitably arranged reflectors, or by light passing through doors, arcades, stained or transparent windows, or the like.

6468 - *see over page*

6657. Lyons, G., and Bevis, H.   April 1.

Incandescent lamps.—Relates mainly to a double holder especially adapted for lamps for stage and like purposes. Fig. 1 is an elevation and Fig. 3 a section. The holders A, A^1, with insulating bases *a*, a^1, are secured together by screwed extensions *f*, f^1 of the contact pieces *e*, e^1 or by screws on the

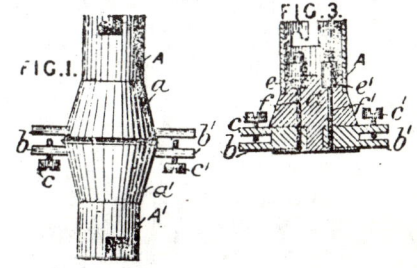

FIG. I.   FIG. 3.

bases. Two terminal clips *b*, b^1 with screws *c*, c^1 are connected with the contact pieces of the two lamps. The clips may be replaced by lugs, applicable also to single holders.

6468. Fitzpatrick, H. D., [*Fuhrmann, A.*]. March 29.

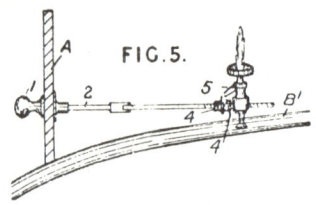

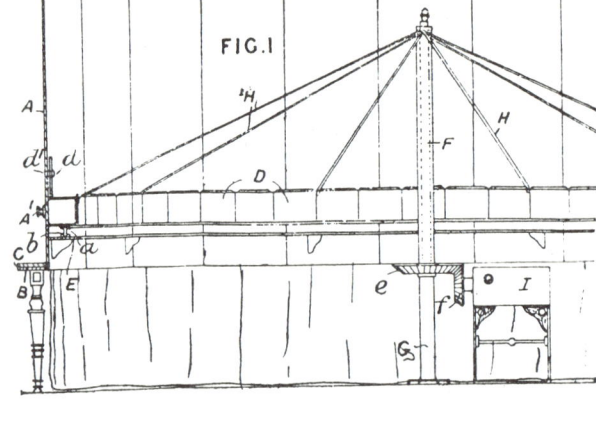

Panoramas. — Fig. 1 is a vertical section of part of a revolving diorama, consisting of a stationary cylinder A in which are a number of eye-pins A¹, and which is supported on an annular table B which is cushioned at C to form an arm rest for observers. Inside the framing is a ring D of stereoscopic-boxes on the underside of which is a grooved rail a running on wheels or rollers b, supported on a ledge E secured to the framing A. The boxes are connected by stays H, H to a tube F which rotates on a central spindle G, and carries a bevel wheel e gearing with a pinion f which is rotated by hand or by clockwork in the casing I. A ring secured to the boxes carries name plates d which are seen through openings d^1. The views are illuminated by gas jets behind, supplied by a pipe B¹. Each jet can be regulated by the observer by means of a rod 2 and knob 1, Fig. 5. The former is screwed and has, mounted on it, nuts 4, 4, between which the lever 5 of the gas tap is held.

7371. Rucker, M. D. April 10.

Tandem bicycles of the "Eiffel" type for advertising and acrobatic purposes. The invention consists in providing the ordinary "Eiffel" bicycle with a low seat I and chain gearing M for a second rider who assists the first rider to mount and dismount. The framing A is constructed as shown, and it supports a seat D and gearing E, F, G for the first rider. The chain is tightened by the lever H carrying the rollers H¹. The steering stem B¹ is carried upwards between the tubes A¹ and provided with a handle-bar B² and low handles

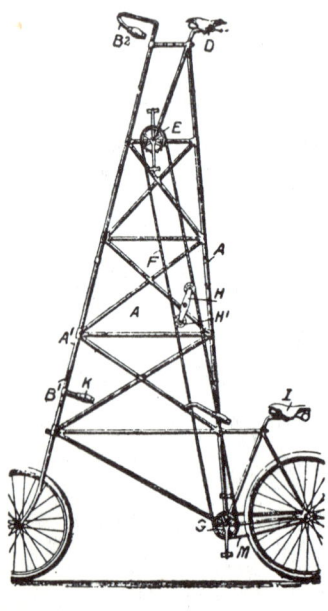

K, so that the machine may be steered when it is being pushed along. The construction of the frame and the arrangement of the gearing may be modified.

8111. Stoll, O. April 24.

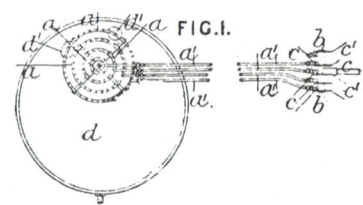

Fountains. — Relates to Pepper's ghost illusions, and consists in arranging behind the glass sheet used a water-spraying or water-projecting appliance so placed with respect to the other objects, that in the images seen the object appears to be in the water, or receiving or discharging water. The Figure shows one arrangement of water pipes &c., the main b having four branch pipes a^1 leading to perforated rings a standing in a trough d. The jets are adjustably controlled by cocks c having handles c^1. The trough may have windows d^1 therein to illumine the fountains from below.

9100. Murphy, J., Engwall, O. F., and **Tiden, C. A.** May 7.

Opera glasses. — Detachable holders are described which can be folded into small compass for convenience of carriage and contain means by which the focussing mechanism can be operated by the finger and thumb of the hand grasping the holder. One form is shown in Figs. 1, 2, and 4, in which the bars a^1 uniting the barrels a, a are connected

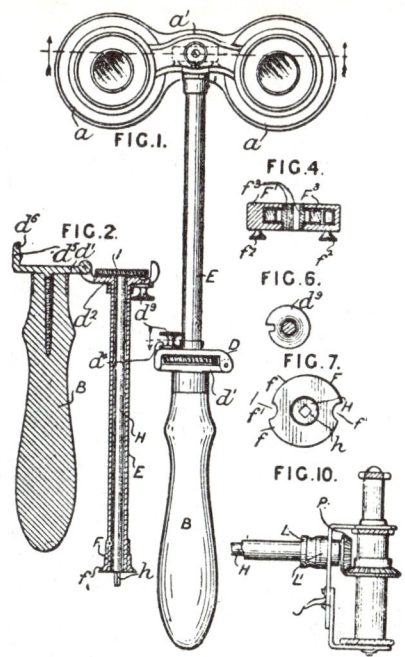

FIG.1.

FIG.4.

FIG.2.

FIG.6.

FIG.7.

FIG.10.

the holder. The holder may be hinged to the glass in place of being detachable, the ends of the spindle being grooved as described above.

9914. Thomas, W. J. May 20.

Sun burners. — Relates to means for lighting theatres, lecture rooms, &c., and forms an improvement on Specification No. 5102, A.D. 1888. Gas enters the receiver *s* by the pipe *r*. Two baffles *u* and *t* prevent solid matter passing to the burner *y*, Figs. 5 and 6. A ring *n* of triangular section forms a shield and deflector for the flame. The burners may also be placed at 45° to the vertical, as in Fig. 1, a deflector *x* being fitted to each burner, as in Figs. 1 and 3.

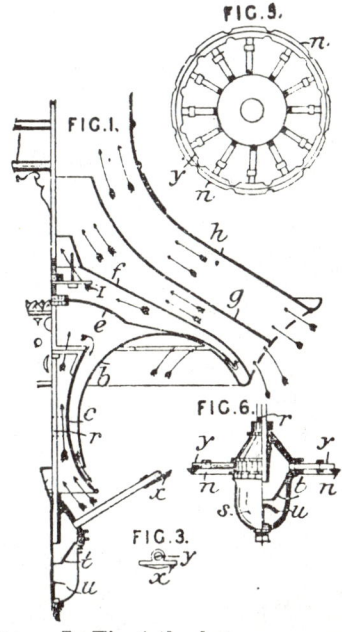

FIG.5.

FIG.1.

FIG.6.

FIG.3.

by a tube F¹ of rectangular section, as shown in Fig. 4. Within this tube slides a slotted bar F³, one side of the slot being cut to form a rack gearing with a pinion f^3 mounted in bearings in the bar F¹. The holder is in two portions B and E, hinged together, as shown at D. The portions d^1 and d^2 of the joint have interfitting projections d^5 and d^4, the former of which is notched at d^6 to receive the rim of the turn-button d^9, which is also notched, as shown in Fig. 6, to allow the parts B and E to be folded, as shown in Fig. 2. The part E is tubular and contains a spindle H having at one end a milled head I by which it is rotated, and at the other has a squared portion *h* which fits a square hole in the pinion f^3. The stem E has at its upper end a sleeve F, which in plan is of the form shown in Fig. 7. To attach the holder to the glass, the notches f^1, f^1 in the sleeve F are passed over the bevelled buttons f^2, f^2 on the bar F¹, and the sleeve F is then rotated to bring the bevelled flanges *f*, *f* under the said buttons. In a modification of the joint D, the parts d^1, d^2 are secured by a spring catch. A holder similar to that described may be fitted to a glass having the usual screw focussing mechanism. A bevel-pinion takes the place of the usual milled head, as shown in Fig. 10, and gears with a pinion P carried by a frame J. The stem E of the holder has a sleeve L which is screwed to a boss L¹ on the said frame J, and the focussing spindle H has a reduced portion to fit a square hole in the pinion P as described with regard to the former arrangement. This bevel-gear arrangement may be fitted to glasses without holders, a milled head taking the place of the spindle H. In a further modification, the holder is secured to the glass by a bayonet-joint and the handle carries the focussing wheel, the spindle of which has a grooved end to fit the similarly formed end of the spindle in the stem of

Reflectors. — In Fig. 1 the hot gases pass through the reflector *b* and between *f* and *g* and cause cold air to be drawn between *f* and *g*, *g* and *h*, and also up *c*. A valve I regulates the draught. Several methods are described for preventing the reflector from cracking, and baffle plates and additional casings therefor may be employed with or without a regulating valve.

11,729. Shaw, W. June 17.

Forced ventilation ; air, aromatizing, disinfecting, &c. — Relates to the ventilation of dwellinghouses, churches, halls, theatres, and other places, by using a fan driven by an electromotor to draw off foul air, or to supply fresh air. Diffusing-apparatus consisting of a number of partitions *i*, such as is shown in section at Fig. 5, is fitted on the end of the inlet shaft *b*, the inlet of air being regulated by a throttle valve *g*. The face of the diffuser is preferably covered with wire gauze. In another form of inlet, the top of the shaft containing the electrically-driven fan terminates in a series of vertical pipes bent horizontal at the top and arranged in a circle. The outlets of the pipes have caps of wire gauze, and they can be turned round

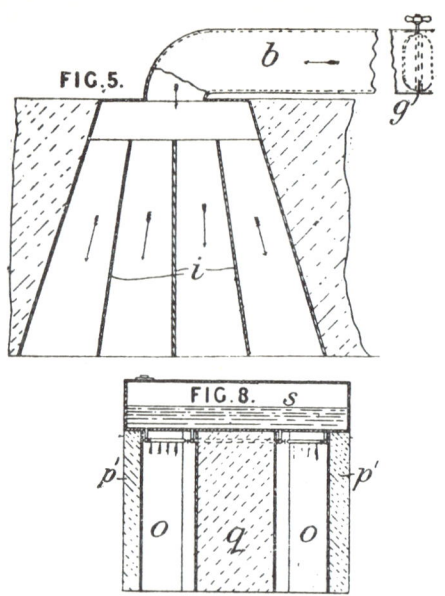

FIG.5.

FIG.8.

11,966. Willway, A. B. June 19.

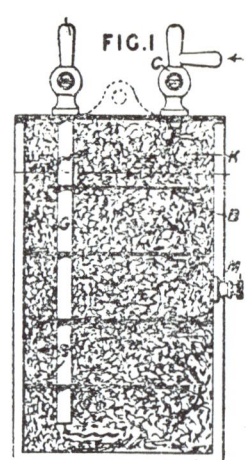

FIG.I.

Limelight apparatus.—Fig. 1 shows the interior of an apparatus for saturating oxygen with ether, gasoline, or the like, which is supplied through an opening closed by a stopper K. The box may be made in halves connected by flanges and is divided by diaphragms B, B which cause the gas to take a sinuous course from the inlet cock C to the outlet pipe G. The box contains cotton-waste or other absorbent, and is filled up to the level of the overflow plug M with liquid. In a modified form of apparatus the gas is supplied to the bottom of the box and passes away from the top. It is thus dried by passing through the upper layers of cotton-waste.

so as to discharge the air in any required direction. Fig. 8 is a vertical section of a conduit through which the air may be drawn by a fan. In the centre of the conduit is a deflector q, diamond-shaped in horizontal section, and encased in blanket to absorb water, disinfectant, or scent falling from the cistern s, the air thus gaining disinfecting or scenting properties. Flap valves may be fitted at the sides to close the passages o o.

11,903. Rignall, G. June 19.

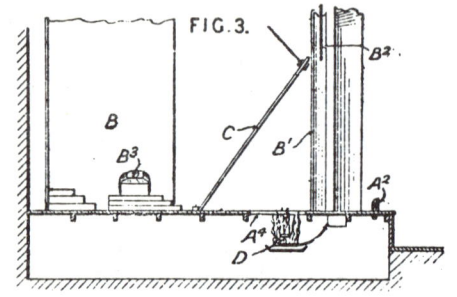

FIG.3.

Conjuring apparatus.—Relates to optical illusions, in which persons or objects are apparently enveloped in flame, or move or dance about therein, or are being consumed thereby. The stage is provided with footlights A^2, curtains B, B^1, B^2, and an inclined mirror C. Beneath an opening A^4 in the stage is a fire D, preferably obtained by burning a hydrocarbon in a suitable grid. The flames are seen reflected at the place B^3, where the actors may lie, move, or dance as required in the illusion.

13,076. Locke, C. W. July 6.

Oxyhydrogen lamps.—Oxygen and hydrogen supplied through tubes B, B^1 respectively mix in a vertical tube D and pass to a deflecting cone E in the mixing chamber A having fine perforations F, F^1 through which the mixed gases pass to the burner tube G. For the jet slides two tubes H, H^1, Fig. 2, are connected by a metal bridge I and telescope into two other tubes K, K^1 attached to the lantern. The bridge I carries the jet pin J.

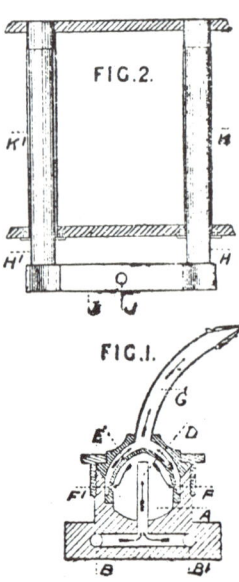

FIG.2.

FIG.I.

13,416. Walters, A. July 12. *Drawings to Specification.*

Reflectors for electric arc lamps. A removable reflector, hinged to the lamp, is provided with a central aperture for the passage of one of the carbons.

13,926. Hipwell, D. E. July 22.

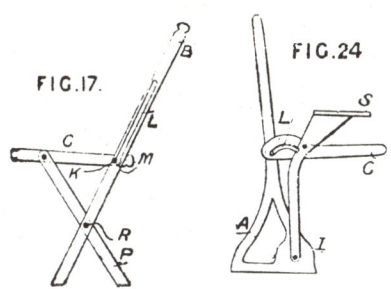

FIG.17. FIG.24.

Seats and stools.—The seat C and back B are pivoted to each leg P. Pins K are fitted to slide in grooves L and allow the seat to be reversed. Various modifications may be obtained by arranging the grooves L in seat or legs P. A folding theatre seat with arms S is shown in Fig. 24.

14,598. Edwards, W. Aug. 1.

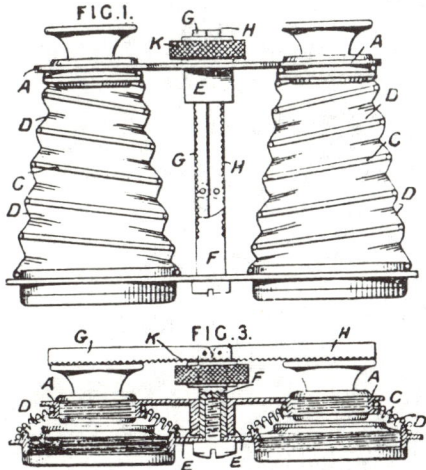

Opera &c. glasses.—The barrels of the glasses are formed of a coiled spring C covered with flexible material D. The central post F is square, and the greater part of it is formed of two hinged legs G, H, the whole being screw threaded at its corners for the milled nut K. The eye-lens plate A has a lug E with square hole fitting F, and when the glasses are closed the parts G, H are turned down, Fig. 3, and the nut K run back so as to engage fingers on the legs G, H and hold them in position.

16,070. Chase, C. A. Aug. 27.

Panoramas. — Views, representing the horizon, are thrown on a spherical, cylindrical, or polyhedral wall A by steropticons or magic lanterns carried by a cage E suspended by wires F. A canopy is suspended below the roof, and the

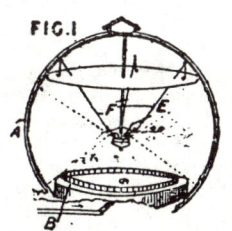

spectators take their places on a platform B.
A series of pictures are arranged in a ring, and a new complete picture may be projected by rotating the ring by means of a rack and pinion. The stereopticons are mounted on slides or carriages, and are adjustable by pinions and racks. Converging slides controlled by screws are fitted at the front of each lantern to cut off the overlapping edges of the light, and produce an evenly blended picture. Cloud and water effects may be produced by manipulating auxiliary stereopticons arranged below the main ones. The lanterns may be lighted by electric arc lamps or other suitable means.

16,901. Butcher, W., Butcher, W. F., and **Drake, H. O.** Sept. 10.

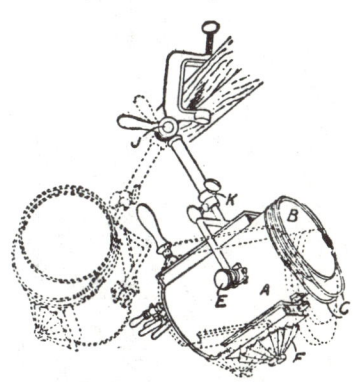

Theatrical appliances.—Relates to the lime-light "boxes" used in theatres and other places to obtain a brilliant illumination. The usual square wooden box is replaced by a metal drum or cylinder A carrying the lime-light apparatus, the lens B, the coloured tinters C, and a cowl F, which is made loose to facilitate packing. The screw joints J, K, E permit of the drum A being readily manipulated to turn the light in any direction, as indicated by the dotted lines.

17,652. Rodeck, C. G. Sept. 21.

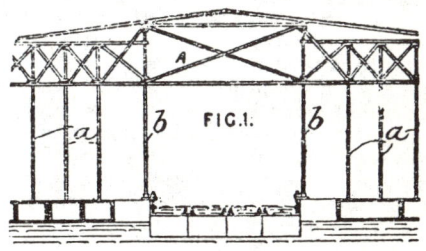

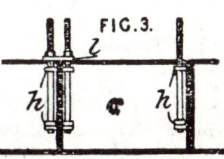

River dwellings &c.—A number of pontoons, of box like or other form, are connected together by straps *l* to form a floating base, on which a superstructure A is built of any convenient shape and supported on columns *a*, *b*, which latter are carried by suitably formed thimbles *h*. Some of the pontoons may be placed below the level of the water to form a reservoir or basin, which may be used as a swimming bath or washing trough, or upon this floating base a building, for use as a theatre, circus, ball-room, or the like, may be erected.

18,935. Probert, I., and Moy, E. F. Oct. 9.

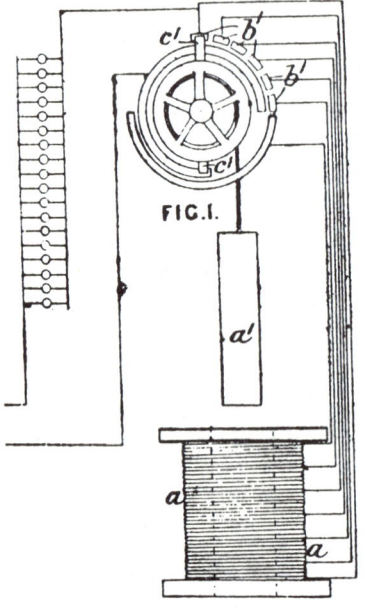

FIG. 1.

Switches for regulating the current in alternating current circuits for theatre lighting &c. Fig. 1 shows one form. A choking coil *a* is divided into sections, and connected as shown to the contacts b^1 of a switch. By turning the switch arm c^1, more or less of the choking coil is put in the circuit. At the same time a core a^1 is lowered into or raised from the coil to make the changes in the E.M.F. more gradual. The core may be fixed, and a screen be raised or lowered over it. In a modified form the coil is continuous, and resistances are arranged between the contacts on the switch. Where several circuits have to be operated, either simultaneously or independently, the switches are connected by gearing to check wheels arranged on a board or platform. On the axles of the check wheels worm-wheels are mounted, and are driven by a worm or worms. A spring pin is adapted to lock the check wheels with the worm wheels when several are to be operated at the same time.

19,841. Kilányi, E. von. Oct. 22.

Theatres; apparatus for exhibiting tableaux vivants. A series of platforms or cars A, carrying the groups or persons properly posed, are moved on rails C behind a frame D or aperture in the scenery by friction wheels I^2, I^3, which grip bars or blades E below the cars, and are driven by a crank handle J^1, worm J^2, and worm wheel I. A suitable background or scenery Z is unwound from a roller Y

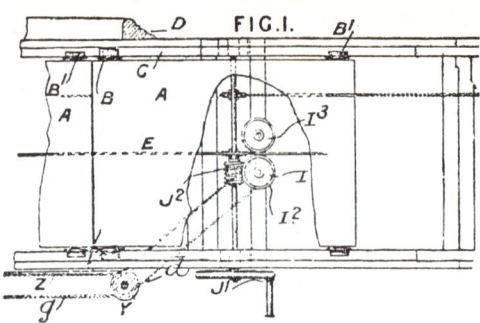

FIG. I.

and wound on a parallel roller driven by chains *g*, *d* and a sprocket wheel on the spindle of the roller I^2. When the car is at the end of its travel, the broad and narrow wheels B, B^1 sink through wide and narrow recesses or slots in the rails C on to inclined rails, and the empty cars are returned to the starting point, to be used over again, along horizontal rails below the rails C. Projections from endless carrier chains below the lower rails engage with hooks underneath the cars. Wide and narrow gauge inclined rails are arranged at the starting point for the purpose of enabling the cars to be drawn to the proper level, and switches pivoted to the rails C are raised by the wheels B, B^1, and fall again after the wheels have passed them.

20,208. Tollerton, J. Oct. 26.

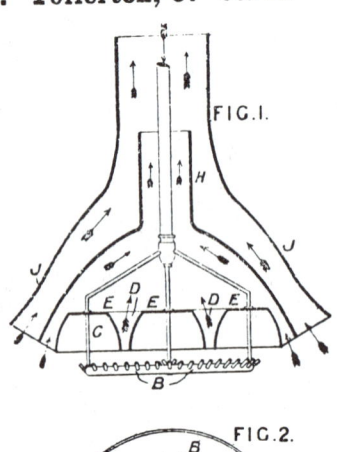

FIG. I.

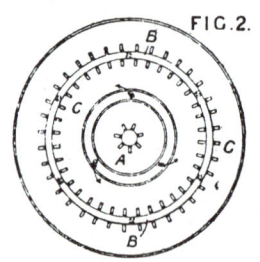

FIG. 2.

Sun burners.—Reflectors A, C with perforated tops E are arranged to correspond with the ring or cluster burners B, which are ignited by pilot jets. The heated gases which do not ascend through the perforated tops E are deflected back on to the flames on their way to the outlet passages D. The casing H is supplemented by a second casing J to increase the ventilation of the building.

21,101. Boisset, W. W., Boisset, A. H., and Boisset, F. M. Nov. 7.

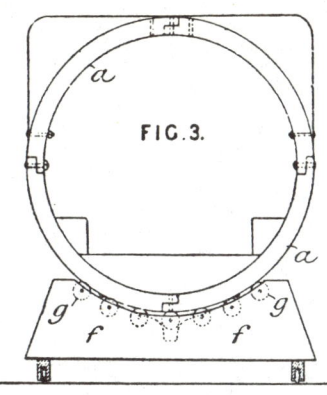

FIG. 3.

Theatrical appliances.—Boats and ships for theatrical displays are formed of hollow cylinders *a* constructed in segments bolted together and supported by friction rollers *g* in a cradle *f*. The apparatus is provided with a winch or crab for rocking the vessel from side to side, and, if necessary, a steam or gas engine may supply the motive power. Suitable clips are furnished for attaching scenery, and the masts and funnels are made easily detachable.

22,515. Gwyer, G. W. Nov. 25.

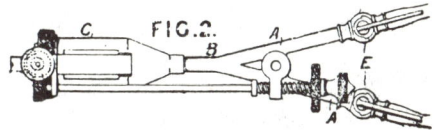

FIG. 2.

Lime-light apparatus.—To ensure a more complete mixture of the oxygen and oxy-ether gases the respective supply pipes A are arranged to discharge into a common pipe B, thus being partially mixed before entering the coned end of the mixing chamber C. Valves E are provided for the regulation of the supply of either gas.

1896

580. Farrell, H. H. Jan. 9.

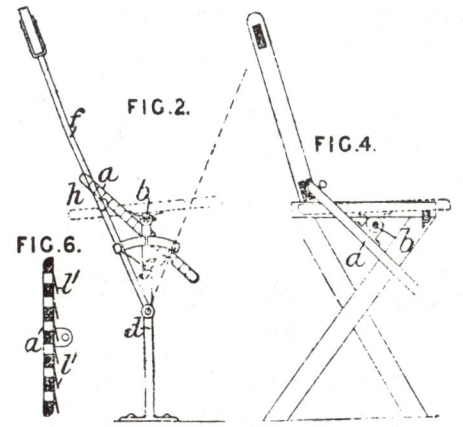

FIG. 2.   FIG. 4.   FIG. 6.

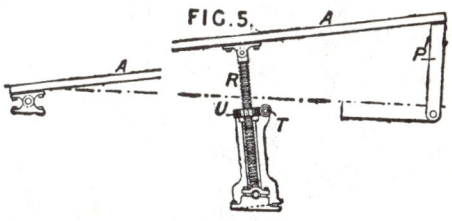

FIG. 5.

Chairs ; seats.—The seat *a* of a theatre, garden, or outdoor, or omnibus, tramcar, or steamer seat is pivoted at *b* to the standards *d* in such a way that when vacated it turns till one of the recesses abuts on the cross bar *h* on the reversible back *f* and so presents the lower surface to the weather. The back abuts against one of the stops *g*. Fig. 4 shows a chair with a similar reversible seat. The bottom may be plain or barred, or partly plain and partly barred, a plate on the underside serving for use as an advertising or notice board. The seat may be lowered as in Fig. 6 ; the louvres *l'* may be advertised on. In the Provisional Specification, it was stated that waterproofed aprons on spring rollers might be provided to protect the seats from the weather.

1626. Horsfall, W., and Berry, R. Jan. 23.

Floors.—The floors of theatres, music halls, schoolrooms, &c. are pivoted centrally or at the ends so that they can be tilted to allow the people at the back to have a good view of the stage or platform. In the arrangement shown in the Figure, the floor A is tilted by a series of screws R working through worm-wheels U operated by screws T on a transverse shaft. Pivoted legs or struts P[1] support the floor in an inclined position. The floor may be tilted by hydraulic jacks, or by a winding drum operated by a worm and wheel, and may be balanced by weights and cords.

2991. Boisset, F. P. Feb. 10.

Acrobatic apparatus.— A pair of standards *c'* carries a shaft *c* upon which a frame *a* or its equivalent is rotated by means of chains *d* passing around sprocket wheels *e*, *f*, the latter of which are on a shaft *g* furnished with cranks, which are operated by a performer *h*. The latter supports himself by holding grips *i*. The rotating frame carries trapezes or hori-

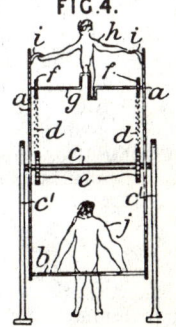

FIG. 4.

zontal bars *b* upon which while revolving one or more acrobats *j* perform.

3249. **Lytton, E.** Feb. 13.

Theatres.—The lower central corners of tableaux curtains A, B are attached to links *c* connected to links *d*, pivoted to blocks or posts at the sides, and are raised simultaneously by cords E, F passing through curtain rings G and over pulleys to a common cord E[1]. The weight of the jointed rods *c, d* tends to close the curtains, preferably so as to overlap one another. The upper edges of the curtain may be fastened to a horizontal beam L which can be raised with the curtains above the proscenium. The rods *d* are pivoted to blocks H, capable of sliding on vertical rods J, or to small carriages running on vertical guide-rails. In order to prevent jamming, the carriage or block H may be connected to the beam by a rod or chain K.

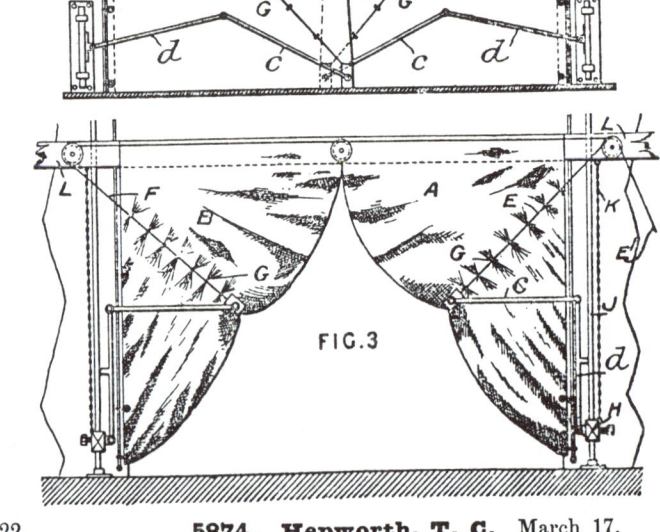

4025. **Niblett, J. T.** Feb. 22.

Theatrical appliances.—Electric lamps are covered with translucent petals or leaves of artificial flowers, or are shaped to represent roses, flowers, &c., or gems, precious stones, &c. may be represented by covering the lamps with coloured glass or material. Or light may be projected from hidden electric lamps on the flowers, ornaments, dresses, scenery, &c. Electricity may be supplied to the lamps by flexible wires, or the performers may carry portable batteries. The luminosity of the lamps may be varied by rheostats or variable resistances controlled by hand, clockwork, or an electrically-driven motor. Each circuit is controlled by a switch operated by the performer or from the wings.

5473. **Hatch, O. B.,** and **Dougall, J. W.** March 11.

Umbrella stands.—A ring A is hinged to a plate B fixed by screws *d* or a clamp to a chair, theatre or other seat, table, counter, &c. The spring D acts on a flat on the part *a* to keep the ring in place. A receptacle C to catch drippings is fixed by a pin and slot *c*[1] to the lower part of the article. The ring may be split and may be of vulcanite, bone, &c. ; it can be hinged so as to turn up or sideways under a counter or table. Instead of a hinge, as shown, the ends of the ring may be sprung into recesses in a projection on the chair &c.

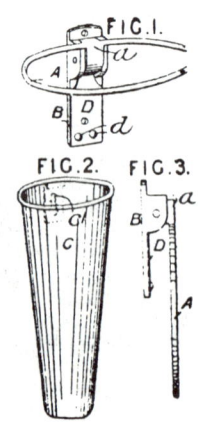

5874. **Hepworth, T. C.** March 17.

Arc lamps.—Carbons for projection lamps using alternating currents are made with soft cores B placed eccentrically in the carbons, as illustrated in section, to produce a better light in one direction. The carbons may be of forms other than round.

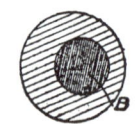

5921. **Shepherd, T.,** and **Simplex Cash Register Syndicate.** March 17.

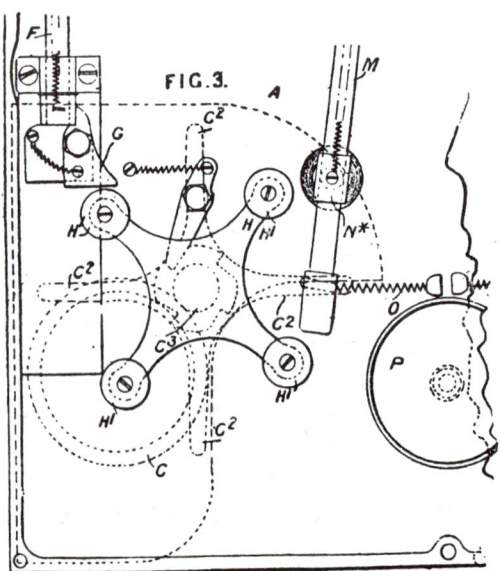

Admission-fees, registering and checking.—The check-issuing window is covered by a grating having one aperture large enough to pass any coin, but too small for the checks. On the table A (an under-plan of which is shown in Fig. 3) is a slotted cylinder C for the checks, on the top of which are placed weights. If variously-priced checks are to be issued, several cylinders are provided of different diameters or shapes. The checks are issued *seriatim* by the arms C², C² on the shaft C³, which is turned through a quarter of a revolution at each actuation of the push-rod F. This is effected by the spring slip pawl G striking the roller H¹ on one of the arms H, also secured to the spindle C³. Simultaneously, another roller pushes back the rod M, sliding in a pivoted sleeve N°, and operates the counting-mechanism. The rods F and M are returned to normal position by springs, and the latter carries the spring hammer O of the bell P, which then rings for each check issued.

6591. Boult, A. J., [*Elton, S.*]. March 25.

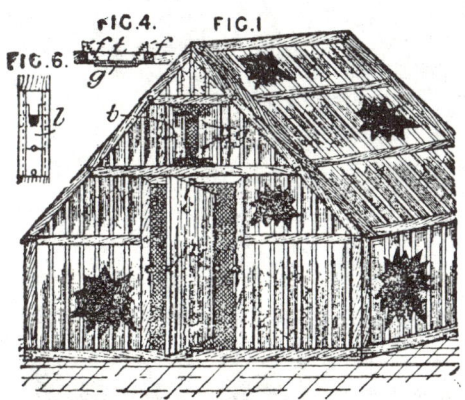

Theatrical appliances.—A canvas or other structure on a wooden framing is painted to represent a greenhouse or the like, and is fitted with a door adapted to turn on central vertical pivots c or horizontal pivots a, and a gable window t, which can be opened inwards or outwards, and is automatically closed by springs f and rubber bands g. Holes in the canvas or other covering are made with jagged edges to represent broken glass, and are temporarily covered by pieces of canvas attached by cotton threads. When an acrobat or performer jumps through one of the holes, he carries the piece of canvas with him, and exposes the jagged hole. The door pivots are retained by forked slides or bearings l, and either pair of pivots can be released by withdrawing the slides.

7511. Cox, F. P. April 9.

Exhibitions, scenic and spectacular; theatres.—

Signs and other devices for advertising and for scenic and spectacular purposes are produced by means of glass or burnished rotating rods or prisms a, which are illuminated by a light h placed in

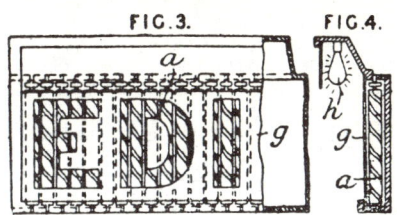

front or behind. Devices &c. may be formed on a front g or otherwise. By spirally grooving the rods &c., and by suitably arranging them, and also by means of reflectors &c., a representation of flowing water, cascades, and other effects may be produced.

9204. Steward, J. H. May 1.

Opera and field glasses.—The eye-glasses H, H¹ are carried by tubes F, F¹ sliding in the outer casing, shown in dotted lines. The tubes are connected to a bridge E, E, which is adjusted for focussing by turning the wheel A, A on the tube B, the slot C acting upon a pin D on a tube working within B and attached to the bridge.

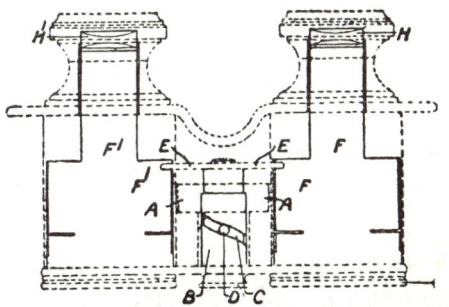

9758. Fanta, F. May 7.

Theatres. — Relates to carpets and other floor coverings having electric conductors therein and to shoes provided with contacts or switches for use in connection therewith for producing lighting effects on the stage. Wires or strips of metal or wire gauze are incorporated

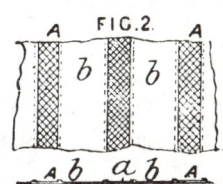

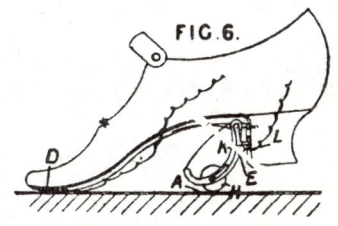

with the carpet during manufacture, or are afterwards attached. Fig. 2 shows an example in which a backing *a* has attached to it conductors A, the intermediate spaces being covered with fabric *b*. Adjacent conductors are connected to opposite poles of the electric battery or generator. The shoes of dancers are fitted with electric contacts in the soles, or heels, or both, or with switches. Fig. 6 shows a shoe with a contact D in the sole, and under the instep a metallic roller H which makes a contact with a strip A in the carpet. When the heel is depressed the circuit is broken owing to the point K on the lever E moving away from the plate L on the heel.

10,063. Bierstadt, A. May 12.

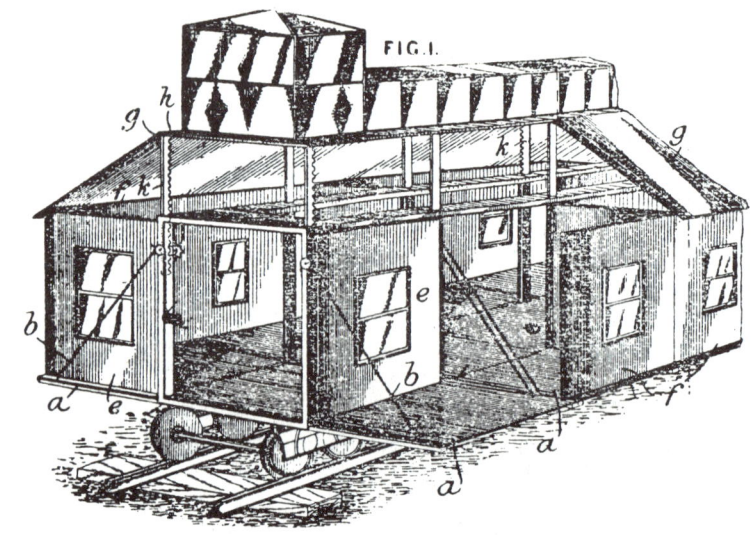

FIG.1.

Portable; collapsable; churches; theatres; concert halls &c.—The sides *a* of a railway car are arranged to be lowered by chains *b* to provide extended floor space, while other hinged parts *c, f, g* are extended to form the sides and roofs. The main roof *h* is raised by racks *k* to provide additional space for light and air. Two carriages may be placed near one another and the adjacent sides connected so as to form one hall. Arrangements may be made by which the expansion and contraction of all parts of the building are made simultaneously from one source of power.

11,013. Courtneidge, R. May 21.

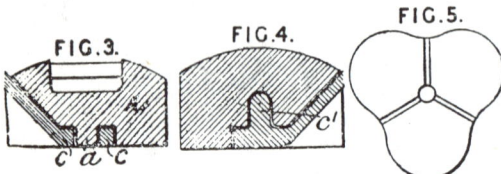

FIG.3.   FIG.4.   FIG.5.

distance between the glasses may be adjusted for focus. Detail may be varied.

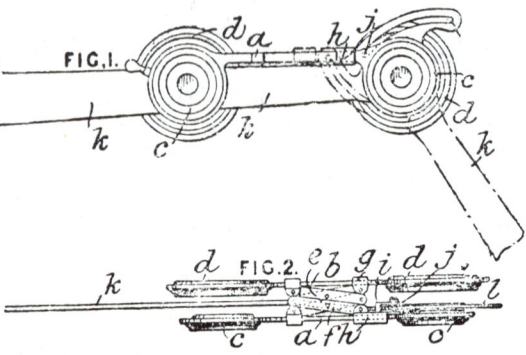

FIG.1.

FIG.2.

Theatres.—The braces or iron rods C, fixed to the scenery, are held down on the stage floor by recessed weights A, which are provided with central pins *a* adapted to enter eyes or holes in the braces. In a modification, shown in Fig. 4, a pin *c* of the brace enters a hole in the weight. The weights may be circular in plan, or of the form shown in Fig. 5.

11,544. Bloch, E. May 27.

Opera glasses.—Relates to the type provided with a long handle. The object glasses *d, d* and eye-glasses *c, c* have their frames *a, b* connected by lazy-tongs *e, f*, one lever of each being secured to the frames and the others to sliding sockets *g, h*. The handle *k* turns about one of the eye-glasses, and has a slotted extension *l* engaging a pin *j* projecting from the bracket *i* on the socket *h*. By turning the handle through a required angle, the

11,922. Dalman, G. H. B. June 1.

Tickets.—Railway, steamboat, omnibus, tramway, theatre, or other tickets are made in the form of cases, in which may be placed an insurance voucher or policy. The case A, which may be of fine paper strengthened with textile fabric or of other suitable material, may have a flap

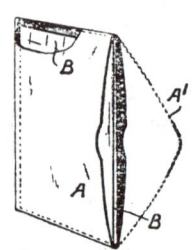

A[1] closed by ordinary
means. The policy B may
be a card or folded sheet, held in place by fitting
tightly or with the aid of gum. For railway and
like tickets, the policy may have a map of the
route on the back, with suitable information re-
garding the journey &c., the spare spaces being
filled with advertisements.

17,132. Schmidt, A. E. Aug. 1.

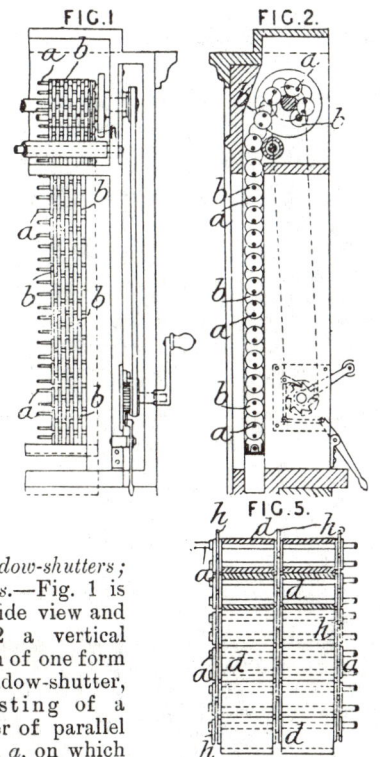

*Window-shutters;
theatres.*—Fig. 1 is
an inside view and
Fig. 2 a vertical
section of one form
of window-shutter,
consisting of a
number of parallel
rods *a, a*, on which
are threaded metal
discs *b, b*. In place
of discs, rings may be used, or, as shown in Fig. 5,
tubes *d, d* may take the places of the rings and
discs. A pair of rods *a, a* is passed through each
tube, and one rod of each pair is connected to one
of the adjoining pair by links *h, h*. Fireproof
curtains for theatres may be similarly constructed.

19,251. Walters, A. Sept. 1.

Chairs; seats; shelves and shelving.—A shelf
to receive a hat, parcel, &c. is hinged at *c*[1] to a
frame *b*, having cross-bars *b*[1], pivoted at *b*[x], and is
supported at the front by a chain &c. *c*[2]. When not
in use the shelf is folded as in Fig. 1, and retained
by a catch *d*. The shelf may be supported by a
lazy-tongs arrangement, Figs. 4 and 5, so arranged
that the catch *e*[1] is released on pressure being put on
the seat.

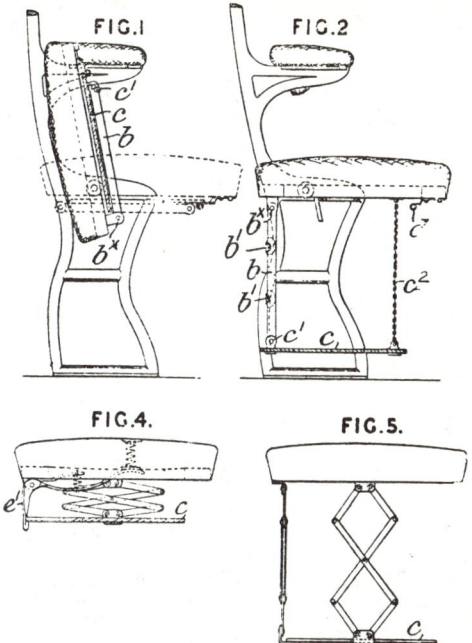

23,549. Conquest, G. A. O. Oct. 23.

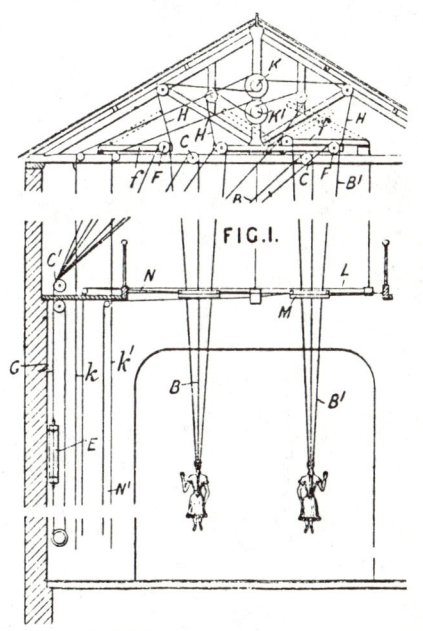

Theatrical appliances.—Relates to apparatus for
raising figures such as fairies in pantomimes, and
tilting them, or moving them across the stage. A
central lifting-wire B is attached to the upper part
of each figure near the neck, and side tilting wires
B[1] are attached to the waist. These wires pass
between guide - pulleys of horizontal sliding
travellers M over pulleys C, F, C[1], and are

attached to a weight E carried by an endless operating wire G. Levers *f* carrying the pulleys F are raised for the purpose of tilting the performers by wires H, H¹ from drums K, K¹, which are operated by hand-wires *k*, *k*¹. The travellers or runners M are moved along horizontal guide and supporting wires L by wires N, N¹.

24,883. Aitchison, J. Nov. 6.

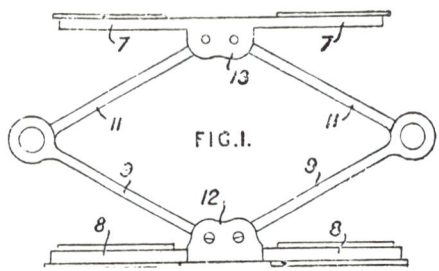

FIG. 1.

Telescopes &c.—Relates to improvements in the glasses described in Specification No. 1016, A.D. 1891. The collapsable barrels are dispensed with, and the frames 7, 8 of the eye and object glasses are connected by double hinged links 9, 9, 11, 11 pivoted in the cases 12, 13. where they are geared so as to ensure the parallelism of the frame 7, 8 and coincidence of the axes of the glasses. This gear may consist of forks at the ends of the links engaging studs on plates sliding parallel to the optical axis. The links 9, 9, 11, 11 are curved so as to clear the line of sight. The mechanism, in a modified form, may be applied to monoculars &c

26,783. Grant, L. Nov. 25. *Drawings to Specification.*

Bar-bells.—Relates to employing light bar-bells or wands, either with plain or ornamental ends, for the use of dancers.

26,795. Stott, J. Nov. 26.

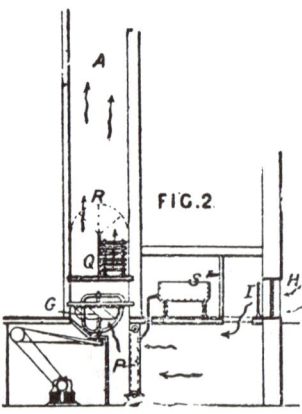

FIG. 2

Heating buildings.—Relates to a method of ventilating theatres, churches, and the like, in which the air may be heated, cooled, or otherwise treated. Fig. 2 shows in section the arrangements

by which air is admitted into the building. Entering by an inlet H near the ground, the air passes through a radiator I consisting of pipes heated by hot water or steam, then through an endless rotating screen P (as described in Specification No. 5086, A.D. 1894), which may be moistened with scent, then through the air-propeller G (driven by an electromotor), then through a second heater Q into the shaft A which leads to a receptacle over the ceiling. From this receptacle the air is discharged through a number of openings into the room or space to be ventilated. The foul air is drawn off through doors or hit-and-miss ventilators placed near the floor, and connected to uptake shafts leading up to the roof of the building.

27,472. Gaitton, E. Dec. 2.

Theatrical appliances.—In order to produce a racing scene on the stage, the animals are placed on endless bands or tracks B which are mounted on rollers F and driven by endless bands E in a direction opposite to the motion of the animals. The roller spindles are mounted on anti-friction wheels running in an oil bath, or are held in bearings by sliding detachable notched plates and clips.

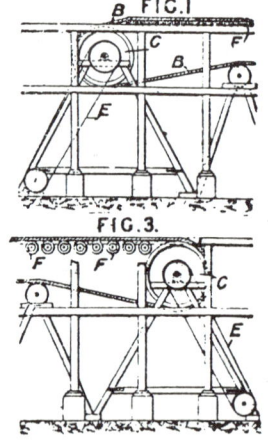

FIG. 1

FIG. 3.

The driving-drums C are preferably constructed of transverse wooden slats, nailed to sheet-metal drums on skeleton frames. A panorama screen and scenery are caused to travel in a direction opposite to the horses, and currents or blasts of air are blown on the jockeys. Booths, bookmakers, tumblers, jugglers, &c. are represented about the course.

29,620. Tabulewitch, V. Dec. 23.

Theatrical appliances.—An electric lamp for theatrical effects is provided with carbon positive and steel negative electrodes, which are pressed together by a spring or weight but are separated electromagnetically, so that a rapid succession of electric discharges is produced between them. Coloured light may be produced by adding pyrotechnic salts to the carbons. In the portable lantern illustrated, the steel electrode 19 is made with a head which is held between springs in a socket 23, carried by rods 20. The carbon 18 is clamped in a split tube 6, held up by a lever 8 and spring 15. The upper part of the tube 6 is of iron, and is drawn down with the carbon by a surrounding coil 1 in series with the carbon, when a sufficient current passes. The lamp may be inverted, in which case the carbon-holder falls by

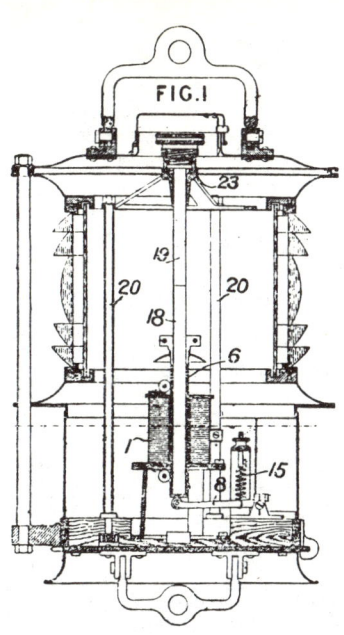

FIG.1.

gravity, and is raised by the coil. To increase the light produced, the current to the lamp passes through a number of parallel self-induction coils; these are wound on soft iron cores projecting from an iron bar. Several such sets of coils may be connected in parallel.

1897

1274. Grogan, S. Jan. 18.

Theatrical appliances.—
A tunic B, fastened at the back by hooks and eyes, or other fastenings, has the belts and accoutrements of a lancer, Uhlan, or cavalryman stitched to it in place, and a short skirt reaching to, or below, the knees of the actress, has rows of military braid stitched to the sides after the manner of trouser stripes. The performers are provided with lances and pennants, and go through various military exercises and dances on the stage.

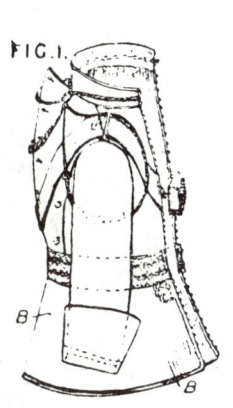

FIG.1.

3102. Kunkel, C. Feb. 5.

Door and gate opening apparatus; hinges.—
Relates to means for enabling the fastenings of the doors and gates, either single or double, of a large building, theatre, &c. to be opened from a central place. A divided sliding-bolt s, s^1 is maintained in the locked position shown by a spring hook f^3 engaging with a lever h which can be moved sideways to release the hook and bolt by expanding the pneumatic bulb b or by depressing the hand-lever h^1, causing a rod s^2, having a wedge-shaped upper end, to rise and displace the lever h. The bolt is disengaged by a spring f. A locking-

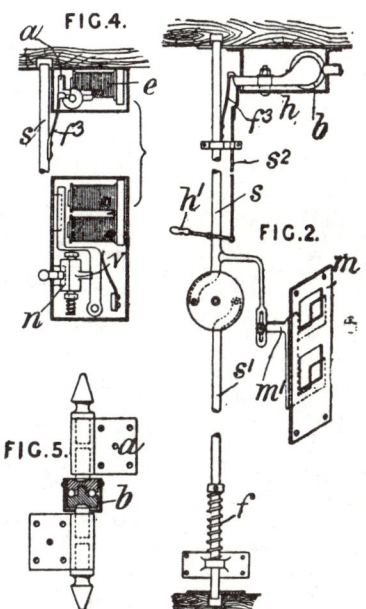

FIG.4. FIG.2. FIG.5.

plate m^1, sliding behind the striking-plate m, falls with the bolt s, s^1, and allows the halves of a double door to open without retracting the lock bolts. The pneumatic release may be replaced by an electromagnetic one, Fig. 4. On completing a circuit, the armature a of an electromagnet e is attracted, releasing a lug v on a cylinder n, and allowing the latter to rotate and release the hook

f^3, previously engaging with a notch on the cylinder. Springs of any desired construction are provided to open the doors when the fastenings are released. To ensure easy opening, the flaps a, Fig. 5, of the hinges are connected by a ball bearing formed in enlarged ends b secured to or in one with the flaps.

3419. Atroy, J. Feb. 9.

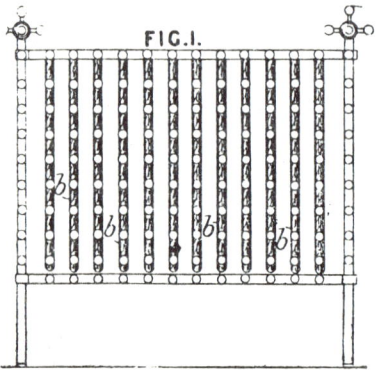

FIG. I.

Exhibitions, theatres, &c.—Relates to bells played by agitating the ropes b on which they are carried. The ropes are also furnished with electric lights and produce a spectacular effect. Electric lights may also be placed on the frame which supports the ropes.

4400. Armour, J. G., and **Southorn, C.** Feb. 18.

Chairs. — A set of standards 1 for a row of theatre seats simply rest on the floor or slide into fixed socks 20, Fig. 9; they are connected at the base by rods engaging screws 5 and fixed by nuts 6; they are bound together at the top by the seat backs, which have shoulders resting on the parts 18 and studs engaging keyhole slots 14. The arms have studs engaging keyhole slots 14; the studs are dropped in, and the arms slid forward, after which the backs are put ⟩and prevent the arms from moving back. Pivots on the seats drop into slots 9. Flanges

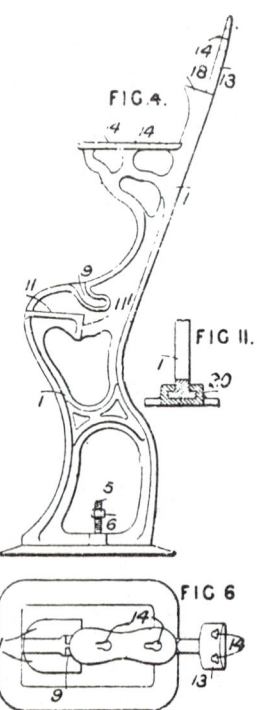

FIG. 4.

FIG II.

FIG 6

11, 11^1 hold the seat in a horizontal or turned-up position. Any arm, back, seat, or standard can be removed for upholstering &c. The backs and arms may have dovetailed projections engaging corresponding recesses in the standards. The end standards have the flanges 11, 13 and sockets 9 on one side only.

6389. Hengler, A. March 11.

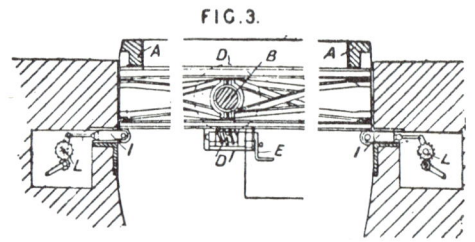

FIG. 3.

Circuses; theatres; floors.—A circular stage A is mounted on horizontal trunnions B, and is tilted or reversed, for producing scenic effects, by a crank E, worm D^1, and worm-wheel D. When in position, the stage is supported at opposite sides by bolts I operated simultaneously by shafts L, cranks, and connecting-rods. The stage may be fitted with trap-doors and scenery, and one side may be formed as a trough to hold water.

8645. Batault, E. April 5.

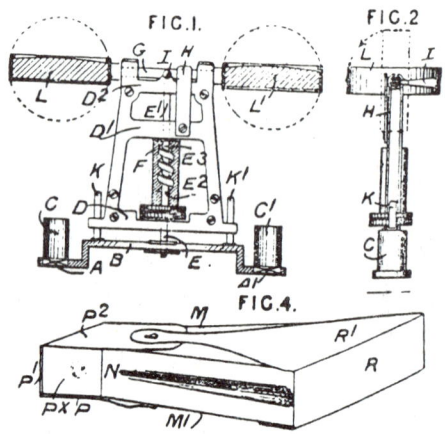

FIG. I.   FIG. 2.

FIG. 4.

Opera glasses, folding. The object-glasses L, L^1 are carried by a spindle G, pivoted in the spring arms of a frame D, D^1, D^2, which can be set in either of two positions at right-angles, and held there by flat faces on the spindle being engaged by the spring H and by the handle I coming against stops. The eye-glasses A, A^1 are carried by a bar B, and have small tubes C, C^1, which act as diaphragms. The focussing-adjustment is effected by a nut F acting on a screw E^2, E^3 on the rod E, E^1 secured to the bar B, the motion being guided by pins K, K^1. Preferably the glasses are secured to the casing shown in Fig. 4, which excludes extraneous light when the glasses are in use. This consists of an upper and lower plate M, M¹ connected by collapsable sides N, a rigid case P× surrounding the eye-glasses, and two flaps P, P¹, P² and R, R¹ which, when carrying the glasses, are folded as shown. When it is desired to use the opera-glass the flap P, P¹, P² is folded flat on the plate M¹, the part R folds over to secure them, and the part R¹ acts as a handle.

8983. Schmidt, A. E.   April 8.

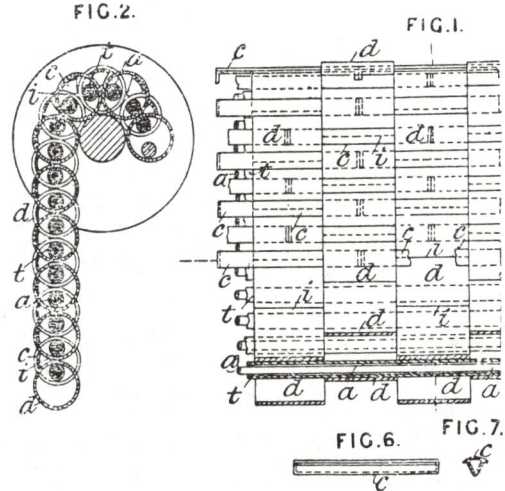

FIG.2.   FIG.1.

FIG.6.   FIG.7.

Window-shutters ; theatrical appliances.—A roller shutter screen or theatre curtain is made up of a number of rings or short tubes d which are placed so as to break joint and which are connected by tubes t through which pass rods a connected at the ends by links. Filling-pieces c, Figs. 6 and 7, of suitable lengths are inserted endwise and fill up the intermediate hollows i and prevent the insertion of burglars' tools. Triangular rods or tubes may be used instead of the filling-pieces C.

12,735. Reinold, J., and Reinold, P. J. May 22.

Chairs ; seats.—The back D is fixed to the sides of a railway or tramway carriage compartment or to the upright standards of a theatre chair, bench, form, &c. The lath seat a, a^i is connected at the front to parts H sliding on guides. The legs are telescopic, or are in parts capable of sliding one on the other, or are provided with pins and slots to allow the seat to slide. The legs are pivoted at each end and are pressed forward by springs Q. The seat is further supported by an L-shaped piece L and a fixed guide M. Rollers R and a guide F¹ facilitate the entrance of the seat behind the back. The cushion U, U¹ is in two parts, hinged together and to the seat and back.

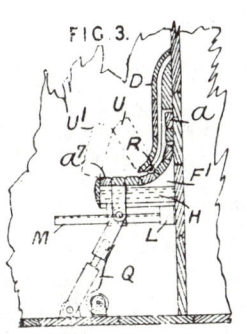

FIG.3.

14,882. Walters, A.   June 19.

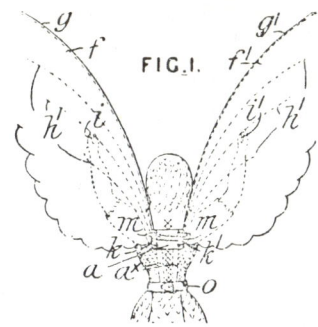

FIG.I.

Theatrical appliances.—The stage artiste is dressed in a suitable costume provided with a pair of wings f, f^1, and a realistic bird effect is produced by the aid of coloured lights. The wings are made of white silk or other material supported by spring ribs g, g^1, h, h^1, and are attached to flaps k, k^1, pivoted to a back-plate a. Loops or tags i, i^1 are attached to the wings for the purpose of manipulation, and springs m cause the flaps to project at right-angles to the back-plate when the wings are released. The back-plate is constructed of two parts connected by eyes or staples and a locking-pin. Each part carries a shoulder strap, hook, or spring, and a flat spring or plate $a×$ which is attached to the waist band or belt o. The wings can be moved backwards or forwards, or up and down, or be folded over the body.

15,723. Schmidt, G.   July 1.

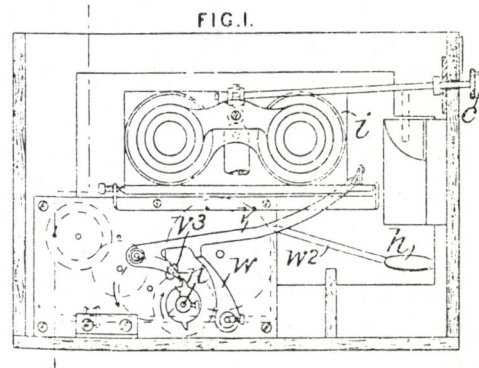

FIG.I.

Hiring opera-glasses and telescopes.—The coin depresses the plate h which is connected by the lever w^2 to the lever w, the movement of which allows the lever v to fall, swinging the plate i connected therewith from in front of the glasses. A pin v^3 on the lever v at the same time moves so as to allow the clockwork to start, its motion being continued until one of the projections on the wheel n lifts the lever v, bringing the levers &c. into their former condition and stopping the motion. The apparatus is rotatably mounted on a vertical axis and can be also raised and lowered, while the glasses are adjusted by the button c.

17,229. Shipman, F. W. July 21.

Theatrical appliances.—A series of plane vertical mirrors *a*, at the back of the stage, and revolving columns *b*, *c* having mirrors fixed to the sides, are arranged in a semicircle to produce multiple images of persons, scenery, and objects on the stage.

FIG.I.

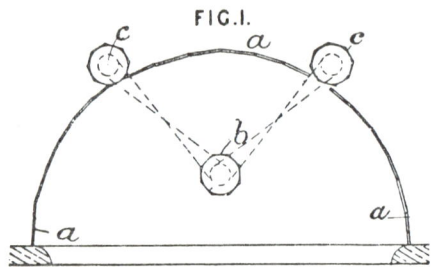

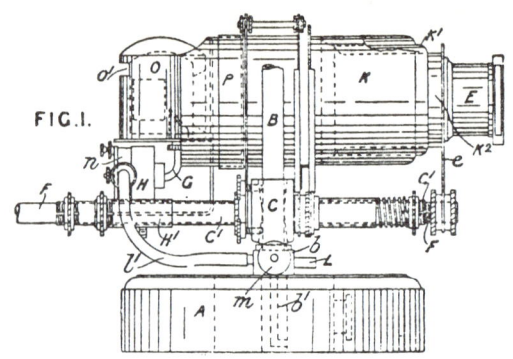

FIG.I.

17,438. Sweetser, A. July 24.

Limelight apparatus.—The oxygen gas from the supply pipe L partly passes through the block *b* and the flexible pipe *l*[1] to the mixing-chamber H, and partly descends the passage *b*[1] to the ether or hydrocarbon saturator formed by the hollow base A, thence traversing a similar block *b* and flexible pipe on the opposite side of the lantern to the mixing-chamber H. Cocks *m* control the gas supplies through the plugs *b*, and the flexible tubes may be connected to the hollow arms of a plug *n*, by turning which the communication with the mixing-chamber H is cut off, except for a small bye-pass. The refractory combustion chamber O has an opening O[1] for the escape of the heat and fumes from the jet. Two or more lanterns may be mounted on the hollow pillars B, which then carry the gases to the upper lantern or lanterns; the parts of the lantern may be adjusted longitudinally by means of the sliding tubes F, C[1], H[1]; and the whole lantern may be rocked upon the supports C for the purpose of adjusting the position of the disc on the screen without necessitating the tilting of the base of the lantern.

17,665. Leighton, J. T. July 28.

Theatrical appliances.—Devices for producing stage effects consist of a corrugated &c. front plate of glass which is let into a frame and backed at some distance with foil or the like to produce a lustrous effect. The interior may be fitted with mirrors at the sides. The designs &c. which are put on the front may be illuminated by a lamp at the rear. Advertisements may also be placed within the frame at the back.

17,747. Boult, A. J., [*Bellet, F.*]. July 28.

FIG.2.

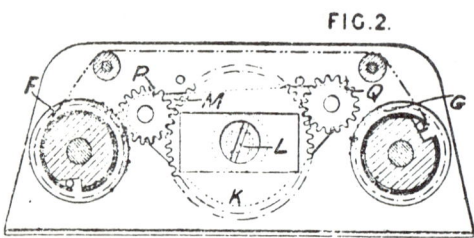

Panoramas.—Relates to reversing-gearing applicable in all apparatus in which a film, band, ribbon, or the like is to be moved or wound up in one or the other direction, such for instance as roller devices for photographic, stereoscopic, or panoramic apparatus, graphoscopes, magic-lanterns, registering-apparatus, type-writers, &c. The driving-spindle L, turned by means of a milled head, carries a toothed wheel K and a loose plate M upon which are mounted pinions P, Q in gear with the wheel K and adapted to engage alternately with wheels F, G secured upon the rollers. The plate is tilted to change the gear, when the direction of the rotation of the spindle L is changed, by frictional connection with the wheel K against which it is pressed by a spring.

18,925. Moss, R. J. Aug. 16.

Magic-lantern lamps.—When two or more burners *p*[1], *p*[2] are used, each burner is connected by separate supply pipes *b*[1], *b*[2] and gas cocks *c*[1] with the main supply pipe *a*[2]. This pipe terminates in a sleeve *a*[4], which, by means of a set-screw, may be adjusted both vertically and horizontally upon the pillar *r*; and the reflector *g* may be vertically adjusted upon the rod *e*, which is carried by connected sleeves *d*[1], *d*[2], capable of sliding horizontally upon the burner tubes *b*[1], *b*[2].

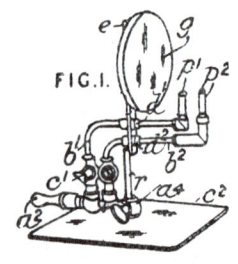

FIG.I.

19,255. **Barton, J. H.,** and **Stuart, J.** Aug. 20.

Opera and field glasses.—Relates to glasses of the prismatic type, designed for reducing the length of the instrument. The two prismatic telescopes are mounted in bodies or casings *a, b* which can turn about the axes of the objectives so that the distance apart of the eye-pieces *j, j* can be varied to suit different persons without altering that between the objectives. Simultaneity of movement is ensured by the toothed sectors *l, m,* a recess *m²* and pin *n* limiting the motion. Focussing is effected by turning a milled head *f²,* the spindle *f* of which carries a screw working in a wedge-shaped block *e.* The eye-pieces slide on tubes *k, k,* and are connected by arms *h, i* with the plates *g, g²,* the arms being pivoted to turn about the axis of the objectives.

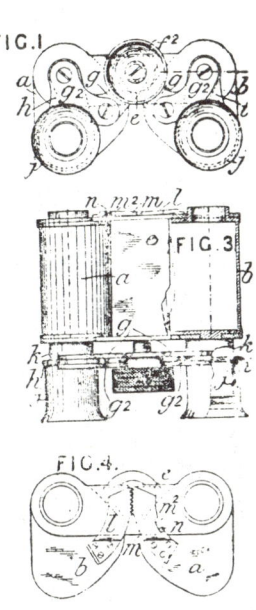

19,472. Vernici, I. Aug. 24.

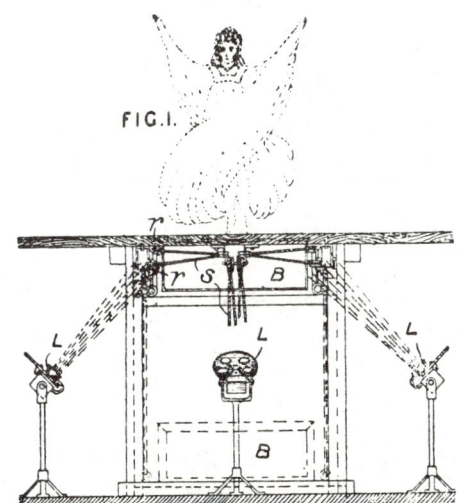

Theatrical appliances.—A serpentine dancer goes through her performance on a glass plate level with the stage, and is illuminated from below by lights projected by reflectors L at the sides and front. The glass platform is secured in a frame B which can be raised and lowered by cords *s* passing over pulleys *r.*

25,864. **Meysel, G.,** (*called* Myselli). Nov. 6.

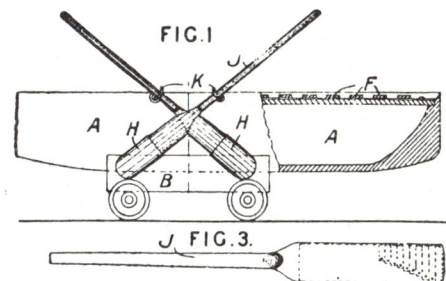

Theatrical appliances.—A novel musical performance is given on the stage by means of instruments attached to, or forming parts of, boats, sculls, bicycles, and chest pads for boxers. Fig. 1 shows a boat A mounted on a carriage B, and provided with strips of glass or metal F which

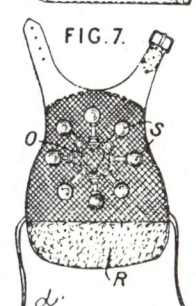

are struck by hammers. The boat is divided transversely into halves which are connected together by screws and wing nuts. The oars J fit in pockets H and hooks K at the side of the boat, and each blade is in the form of a Pan's-pipe. A bicycle for producing a comical effect is made without pedals and with abnormally thick india-rubber tyres. The handle-bar carries a number of tuned bells which are sounded by hammers acted on by coiled springs controlled by knobs, levers, springs, &c. Fig. 7 shows a boxing doublet or jacket fitted with india-rubber air balls S and musical pipes or wind instruments which are sounded when the balls are struck. The doublet is made of two layers of linen lined with wire gauze, and is stuffed with seaweed, wood wool, or the like at the lower part R. A central heart-shaped sound-hole O is provided, or several apertures may be made to allow the sound to escape.

26,387. Ormerod, J. B. Nov. 12.

Theatrical appliances ; struts.—The object of the invention is to prevent damage to canvas scenes when packed for transport. Instead of using projecting eye screws, the hooked diagonal struts *e* engage with eye plates *a* hinged to the frames *b.* These plates fold into recesses in the frame when the struts are detached.

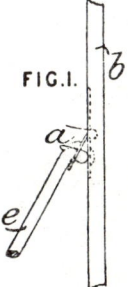

26,413. Schumann, A. Nov. 12.

Circuses; theatrical appliances.—A bed or sofa for a performing horse or other animal is mounted on wheels, and provided at one end with a cushion, against which the animal pushes with its head in order to wheel the bed into the arena. The animal fetches a mattress, pillow, and counterpane, and after getting into bed pulls a handle or cloth C at the end of a rope attached to a catch which

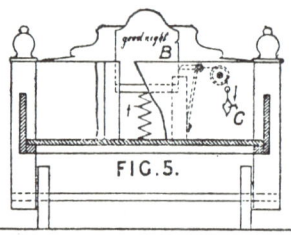

FIG. 5.

holds a board B in a concealed position. This board is marked with an inscription such as 'good night,' and is forced upwards by a spring or weight when the catch is withdrawn.

26,611. McLennan, K. Nov. 15.

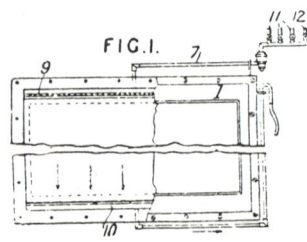

FIG. I.

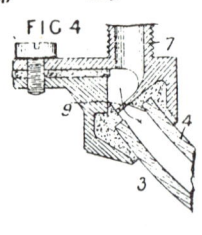

FIG 4

Theatrical appliances.—Changeable coloured lighting effects are produced by placing a narrow glass tank or frame 1, containing coloured liquid, in front of the source of light.

Three pipes 11 supply red, blue, and yellow liquids to the inlet pipe 7, and water is supplied by a pipe 12. These pipes are provided with valves or cocks so that any desired tint of liquid can be obtained. As fresh liquid is supplied through a perforated strip or cover 9, an equal quantity escapes through an outlet channel and pipe 10. The sheets of glass may be moulded with figures, ornaments, lettering, advertisements, &c. In a modification shown in Fig. 4, convex sheets of glass 3, 4 are secured in a circular frame.

28,602. Geller, J. Dec. 3.

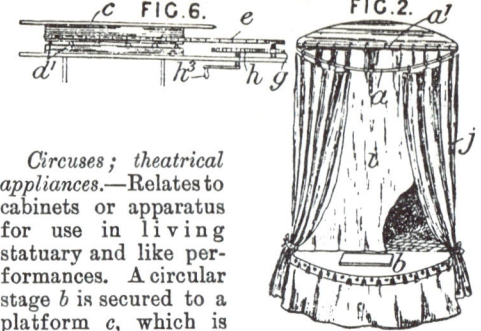

Circuses; theatrical appliances.—Relates to cabinets or apparatus for use in living statuary and like performances. A circular stage *b* is secured to a platform *c*, which is mounted on rollers *d*[1] and can be rotated on a central pivot by a handle *h*[3], toothed wheels *h, g*, and an endless chain *e*. Black velvet or other curtains *i, j* are suspended from a cross-bar *a*[1] and ring *a* supported by vertical jointed tubular rods. The central curtain *i* divides the cabinet into two parts, one of which may be used as a dressing-compartment. When arranged in a circus ring, the platform is rotated to bring the performers into the view of the audience in all parts of the circus.

28,859. Stewart & Co., D., and **Lyon, H.** Dec. 7.

Switches.—Liquid resistances with dipping cones, such as are described in Specification No. 5474, A.D. 1890, are used in pairs, with supporting cords and pulleys, for supplying either of two motor circuits, or any of a number of circuits for stage lighting, or, as illustrated, for controlling motors for cranes and other purposes. In this arrange-

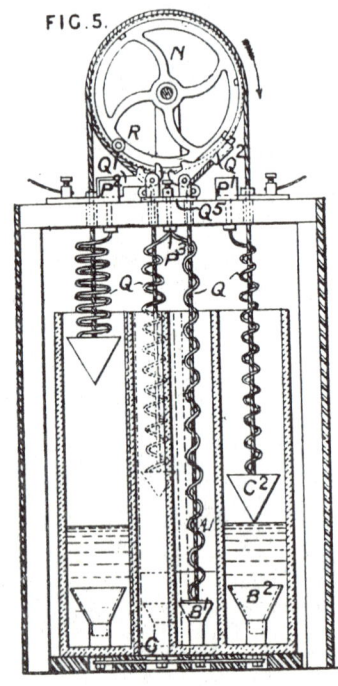

FIG. 5.

ment, four earthenware or other jars contain resistant liquid and four hollow metal cones B^1, B^2, all connected to one supply conductor C. Four other cones C^2 are hung from a pulley N, one pair at each side, and are connected electrically by flexible conductors Q. Two of these, on opposite sides, and optionally with smaller jars, are connected through the terminal P^3 to one end of the shunt field circuit of the motor, which is thus gradually supplied with current in one direction when the pulley N is turned in either direction. The other two upper cones are connected by terminals P^1, P^2 to the motor armature. Switches Q^1, Q^2, operated by a roller R on the pulley N, connect either terminal P^1, P^2, the cone of which is raised, with a plate Q^5 connected to the second supply conductor. The armature is thus supplied with a regulated current in either direction, depending on the direction and extent of turning of the pulley N. For regulating stage lighting, the pulleys of a number of pairs of cells are placed on one long shaft, on which they may be separately turned or fixed by screw handles, and the shaft may be turned by gearing; the cells may be connected with various circuits by plug couplings.

1898

4007. Boult, A. J., [*Schaffhirt, O.*]. Feb. 17.

Opera-glasses.— The objective and eye-glass frames *a, g* are connected by collapsable bellows *h, h*. They carry respectively guide-rods *b, f* to parts *c, c* and *x, x* on which are pivoted the ends of lazy-tongs *d, d, e, e* operated by finger-pieces d^1, d^2. The right-hand parts *c* and *x* slide on the guide-rods as the glasses are folded. To retain the focus adjustment when once found, a screw stop *l* is arranged on a screw *k*; or this may be on a separate spindle adjusted by a milled head from the side.

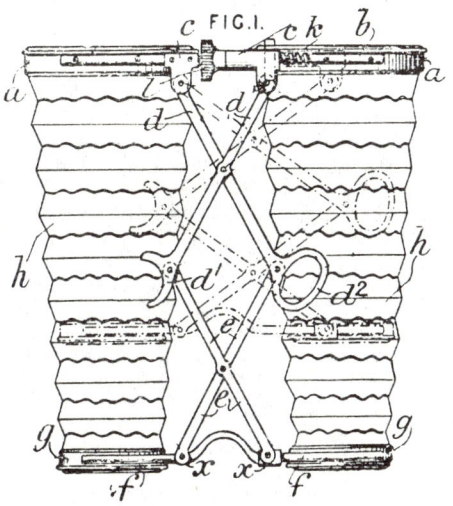

4761. Emmott, W. Feb. 26.

Lighting, systems of; switches.—Relates to a means for controlling the light from lamps, such as theatre lamps, supplied with alternating current. An impedance coil, divided into sections, is included in the circuit, and a switch is provided for varying the number of sections in the circuit. In the arrangement shown in Fig. 1, the impedance coil 1 is of the construction described in Specification No. 21,236, A.D. 1896, and its sections are connected to the contacts of a switch 10. In a modified arrangement, adapted to be operated by clockwork or otherwise for advertising purposes, a rotary drum fitted with contacts rubs on circularly-disposed contacts.

4886. Clark, H. M. Feb. 28.

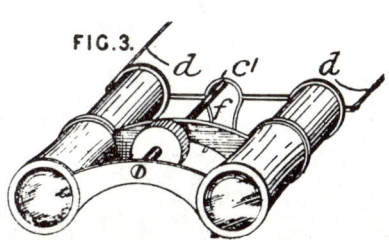

Opera and field glasses.—Opera-glasses, binoculars, and the like are fitted with spectacle bows *d, d*, a bridge c^1, and a resilient nose clip *f*, so that they can be worn and leave the hands free.

5532. Barber, T. W. March 7.

Exhibitions, scenic and spectacular; panoramas.—Relates to optical lanterns for projecting cycloramic views on a cylindrical screen. The lantern comprises eight or more projecting lenses A, with condensers D, mounted on a horizontal annular table C so as to be capable of angular and radial adjustment. The condensers D are of rectangular form, and fit loosely in the cells W. The slide-carriers F are operated simultaneously, to change the pictures, by rack-and-pinion gearing, and adjustable diaphragms are provided for registering the different segments of the

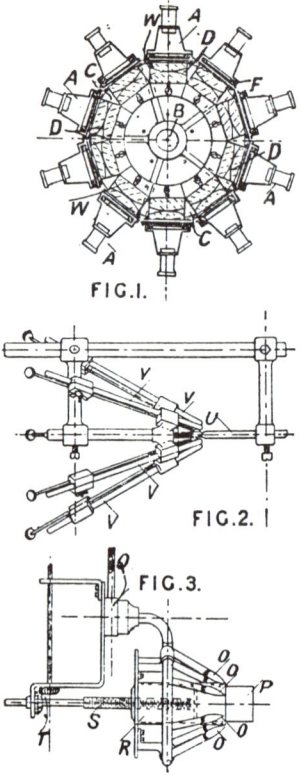

FIG.1.

FIG.2.

FIG.3.

picture on the screen. The projecting-light consists of a centrally-arranged lamp B, which may be an arc lamp having a single positive carbon U and several adjustable negative carbons V, Fig. 2, or a lime-light having a series of jets O &c. surrounding the lime P and supplied from a mixing-chamber B. Two or more limes P are placed in the tube R, and are fed forward to the jets, as required, by the screw S and bevel gearing T. When portions only of the views are to be projected, to form a background for kinematographic pictures, those portions of the views which are not to be projected are masked by suitably-shaped pieces of opaque material, such as paper, and the material from which such pieces have been cut is used to mask and register the kinematographic pictures.

5694. Grade, G. March 8.

Acrobatic apparatus.—Rotating apparatus for enabling several acrobats to perform at one time. A vertical shaft *a*, rotated by a pulley *i* and chain *k*, is enclosed within a tube *b* supported by a disc *s* and held in position by legs *c* and guy ropes *d*. The shaft *a* supports a hoop *r* which rotates with the shaft, and which carries four separate acrobatic devices, namely, the two balancing &c. devices I, II, the trapeze III, and the platform IV. Each balancing-device consists of two hollow arms *l* adjustable on the hoop, which are braced together, and have adjustable rods *n* with handles *e* sliding therein.

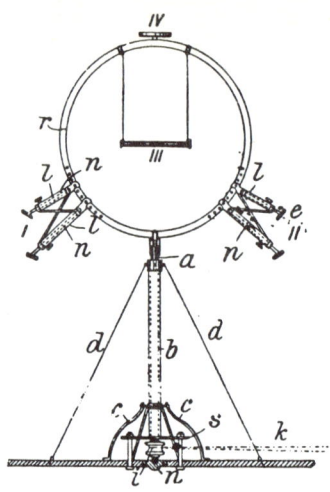

8261. Winslow, F. E. April 6.

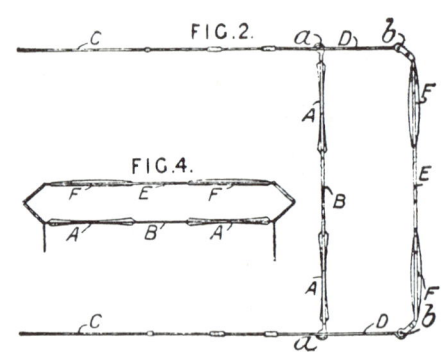

FIG.2.

FIG.4.

Spectacles and eyeglasses; opera-glasses.— An opera-glass arrangement of lenses A, A, F, F is mounted in frames B, E connected by sliding bars D, D and ordinary wings C, C so that the lens frames can be pulled apart as far as is required. When not in use, the frames may be pushed together and the pivots *a*, *a*, *b*, *b* of the wings and bars then come over each other so that the wings and bars can be folded in the ordinary manner. Fig. 4 shows another method of connecting the frames. The invention may also be applied to lorgnettes or "quizzing glasses." In this case the two sides of the case are hinged together near the bottom and each carries a lens frame. By squeezing the two sides of the case together at the bottom, against the action of a spring, the upper ends can be separated as required, while the parallelism of the lens frames is maintained by a lazy-tongs linkage. Spring catches are provided for holding the lens frames in their open or closed position.

8286. Parsonage, C. April 7.

Magic-lanterns.—The slides of magic-lanterns for advertising and other purposes are carried on holders A which are hinged together to form an endless chain passing over four pivoted boxes or blocks B. One of the latter is actuated by clock-work &c. so as to move the slides intermittently, an interval of rest of a few seconds being allowed for the display of each slide.

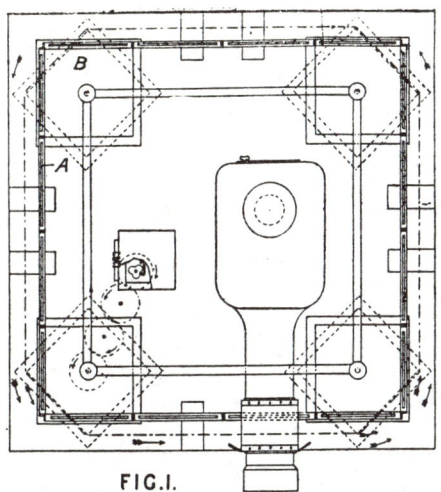

FIG.I.

8559. Kirby, G. April 12

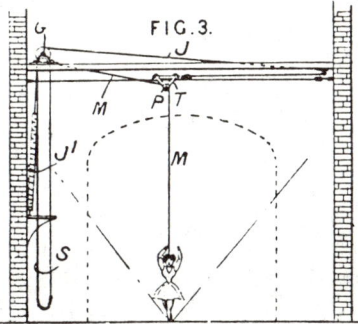

FIG.3.

Theatrical appliances.—Relates to 'flying' apparatus. Fig. 3 shows an arrangement for lifting or lowering an artiste from or to either side of the stage. The rope M, which passes round the pulley P of the traveller T, is wrapped round a sheave on the drum G, and the rope J attached to the traveller is wrapped round another sheave on the same drum. Two other sheaves on this drum, having their ropes wrapped in opposite directions, are connected by the bight S, while the rope of a fifth sheave is connected to the india-rubber cord J^1 shackled to the stage. Modifications are described for lifting or lowering one or two artistes vertically.

9511. Clémançon, C. E. April 25.

Regulating ; lighting, systems of.—Rheostats applicable for regulating lamp circuits for stage lighting, and for other purposes, may be rotated by hand, or by electric, gas, water-pressure, or other motors, which may be controlled from a distance. The rheostat may consist of wire fixed on the surface of a drum a in a zig-zag manner, or

wound on the rim of a wheel. One end of the wire is connected with a contact ring and brush, and the drum or wheel is rotatable so that any part of the wire may be brought in contact with mercury in the trough c below it. A method of controlling an electric motor f for this purpose is specified. The field of the motor is connected directly between the mains + —. The armature f is connected through a reversing-switch h, a speed-regulating rheostat k, and a cut-out j to the mains. In order to indicate near the switches the position of the main rheostat a, the drum of this carries a number of projecting studs e and springs, which come in contact with a lever n, and thus

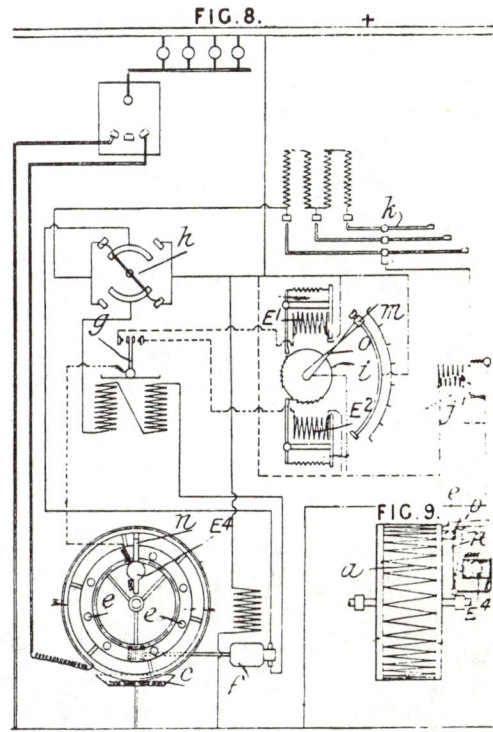

intermittently close an indicator circuit. This circuit includes the armature g of a polarized relay, the magnet of which is in the motor armature circuit, so that the relay armature completes the indicator circuit through either of two magnets E^1, E^2, depending on the direction of the motor current. These magnets have spring-actuated armatures formed as pawls, acting oppositely on a ratchet-wheel i, which carries a pointer o. Each current received from a stud e on the main rheostat a thus moves the pointer a step forward or backward in accordance with the direction in which the motor and rheostat are moving. In order that reversal of the motor current while the lever n is on a stud e may not operate the indicator, the indicator circuit includes an electromagnet E^4, which lifts the contact-lever n from each stud on to an adjacent supporting-spring p, immediately after contact has been made. A movable piece m

may be placed at any point in the path of the pointer o, and is connected in a circuit with a magnet controlling the cut-out j previously mentioned, so that the motor armature circuit is opened automatically, when the pointer comes in contact with the movable piece m.

12,592. Hont, J. June 4.

Theatrical appliances.—Gelatine is moulded into leaves, flowers, statuary, medallions, and theatrical scenery, or is applied in the sheet form to picture frames or to papier-mâché, plaster, or other articles. Electric or other lights are arranged round or behind the articles or scenery to illuminate the gelatine.

13,837. Boughton, J. W. June 22.

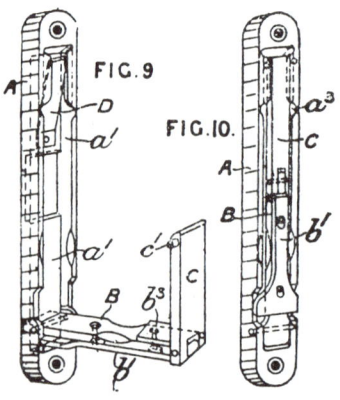

Theatrical appliances.—Folding or collapsable brackets for supporting curtain poles, pictures, &c. on theatrical scenes consist of a back-plate A, for fixing, and a plate B pivoted to A and a plate C pivoted to B. The plates B, C fold into a groove a^1 in the plate A ; the pins c^1 enter notches a^3 in undercut flanges, and a spring D keeps the parts folded. A plate b^1 capable of a short sliding motion on the plate B bears against the plate A and against the extension of the plate C beyond the pivot, and so keeps the parts rigidly in the position shown in Fig. 9 ; the plate C also butts against a short plate b^3 on the upper side of B. Thumb notches are provided to facilitate the drawing out of the arms. When the scene &c. to which the bracket is fixed is placed in a horizontal position the bracket may be so arranged as to close automatically.

14,513. Cox. C. H. July 1.

Theatrical appliances.—Spectacular effects are produced by means of high-tension electrical discharges through tin foil or sheet-metal pieces a attached to a plate of ebonite, glass, or insulating-material. A sheet or similar pieces of tin foil are fixed to the back of the plate, and the opposite sides are connected to the ends of the secondary circuit of a Ruhmkorf coil or the like. If desired, the metallic backing may be dispensed with, and the ends of the secondary coil may be attached to

the pieces a at opposite ends of the plate. Arches, columns, floral, and other designs may be thus arranged and illuminated to the accompaniment of a crackling sound characteristic of such electric discharges. The performers may carry insulated plates or devices with metal pieces on the surface. The conducting-wires pass through an ebonite or glass tube or handle e, and the controlling-switch may be operated by the foot of the artiste, or otherwise. Incandescent or arc lights may also be used.

14,514. Cox, C. H. July 1. *Drawings to Specification.*

Switchboards for use in theatres &c. are built up of metal boxes supported and connected by metal tubes. The switches and cut-outs are fitted in the boxes, and the conductors are led in through the tubes. The whole may be supported on a metal framework.

15,825. Cox, C. H. July 20.

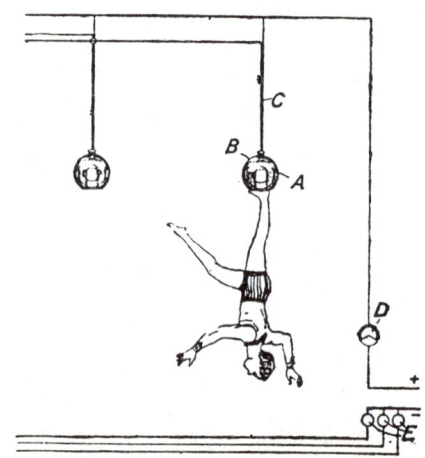

Acrobatic apparatus.—Relates to apparatus for suspending an acrobat in the air. A series of brass balls B is suspended from the ceiling by the leads C carrying electric currents, preferably from secondary batteries, to electromagnets A within the balls. An am-meter D is arranged in circuit, and also a number of switches E, so that, as one magnet is energized, another one may be de-energized. The performer has iron soles on his feet to walk in an inverted position, or on the gloves on his hands to swing feet downwards.

16,378. Wulff, E. July 27.

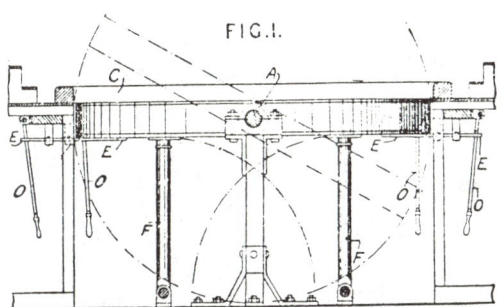

FIG.1.

Theatres ; circuses.—The stage C is mounted on a horizontal axis A, so that it can be reversed for the purpose of bringing fresh scenery or apparatus into use. The scenery or apparatus can be fixed underneath the stage while the performance is going on on the upper surface of the stage. Sliding bolts E operated by levers O support the periphery, and pivoted columns F help to sustain the middle of the platform. For water performances in circuses a canal is provided at the circumference of the arena to carry off the water when the arena is tilted.

16,927. Spencer, R. Aug. 5.

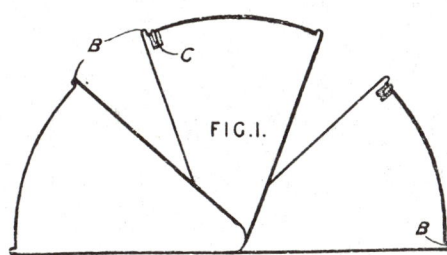

FIG.1.

Advertising.—Relates to a fan which may be used as a programme, menu card, or the like or for advertising purposes. The slats or blades are fastened together at their narrow ends by an eyelet, and are also connected together by a cord or ribbon made to adhere to their adjacent edges or by an endless cord threaded through holes in them or, as shown in Fig. 1, by hooks C which fit over the top edges of the adjacent blades and are prevented from slipping off by the pieces B projecting from the ends of each blade.

17,095. Bynoe, F. O., and **Cubison, H. J.** Aug. 8.

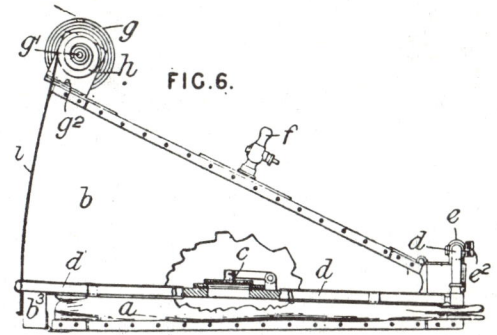

FIG.6.

Gas supply.—Relates to apparatus for delivering gas at constant pressure to the lime-light or gas light of a magic lantern or for other purposes. Gas passes to the receiving-bellows a by a pipe d communicating through a non-return valve or stop-cock e, which is normally kept open by a spring e^2, with a gas generator or holder. The valve e is closed by pressing a lever attached thereto, and on continuing the pressure the bellows a collapse and drive gas through a non-return valve c or stop-cock into the pressure bellows h. Gas is expelled at constant pressure through a cock f by the action of a spring g, one end of which is fixed to a pin g^2 and the other end to a spindle g^1 carrying two fusees h, over which pass cords i secured at their lower ends to the frame b^3.

19,240. Arber, W. H. Sept. 9.

Signals, indicator or visible, and bell.—Relates to indicators for exhibiting programme numbers in places of amusement &c. The numbers a are arranged as shown, on a board or clock face, and behind each number an electric lamp is mounted. The lamps are separated from each other by partitions, and are connected to a central switch, by means of which any desired lamp may be switched in and the corresponding number illuminated. The Provisional Specification also states that the operation of the switch may actuate an electric bell or gong at the indicator, to announce audibly the changes of the numbers.

FIG.1.

EXTRA TURN

19,620. Parsons, A. J., and **Bastian, C. O.** Sept. 15. *Drawings to Specification.*

Theatrical appliances.—To give optical effects for advertising, stage purposes, and the like, tablets or signs are used consisting of two sheets of wire gauze, muslin, or perforated metal &c., secured, one to the front and the other to the back of a frame, the advertisements &c. being displayed on both sheets or on one only. The movement of the observer gives an apparent motion to the surface of the tablet. One of the surfaces may be moved relatively to the other, or the tablets as a whole may be moved, and the effect may be heightened by coloured light. The Provisional Specification states that the back sheet may be, instead of gauze &c., plain and transparent or coloured and provided with a pattern, and that a corrugated sheet of glass &c. may be used for the woven material or gauze &c.

21,413. Ganem, C., and **Quinson, G.**
Oct. 11. *Drawings to Specification.*

Hiring opera-glasses &c.—The instrument to be hired is made as a box in the usual opera-glass form, a sliding lid carrying the eyeglasses and the bottom of the box the objectives. The space between the optical tubes is used for storing sweetmeats, a scent bottle, &c.

21,853. Hollingsworth, C. M. Oct. 17

Exhibitions, scenic and spectacular; panoramas.—An approximately-spherical shell A, mounted on rollers *c*, is painted externally in relief to represent the earth or one of the planets, and at night the outlines of seas and continents may be marked off by coloured electric lights. Volcanos can be shown in action, and pyrotechnical displays can be given from various parts of the

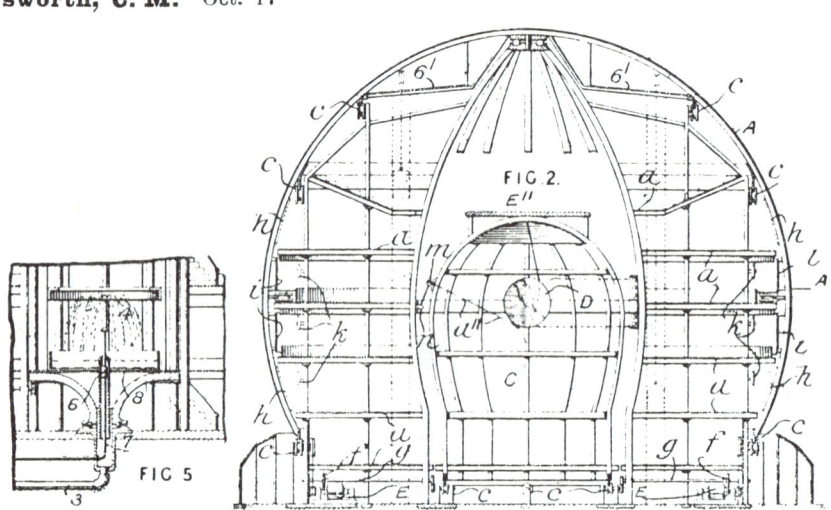

sphere. The shell is rotated by electric motors E and endless belts, and carries internally panoramic or other spectacular views *h*, *i*, illuminated by electric incandescent lamps *k*. A central circular structure C, carrying a band stage E^{11} and a large globe D, is mounted on rollers, and is rotated by toothed wheels *f* and shafts *g*. The globe D is suspended by invisible wires, and is rotated about an inclined axis by a friction-wheel *n* and an endless band a^{11}. It is lighted on one side by lamps to show the succession of day and night and the seasons of the year. The spectators reach the different floors *a* to view the panoramic and scenic effects by staircases or lifts. To allow for ventilation and permit pyrotechnic displays, the upper part of the shell consists of wire gauze provided with apertures, and carries a floor 6^1 which slopes outwards to carry off rain-water. In a modification, the shell with the floors is mounted on an annular base or air chamber which floats in an annular basin of water. This base is centered and rotated by cables passing round the periphery and round pulleys operated by motors. Circular rails carrying the panoramic views are rotated by motors and endless bands. In another modification shown in Fig. 5, a fountain is arranged in the central space. A rotary basin 8 carries the nozzle 4, which is connected to the supply pipe 7 by a swivel joint 6. Water from the basin escapes through a pipe 3. The shell may be made of a cylindrical shape with a dome-shaped roof, and may revolve or be made stationary.

22,858. Prestwich, E. E., and **Burt, L. N.,** [*trading as* Prestwich & Burt]. Oct. 31.

Regulating; switches.—Relates to regulating the supply of current to multiple circuits containing lamps or motors &c., and is especially applicable in theatres. A resistance, either a choking coil or an ohmic resistance, is inserted in each circuit. Figs. 1 and 2 show the arrangement for use with alternating currents. A number of choking coils J are arranged in the circuits, and the cores *j* may

be moved simultaneously or in combinations. On a shaft A are fixed a set of notched wheels D and loose pulleys E, the latter carrying cords *i* connected to the cores *j*. The pulleys carry telescopic handles F fitted with detents *g* by which any one or set of pulleys may be locked to the shaft. The shaft is rotated by worm or other gearing B. For continuous currents, adjustable resistances replace the choking coils, the cores J carrying contacts *o* for short-circuiting the coils when in the lowest position.

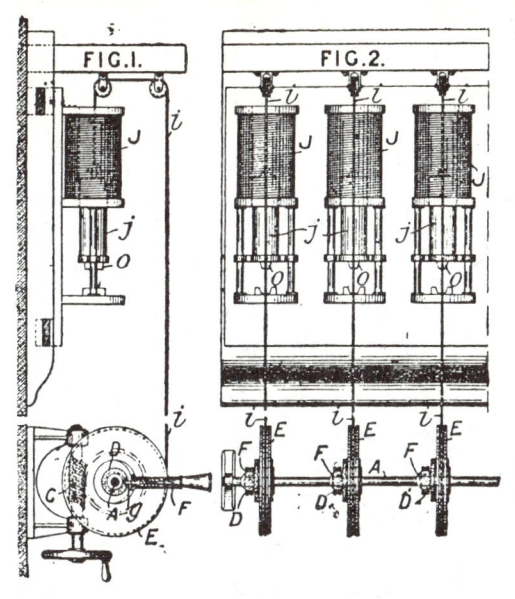

23,382. Beauchamp, F. Nov. 7.

Magic-lanterns.—A glass disc bearing advertisements F[1] is rotated intermittently by means of chain gearing which is actuated by an arm operated by a cam, so as to bring the advertisements in the upper part of the disc, which are inverted, before a magic-lantern arrangement for being cast on a screen.

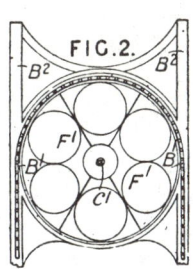

23,508. Potter, T. Nov. 8.

Seats.—Fig. 6 shows a method of constructing fireproof seats for theatres &c. Concrete risers C are cast above the iron or steel joists H ; corrugated or plain metal sheets K are laid on the risers and flanges of the joists ; concrete L is

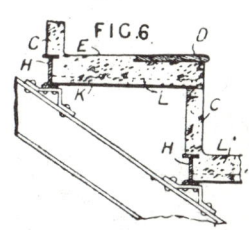

deposited on the plates ; wood seats D are laid on the concrete ; and cement E is applied to form rounded corners to prevent the accumulation of dust.

23,070. Bálint, D., Monostor, A. B. de, Laszky, A., and Laszky, S. Nov. 2.

Hiring opera-glasses.—A pair of glasses attached by a cord *s* rests on a spring shelf *f* in a fixed box B, the door of which is fastened till after prepayment.

Coin action ; coin-discharging mechanism.—The coin drops from the shoot *q* into a loop *o* upon a lever *g*, so that, when the lever is pulled by a handle *t*, the coin is drawn off a shelf *s³* and makes a bell crank *j* lift the latch of the door.

Signals ; registers.—The shelf springs up after removal of the glasses, and completes an electric circuit L containing a signal.

25,275. Boult, A. J., [*Carré, P.*]. Nov. 30.

Fireproof compositions.—Relates to a fireproof composition to be used as a coating for rendering materials non-inflammable. It may be applied to wood, fabrics, curtains, gauze, silk, muslin, &c., theatrical scenery, lamp shades, &c. It is formed of an aqueous mixture of boracic acid, sulphate, hydrochlorate, or carbonate of ammonia and borax. Glue and colouring-matter may also be added to the composition.

27,000. Sachs, E. O. Dec. 21.

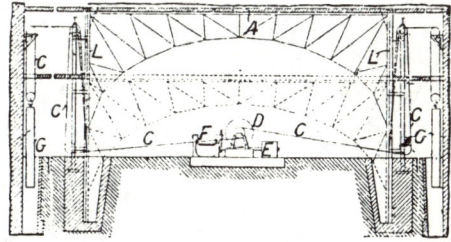

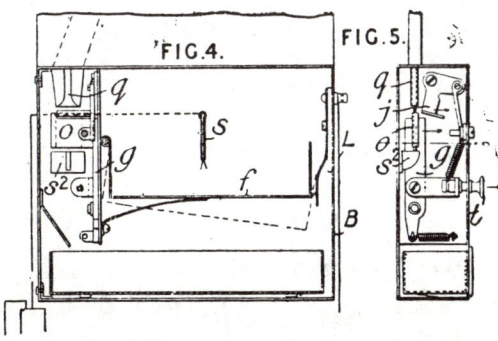

Fraud, preventing ; signals.—If the attachment cord is severed, an electric circuit is broken to release a key which completes the circuit of an alarm bell.

Theatres ; floors.—The stage floor is made up of sections A supported by trussed girders or arches attached to vertical sliding columns L which are connected by ropes C to counterweights G and winches D. Each winch can be worked by an electric or other motor E, or by hand-gear F, in order to raise or lower the corresponding section of the stage.

1899

1382.   Sanson, R. A. G.   Jan. 20.

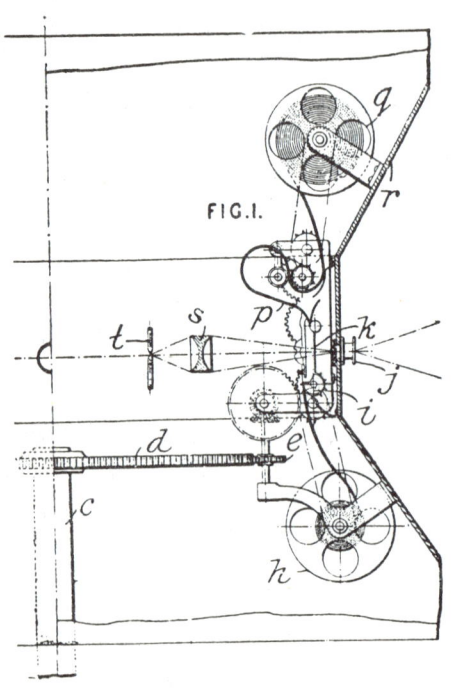

Panoramas.—Relates to the projection upon screens from a series of instruments of panoramic views which have been taken from below the car of

an ascending and descending balloon, in such a way as to produce upon spectators the illusion of a balloon excursion. Fig. 1 shows in elevation one of the kinematographs, which, screened by walls *r*, in imitation of a car, are arranged in a circle. Canvas may be employed, at the changing of the views, to represent clouds, and thereby to heighten the illusion.

2742.   Bowles, E. W.   Feb. 7.

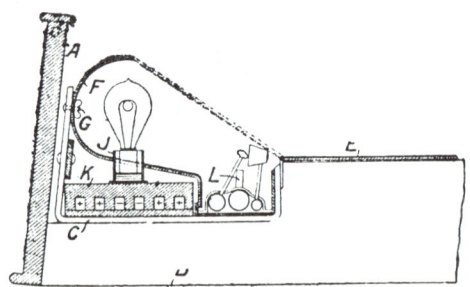

Footlights ; reflectors.—Electric lamps are set in nsulating-sockets J on the wood casing K, which is supported on angle-irons C, attached to the woodwork B, A. Reflectors F, curved as shown, and having holes to receive the sockets J, are bolted at G to the irons. Ordinary gas lamps L may also be provided. A white enamelled or painted cover E is hinged to the irons so as to lie flat on the stage, or to turn up against the reflector and enclose the lamps. Battens and side lights may be arranged similarly.

3072.   Dalman, J. C.   Feb. 11.

Chairs ; seats.—Two or more seats *a* are pivoted by means of eye plates *d* on a rod *e* fixed or bearing in eye pieces b^3 on two end standards *b*, b^1 and on central projections. When in use, the seats

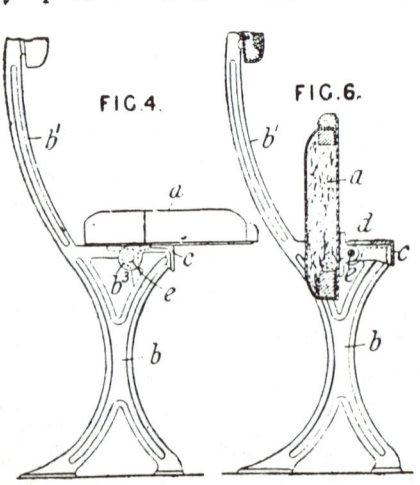

bear on an angle-iron *c* carried by the end standards. When turned up, a suitable stop bears against the underside of the angle-iron *c*, or other suitable stops or rails are provided to limit the motion. Buffers may be provided.

3081.   Wigley, H.   Feb. 11.

Fireproof compositions.—In fireproofing muslins, curtains, theatrical scenery, &c., the fabrics &c. are treated with a composition consisting of a specified proportion of ammonium sulphate and creosote, or, when used with distemper colours, of ammonium sulphate, gum arabic, and acetic acid.

3298. Cumine, J. A., and Reinolts, G. von. Feb. 14.

Conjuring - apparatus. — The knob a^1 is secured to the walking-stick a by means of a disc b having a flanged rim which is enclosed between pairs of plates c, c^2 secured in the head and the upper end of the stick respectively. Notches b^3 are formed in the disc, which is free to rotate so that a knife or other article may be passed through the joint without destroying the connection. The disc

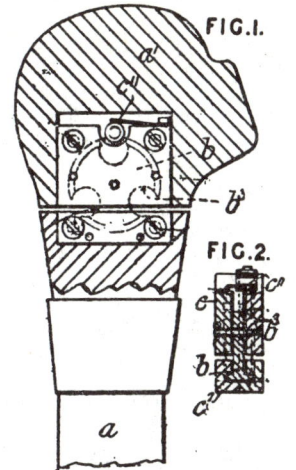

is provided with a spring stop c^{11}. The device is stated to be applicable for other purposes.

arms 11 and the pivoted back 16. On lifting up the seat, pins 18 act on slotted plates 17 on the back, and force the bottom part of the back backwards, thus withdrawing a key or pin 23, pivoted to a cross-bar on the back, from registering holes in the cap 3, 5 and head 4 ; the seat and back are now caused, by the inclines 27, to automatically rotate through 90°, leaving lanes between each pair of chairs, which fold back to back. The seats are locked in the folded position, as the pin cannot enter the hole in the head 4, and cannot be brought down till the chair has been rotated to its front. The standard is preferably eccentric to the chair. Fig. 8 shows a modified standard, without the cap and having a projection 25 and pin 26 to form a stop.

5055. Lacey, H. H. March 8.

Hat holders. — Relates to racks or hat holders to be fixed either horizontally or vertically beneath the seats, or on the backs, of chairs, benches, pews, or seats in churches, theatres, railway vehicles, &c. The rack is preferably bent from one piece of wire, but may be stamped from sheet metal or cast, and has three prongs or hooks c, c^1 to receive the brim of the hat and eyes e for receiving fixing-screws.

4613. Hosmer, A., and Silliman, C. H. March 2.

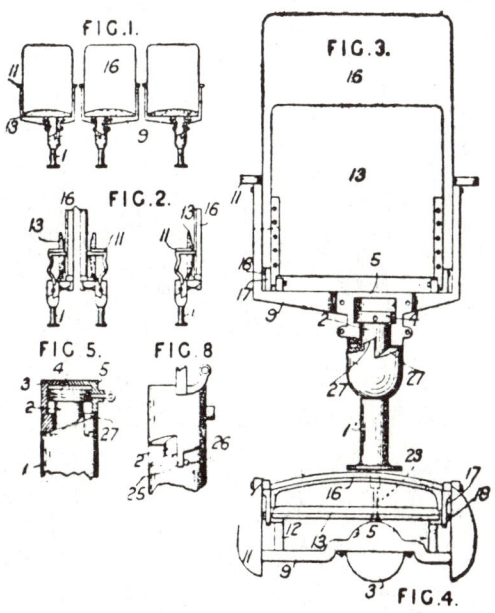

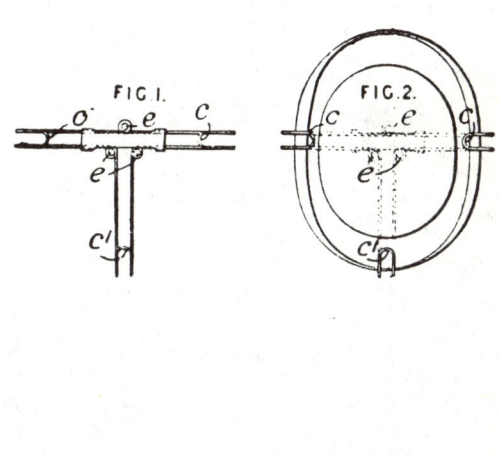

Chairs. — The standard 1 of a chair for use in theatres, halls, &c. has a head 4, neck 2, and flange with a pair of ratchet inclines 27. The seat 13 is pivoted to lugs 12 on a cross-bar 9, which is formed with one part 5 of a two-part cap 3, 5, bolted together over the head 4. The lower part of the cap has inclines corresponding to the inclines 27. The bars 9 project upwards, and support the

5732. Silbon, W. March 16.

Gymnastic apparatus ; trapezes.—The framings or platforms in combination with trapezes are arranged in such a way that, when either of them are not immediately required, they may be turned up out of the way. Fig. 1 is a diagrammatic view of the whole arrangement. The two parts A, A^1 of the main platform are hinged together at A^3, from which start the additional and triangular

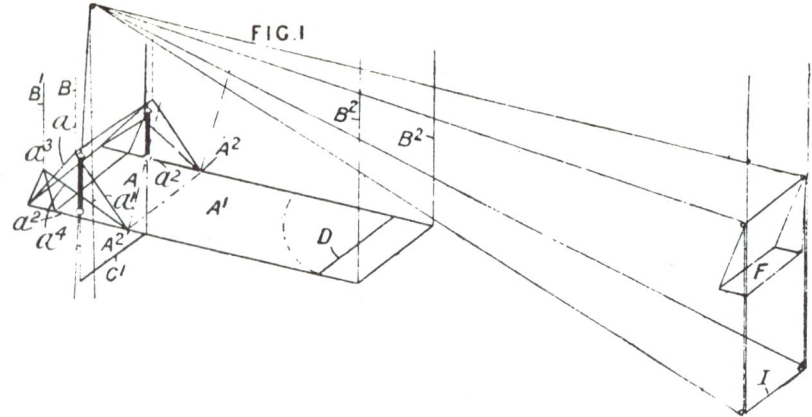

FIG. I

framings a^1, a^2 and a^3, a^4, the arms of the latter projecting laterally. By means of the ropes B^2, B^2, the part A^1 may be raised so as to occupy out of use the position shown in dotted lines. The part A with its triangular framings is supported by cords B, B^1. Spring pendants support a trapeze C^1. The bar D is hinged in such a way as to be swung out of position and to be secured parallel to one of the side rods. An auxiliary platform F is so hung that, when swung out of its normal position, it shall be horizontal. A trapeze I is also hung from this end, the height of the platform and trapeze being adjusted by cords at the main platform end.

6268. Cinquevalli, P. B. March 23.

Conjuring-apparatus.—Relates to dresses and apparatus to be used in humorous sketches in which one performer appears dressed as a servant or the like and a number of articles are drawn from his person. Pockets closed by suitable flaps are made in all parts of coats and other garments and contain such articles as writing-necessaries, a letter-box, washing-apparatus, a brush and comb, a couch, clock, bell, telephone, cigar box, matches, drinking-appliances, &c. The trousers and boots also serve to conceal various articles. A lamp is fitted in and concealed by a wig worn by the servant, and his hat is provided with telescopic legs to convert it into a stool and also serves as a receptacle for a towel &c. Revolvers, which may have the barrels cut off, are fixed to a plate provided with hooks by which it is attached to the servant's waist belt. He also carries a box which contains a telephone call bell, a pillow, &c. Fig. 12 shows the couch ready for use. It consists of a number of boards n^{10}, n^{20}, n^{30} which may be slid one on the other and be fastened together so as to occupy a small space concealed by the coat tails, and the boards are covered by a strip of fabric n^5 which is wound off a roller n^6. An awning is formed by a strip of fabric n^9 which is wound off a roller n^8 and is supported by a stick n^{13}. The couch is supported by the box o, or the boards are provided with telescopic legs for this purpose.

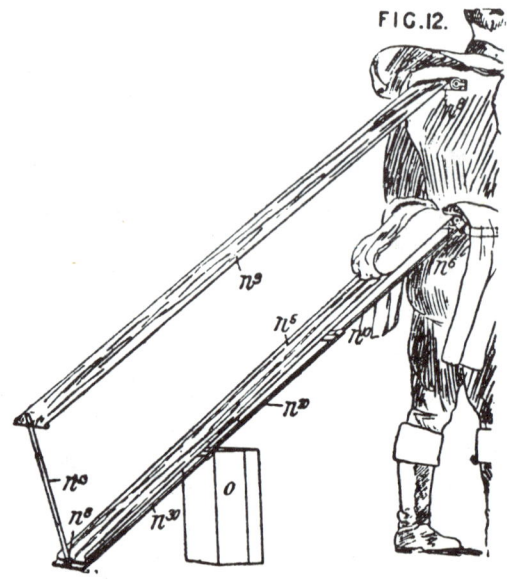

FIG. 12.

6526. Horst, M., [*trading as* Horst & Co., M.].
March 27.

Chairs. -- Relates to arm chairs for theatres, churches, &c. The back 6 and seat 4 are hinged or pivoted to one of the supports 5, so as to be capable of turning up against it as shown in Fig. 3. The back may be hinged along one of its s i d e s, instead of pivoted at one end as shown. Suitable springs or spring hinges may be fitted to make the movement automatic, in which

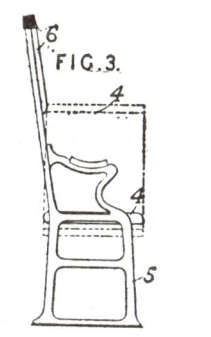

case the back is provided with spring catches to hold it in its unfolded position.

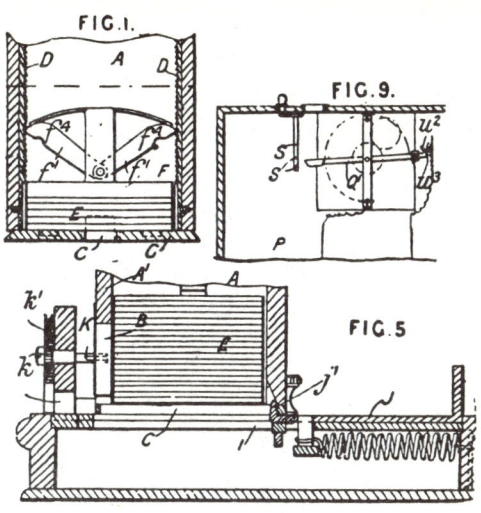

6534. Ballance, W. *April 13.*

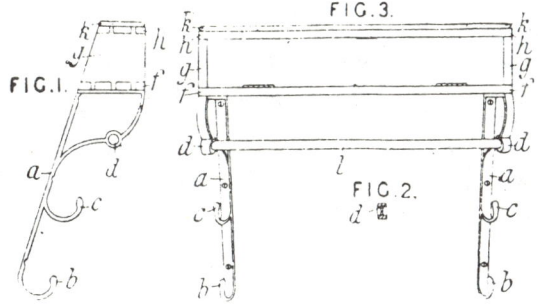

Brackets; chairs; seats; clothes-hanging hooks and rails; shelves and shelving; book cases and shelves.—Shelves *f*, *h*, fitted with a rim *k*, end pieces *g*, and with or without a lock-up let-down flap door, are supported by brackets *a*, with clothes-pegs *b*, *c* and a coat-rail *l*, to the back of a chair seat or pew in a church, theatre, &c. The rail *l* is fitted into a double socket *d*, Fig. 2, on each bracket *a*. The shelves &c. are for supporting books, drinking-vessels, opera glasses, smoker's requisites, &c., and the brackets or racks may be used for umbrellas, coats, hats, &c.

6959. Marsh, A. March 30.

Admission-fees, registering and checking.—Relates to a check issuing and receiving system for theatres &c. by which the issue and receipt of each check is electrically signalled to the manager's room. The tickets or checks E of different values are piled up in separate magazines A, each with a front A[1] sliding in grooves and a bottom C in which is a slot *c*. The magazine is bound at the top with a strengthening-band and fitted with a strap by which it can be carried, and the sliding front is locked at the top. A fastening B at its lower end has a bolt which, while the magazine is being carried about, closes the slit through which the tickets are issued; when, however, the magazine is placed on the issuing - apparatus,

Fig. 5, the bolt is shot back by a key K turned by gear *k*, *k*[1], in which position the key is fixed in the lock so that the magazine cannot be withdrawn until the bolt is again passed over the issuing slit. A weight F, with spring-pressed detents f^1, f^1 engaging racks D, D at the side of the magazine presses the tickets down, and prevents one from being inserted at the bottom, a pair of spring catches situated in recesses in the plate C further ensuring this result. The tickets are issued by pushing forward the spring slide J having a projection j^1 working in the slots *c*, I. This slide has a laterally-projecting arm which actuates a set of Geneva-geared counting-wheels and closes circuit for an electric counter in the manager's room. A specially-formed hooked instrument is provided for lifting the weight F when necessary, the hooks taking into the recesses f^4, f^4 under the detents f^1, f^1 and freeing them from the racks D, D. The checks when delivered up to the attendants are passed through a slit into a box P, Fig. 9, and fall upon a counterbalanced lever Q^1 which, rocking on its pivot, actuates a counter and also completes circuit at u^2, u^3 for an electric counter in the manager's room. A rod S can be moved so that pins *s*, *s* upon it embrace the end of the lever Q^1 while the box is being carried about and prevent its movement: the entrance slit to the box is closed by the same action.

7790. Lion, A. L. April 13.

Air, purifying.—Air for ventilating barracks, dormitories, schoolrooms, hospitals, restaurants, theatres, &c. is freed from dust germs and other impurities by washing. The air passes through a trunk *a*, Fig. 1, down which a number of jets of water *i* fall, rotating a fan which serves to mix the water and air intimately. The air escapes by the trunk *b* and the dirty water by the pipe *t*. Instead of a number of jets, a single one *q* may be employed, as in Fig. 5, which shows the invention applied to a locomotive or other chimney *s*. A jet of steam may be used instead of water.

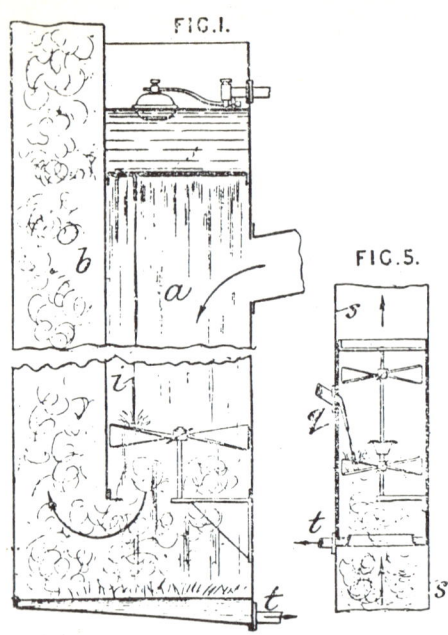

FIG.I.

FIG.5.

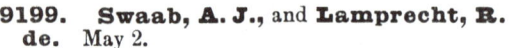

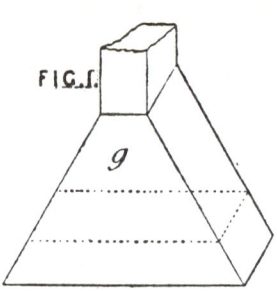

FIG.I.

and other purposes. The powder is contained in compartments b of a casing a, which is provided with electrical contact-pieces c corresponding to the spring contacts e on the separate stand d. The powder in either of the compartments b is ignited as required by sending, by means of a switch f, a current through the respective incandescing or sparking wire w. A chimney g, supported above

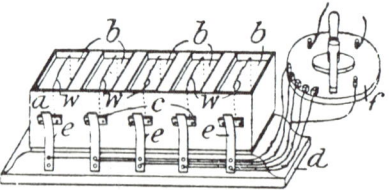

9199. Swaab, A. J., and Lamprecht, R. de. May 2.

Magnesium &c. lamps.—Relates to powder flash lights for use with apparatus for exhibiting views

the apparatus, is packed with a mixture of sawdust and iron filings or turnings to condense or retain the smoke and fumes.

13,026. Justice, P. M., [*Long-Arm System Co.*]. June 22.

Theatrical appliances. — Relates to improvements on the apparatus described in Specifications No. 16,013, A.D. 1896, and No. 18,248, A.D. 1897. It is shown as applied to the opening and closing of ships' bulkhead doors, but may also be employed to lower simultaneously the fireproof curtain and open all the exits from a theatre. The door B, Fig. 4, carries a cylinder B^1 moving on a hollow rod A^3 secured to the bulkhead. A pipe A^4 passing through this rod supplies fluid under pressure to the lower end of the cylinder, while the annular space between the pipes and the rod serves as a supply and exhaust passage for the upper end of the cylinder. The door. D is a valve arrangement by which the opening and closing of the door is controlled. The valve casing is divided into two chambers, to one of which, as shown in Fig. 8, the fluid under pressure is led by a pipe E. The other

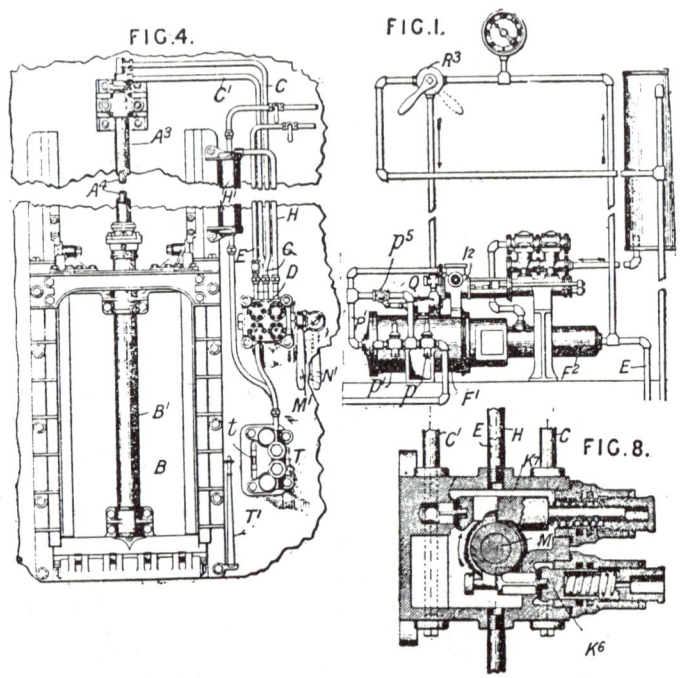

FIG.4.

FIG.I.

FIG.8.

communicates through a pipe H with the reservoir H¹, Fig. 4. In the pressure chamber shown there are two valves; one K^7 controls the admission to the pipe C^1 leading to the upper end of the cylinder, and the other K^6 controls the admission to the pipe C and the lower end of the cylinder. Two valves in the exhaust compartment similarly control the exhaust from the cylinder. The valves are controlled by a spindle M on which is a hand-lever M¹, Fig. 4. A second lever N¹ on the other side of the bulkhead is connected to M¹ by bevel gear. The springs are adjusted to hold the valves closed against the ordinary working pressure. By considerably increasing this pressure, however, all the doors can be simultaneously closed, the pressure being then sufficient to raise the valve K^6. Any door can at any time be opened by hand, and is automatically closed when the hand-lever is released. In event of any breakdown in the pressure-generating gear, the door can be opened or closed by means of a hand-pump T, Fig. 4, actuated by a lever T¹ which is placed in the slot t. As shown in Fig. 1, the pressure in the system is maintained by a steam or other fluid-pressure accumulator, in which F¹ is the steam cylinder and F² the ram cylinder. Steam is supplied to the cylinder F¹ through two reducing-valves p, p^1, and thence to the pump cylinder I² by the pipe P¹. When the pressure in the mains is to be increased to close all the doors on an emergency, the valve R^3 is opened to admit fluid under pressure from the pipe E to a spring-pressed piston in the cylinder Q. This piston is thus moved to open the valve P^5, and admit steam from between the two reducing-valves to the pump I². In a modification, compressed air is used in the normal working of the system, while each door can be opened or closed, by hand, by means of a liquid supplied by a hand-pump. The liquid reservoir is provided with special means for separating and releasing the air which enters it with the exhaust water.

14,293. Berresford, A. W. July 11.

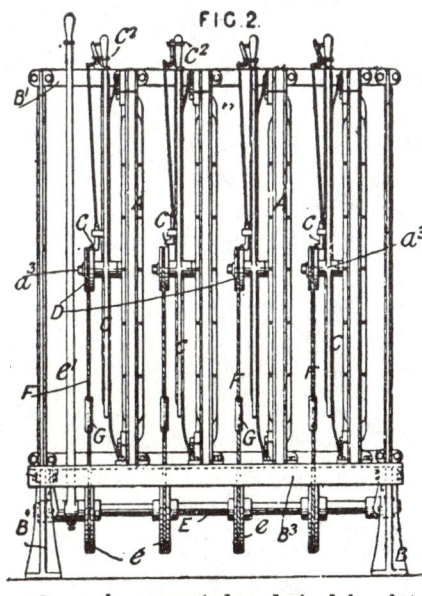

FIG. 2.

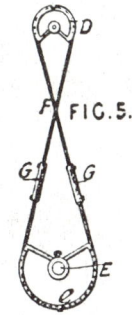

FIG. 5.

Lighting, systems of; switches.—Relates to the means for altering the lights on the stage of a theatre and obtaining different combinations. The resistance plates A are independently mounted in the frame B, B¹, B³, and screwed to the same so that any one of them can be removed without disturbing the rest of the apparatus. The switch levers C, which work over contact-points on the plates, are loosely pivoted on stub-shafts a^3, which also carry sectors D connected by wire ropes F with sectors e on the shaft E. The levers C and sectors D may be connected as desired by clutches c on slipping down rings c^2 at the top of the lever. The shaft E carries a master lever e^1 by which it and the sectors e are moved simultaneously, and with them such of the switch levers C as have been coupled. The wires F may be crossed, or not, to give the desired direction of movement to the levers C. G, G are adjustable insulating-couplings for the rope F. The shaft E is made vertically and horizontally adjustable in its supports.

15,890. Mills, J. Aug. 3.

Theatrical appliances.—To make it appear as though a person is performing, as in the serpentine dance, below the surface of water, a water screen D is interposed between the performer and the auditorium. Water is discharged from overhanging imitation rockwork from a pipe A and allowed to trickle over the surface of gauze or glass B which, to set the water further in motion, may be

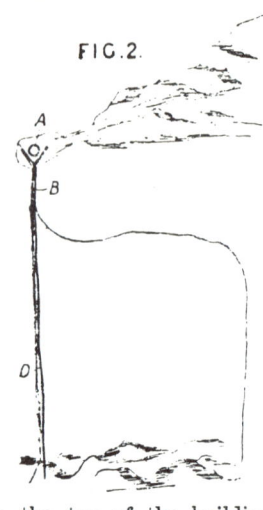

FIG.2.

continuous ladder from the top of the building to the bottom. The apertures in the wall are closed by hinged covers *g*, and rollers *n* are provided for the ladder sections to run on. In a

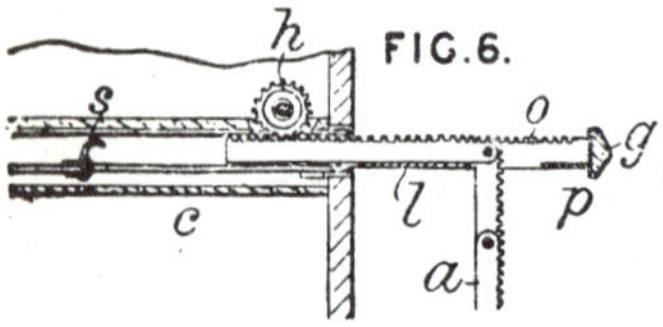

17,109. Achew, J. Aug. 23.

Theatrical appliances.—A lamp is made with an opaque top *a*, a front *b* of white opal glass or the like, a space *c* upon which may be displayed the name of a place, and internal vertical grooves for receiving sheets of differently - coloured glass which can be let down before the front by hand-

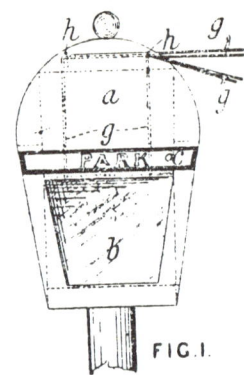

FIG.1.

cords *g*, which pass through eyes *h* and extend to the wings or back of the stage. The apparatus is intended for use in a variety stage performance in which wagers are made concerning the change of colour. The attendant changes the colours according to a predetermined code of instructions. Instead of mounting the coloured glass plates in guides they may be hinged, or mounted in hinged frames.

FIG.6.

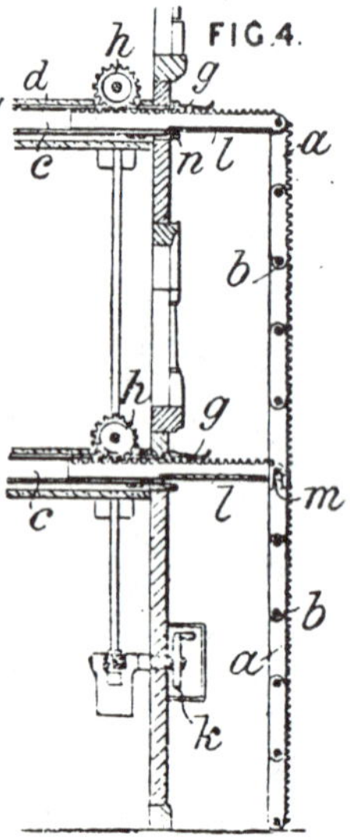

FIG.4.

modification shown in Fig. 6, the ladder is arranged to slide within a frame *o* mounted in the guides *c*. The frame *o* carries a door or cover *g*, and platform *l*, *p*, and is formed with rack teeth which engage with the pinions *h*. When the ladder is raised and withdrawn, it slides within the frame *o* until the top rung comes in contact with a double hook pivoted to the frame. The ladder and frame then slide together within the guide *c*. Folding hand-rails may be pivoted to the platforms.

17,641. Taylor, H. D. Aug. 31.

Telescopes and opera glasses. — A low - power negative eye - piece is formed by combining a positive meniscus lens F (nearly convexo-plane), made of crown glass of low refractive and dispersive powers, with a double concave lens E (nearly plano - concave) placed very close to it. The lens E has a power approximately 1·8 times

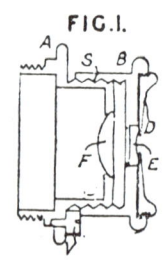

FIG.1.

that of the lens F, and is made of dense flint glass. The eye-diaphragm D has a sharp edge, and is placed close to the lens E. If it is desired to vary the power of the combination, the lens E is mounted in the tube B, which screws on to the part A at S ; the movement is controlled by a stop, the adjustment being effected with the help of a scale on the surface of B and a reading-mark on the stop V. The Specification gives exact data for one preferred form of eye-piece, but the construction may be somewhat modified.

20,255. Grismer, J. R. Oct. 9.

Theatrical appliances.—
Relates to apparatus for
producing a realistic snow
storm on the stage. Paper
flakes, discharged by a
flake dropper 2^a, and sand,
salt, meal, or other
granular substances, dis-
charged by perforated
rotary cylinders 2, are
driven across the stage
and against the windows,
doors, and scenery by air
from fans 3 worked by
electricity or hand power.
An ordinary flake dropper
is used, consisting of a
perforated hopper or
casing of wire netting,
suspended by cords 2^g,
and operated by cords 2^h
in the usual manner.

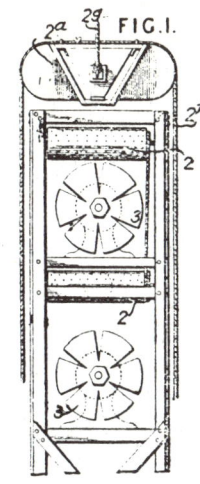

20,623. Supthut, H. Oct. 14.

Spectacles and eyeglasses ; opera-glasses.—Consists
of a combined fan and lorgnette or opera-glass.
The lorgnette may be simply pivoted to one of the
bars of the fan, so that it can be raised or lowered
by hand, but it is preferably so mounted that the
raising and lowering is automatically effected by
the opening and closing of the fan. In the form
shown in Fig. 1, the lorgnette b is secured to an
arm c, pivoted at c^1 to a bar a of the fan. On the
arm c is a pulley d connected by a crossed cord k
to a pulley e. The pulley e is rigidly connected to
a lever f, on the outer end of which is a pin guided
by a rod g on a bar i of the fan, so that when the
fan is opened or closed the lever f and lorgnette b
are moved. A helical spring may be provided on
the pivot c^1, tending to retain the lorgnette in

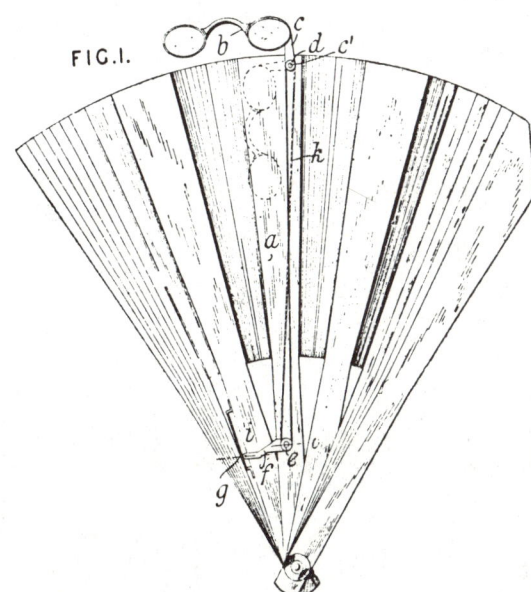

either the closed or the open position. In this
case a single cord, secured to a cranked extension
of the link c, and provided at the end with a ball
adapted to engage with a suitable catch on the bar
a, may be used to actuate the lorgnette. A light
opera-glass may be mounted in a similar manner.

22,180. Boult, A. J., [*Fuller, M. L.*].
Nov. 6.

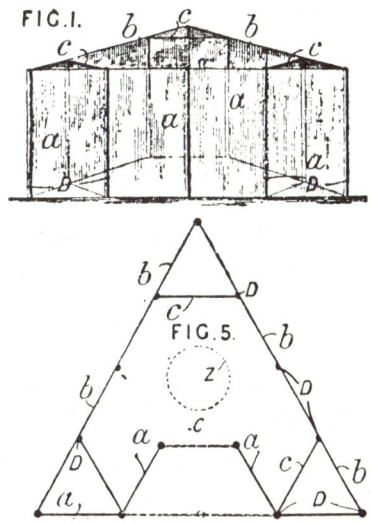

Theatrical appliances.—Relates to combinations
of transparent glass plates and mirrors for producing multiple reflections on a stage. The
mirrors b are arranged at the back of the stage in
two or more planes, and the clear glass plates a, c
are arranged at suitable angles with the mirrors.
Cylindrical or prismatic columns Z, constructed of
mirrors or clear glass, may be placed within the
spaces enclosed by the reflectors. The junctions
of the glass plates and mirrors may be covered
with opaque material D, representing columns,
trees, or the like, or they may be left uncovered.
The glass plates act as reflectors, and also allow
light to pass through them.

23,473. Fuller, I. M. Nov. 24.

Theatrical appliances.—
Relates to means for
simulating fire on the
stage. Streamers 12, of
red, coloured, or darkened
translucent or transparent
material, are attached by
loops to the wires of a
gridiron or perforated
screen secured in the
floor, and are fluttered by
blasts of air produced by
fans 13^a. The streamers
are illuminated from

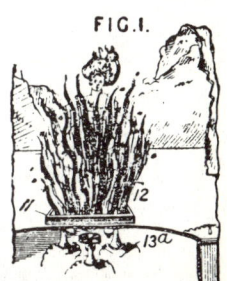

below by electric light, and coloured slides or
sheets of glass or gelatine may be interposed to
produce luminous effects. The effect of sparks
is obtained by introducing spangles or bits of

coloured paper into the air currents. The axes of the fans converge towards the grating, and an inclined reflector throws the light in the required direction. A flange or kerb 11 is placed at the front and sides of the opening in the stage floor.

24,539. Conquest, G. A. O. Dec. 9.

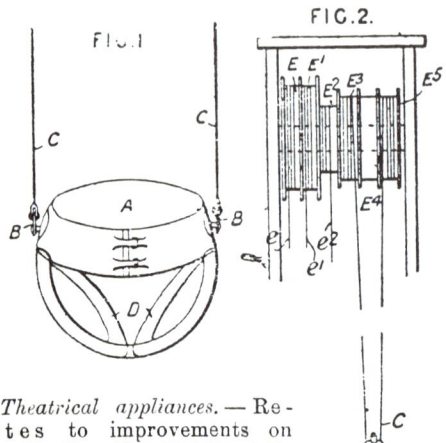

Theatrical appliances. — Relates to improvements on Specification No. 23,549, A.D. 1896. Fairies or acrobatic or other performers are suspended from the hips by wires C connected by links B to a belt A provided with padded leg rings or bands D. The wires C are wound in the same direction on drums E^3, E^5, which are rotated to raise or lower the performer by wires e, e^1 wound in opposite directions on drums E, E^1. A wire e^2 wound on a central small drum E^2 is attached to an arrangement of springs. With this apparatus the performer can turn somersaults &c. In a modification, the wires are attached to the back of the performer, and pass round drums of slightly different sizes so that the performer is automatically tilted when raised. In another arrangement, a tilting wire is used in combination with the two wires attached to the hip belt.

24,887. Digby, T. J. Dec. 14.

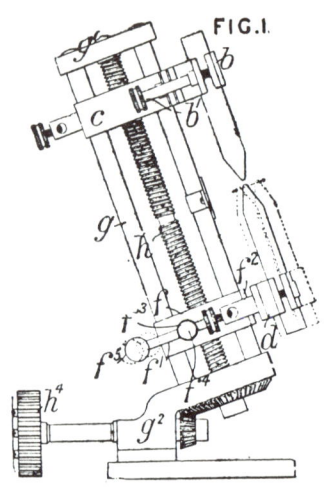

Arc lamps for stage lighting or other purposes. Variation in the amount of light emitted to a projecting lens or reflector is effected by moving one electrode out of line with the other, independently of their ordinary longitudinal feed, which may be automatic. In the lamp shown in Fig. 1, the carbons are carried by screw clamps b, b^1, d, insulated from blocks c, f, which slide on a frame g, g^1, g^2, when moved by a screw h geared to an ebonite hand-wheel h^4, to regulate the arc. The lower clamp d is carried by two side rods f^1, which slide in two cross-pieces f^2, f^3 on the block f when moved by a handle f^5, or may be fixed by a screw f^4. Other adjusting-means may be used.

1900

230. Bradley, T.
Jan. 4.

Public baths; pavilions; circuses; theatres. — Relates to the construction of a floating bath, which may be moved to or form a part of a floating pier, and which may be used as a theatre, circus, or for other entertainments. Fig. 1 shows a cross-section, and Fig. 4 a part sectional plan of a bath. The hull is divided into a number of water-tight compartments *a*, *a* at the sides, the central portion forming the bath. Water is admitted to the bath through a valve in the central chamber *p*. The bath has a movable bottom *d*, which is divided into compartments and is retained at the bottom of the bath by locking-bolts operated by hand. When these bolts are withdrawn, the bottom floats upwards and forms a floor. By admitting water to the compartments, the floor is lowered again when required. Surrounding the bath are tiers of seats, promenades, and accommodation for animals when the stage is used as a circus. Small swimming and other baths, bandstands, lounges, &c. may also be constructed. At one side is a stage *t*, which may be arranged to be raised and lowered in the same manner as the bottom of the bath. Canals and basins *t¹* extend laterally from the stage to enable miniature naval displays to be given.

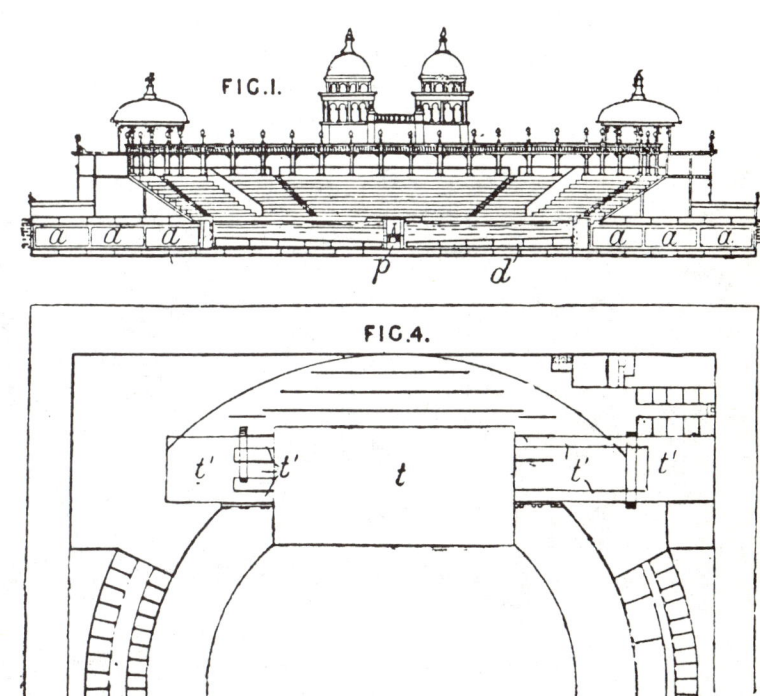

FIG.I.

FIG.4.

256. Huet, H. L.   Jan. 4.

Opera and field glasses. — In reflecting-binoculars, especially of the kind described in Specification No. 9805, A.D. 1898, the width of the instrument is reduced by arranging the eye and object glasses *b, c* in the same relative position in the two barrels *a*, instead of in symmetrical positions. The barrels are adjusted, to suit the distance between the eyes, by means of racked guide-bars *d, d¹* and gear *f, h, j* operated by a milled nut *e*. The focussing of each optical system may be independent.

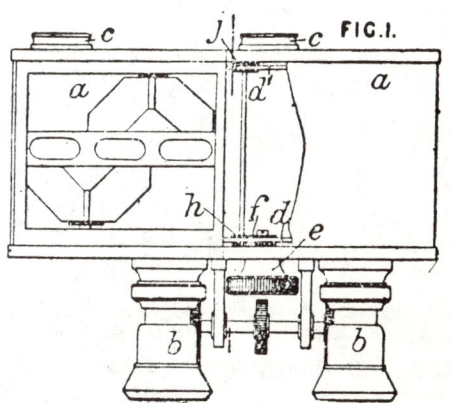

FIG.I.

1182. Robertson, J. Jan. 19.

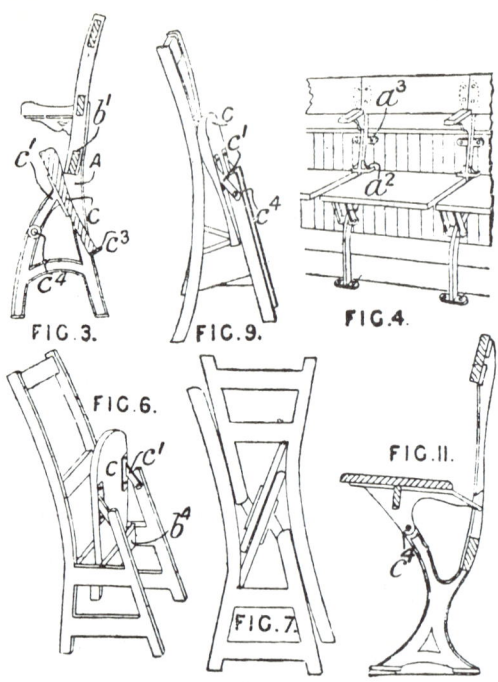

FIG.3.   FIG.9.   FIG.4.

FIG.6.

FIG.II.

FIG.7.

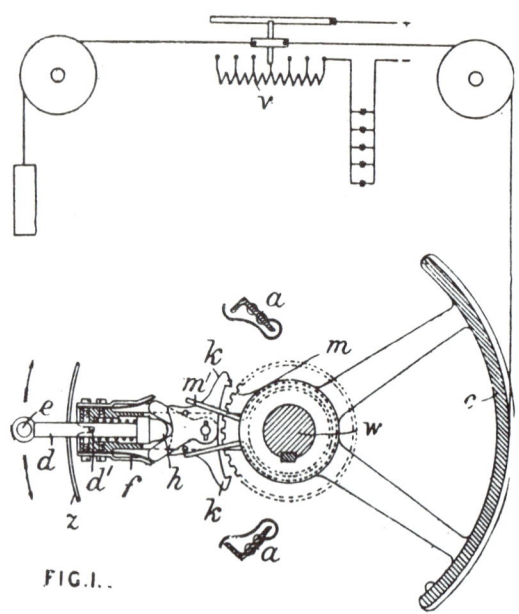

FIG.I.

Seats; chairs.—Relates to theatre seats, and has for its object to make the seat capable of folding to allow persons to pass. The seat C is carried by a pair of levers c^1, pivoted at c^1. When in use, the projection c^3 abuts against the cross-bar b^1 of the back, and the centre of gravity of the seat is forward of the pivots ; by a slight push the seat may be caused to occupy the position shown in Fig. 3. The standards A may be arranged in isolated pairs supporting one seat, or in a row as shown in Fig. 4, where they are fixed to the steps of an ascending gallery by means of lugs a^3 ; in this case stops a^2 replace the cross-bar b^1. Fig. 6 shows the invention applied to a chair ; when the seat is folded, it abuts against a bar b^4, and two such folded seats can be packed together as shown in Fig. 7. Modifications are shown in Figs. 9 and 11.

consists of rheostats c, in circuit with the groups, and separately connected by weighted cords with sector levers c, which are mounted on a single shaft w so that each lever, rheostat, and group of lamps may be separately regulated, or the whole may be varied together, either to increase or to diminish the light, commencing from the parts in any positions, by turning the shaft with all the levers by a hand-wheel and toothed gearing, not shown. For this purpose each sector lever is loose on the shaft but can be engaged with a toothed wheel m, fixed thereon by pawls k pressed inward by springs f. The pawls can be disengaged by inserting between them a cam h, supported on the lever by a sliding rod d, which is provided with a spring pressing it inward, and a handle e and a pin d^1 for moving and holding it out. A pointer on each lever indicates its position on a stationary scale z. When the shaft w is turned so that a lever reaches an extreme position, the driving-pawl comes in contact with a spring stop a, and is disengaged from the toothed wheel, so that the shaft may continue to turn ; an arm of a spring m^1 carried frictionally on the shaft then lifts the second pawl from the toothed wheel, to prevent noise by passage of the teeth under it.

1671. Winkler, A. Jan. 26.

Belts.—Belts a with one or two side loops b are worn by acrobats &c. to allow them to assist one another in their performances, the loops giving a secure hand-hold.

FIG.I.

2356. Siemens Bros. & Co., [*Siemens & Halske Aktiengesellschaft*]. Feb. 6.

Regulating.—An apparatus for controlling the lighting of a theatre stage by groups of lamps

4879. Jacobsen, B. H. March 14.

Theatres.—The stage a is mounted on wheels b, c, adapted to run on rails d, e, so that it can be moved to one side, or backwards, and a fresh stage and scenery can be introduced. The centre of the stage is supported by pivoted arms g, which can be folded against the walls f. The wheels b, c are movable vertically by bevel, worm, and screw gearing, so that either set can be brought into action. At the points where the rails cross one another, short pieces of rail are pivoted so as to turn in the direction required. The rails may be

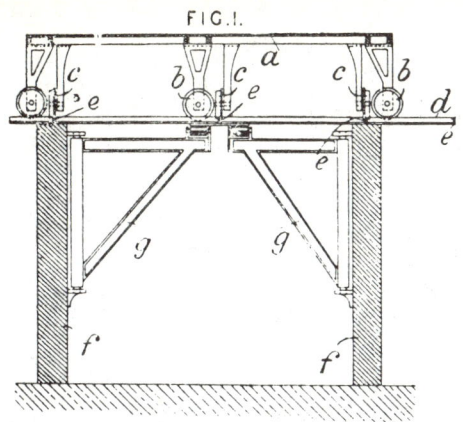

FIG. 1.

made of angle or channel iron with the flanges cut away or omitted at the crossings. Ordinary turntables may be used to move the stages from one set of rails to other rails at an angle with the first set. By this invention, a winter landscape with natural ice can be pushed from a refrigerating-room to the front, or a tropical scene with natural plants can be moved forward from a hot-house. A water basin f is constructed below the stage for water performances.

6544. Biver, M. A., and **Hénard, A. E.** April 7.

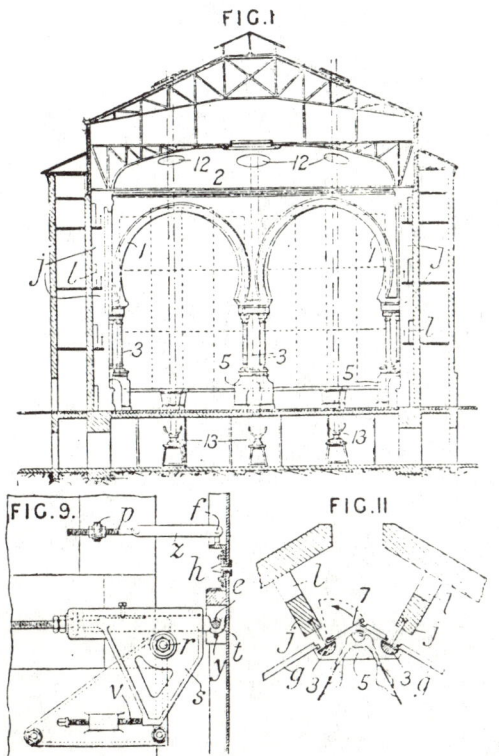

FIG. 1.

FIG. 9.   FIG. 11.

Theatrical appliances; exhibitions, scenic and spectacular.—A hexagonal or polygonal multiple reflecting-chamber is constructed with reflecting-walls, each consisting of a number of mirrors which are adjustable, as shown in Fig. 9, so as to come into the same plane. Each mirror is secured in a braced metal frame h with a narrow black border, and is suspended by adjustable bolts e resting on adjustable screwed hooks t carried by frames s, which are mounted on pivots r, and bear against adjustable screwed stops v. Hooks f at the lower end of the frame engage with eye-bars z connected to screwed rods which pass through fixed eye-bars p, and are adjustable by means of nuts. The hooks t fit between collars on the bolts e, and stop pins y prevent the frames from becoming unhooked. An elliptical vaulted roof 2 is supported on arches 1, and is pierced with openings 12 opposite to similar openings in the floor. Electric-light projectors 13 below the floor project cylindrical or conical beams of light upwards so as to illuminate suspended objects such as birds, insects, dancing girls, scenery, &c., or spiral jets of water, cascades of metal drops, flowers, &c. At the angles of the walls, half columns 3 of transparent material are arranged, and the angles are filled in with narrow mirror sections 7 mounted on pedestals 5. The sections 7 are pivoted so as to allow performers with flags &c. to pass on to the pedestals from behind. Doorways, passages, and staircases are arranged to give access to the adjustable devices of the mirrors, and manholes l are made through masonry buttresses j, which support the mirrors. The mirrors are bedded in felt or plastic material in the frames, so as to allow for expansion and contraction. An orchestra or automatic instrument may be placed below the floor.

7973. Barton, J. H. April 30.

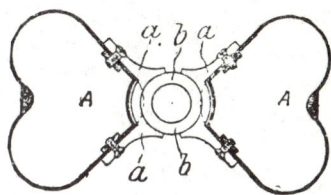

Field and opera glasses.—The bodies of prism binoculars A, A are secured by screws in forked extensions a, a of the central pivot b.

8946. Wrightnour, J. S. May 15.

Air, oxygenating.—Consists in evaporating in a special manner nitrogen from liquid air and utilizing the remainder when evaporated for oxygenating the atmosphere of auditoriums, hospital wards, private apartments, &c. Liquid air is passed into a container 3, in the bottom 4 of which is formed the receptacle 5. The lower portion of the container around the receptacle is sealed hermetically, and constructed of and covered by materials not readily conducting heat, as, for instance, lead, glass, wool, &c., or glazed tiles with hollow or porous interiors into which liquid air or gases

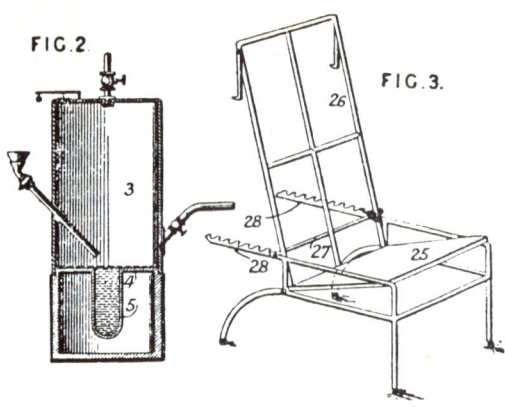

FIG.2   FIG.3.

therefrom may percolate. The upper part of the container is formed of good heat-conducting material, so that, on the liquid air flowing from the receptacle 5 over the bottom 4, the nitrogen will first evaporate. This nitrogen is first drawn off, after which the remaining oxygen will be passed through suitable pipes to the apartments to be oxygenated. In order to heat the oxygen as it passes to an apartment, in the flexible pipe which conveys the gas, a metallic portion is inserted. For supporting and tilting the container during the operation, the stand, Fig. 3, having the pivoted back 26 and bottom 25, may be employed, the inclination being dependent upon the position of the rod 27 on the racks 28.

12,440. Hagen, C. L. July 10.

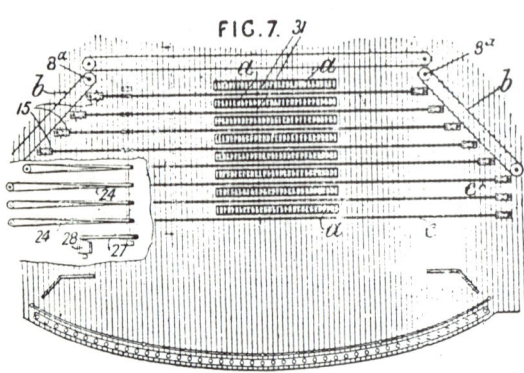

FIG.7.

Theatrical appliances.—Relates to scenic apparatus for producing horse, chariot, and other races on the stage. The horses or performers are arranged to run on endless moving tracks *a* in front of scenery attached to endless travelling bands *b* at the back and sides of the stage. The appearance of moving ground is represented by series of endless travelling belts *c*, mounted between the tracks *a* above the stage. The belts increase in depth towards the back of the stage, and are driven at a slower rate in order to produce a perspective effect. The bands *b*, forming the background, are suspended from slotted overhead tracks by rods fitted with rollers mounted on ball bearings, and are driven in the same direction by

a motor, endless driving-bands, and toothed gearing. The overhead tracks are supported by outrigged frames or braced structures, and the frames carrying the side bands can be turned to the back of the stage about the vertical driving-shafts 8^a when the performance is over. The braced frames carrying the side bands are mounted on rollers, and side struts hinged to the braced frames can be fastened to the floor by pins &c. The belts *c* are driven by a motor 28 and endless bands 27, 24, and are guided between rollers 15, and vertical grooved pulleys.

12,538. Stuart, J., and Hasselkus, J. W. July 11.

Opera and field glasses.—Relates to prismatic instruments. The focussing-adjustment consists of a spindle C secured in the hinge of the plates *b* by a screw b^1 and passing through the hinges of the plates *a*. This spindle engages the screwed hollow shaft D by its screws *c*, the sleeve E being held between the collets a^3, a^3, which hold together the cutaway and overlapping parts of the hinges connecting the plates *a*. The hinge of the plates *b* is formed and held in a similar manner. A screw *e* locks together the hollow shaft D and sleeve E, and the adjusting milled head d^2 is secured to the shaft. A screw *f* passes into the plate at the end of the sleeve E. This frictional arrangement prevents overwinding of the milled head from doing harm, as the spindle C, shaft D, and sleeve E can all turn together under the application of force. The focussing-adjustment and eye-piece tubes can

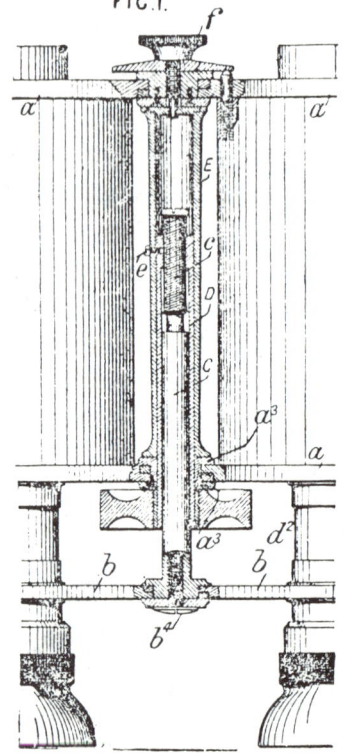

FIG.I.

be removed, after taking out the screws *f*, *e*, for

the instrument to be adjusted for coincidence for the eye-piece images.

13,072. Rossman, J. G. July 19.

Theatrical appliances. — Braces B for stage scenery are formed with hinged foot irons or portions *a* carrying wood-screws *c*, which are made with collars adapted to fit in recesses in the foot-irons. A portion a^4 of the foot-iron is detachable, and is secured to the main part by screws a^5. The inclination

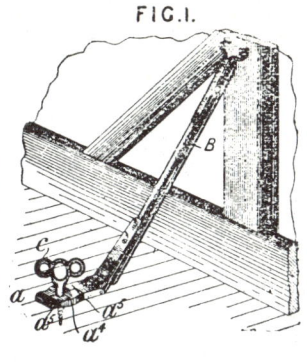

FIG. I.

of the brace can be varied, and the screw cannot get lost accidentally.

13,529. Walmsley, F. July 27.

Theatrical appliances. — Relates to apparatus for pasting or applying plain or crimped strips of gilt foil, or tinsel, to stage scenery &c. The tinsel or foil paper is drawn from a roll O, passes between a pair of plain or crimping rollers A, B, is pasted underneath by an endless band K dipping into a trough E, and is cut off by a serrated knife M operated by a trigger m^3, rod m^2, and bell-crank lever. The paste trough is pivoted to the frame C, and is adjusted by a screw e^2. A cover G is formed with guides for supporting the frame carrying the endless band, and is fitted with a slide g^4 for removing surplus paste from the band. A slotted guide-trough D, for supporting the strip, is formed with a tongue which enters a central groove in the periphery of the wheel B. This trough carries

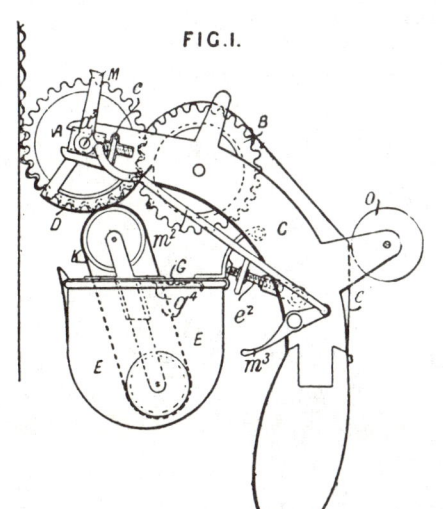

FIG. I.

bearings for the axle a^3 of the wheel A, which is adjusted by screw-nuts *c*. A flat spring c^1 bears against the roll O.

15,377. March, E. Aug. 29.

Chairs; brackets. — A shelf *b* is hinged by means of lugs *m* and *l* to hollow strips *g* fixed to the back of a music-hall chair, wall, &c. A guard-rail *c* is similarly hinged to the upper part of the strips *g*, and is supported by uprights *d* pivoted to the shelf *b* and swivelling on the rod *c*. Springs *h*, acting on the lugs *j*, *m*, hold the shelf in the open or folded positions shown in Figs. 3 and 4.

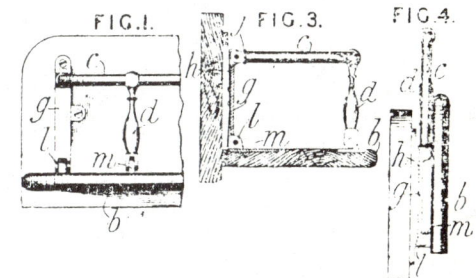

FIG. I.   FIG. 3.   FIG. 4.

16,687. MacKenzie, N. K. Sept. 19.

Chairs. — Relates to chairs having reversible seats, for use on ships' decks, or in theatres, gardens, &c. The seat is pivoted at or near its longitudinal central line, in such a manner that it automatically turns over when vacated. When in use, its back end bears on the under-side of a cross-bar 12 on the supports of the fixed or reversible back. The bars 12 are capable of slight vertical movement in slots in the uprights 13, and their weight gives an initial turning impulse to the seat. Projections 20 and recesses 21 may engage the bars 12, and so keep the seat and back

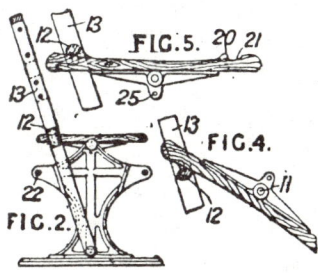

FIG. 5.   FIG. 4.   FIG. 2.

in place. Cross-bars 22 may be fitted to prevent accident when a person attempts to sit down before reversing the seat. The seat may be held in its inclined position by a pin passed through the hole 25 and frame. Shot, weights, or a liquid may be contained in a suitable cavity under the seat to assist gravity in reversing the seat.

18,946. Edwards, E., [*Engelsmann, A.*]. Oct. 23.

Lighting, systems of ; search-lights ; signal lamps ; lenses ; reflectors ; miners' and like safety lamps.—
An apparatus for projecting light from one or more lamps to a position at some distance is applicable for lighting, producing colour effects, illuminating fountains, lighting places containing explosive gases, optical signalling and telegraphy, and other purposes. In the form shown in Fig. 1, a horizontal base *m* carries several lanterns *b*, a casing *g*, and a number of reflectors *i* adjustable on ball-joints and slides. Each lantern *b* contains an electric incandescent lamp and four lenses directing the light through apertures in the sides and top of the casing *g* ; that passing through the side apertures *h* may be reflected by the mirror to any position *x*, where a glass ball may be placed.

A drum *f*, provided with apertures filled with coloured glass or gelatine, is supported in the casing by a central pivot *u*, and is rotated by a clock or other motor, such as a fan *r* driven by the hot air rising from the lamps. In a modification, an alternating-current arc lamp has its carbons arranged in line with the position to be lighted, the arc being surrounded by two circles of condensing lenses, the outer ones receiving light passing between the inner lenses ; the reflectors may be fixed in a curved casing, and the coloured glasses carried in apertures in a disc which rotates in front of the casing. In another modification of this construction, a continuous current arc is placed somewhat in front of a circle of inclined lenses.

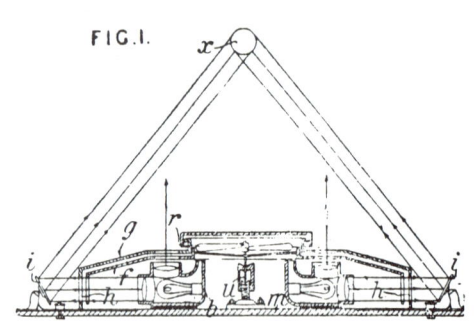

FIG. 1.

21,879. Digby, T. J. Dec. 3.

Acetylene and like lamps ; limelight apparatus &c. for lighting theatre stages. Gradual and practically-imperceptible variations in the colour or intensity of the light projected by a single acetylene, limelight, or similar apparatus upon theatre stages are effected by the use of screens of frosted gelatine, isinglass, or like material, which are mounted in frames and applied like photographic shutters in combination with the ordinary transparent screens of different colours. The frosted screen is prepared by pouring the liquid gelatine or other material upon a sheet of frosted glass, spreading it by rollers into a thin film of uniform thickness, removing the film *e* from the glass and placing it between two flat pieces *e¹* of thin wood or cardboard, and binding the side and bottom edges *e²* with linen or other thin material. The screen is then placed loosely between the side frames of the lantern or projector, from which it is prevented from falling by a metal guard *a¹*. When the ordinary transparent coloured screen is displaced or superseded by a second similar screen, the frosted gelatine obliterates or diffuses the line projected by the adjoining edges of the two screens, thereby avoiding the use of a second lamp or projector.

FIG. 2.

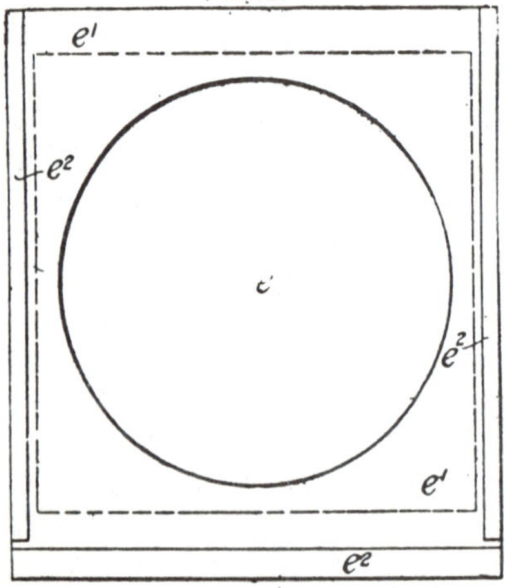

FIG. 3.

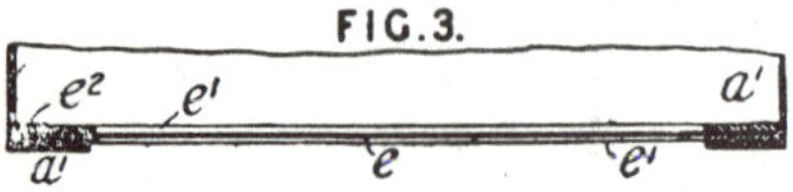

21,985. Mackenzie, J. W., [*Yberri-Fitch, D. de Santa M. d'*]. Dec. 4.

Panoramas ; theatrical appliances.—A stereopticon *e* is placed in the gallery, and a second stereopticon *e¹* is employed at the back of the stage *a¹* to throw images on front and back screens *b, d* on the stage, The part *b²* of the front screen consists of thick opaque cloth with a white or grey face. The central portion *b³* is formed of fine lace, gauze, or reticulated material, on which an image can be thrown, or through which an image on the screen *d* can be viewed. The screen *d* is made of thin

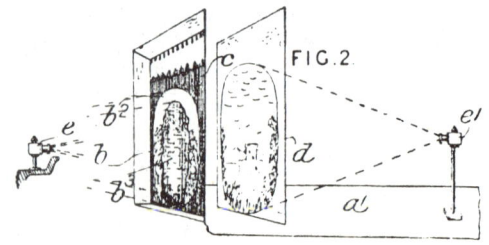

FIG. 2.

muslin or silk, and a dark opaque curtain *c* is
draped round the proscenium opening.   The
images on the screens are combined to produce
varying effects, and artistes may perform between
the screens.

23,203.   Downes, E.   Dec. 19.

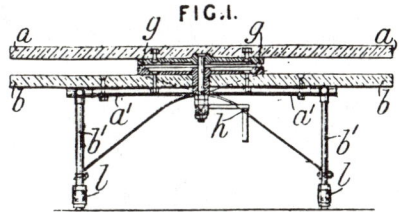

Theatrical appliances: circuses.—A revolving
stage *a* for circuses and theatres is mounted on a
central spindle and ball bearings *g*, and is rotated
by a handle *h* in a direction opposite to that of
ponies, animals, or human beings running on the
stage.   A lower table *b* is fixed to a tubular braced
supporting-frame *a*^{1}, *b*^{1}, mounted on adjustable
legs *l*.

The Indexes

Name Index

Barton	John Henry	Mechanician	1900	7973
Bastian	Charles Orme	Electrical engineer	1898	19620
Batault	Emile	Profession not stated	1897	8645
Beauchamp	Francis	Engineer	1898	23382
Beeton	Christopher Joseph	Retired schoolmaster	1892	16554
Bell	Henry	Profession not stated	1878	3862
Bell	James	Profession not stated	1878	3862
Bell	James	Profession not stated	1879	2970
Bellet	Ferdinand	Engineer	1897	17747
Bellini	Henry Linari	Profession not stated	1875	3215
Bennett	Henry Mellor	Iron founder	1882	394
Berlyn	Frederic Harman Peter	Electrical engineer	1891	13683
Berresford	Arthur William	Manufacturer	1899	14293
Berry	Raymond	Architect	1896	1626
Betts	William John	Merchant	1890	19642
Bevis	Henry	Electrician	1895	6657
Bierstadt	Albert	Artist	1896	10063
Bishop	William	Gentleman	1888	356
Bissmire	Catherine Elizabeth	Artiste	1890	4364
Biver	Mathias Alfred	Glass-works manager	1900	6544
Bloch	Edmond	Engineer	1894	20054
Bloch	Edmond	Profession not stated	1896	11544
Boehle	Herrmann	Profession not stated	1884	12382
Boisset	Albert Hotton	Gymnast and pantomimist	1895	21101
Boisset	Frank Mendoza	Gymnast and pantomimist	1895	21101
Boisset	Frederick Perkins	Gymnast	1896	2991
Boisset	William Welch	Gymnast and pantomimist	1895	21101
Bolton	Charles	Upholsterer	1863	3209
Bond	Henry	Newspaper manager	1889	19926
Booth	Harold Sims Joseph	*Agent for* C. Hermann	1892	5528
Booth	Lawrence	Architect (F.R.I.B.A.)	1887	13025
Boughton	John Waters	Gentleman	1898	13837
Boulard	Madame	Profession not stated	1856	2751
Boult	Alfred Julius	*Agent for* W.C. Shaffer	1887	10402
Boult	Alfred Julius	*Agent for* M.L. Fuller	1893	10221
Boult	Alfred Julius	*Agent for* S. Elton	1896	6591
Boult	Alfred Julius	*Agent for* F. Bellet	1897	17747
Boult	Alfred Julius	*Agent for* O. Schaffhirt	1898	4007
Boult	Alfred Julius	*Agent for* P. Carré	1898	25275
Boult	Alfred Julius	*Agent for* M.L. Fuller	1899	22180
Boulter	Cornelius Alfred	Optician	1891	16223
Bourieff	Jean Baptiste Marie Amédée	Profession not stated	1866	2755
Bowles	Edward Wingfield	Civil engineer	1899	2742
Boys	Charles Vernon	Professor of physics	1892	3942
Bradley	Herbert	Gent	1874	4479
Bradley	Thomas	Engineer	1891	1016
Bradley	Tom	Architect and surveyor	1900	230

Bramham	Philip	Optician	1888	2192
Broadbridge	Edward	Furniture dealer	1891	2399
Brooman	Clinton Edgecumbe	*Agent for* J.B.M. Bourieff	1866	2755
Brooman	Richard Archibald	*Agent for* Madame Boulard	1856	2751
Brooman	Richard Archibald	*Agent for* Messrs Demangeot and Co.	1859	2564
Brown	Andrew Betts	Engineer	1875	3593
Brown	Joseph	Gas engineer	1887	8627
Browne	Newnham	Chartered patent agent	1893	10296
Buatier	Joseph	Egyptian Hall, Piccadilly	1886	16388
Buatier	Joseph	Egyptian Hall, Piccadilly	1886	16389
Buatier	Joseph	Egyptian Hall, Piccadilly	1887	9798
Buatier	Joseph	Gentleman	1891	5172
Bull	William	Gent	1874	4479
Burgess	Neilson	Profession not stated	1890	20976
Burt	Leslie Newman	Electrical engineer	1898	22858
Busby	Albert Gibbons	Profession not stated	1872	1186
Butcher	William	Photographer	1895	16901
Butcher	William Frederic	Photographer	1895	16901
Butterworth	Robert Harry	Private tutor	1894	3954
Bynoe	Frederick Oatley	Manager to a scientific instrument manufactory	1898	17095
Cabanes	Henri	Profession not stated	1867	722
Calcott	William	Artist	1861	2500
Calcott	William	Scenic artist	1864	826
Calvert	Charles Alexander	Profession not stated	1870	178
Calvert	Charles Alexander	Profession not stated	1871	2776
Campbell	Stafford	Shipwright	1888	1302
Cardwell	William Alexander	Lieutenant Colonel in the Army	1887	17107
Carré	Ernest	Clerk	1889	5287
Carré	Paul	Chemist	1898	25275
Carter	John Henry	Profession not stated	1874	2864
Carter	John Henry (younger)	Profession not stated	1874	2864
Castan	Gustav	of Gebrüder Castan	1888	5254
Castan	Louis	of Gebrüder Castan	1888	5254
Cattreut	Louis	Shorthand writer	1884	10358
Cawdery	John William	Theatrical machinist	1890	5771
Celrain	John	Profession not stated	1879	299
Chadwick	John George	Profession not stated	1892	10345
Chadwick	Thomas Henry	Profession not stated	1892	10345
Challis	James	Commercial traveller	1894	37
Chandler	Henry	Upholder [sic]	1860	2080
Chandler	William	Profession not stated	1894	21844
Chantler	Henry	Clog-maker	1885	1373
Chapman	Frank Montileoues	Theatrical manager	1890	13201
Chase	Charles Arthur	Profession not stated	1895	16070
Cheffins	William	Photographer	1891	3727
Chèradame	Antoine Leopold	Profession not stated	1872	2053
Christy	Thomas	Merchant	1890	12230

Cinquevalli	Paul Braun	Artist	1894	6834
Cinquevalli	Paul Braun	Professional juggler	1899	6268
Clark	Alexander	Gent	1882	2935
Clark	Alexander	Gent	1883	2601
Clark	Alexander Melville	*Agent for* A.J. Martin,E. Tessier	1879	117
Clark	Alexander Melville	*Agent for* G. Meyer	1883	941
Clark	Alexander Melville	*Agent for* G. Trouvé	1884	5157
Clark	Henry Munday	Gentleman	1892	20137
Clark	Henry Munday	Gent	1898	4886
Clark	William	*Agent for* T. Foucault	1861	1784
Clark	William	Engineer and *Agent for* Count W. F.De Douhet	1861	2083
Clark	William	*Agent for* B. Subra	1863	3015
Clarke	John Algernon	Farmer	1875	1804
Clarke	Maximilian William H.	Architect	1887	12817
Clegg	John	Profession not stated	1872	999
Clémançon	Claude Edouard	Engineer	1898	9511
Cloquet	Louis	Engineer	1895	4807
Cockman	Alfred Ebenezer	Conjuror	1888	17005
Cogswell	Henry Daniel	Gent	1881	3725
Colby	Edward John	Mechanical engineer	1889	9955
Coleman	Joseph James	Profession not stated	1878	3862
Coleman	Joseph James	Profession not stated	1879	2970
Colt	James Bennett	Manufacturer	1889	14671
Coninck	Frank de	Profession not stated	1888	3795
Conquest	George A. Oliver	Theatrical manager	1899	24539
Conquest	George Augustus Oliver	Theatrical manager	1896	23549
Cooper	Ernest Sewell	Yorkshire dyer	1893	18623
Cooper	William	Bonnet manufacturer	1846	11512
Cornelius	Mrs.Ellen Francis J.	"Of no occupation"	1889	15168
Coulson	Richard	Architect	1892	242
Courtneidge	Robert	Theatre manager and author	1896	11013
Cox	Charles Horace	Commercial traveller	1898	14513
Cox	Charles Horace	Commercial traveller	1898	14514
Cox	Charles Horace	Commercial traveller	1898	15825
Cox	Frederic Percy	Clerk	1896	7511
Cox	George	Profession not stated	1863	449
Cresswell	Maud Beatrice	Spinster	1893	24038
Crowe	William James	Merchant	1890	19642
Cryer	Abraham	Stage artiste	1892	22952
Cubison	Herbert Jelfs	Secretary to a public company	1898	17095
Cumine	James Alexander	Model maker	1899	3298
Cunynghame	Henry Hardinge Samuel	Barrister at law	1892	3942
Dade	Daniel Henry	Profession not stated	1881	1196
Dallmeyer	John Henry	Optician	1870	2750
Dalman	George Henry Bennett	Merchant	1896	11922
Dalman	James Charles	Manufacturer	1899	3072

Dando	Walter Pfeffer	Profession not stated	1875	3067
Dando	Walter Pfeffer	Theatrical manager	1890	16699
Dando	Walter Pfeffer	Stage manager	1893	24064
Dando	Walter Pfeffer	Stage manager	1894	17077
David	Henri	Profession not stated	1882	63
Davies	George	*Agent for* A.G. Busby, W.B. Woodbury	1872	1186
Davis	Alfred	Gent	1871	3352
Davis	Henry Thomas	Profession not stated	1875	1874
Day	St. John Vincent	*Agent for* W. Stanton	1888	19024
De Douhet	William F., Count	Profession not stated	1861	2083
De Monostor	Adalbert Béky	Journalist	1898	23070
De Santa Maria d'Yberri-Fitch	Dolores	Danseuse	1900	21985
Dean	Albert Reuben	of A.R. Dean and Co.	1894	4407
Defries	Coleman	Gas (lighting) engineer	1864	22
Defries	Coleman	Gas engineer	1864	1643
Defries	Coleman	Gas engineer	1864	2393
Defries	Coleman	Jonas Defries and Son	1866	2301
Demangeot & Co.	Messrs.	Messrs. Demangeot & Co.	1859	2564
Dengg	Carl	Profession not stated	1882	2889
Dennett	Charles Colton	Builder	1863	1998
Denstone	William Huskisson	Profession not stated	1879	5185
Dickinson	Basil Bentham	Gentleman	1894	7673
Digby	Thomas Joseph	Electrical engineer	1899	24887
Digby	Thomas Joseph	Electrical engineer	1900	21879
Dinsmore	John Henry Richardson	Engineer	1888	5247
Dircks	Henry	Civil engineer	1863	326
Doubell	Edward Henry	of Childe and Doubell	1880	5105
Dougall	John Wilson	Chemist	1896	5473
Downes	Edward	Music hall artist	1900	23203
Drake	Hugh Oakley	Photographer	1895	16901
Du Fay	Alcide Sanial	Profession not stated	1870	673
Dufossé	Eugène	Profession not stated	1860	1318
Duncan	Charles Stewart	Profession not stated	1862	980
Duncan	William Henry	Engineer	1884	934
Duncan	William Henry	Engineer	1884	1378
Duncan	William Henry	Engineer	1884	1597
Duplany	Claude Marius	Theatrical manager and actor	1887	13740
Dutton	Joseph	Profession not stated	1881	4343
Dutton	William Harry	Gentleman	1887	13258
Edwards	Edmund	Engineer	1873	2888
Edwards	Edmund	Engineer	1874	3604
Edwards	Edmund	*Agent for* E. Lüddeckens	1891	18598
Edwards	Edmund	*Agent for* A. Engelsmann	1900	18946
Edwards	William	Engineer	1895	14598
Edwin	Walter	Profession not stated	1865	131
Elton	Sam	Profession not stated	1896	6591
Emerson	James Ezekiel	Manufacturer	1887	6882

Emmott	Walter	Electrical engineer	1898	4761
Engel	Freidrich Herman F.	Profession not stated	1891	7487
Engelsmann	August	Engineer	1900	18946
Engwall	Oscar Frederick	Mechanician	1895	9100
Erlanger	Abraham Lincoln	Theatrical manager	1891	21877
Fairfax	Joseph Sinclair	Consulting engineer	1887	5202
Fanta	Ferdinand	Consulting engineer	1896	9758
Farini	Guillermo Antonio	Profession not stated	1870	1572
Farini	Guillermo Antonio	Profession not stated	1875	4404
Farini	Guillermo Antonio	Profession not stated	1877	4587
Farini	Guillermo Antonio	Gentleman	1887	1906
Farrell	Henry Havelock	Commission agent	1896	580
Felbermann	Louis	Profession not stated	1892	14948
Finger	Louis	Profession not stated	1870	1584
Fisher	Joseph Alfred	Manager, United Asbestos Co. Ltd.	1887	13025
Fitzpatrick	Hugh Donald	*Agent for* A. Fuhrmann	1895	6468
Forret	John Alexander	Chemist and druggist	1891	10482
Foucault	Théophile	Manufacturer	1861	1784
Franck-Valery	Emile	Profession not stated	1891	21716
Franck-Valery	Paul	Profession not stated	1891	21716
Franquin	Pierre	Profession not stated	1884	9200
Friese-Greene	William	Photographer	1893	22954
Frome	Charles Henry	Profession not stated	1880	3416
Fuhrmann	August	Panorama proprietor	1888	7067
Fuhrmann	August	Panorama proprietor	1895	6468
Fuller	Ida May	Stage artist	1899	23473
Fuller	Marie Louise	Professional dancer	1893	10221
Fuller	Marie Louise	Dancing actress	1893	10296
Fuller	Marie Louise	Professional dancer	1893	10301
Fuller	Marie Louise	Profession not stated	1899	22180
Gaitton(sic)	Emile	Engineer	1896	27472
Ganem	Chakri	Manufacturer	1898	21413
Gardener	Cuthbert	Contractor	1887	14101
Gardner	Edward Vincent	Professor of chemistry	1875	4486
Garthwaite	Charles Wheatley	Cabinet maker	1881	2022
Geddes	William	Merchant	1887	12304
Geller	John	Gymnast	1897	28602
Gibbs	George Cantrell	Profession not stated	1880	3416
Gibbs	Joseph	Engineer	1833	6408
Gibson	James Hume	Ironmonger	1884	9604
Gillett	William Frederick	Architect	1885	1173
Glazier	William	Joiner	1884	9604
Gleason	William James	Attorney at law	1889	10884
Gooding	Richard Alpheus	Profession not stated	1870	2726
Goodwin	Thomas	Teacher of woodwork and carpentry	1894	17604
Grade	Gustav	Artist	1898	5694
Granger	Louis Edwin	Gent	1889	15496

Grant	Lewis	Professor of dancing	1896	26783
Gray	Charles	Optician	1889	6999
Graydon	James Lawrence	Licensed victualler	1892	16183
Green	James	Jeweller	1890	7448
Grieve	Thomas Walford	Artist	1873	294
Grieve	Thomas Walford	Artist	1879	259
Grismer	Joseph Rhode	Profession not stated	1899	20255
Grogan	Samuel	Artiste "at present on tour"	1897	1274
Grottendieck	William Geldolph	Electrical engineer	1894	24821
Gudgeon	Robert Horsley	Cabinet manufacturer	1890	3150
Guitton	Emile	Engineer	1896	27472
Gwinner	Robert	Profession not stated	1882	2889
Gwyer	George Wright	Gentleman	1894	2365
Gwyer	George Wright	Engineer	1895	22515
Gwynne	James Eglinton A.	Engineer, Brooke Street Works	1894	17077
Gye	Frederic	Profession not stated	1861	927
Gye	Frederic	Profession not stated	1878	4473
Hackforth	Matthew	Painter and decorator	1863	351
Haddan	Herbert John	*Agent for* E. Molera, J. Celrain	1879	299
Haddan	Herbert John	*Agent for* T. Trivier	1882	902
Haddan	Reginald	*Agent for* F.H.F. Engel	1891	7487
Hagen	Claude Lavrain	Stage machinist	1900	12440
Hall	Frederic Thomas	*Agent for* E. Heit	1868	1487
Hall	Joseph	Clerk	1866	1491
Hall	Thomas	Profession not stated	1874	3669
Halske & Co.		Electrical engineers	1894	21140
Hamlet	Thomas	Gymnast	1877	2356
Hargreaves	William	Physician	1893	9289
Harradine	William Newton	Professional ventriloquist	1888	13105
Harris	Henry Inkson	Electrician	1889	10285
Harrison	Thomas	Cabinet maker	1881	2022
Harrison	William Henry	Profession not stated	1866	3110
Hart	Frederic William	Manufacturer of scientific appliances	1888	356
Hart	Frederic William	Manufacturer of scientific instruments	1889	3279
Hartley	Frederick William	Gas engineer	1868	46
Harvey	William Henry	Journalist	1894	22211
Hasselkus	John William	Engineer	1900	12538
Hatch	Oswald Birch	Oil merchant	1896	5473
Haviland	Robert J. Langstaff	Profession not stated	1882	2107
Hawker	Thomas Henry Seymour	Engineer	1880	15
Hayes	George	Civil and mechanical engineer	1892	6940
Hayward	Suter King	Engineer	1893	5936
Heath	Thomas Theodore	Artist	1863	894
Heath	William Edwin	Army captain	1887	12304
Hedgman	Elward Radford	Electrical engineer	1888	17559
Heit	Edouard	Profession not stated	1868	1487
Held	Heinrich	Manufacturer	1890	1959

Hempson	Amis	Gent	1860	2080
Hénard	Alfred Eugène	Architect	1900	6544
Hengler	Albert	Circus proprietor	1897	6389
Hengler	Albert Henry	Hengler's Circus	1890	9047
Hepworth	Thomas Cradock	Lecturer	1896	5874
Hermann	Charles	Manufacturer	1892	5528
Hertz	Carl	Illusionist	1890	16903
Heysinger	Isaac W.	Physician	1885	8727
Hillman	William	Engineer	1889	12847
Hipwell	Daniel Edward	Merchant	1895	13926
Hobson	Charles Walshaw	Outfitter	1889	540
Hoffman	John William	Profession not stated	1863	2019
Holbrook	Benjamin	Manufacturer	1887	2315
Hollingsworth	Charles M.	American gent	1898	21853
Hont	James	Artist	1898	12592
Horsfall	William	Ironfounder	1896	1626
Horst	Marius	Inventor of Horst & Co.	1899	6526
Hosmer	Arthur	Lumberman	1899	4613
Houldershaw	William	Dealer in optical goods	1895	2195
Huet	Henri Louis	Optical instrument manufacturer	1900	256
Hughes	Alexander	Optician	1889	18583
Hughes	De Bosco	Scenic artist	1863	2841
Hughes	William Charles	Optician	1875	2683
Hughes	William Charles	Optician	1889	1570
Hughes	William Charles	Optician	1889	3839
Hughes	William Charles	Optician	1890	611
Hughes	William Charles	Manufacturing optician	1891	4387
Hughes	William Charles	Manufacturing optician	1891	5106
Hughes	William Charles	Manufacturing optician	1892	10568
Hunt	Bristow	*Agent for* L. Finger	1870	1584
Hunt	William Leonard	*Agent for* G.A.Farini	1875	4404
Hunter	William Anthony	Profession not stated	1869	1077
Imray	John	*Agent for* K. Pfaff	1882	437
Jackson	Alfred Charles	Optical instrument maker	1893	17701
Jacobsen	Bernhard Holger	Managing director	1900	4879
James	Alfred	Photographer	1888	2730
Jefferson	Charles Burke	Theatrical manager	1891	21877
Jensen	Peter	*Agent for* H.S. Suillot,H. David	1882	63
Jensen	Peter	*Agent for* R.J.L. Haviland	1882	2107
Jensen	Peter	*Agent for* Mac Kaye Manufacturing Co.	1883	5307
Jensen	Peter	*Agent for* L.van Steene,L. Cattreut	1884	10358
Jensen	Peter	*Agent for* H.G. Underwood	1890	1884
Johnson	Edward	Dairyman	1892	21673
Johnson	James Yate	Gentleman	1893	21960
Jones	Edmund Cyril	Machinist	1889	10884
Jones	George William	Engineer	1886	10500
Jones	Thomas Lloyd	Mechanical engineer	1881	4267
Jordan	William	Mechanical engineer	1891	2399

Jordan	William	Mechanical engineer	1891	20576
Justice	Philip Middleton	*Agent for* V. Vankeerberghen	1882	4073
Justice	Philip Middleton	*Agent for* I.W. Heysinger,J. Pusey	1885	8727
Justice	Philip Middleton	*Agent for* Long-Arm System Co.	1899	13026
Kaufmann	Nicholas Edward	Champion trick rider	1891	2041
Kautsky	Johann	Profession not stated	1882	2889
Keeling	Enoch Bassett	Architect	1863	31
Keevil	Henry	Profession not stated	1877	2241
Keith	Charles Henry	Circus proprietor	1882	753
Keller	John	Printer	1890	9884
Kemp	Henry	Optician	1889	6999
Kerr	Walter	Manager of the Electric and Lime Light Co.	1865	3286
Kershaw	Abraham	Scientific instrument maker	1892	16026
Kidd	Robert Leamon	Profession not stated	1882	2780
Kilányï	Eduard von	Scenic artist	1895	19841
Kilham	John Thomas	Artist	1888	7498
King	Horatio Nelson	Photographic artist	1863	1744
King	William Falconer	Engineer	1894	1433
Kiralfy	Imre	Dramatic author	1894	18083
Kirby	George	Carpenter	1898	8559
Klaw	Marc	Theatrical manager	1891	21877
Klinkerfues	Wilhelm	Professor and Director of the Royal Observatory, Göttingen, Hanover	1870	3228
Knell	James W.	Actor	1883	3010
Knell	James William	Actor	1889	9068
Knell	James William	Actor	1890	3847
Knott	Kennard	Profession not stated	1877	3607
Kreittmayr	Joseph	Formator of the Bavarian National Museum	1875	959
Krüger	Simon David	Profession not stated	1876	2180
Kunkel	Carl	Locksmith	1897	3102
Lacey	Horace Harry	Surveyor	1899	5055
Lacomme	Jean Marie Auguste	Doctor of Medicine	1870	2202
Lacomme	Jean Marie Auguste	Profession not stated	1879	92
Laine	Louis	Profession not stated	1867	2737
Lake	Henry Harris	*Agent for* B. Holbrook, H.N. Mann	1887	2315
Lake	Henry Harris	*Agent for* J.W. Knell	1889	9068
Lake	Henry Harris	*Agent for* J.W. Knell	1890	3847
Lake	Henry Harris	*Agent for* N. Burgess	1890	20976
Lake	Henry Harris	*Agent for* M.L. Fuller	1893	10301
Lake	William Robert	*Agent for* A.L. Chèradame, A.E. Le Dreux,V.C.J. Oursel	1872	2053
Lake	William Robert	*Agent for* T. Jones	1881	4267
Lake	William Robert	*Agent for* H.S. Maxim	1881	5663
Lake	William Robert	*Agent for* J.W. Knell	1883	3010
Lake	William Robert	*Agent for* J.B. Colt	1889	14671
Lamprecht	Rodolphe de	Gentleman	1899	9199
Lancaster	Frederick John	Assistant at the Metropolitan Board of Works, London.	1888	7732
Lane	John	Brewer	1888	246
Laszky	Albert	Composer	1898	23070

Laszky	Sigismund	Engineer	1898	23070
Latelle	Cornelius	Tightrope and trapeze artist	1892	8708
Latelle	Richard	Tightrope and trapeze artist	1892	8708
Le Dreux	Alexander Eugène	Profession not stated	1872	2053
Le Mesurier	Harry Brooke	Chief Constable of Exeter	1889	8772
Lecoq	Louis Gustave	Profession not stated	1861	1711
Lee	Robt. Bristow	Engineer of the Titancrete Co.	1888	3708
Lee	William	*Agent for* W. Lee, J.T. Pullon, W. Sykes	1876	474
Leighton	John Taylor	Manufacturer	1897	17665
Leslie	Henry J.	Theatre proprietor	1890	5474
Letta		Equilibrist	1891	8891
Levi	Samuel Joseph	Optician	1889	5287
Lion	Alexandre Léon	Manufacturer	1899	7790
Locke	Charles Woolnough	Optical lantern expert and manufacturer	1895	13076
Long Arm System Co.			1899	13026
Louit	Jean Baptiste Emile	Gent	1863	264
Lowe	Albert Henry	Profession not stated	1882	1355
Lüddeckens	Ernst	Doctor	1891	18598
Luis	José	*Agent for* Anon	1858	2170
Lutticke	George Frederick	Gentleman	1891	2165
Lutticke	George Frederick	Gentleman	1891	13765
Lynn	Hugh Simmons	*Agent for* T.W. Tobin	1874	3228
Lyon	Henry	Electrician	1890	5474
Lyon	Henry	Electrical engineer	1897	28859
Lyons	George	Electrician, Savoy Theatre, London	1895	6657
Lyons	Lawrence Nathaniel	Profession not stated	1894	5155
Lytton	Edward	Theatrical manager	1896	3249
Maas	Joseph	Accountant	1874	2286
Mac Kaye Manufacturing Co.			1883	5307
MacKenzie	Neil Kennedy	Parish minister	1900	16687
Mackenzie	John William	*Agent for* De Santa Maria d'Yberri-Fitch	1900	21985
Maitland	William Henry	Profession not stated	1870	2933
Maitland	William Lauderdale	Profession not stated	1870	2933
Malden	Benjamin John	Gentleman	1894	1024
Mann	Henry Nepthali	Manufacturer	1887	2315
March	Edward	Engineer	1900	15377
Marsden	Charles	Ventilating engineer	1856	28
Marsh	Albert	Actor and theatre manager	1899	6959
Martin	Abel Jean	Profession not stated	1879	117
Martin	William	Iron merchant	1894	243
Maskelyne	John Nevil	Illusionist	1875	1804
Maskelyne	John Nevil	Illusionist	1880	1148
Maskelyne jnr	John Nevil	Egyptian Hall	1892	9033
Mason	William Havelock	Musical instrument dealer	1892	4668
Matthews	Lambert	Gentleman	1893	10238
Maurice	Joseph	Profession not stated	1864	2564
Maurice	Joseph	Dentist	1868	1049

Maxim	Hiram Stevens	Profession not stated	1881	5663
McCarty	William Fitz-Charles	Colonel	1878	5255
McDade	John Joseph	Engineer	1892	3209
McIlvenna	Charles	Profession not stated	1878	5109
McLennan	John	Horologist	1882	858
McLennan	Kenneth	Scenic artist	1882	858
McLennan	Kenneth	Draughtsman	1890	13056
McLennan	Kenneth	Artist	1897	26611
McMullin	Mary	Spinster	1887	1667
Melven	George de	Conjuror	1888	17005
Melville	Andrew	Grand Theatre, Birmingham	1887	12328
Menotti	Otto	Wire walker artist	1892	21280
Meyer	Gaspard	Profession not stated	1883	941
Meysel	George	Artiste	1897	25864
Mia-Mia		Ventriloquist	1891	21887
Midgeley	Thomas	Manufacturer	1887	6882
Millis	Frederic William	Ventriloquist	1891	21887
Mills	Jennie	Dancer	1899	15890
Molera	Eusebius	Profession not stated	1879	299
Moreton	Henry Burrell	Paint manufacturer	1885	1173
Morgan	Jacob	Stone merchant	1881	1769
Morgan	William	Sculptor	1881	1769
Morgan	William Thomas	Profession not stated	1882	2780
Morgan-Brown	William	*Agent for* J. Peiffer, W.F.C. McCarty, Prince Perigord de Sagan	1878	5255
Morgenstern	Louis	Artist	1890	15024
Morgenstern	Louis	Artist	1890	15025
Morgenstern	Louis	Artist	1890	20392
Morris	John	Profession not stated	1874	2334
Morris	Joseph Matthew	Profession not stated	1873	2163
Morritt	Adelaide	Profession not stated	1892	13597
Morritt	Charles	Egyptian Hall	1892	9033
Morritt	Charles	Brewer	1893	17429
Morton	Charles	Profession not stated	1864	41
Moss	Richard John	Ironmonger's assistant	1897	18925
Motte	Henri	Artist	1890	12845
Moule	John	Manufacturing chemist	1857	478
Moy	Ernest Francis	Electrical engineer	1895	18935
Mueller	Gustav	Profession not stated	1875	2120
Mulhall	George	Athlete	1892	11675
Munro	John	known as: John Munro Graham	1863	1917
Murcott	Henry John	Profession not stated	1881	2358
Murphy	Jeremiah	Mechanician	1895	9100
Myers	George David	Engineer and printer	1846	11512
Myselli		Artiste	1897	25864
Nagel	Junius	Profession not stated	1882	1468
Nagel	Junius	Chemist	1884	2154
Neale	Wm. Bevoir Buchanan	Gent	1895	2746

Newbold	Henry	Profession not stated	1876	2438
Newton	Frederic	Optician	1877	1957
Newton	Frederic	Scientific instrument maker	1893	18440
Newton	Herbert Charles	Optician	1889	12913
Newton	Herbert Charles	Scientific instrument maker	1894	12572
Newton	William Edward	Civil engineer	1857	1060
Newton	William Edward	*Agent for* H. Cabanes	1867	722
Newton	William Edward	*Agent for* A.S. Du Fay	1870	673
Niblett	Job Thomas	Electrical engineer	1896	4025
Nicholls	Thomas	Carpenter and joiner	1890	9752
Nixon	Edwin	Surveyor	1888	7732
Noakes	David William	Hay salesman	1886	6154
Noakes	David William	Engineer and optician	1892	5541
Nolan	Patrick William	Profession not stated	1873	2648
O'Sullivan	Daniel Robert	Homeopathic surgeon	1887	11646
Ober	William Young	Inventor	1887	16744
Oliver	George	Profession not stated	1871	1234
Oliver	George	Profession not stated	1875	3366
Oller	Joseph	Director of the Nautical Arena, Paris	1886	3920
Ormerod	Joseph Bamford	Theatre proprietor	1897	26387
Oursel	Victor Charles Jules	Profession not stated	1872	2053
Owen	Richard	Merchant	1882	858
Paris	Alfred John	Fireproofer	1889	14515
Parkes	George	Theatrical performer	1866	184
Parsonage	Christopher	Mechanic and stereotyper	1898	8286
Parsons	Arthur Joseph	Electrical engineer	1898	19620
Peebles	David Bruce	Fountainbridge Works	1876	3231
Peiffer	Jules	Profession not stated	1878	5255
Pennefather	De Fonblanque	Cotton broker	1888	5247
Pepper	John Henry	Professor of chemistry and Hon.Director of the Polytechnic Institution	1863	326
Pepper	John Henry	Professor of chemistry	1864	498
Pepper	John Henry	Professor of chemistry	1865	222
Pepper	John Henry	Professor of chemistry	1865	3139
Pepper	John Henry	Professor of chemistry	1866	3278
Pepper	John Henry	Professor of chemistry	1867	3541
Pepper	John Henry	Professor of chemistry	1879	1245
Périgord de Sagan	Talleyrand, Prince	Profession not stated	1878	5255
Petit	Henry Francis Emile	Architect and surveyor	1877	37
Petter	James Bazeley	Ironmonger	1887	12197
Pfaff	Karl	Profession not stated	1882	437
Phillips	Herbert Thomas	Merchant	1890	19642
Pichler	Seraphicus Francis	Profession not stated	1866	3278
Pichler	Seraphicus Francis	Profession not stated	1875	4486
Pichler	Seraphicus Francis	Profession not stated	1876	97
Pickhardt	Gustav	Profession not stated	1882	206
Pickhardt	Gustav	Profession not stated	1883	1078
Plessey	Gabriel	Engineer	1889	1419

Plunkett	Harry Gratton	Actor	1893	24807
Pocock	Alfred Willmer	Engineer	1891	5922
Pocock	Caroline Spilsbury	Gentlewoman	1889	5218
Pocock	Caroline Spilsbury	Gentlewoman	1891	5922
Poilly	Edouard de	Engineer	1875	4068
Porter	Philip	Manager for Lloyd's Maps	1867	2631
Potter	Edward Tuckerman	Profession not stated	1888	14171
Potter	Thomas	Secretary	1898	23508
Pradou	Jules Emile Melon de	Profession not stated	1861	1711
Prestwich	Ernest Edgley	Electrical engineer	1898	22858
Probert	Isaac	Electrical engineer	1895	18935
Prosser	William	Gentleman	1859	2334
Pullon	John Thomas	Profession not stated	1876	474
Puntis	Josiah	Profession not stated	1863	449
Pusey	Joshua	Attorney	1885	8727
Quinson	Gustav	Manufacturer	1898	21413
Racey	George	Profession not stated	1872	498
Rae	Alfred	Retired master mariner	1873	1802
Ramminger	Albert	Cabinetmaker	1891	14423
Ramspacher	Théodore	Civil engineer	1860	187
Ransome	Thomas	Chemist	1885	14949
Rastrick	Robert Joseph Hooper	Chemist	1889	2727
Reddell	Isaac Hadley	Engineer	1816	4035
Redwood	Theophilus Horne	Chemist	1890	401
Reinold	Johann	Manufacturer	1897	12735
Reinold	Peter Joseph	Manufacturer	1897	12735
Reinolts	George von	Gent	1899	3298
Rendell	James Robson	Minister of religion	1890	15292
Resuche	Réné	Gent	1890	7636
Ridgway	Robert	Profession not stated	1882	3932
Rignall	George	Theatrical lessee and manager of Her Majesty's Theatre, Sydney, Australia	1895	11903
Rimington	Alexander Wallace	Artist	1893	24814
Risley	Isaac	Mechanical Engineer	1893	21960
Robertson	James	Cabinet maker	1900	1182
Robertson	John	Engineer	1873	2881
Rodeck	Carl Georg	Engineer and captain of military balloonists	1892	16120
Rodeck	Carl Georg	Engineer	1895	2948
Rodeck	Carl Georg	Engineer	1895	17652
Romah	Robert	Gymnast	1889	934
Rosher	Charles Henry	Civil engineer	1893	22866
Rossman	John Gillespie	Electrical engineer	1900	13072
Roth	Franz	Machinery manufacturer	1882	2889
Rucker	Martin Diederich	Director of Humber & Co. Ltd.	1895	7371
Sachs	Edwin Otho	Architect	1898	27000
Salomons	Sir David Lionel	Baronet	1890	20633
Sanders	William	Boot manufacturer	1891	2725
Sanderson	John Glasgow	Engineer	1883	501

Sanson	Raoul Adrien Grimoin	Engineer	1899	1382
Savage	Henry Thomas	Carver, gilder and picture frame manufacturer	1892	19883
Scantlebury	William	Scientific engineer	1878	1932
Schaffhirt	Otto	Merchant	1898	4007
Schirm	James William Charles Cowen	Landscape painter	1890	11784
Schleicher	Wilhelm	Architect	1889	12547
Schlosser	Eduard	Cabinet maker	1888	13361
Schmidt	August Edmund	Jeweller	1896	17132
Schmidt	August Edmund	Jeweller	1897	8983
Schmidt	Christophe Frédéric	Tailor	1860	187
Schmidt	Gustav	Manufacturer	1897	15723
Schroeder	Frederick	Engineer	1890	18265
Schumann	Albert	Circus Schumann, Francfort on the Main	1897	26413
Scott	Albert William	Photographer and optical lantern exhibitor	1889	17378
Scott	Albert William	Photographer and optical lantern exhibitor	1890	19402
Scott	James Sheppard	Barrister-at-law	1875	4068
Scott	John	Machinist	1889	11738
Scudamore	Fortunatus Augustine	Dramatic author, theatrical manager and actor	1895	976
Selbini	John	Artiste	1894	22132
Seyde	Francis Napier	Gent	1883	5221
Shaffer	William Cass	Electrical engineer	1887	10402
Shaw	William	Profession not stated	1895	11729
Shepherd	Timothy	Engineer	1896	5921
Sherman	John W.	American	1884	6598
Shipman	Fred. Waverley	Theatrical manager	1897	17229
Short	Alfred Joseph	Tinner and inventor of theatrical novelties	1889	4931
Siemens	Brothers & Co.	Electrical engineers	1892	5526
Siemens	Brothers & Co.	Electrical engineers	1894	21140
Siemens	Brothers & Co.	Electrical engineers	1900	2356
Silber	Albert Marcus	Merchant	1870	1467
Silbon	Walter	Gymnast	1899	5732
Silliman	Charles Herbert	Banker	1899	4613
Silvester	Alfred	Photographer	1863	1630
Silvester	Alfred	Photographer	1864	1179
Simmons	Joseph	Profession not stated	1867	3617
Simplex Cash Register Syndicate		Cash register Co.	1896	5921
Simpson	Henry	Lamp manufacturer	1892	8185
Simpson	Henry	Lamp manufacturer	1892	22151
Simpson	Henry	Lamp manufacturer	1893	4644
Simpson	Henry	Lamp manufacturer	1893	24135
Sims	John	Engraver	1868	3542
Sloman	Bernard	Profession not stated	1890	18265
Smith	Albert	Equilibrist	1891	8891
Smith	Alexander Laws	Clerk	1888	11158
Smith	Edward Tyrrel	Theatre manager, Astley's Theatre, London	1863	3272
Smith	George Henry	Profession not stated	1875	3726

Smith	Henry David	Gas engineer	1889	11738
Solomons	Samuel	Gentlemen	1865	2815
Southorn	Charles	House furnisher	1897	4400
Sparkhall	Edward	Printer	1855	313
Spectatoria Co.		Auditorium Building, Chicago, Illinois	1893	1546
Spectatoria Co.		Auditorium Building, Chicago, Illinois	1893	1547
Spence	William	*Agent for* E. Vanderburgh	1860	1448
Spencer	James Robert	Plumber	1885	1373
Spencer	Robert	Musician	1898	16927
Stanley	James Martin	Engineer	1887	13193
Stanley	Thomas Blakemore	Engineers clerk	1887	13193
Stanton	Walter	Profession not stated	1888	19024
Stead	Thomas William	Ironfounder	1888	7962
Steell	George	Nursery florists and bouquet makers	1857	2229
Steell	William	Nursery florists and bouquet makers	1857	2229
Steene	Leopold van	Employee of the Brussels Commune	1884	10358
Stelling	Harry	Gymnastic artist	1895	2432
Stephenson	Rowland Macdonald	Civil engineer	1840	8404
Stern	Moriz	Merchant	1892	9628
Stetter	Konrad	Cabinetmaker	1891	14423
Steward	James Henry	Optician	1889	12972
Steward	James Henry	Optician	1896	9204
Stewart	David	Gardiner [sic], and hothouse builder	1801	2549
Stewart	David	Architect	1811	3417
Stewart & Co. Ltd.	Duncan	London Road Iron Works	1897	28859
Stirton	John Anderson	Costumier	1889	1784
Stocks	Walter	Ironmonger	1890	9934
Stodare	Colonel	Egyptian Hall, Piccadilly, London	1865	1983
Stoddart	Alfred	Profession not stated	1866	442
Stoddart	Alfred	Profession not stated	1866	689
Stoll	Oswald	Theatre proprietor	1895	8111
Stones	John	Engineer and revolving shutter manufacturer	1887	14556
Stott	James	Engineer	1896	26795
Stroud	William	Professor of physics	1890	15292
Stuart	John	Managing director	1897	19255
Stuart	John	Managing director	1900	12538
Subra	Bernard	Professor of maths	1863	3015
Suillot	Hippolyte Simon	Profession not stated	1882	63
Supthut	Heinrich	Merchant	1899	20623
Sutcliffe	William Stansfield	Builder	1872	2112
Swaab	Alfred James	Gentleman	1899	9199
Sweetser	Alfred	Consulting engineer	1897	17438
Sykes	William	Profession not stated	1876	474
Tabulewitch	Vladimir	Profession not stated	1896	29620
Talbot	Romain	Profession not stated	1877	1099
Tanner	George	Theatrical performer	1866	184
Taylor	Alfred Walter	Gent	1869	447

Taylor	Edmund	Managing director of E.& E. Taylor Ltd., Engineers	1894	17830
Taylor	Harold Dennis	Optician	1899	17641
Taylor	Henry	Theatrical Manager, Lyceum Theatre, Crewe	1894	16916
Tee	Harry	Engineer	1875	3024
Tennent	Hector Norman	Gentleman	1893	22665
Tepper	Ernst.	Painter	1887	14543
Terlinden	Gerhard	Manufacturer	1892	6924
Tessier	Eugène	Profession not stated	1879	117
Testo	George	Athlete	1892	11675
Thelwall	Weymouth Birbeck	Artist	1872	1192
Thomas	Robert	Profession not stated	1872	1570
Thomas	Walter John	Gas engineer	1895	9914
Thompson	George Samuel	Carriage builder	1890	18369
Thomson	Benjamin Lumsden	Profession not stated	1882	413
Thomson	Edward Hamilton	Engineer	1876	3304
Tiden	Charles Abraham	Profession not stated	1895	9100
Tinet	Charles	China manufacturer	1867	2902
Tobin	Thomas W.	Profession not stated	1874	3228
Tobin	Thomas William	Architect	1865	222
Tobin	Thomas William	Architect	1865	1983
Tobin	Thomas William	Architect	1865	3139
Tobin	Thomas William	Architect	1867	3541
Todd	Frederick Dundas	Teacher of shorthand	1891	10482
Tollerton	Joseph	Gas lighting engineer	1895	20208
Toms	Henry Luscombe	Optical lantern manufacturer	1893	17701
Tongue	John Garrett	*Agent for* J.M.A. Lacomme	1879	92
Train	Joseph	Manufacturer	1894	16326
Treliving	Joseph	Gentleman	1890	4215
Trivier	Telesphore	Profession not stated	1882	902
Trotman	Frederick	Refreshment contractor of the Zoological Gdns., Regents Park, London	1872	1411
Trouillet	Auguste	Profession not stated	1857	1400
Trouvé	Gustave	Profession not stated	1884	5157
Tubini	Theodore	Gentleman	1890	7479
Tupper	Ernest Du'Solei	Commercial traveller	1893	3756
Underwood	Harold Green	Profession not stated	1890	1884
Urch	William Henry	Upholsterer's salesman	1875	3602
Vailly	Albert	Gent	1890	7636
Vanderburgh	George E.	Profession not stated	1860	1448
Vankeerberghen	Victor	Profession not stated	1882	4073
Vasserot	Charles Frédéric	*Agent for* A.Trouillet	1857	1400
Vaughan	Thomas William	Gas engineer	1887	8627
Vaughan	Thomas William	Gas engineer	1890	19808
Vernici	Ion	Artist	1897	19472
Vilén	Nils	Master-builder	1891	9221
Villiers	Robert Edwin	Profession not stated	1877	4581
Villiers-Stead	Frank	Electrical engineer	1888	17559
Vincent	William	Profession not stated	1866	2318

Walker	Henry Alford	Profession not stated	1872	2723
Walker	James John	Profession not stated	1879	1245
Walker	Lizzie Anna	Profession not stated	1887	13588
Walmsley	Frederick	Scenic artist of Theatre Royal, Portsmouth	1900	13529
Walters	Austin	Engineer	1895	13416
Walters	Austin	Engineer	1896	19251
Walters	Austin	Engineer	1897	14882
Wansbrough	James	Hatter	1846	11512
Wappenstein	Rudolph	Profession not stated	1872	2810
Wappenstein	Rudolph	Profession not stated	1875	1597
Warbrick	John Frederich	Profession not stated	1872	999
Waterhouse	Benjamin	Profession not stated	1874	2410
Watts	Thomas Hodgson	Profession not stated	1873	692
Webb	Henry	Profession not stated	1877	147
Weil	Isidor	Silversmith	1889	6474
Welch	Edward John Cowling	Eden Works, Hampstead	1870	643
Wenig	Emil	Profession not stated	1892	4999
Westaway	James	Commercial traveller	1890	4215
Westcott	George Richard	Profession not stated	1866	2318
Weston	John Henry	Profession not stated	1864	41
White	Frederick	Watchmaker	1870	1467
Wieland	Henry William	Theatrical manager	1890	12762
Wigley	Henry	Musician	1899	3081
Wiles	John Fletcher	Insurance broker	1888	77
Wilkins	Samuel Benjamin	Fire Master of Edinburgh	1882	2066
Williams	Edward Adrian	Theatrical manager	1889	12230
Williams	George	Artist	1891	13683
Willway	Alfred Bush	Engineer	1895	11966
Wilson	Edward	Profession not stated	1876	3867
Wilson	Jas.	Gent	1889	7241
Wilson	Robert	Gymnast	1889	934
Winkler	Alexander	Artiste	1900	1671
Winslow	Forbes Edward	Clerk in Holy Orders	1898	8261
Winson	Joseph	Artiste	1893	17429
Wirth	Frank	*Agent for* J. Kreittmayr	1875	959
Wirth	Frank	Patent solicitor	1882	206
Wirth	Frank	*Agent for* G. Pickhardt	1883	1078
Wise	William Lloyd	*Agent for* W. Klinkerfues	1870	3228
Wise	William Lloyd	*Agent for* Spectatoria Co.	1893	1546
Wise	William Lloyd	*Agent for* Spectatoria Co.	1893	1547
Wood	James Phipps	Woollen draper	1884	6097
Wood	William Henry	Inventor	1894	4735
Woodbury	Walter Bentley	Profession not stated	1872	1186
Woodbury	Walter Bentley	*Agent for* E. Wilson	1876	3867
Woodbury	Walter Bentley	*Agent for* R. Talbot	1877	1099
Woodruff	Henry	Brass finisher	1891	5106
Wrench	Alfred	Manufacturing optician	1889	12860

Wrench	Alfred	Manufacturing optician	1892	18836
Wrench	John Holmes	Profession not stated	1871	604
Wright	Edward	Engineer	1871	621
Wrightnour	John Spratt	Profession not stated	1900	8946
Wulff	Eduard	Circus Director	1894	19698
Wulff	Eduard	Circus manager	1898	16378
Young	George Adam	Surveyor	1867	3523
Young	James	Profession not stated	1872	498

Subject Index

ACROBATICS:
Boisset, Frederick Perkins, 1896, 2991
Dando, Walter Pfeffer, 1875, 3067
Farini, Guillermo Antonio, 1870, 1572
Farini, Guillermo Antonio, 1877, 4587
Letta, , 1891, 8891
Menotti, Otto, 1892, 21280
Mulhall, George, 1892, 11675
Oliver, George, 1871, 1234
Romah, Robert, 1889, 934
Silbon, Walter, 1899, 5732
Smith, Albert, 1891, 8891
Taylor, Alfred Walter, 1869, 447
Testo, George, 1892, 11675
Wilson, Robert, 1889, 934
Winkler, Alexander, 1900, 1671
Wulff, Eduard, 1894, 19698
- *apparatus*: Cox, Charles Horace, 1898, 15825
Grade, Gustav, 1898, 5694
- *bicycles*: Johnson, Edward, 1892, 21673
Kaufmann, Nicholas Edward, 1891, 2041
Latelle, Cornelius, 1892, 8708
Latelle, Richard, 1892, 8708
Rucker, Martin Diederich, 1895, 7371
Selbini, John, 1894, 22132
- *cannon*: Farini, Guillermo Antonio, 1875, 4404
Hunt, William Leonard, 1875, 4404
- *horse*: Schumann, Albert, 1897, 26413
- *illusion*: Boult, Alfred Julius, 1896, 6591
Elton, Sam, 1896, 6591
- *toys*: Pepper, John Henry, 1866, 3278
Pichler, Seraphicus Francis, 1866, 3278
- *unicycle*: Hamlet, Thomas, 1877, 2356
Webb, Henry, 1877, 147

ADMISSIONS:
Aird, Alfred, 1887, 16722
Beeton, Christopher Joseph, 1892, 16554
Calvert, Charles Alexander, 1870, 178
- *registering*: Bain, Levett, 1875, 3602
Bradley, Herbert, 1874, 4479
Bull, William, 1874, 4479
Calvert, Charles Alexander, 1871, 2776
Carter, John Henry (younger), 1874, 2864
Carter, John Henry, 1874, 2864
Davis, Henry Thomas, 1875, 1874

Hall, Thomas, 1874, 3669
Lee, William, 1876, 474
Maas, Joseph, 1874, 2286
Marsh, Albert, 1899, 6959
Maskelyne, John Nevil, 1880, 1148
Mueller, Gustav, 1875, 2120
Newbold, Henry, 1876, 2438
O'Sullivan, Daniel Robert, 1887, 11646
Pullon, John Thomas, 1876, 474
Robertson, John, 1873, 2881
Shepherd, Timothy, 1896, 5921
Simplex Cash Register Syndicate, , 1896, 5921
Sykes, William, 1876, 474
Tee, Harry, 1875, 3024
Thomson, Edward Hamilton, 1876, 3304
Treliving, Joseph, 1890, 4215
Urch, William Henry, 1875, 3602
Walker, Henry Alford, 1872, 2723
Wappenstein, Rudolph, 1872, 2810
Wappenstein, Rudolph, 1875, 1597

Waterhouse, Benjamin, 1874, 2410
Westaway, James, 1890, 4215
Wright, Edward, 1871, 621
- *tickets*: Abraham, Henry Robert, 1856, 807
Anderson, William, 1873, 1200
Bain, Levett, 1875, 1253
Dalman, George Henry Bennett, 1896, 11922
Gooding, Richard Alphaeus, 1870, 2726
Keller, John, 1890, 9884
Trouillet, Auguste, 1857, 1400
Vasserot, Charles Frédéric, 1857, 1400
- *turnstiles*: Clegg, John, 1872, 999
Maitland, William Henry, 1870, 2933
Maitland, William Lauderdale, 1870, 2933
Warbrick, John Frederich, 1872, 999

ADVERTISING:
Achew, James, 1899, 17109
Bastian, Charles Orme, 1898, 19620
Boys, Charles Vernon, 1892, 3942
Challis, James, 1894, 37
Cox, Frederic Percy, 1896, 7511
Cunynghame, Henry Hardinge Samuel, 1892, 3942
Duncan, William Henry, 1884, 1378
Felbermann, Louis, 1892, 14948
King, William Falconer, 1894, 1433

Parsons, Arthur Joseph, 1898, 19620
Petit, Henry Francis Emile, 1877, 37
Spencer, Robert, 1898, 16927
Tupper, Ernest Du'Soleil, 1893, 3756
- *curtain:* Stern, Moriz, 1892, 9628
- *lighting-gas:* Cox, George, 1863, 449
Puntis, Josiah, 1863, 449
- *limelight:* Lacomme, Jean Marie Auguste, 1870, 2202
- *programme:* Stirton, John Anderson, 1889, 1784
- *tickets:* Hall, Frederic Thomas, 1868, 1487
Heit, Edouard, 1868, 1487

ARCHITECTURE:
Bierstadt, Albert, 1896, 10063
Bradley, Tom, 1900, 230
Dennett, Charles Colton, 1863, 1998
Duncan, William Henry, 1884, 1597
Heath, Thomas Theodore, 1863, 894
Keith, Charles Henry, 1882, 753
Rodeck, Carl Georg, 1895, 17652
- *balconies:* Cornelius, Mrs. Ellen Francis J., 1889, 15168
- *decorative:* Savage, Henry Thomas, 1892, 19883
- *floors:* Berry, Raymond, 1896, 1626
Horsfall, William, 1896, 1626
- *murals:* Luis, José, 1858, 2170
- *pit:* Murcott, Henry John, 1881, 2358
- *windows:* Stewart, David, 1811, 3417
Sutcliffe, William Stansfield, 1872, 2112

COSTUMES:
Anton, Georg, 1893, 14600
Cinquevalli, Paul Braun, 1894, 6834
Myselli, , 1897, 25864
Sims, John, 1868, 3542
- *armour:* Davis, Alfred, 1871, 3352
- *bird:* Walters, Austin, 1897, 14882
- *effect:* Browne, Newnham, 1893, 10296
Fuller, Marie Louise, 1893, 10296
- *mechanical:* Day, St. John Vincent, 1888, 19024
Stanton, Walter, 1888, 19024
Thelwall, Weymouth Birbeck, 1872, 1192
- *props:* Meysel, George, 1897, 25864
- *quick change:* Grogan, Samuel, 1897, 1274
Morris, John, 1874, 2334
Stelling, Harry, 1895, 2432
- *wands:* Grant, Lewis, 1896, 26783
- *wig:* Cinquevalli, Paul Braun, 1899, 6268

DISSOLVING VIEWS:
Allen, Samuel Wesley, 1892, 23756
Bond, Henry, 1889, 19926
Busby, Albert Gibbons, 1872, 1186
Davies, George, 1872, 1186
Duncan, William Henry, 1884, 934
Gray, Charles, 1889, 6999
Hughes, Alexander, 1889, 18583
Hughes, William Charles, 1889, 1570

Hughes, William Charles, 1890, 611
Kemp, Henry, 1889, 6999
Newton, Herbert Charles, 1889, 12913
Noakes, David William, 1886, 6154
Steward, James Henry, 1889, 12972
Thompson, George Samuel, 1890, 18369
Woodbury, Walter Bentley, 1872, 1186

DROP SCREENS:
Chadwick, John George, 1892, 10345
Chadwick, Thomas Henry, 1892, 10345

EFFECTS:
McLennan, Kenneth, 1890, 13056
- *coloured-fire:* Jensen, Peter, 1890, 1884
Moule, John, 1857, 478
Underwood, Harold Green, 1890, 1884
- *electrical:* Cox, Charles Horace, 1898, 14513
Fanta, Ferdinand, 1896, 9758
- *fire:* Fuller, Ida May, 1899, 23473
- *flash-box:* Bailey, Francis Gibson, 1892, 5526
Bishop, William, 1888, 356
Engel, Freidrich Herman F., 1891, 7487
Forret, John Alexander, 1891, 10482
Haddan, Reginald, 1891, 7487
Hart, Frederic William, 1888, 356
Hart, Frederic William, 1889, 3279
James, Alfred, 1888, 2730
Lamprecht, Rodolphe de, 1899, 9199
Rastrick, Robert Joseph Hooper, 1889, 2727
Schirm, James William Charles Cowen, 1890, 11784
Siemens, Brothers & Co., 1892, 5526
Swaab, Alfred James, 1899, 9199
Todd, Frederick Dundas, 1891, 10482
Wenig, Emil, 1892, 4999
- *kaleidoscope:* McIlvenna, Charles, 1878, 5109
- *mirror:* Leighton, John Taylor, 1897, 17665
- *paint:* Cryer, Abraham, 1892, 22952
McCarty, William Fitz-Charles, 1878, 5255
Morgan-Brown, William, 1878, 5255
Peiffer, Jules, 1878, 5255
Périgord De Sagan, Talleyrand, Prince, 1878, 5255
- *pantomime:* Lowe, Albert Henry, 1882, 1355
- *rainbow:* Rodeck, Carl Georg, 1895, 2948
- *scenic:* Erlanger, Abraham Lincoln, 1891, 21877
Jefferson, Charles Burke, 1891, 21877
Klaw, Marc, 1891, 21877
- *snow-storm:* Grismer, Joseph Rhode, 1899, 20255
- *tableaux vivants:* Dando, Walter Pfeffer, 1893, 24064
Geller, John, 1897, 28602
Kilányi, Eduard von, 1895, 19841
- *water:* Calcott, William, 1861, 2500
Parkes, George, 1866, 184
Smith, Edward Tyrrel, 1863, 3272
Tanner, George, 1866, 184

EXITS:

- *emergency:* Baird, William, 1887, 12603
Campbell, Stafford, 1888, 1302
Coulson, Richard, 1892, 242
Dutton, William Harry, 1887, 13258
Graydon, James Lawrence, 1892, 16183
Harris, Henry Inkson, 1889, 10285
Held, Heinrich, 1890, 1959
Kunkel, Carl, 1897, 3102
Lancaster, Frederick John, 1888, 7732
Lane, John, 1888, 246
Le Mesurier, Harry Brooke, 1889, 8772
Nixon, Edwin, 1888, 7732
Resuche, René, 1890, 7636
Vailly, Albert, 1890, 7636

FIRE PREVENTION:

Astrop, William, 1882, 3932
Christy, Thomas, 1890, 12230
Clark, Alexander Melville, 1879, 117
Clark, Alexander Melville, 1883, 941
Coninck, Frank de, 1888, 3795
Dade, Daniel Henry, 1881, 1196
David, Henri, 1882, 63
Dutton, Joseph, 1881, 4343
Gardener, Cuthbert, 1887, 14101
Hargreaves, William, 1893, 9289
Haviland, Robert J. Langstaff, 1882, 2107
Hayes, George, 1892, 6940
Jensen, Peter, 1882, 2107
Jensen, Peter, 1882, 63
Kreittmayr, Joseph, 1875, 959
Lake, William Robert, 1881, 5663
Martin, Abel Jean, 1879, 117
Maxim, Hiram Stevens, 1881, 5663
McLennan, John, 1882, 858
McLennan, Kenneth, 1882, 858eral
Meyer, Gaspard, 1883, 941
Owen, Richard, 1882, 858
Paris, Alfred John, 1889, 14515
Ransome, Thomas, 1885, 14949
Ridgway, Robert, 1882, 3932
Schmidt, August Edmund, 1896, 17132
Schmidt, August Edmund, 1897, 8983
Smith, Alexander Laws, 1888, 11158
Stanley, James Martin, 1887, 13193
Stanley, Thomas Blakemore, 1887, 13193
Suillot, Hippolyte Simon, 1882, 63
Tepper, Ernst., 1887, 14543
Tessier, Eugène, 1879, 117
Walker, Lizzie Anna, 1887, 13588
Wigley, Henry, 1899, 3081
Wilkins, Samuel Benjamin, 1882, 2066
Wirth, Frank, 1875, 959
- *architecture:* Abel, Charles Denton, 1884, 9200
Franquin, Pierre, 1884, 9200
- *composition:* Boult, Alfred Julius, 1898, 25275

Carré, Paul, 1898, 25275
- *lamp-shade:* Barbour, William, 1869, 2996
- *scenery:* Boulard, Madame, 1856, 2751
Brooman, Richard Archibald, 1856, 2751
Brooman, Richard Archibald, 1859, 2564
Demangeot & Co., Messrs., 1859, 2564
Spence, William, 1860, 1448
Vanderburgh, George E., 1860, 1448
- *shutters:* Pickhardt, Gustav, 1882, 206
Wirth, Frank, 1882, 206
- *walls:* Thomson, Benjamin Lumsden, 1882, 413
- *water:* Bennett, Henry Mellor, 1882, 394

HEATING:

Bourieff, Jean Baptiste Marie Amédée, 1866, 2755
Brooman, Clinton Edgecumbe, 1866, 2755

HEATING/COOLING:

Cogswell, Henry Daniel, 1881, 3725
Du Fay, Alcide Sanial, 1870, 673
Duncan, Charles Stewart, 1862, 980
Newton, William Edward, 1870, 673
Steell, George, 1857, 2229
Steell, William, 1857, 2229

ILLUSIONS:

Allison, Herbert John, 1884, 6598
Bartlett, William Henry, 1893, 21960
Bissmire, Catherine Elizabeth, 1890, 4364
Biver, Mathias Alfred, 1900, 6544
Boult, Alfred Julius, 1893, 10221
Boult, Alfred Julius, 1899, 22180
Buatier, Joseph, 1886, 16388
Buatier, Joseph, 1886, 16389
Buatier, Joseph, 1887, 9798
Buatier, Joseph, 1891, 5172
Castan, Gustav, 1888, 5254
Castan, Louis, 1888, 5254
Clarke, John Algernon, 1875, 1804
Cockman, Alfred Ebenezer, 1888, 17005
Cumine, James Alexander, 1899, 3298
Denstone, William Huskisson, 1879, 5185
Edwards, Edmund, 1873, 2888
Edwards, Edmund, 1874, 3604
Fuller, Marie Louise, 1893, 10221
Fuller, Marie Louise, 1899, 22180
Hénard, Alfred Eugène, 1900, 6544
Hertz, Carl, 1890, 16903
Johnson, James Yate, 1893, 21960
Kerr, Walter, 1865, 3286
Lynn, Hugh Simmons, 1874, 3228
Maskelyne jnr., John Nevil, 1892, 9033
Maskelyne, John Nevil, 1875, 1804
Maurice, Joseph, 1868, 1049
Melven, George de, 1888, 17005
Mills, Jennie, 1899, 15890
Morgenstern, Louis, 1890, 15024
Morgenstern, Louis, 1890, 15025
Morgenstern, Louis, 1890, 20392

Morris, Joseph Matthew, 1873, 2163
Morritt, Adelaide, 1892, 13597
Morritt, Charles, 1892, 9033
Morritt, Charles, 1893, 17429
Pepper, John Henry, 1865, 222
Pepper, John Henry, 1865, 3139
Pepper, John Henry, 1867, 3541
Pepper, John Henry, 1879, 1245
Plunkett, Harry Gratton, 1893, 24807
Reinolts, George von, 1899, 3298
Rignall, George, 1895, 11903
Risley, Isaac, 1893, 21960
Sherman, John W., 1884, 6598
Shipman, Fred. Waverley, 1897, 17229
Short, Alfred Joseph, 1889, 4931
Simmons, Joseph, 1867, 3617
Stodare, Colonel, 1865, 1983
Stoddart, Alfred, 1866, 442
Stoddart, Alfred, 1866, 689
Tennent, Hector Norman, 1893, 22665
Tobin, Thomas W., 1874, 3228
Tobin, Thomas William, 1865, 1983
Tobin, Thomas William, 1865, 222
Tobin, Thomas William, 1865, 3139
Tobin, Thomas William, 1867, 3541
Walker, James John, 1879, 1245
Wieland, Henry William, 1890, 12762
Winson, Joseph, 1893, 17429
Wood, James Phipps, 1884, 6097
- *horse race:* Burgess, Neilson, 1890, 20976
Chapman, Frank Montileoues, 1890, 13201
Gaitton(sic), Emile, 1896, 27472
Guitton, Emile, 1896, 27472
Hagen, Claude Lavrain, 1900, 12440
Knell, James W., 1883, 3010
Knell, James William, 1889, 9068
Knell, James William, 1890, 3847
Lake, Henry Harris, 1889, 9068
Lake, Henry Harris, 1890, 20976
Lake, Henry Harris, 1890, 3847
Lake, William Robert, 1883, 3010
Williams, Edward Adrian, 1889, 12230
- *optical:* Bolton, Charles, 1863, 3209
- *panoramic:* Fairfax, Joseph Sinclair, 1887, 5202
- *Pepper's Ghost:* Calcott, William, 1864, 826
Dircks, Henry, 1863, 326
Hawker, Thomas Henry Seymour, 1880, 15
Hoffman, John William, 1863, 2019
Hughes, De Bosco, 1863, 2841
Jones, George William, 1886, 10500
King, Horatio Nelson, 1863, 1744
Maurice, Joseph, 1864, 2564
Morton, Charles, 1864, 41
Munro, John, 1863, 1917
Pepper, John Henry, 1863, 326
Pepper, John Henry, 1864, 498

Silvester, Alfred, 1863, 1630
Silvester, Alfred, 1864, 1179
Stoll, Oswald, 1895, 8111
Weston, John Henry, 1864, 41
LIGHTING:
Aronson, Joseph Norman, 1882, 305
Celrain, John, 1879, 299
Grieve, Thomas Walford, 1879, 259
Hackforth, Matthew, 1863, 351
Haddan, Herbert John, 1879, 299
Keeling, Enoch Bassett, 1863, 31
Louit, Jean Baptiste Emile, 1863, 264
Molera, Eusebius, 1879, 299
Reddell, Isaac Hadley, 1816, 4035
- *carbon-arc:* Hepworth, Thomas Cradock, 1896, 5874
- *dimmers:* Leslie, Henry J., 1890, 5474
Lyon, Henry, 1890, 5474
- *effect:* Aronson, Joseph Norman, 1878, 2008
Broadbridge, Edward, 1891, 2399
Clark, Alexander Melville, 1884, 5157
Clark, William, 1861, 2083
De Douhet, William F., Count, 1861, 2083
Engelsmann, August, 1900, 18946
Frome, Charles Henry, 1880, 3416
Fuller, Marie Louise, 1893, 10301
Gibbs, George Cantrell, 1880, 3416
Harrison, William Henry, 1866, 3110
Hont, James, 1898, 12592
Jordan, William, 1891, 20576
Jordan, William, 1891, 2399
Lake, Henry Harris, 1893, 10301
McLennan, Kenneth, 1897, 26611
McMullin, Mary, 1887, 1667
Rimington, Alexander Wallace, 1893, 24814
Sanderson, John Glasgow, 1883, 501
Scantlebury, William, 1878, 1932
Scott, John, 1889, 11738
Smith, Henry David, 1889, 11738
Spectatoria Co., , 1893, 1547
Trouvé, Gustave, 1884, 5157
Wise, William Lloyd, 1893, 1547
- *electric-lamp:* Heysinger, Isaac W., 1885, 8727
Justice, Philip Middleton, 1885, 8727
Pusey, Joshua, 1885, 8727
- *flash-box:* Redwood, Theophilus Horne, 1890, 401
- *footlights:* Bowles, Edward Wingfield, 1899, 2742
Hillman, William, 1889, 12847
- *globes:* Krüger, Simon David, 1876, 2180
- *lenses:* Dando, Walter Pfeffer, 1894, 17077
Gwynne, James Eglinton A., 1894, 17077
- *limelight:* Anderson, James Edward, 1892, 18836
Barton, John Henry, 1893, 5554
Butcher, William Frederic, 1895, 16901

Butcher, William, 1895, 16901
Cooper, Ernest Sewell, 1893, 18623
Digby, Thomas Joseph, 1900, 21879
Drake, Hugh Oakley, 1895, 16901
Goodwin, Thomas, 1894, 17604
Gwyer, George Wright, 1894, 2365
Gwyer, George Wright, 1895, 22515
Gye, Frederic, 1861, 927
Houldershaw, William, 1895, 2195
Hughes, William Charles, 1875, 2683
Hughes, William Charles, 1889, 3839
Hughes, William Charles, 1891, 4387
Hughes, William Charles, 1891, 5106
Hughes, William Charles, 1892, 10568
Jackson, Alfred Charles, 1893, 17701
Kershaw, Abraham, 1892, 16026
Locke, Charles Woolnough, 1895, 13076
Malden, Benjamin John, 1894, 1024
Matthews, Lambert, 1893, 10238
Newton, Herbert Charles, 1894, 12572
Noakes, David William, 1892, 5541
Prosser, William, 1859, 2334
Scott, Albert William, 1889, 17378
Simpson, Henry, 1892, 8185
Sweetser, Alfred, 1897, 17438
Talbot, Romain, 1877, 1099
Taylor, Henry, 1894, 16916
Toms, Henry Luscombe, 1893, 17701
Welch, Edward John Cowling, 1870, 643
Willway, Alfred Bush, 1895, 11966
Woodbury, Walter Bentley, 1877, 1099
Woodruff, Henry, 1891, 5106
Wrench, Alfred, 1892, 18836
- *musical effect:* Atroy, James, 1897, 3419
- *oil:* Silber, Albert Marcus, 1870, 1467
White, Frederick, 1870, 1467
- *reflectors:* Boehle, Herrmann, 1884, 12382
- *substage:* Cresswell, Maud Beatrice, 1893, 24038

LIGHTING, ELECTRIC:
- *arc-flash:* Tabulewitch, Vladimir, 1896, 29620
- *carbon-arc:* Digby, Thomas Joseph, 1899, 24887
Gye, Frederic, 1878, 4473
- *control:* Berresford, Arthur William, 1899, 14293
Burt, Leslie Newman, 1898, 22858
Clémançon, Claude Edouard, 1898, 9511
Cox, Charles Horace, 1898, 14514
Emmott, Walter, 1898, 4761
Lyon, Henry, 1897, 28859
Prestwich, Ernest Edgley, 1898, 22858
Siemens, Brothers & Co., 1900, 2356
Stewart & Co. Ltd., Duncan, 1897, 28859
- *effect:* Edwards, Edmund, 1900, 18946
Niblett, Job Thomas, 1896, 4025
Vernici, Ion, 1897, 19472
- *lamp holder:* Bevis, Henry, 1895, 6657

Lyons, George, 1895, 6657
- *reflectors:* Walters, Austin, 1895, 13416
- *switches:* Halske & Co., , 1894, 21140
Moy, Ernest Francis, 1895, 18935
Probert, Isaac, 1895, 18935
Siemens, Brothers & Co., 1894, 21140

LIGHTING, GAS
- *control:* Brown, Joseph, 1887, 8627
Klinkerfues, Wilhelm, 1870, 3228
Newton, William Edward, 1857, 1060
Peebles, David Bruce, 1876, 3231
Poilly, Edouard de, 1875, 4068
Scott, James Sheppard, 1875, 4068
Vaughan, Thomas William, 1887, 8627
Wise, William Lloyd, 1870, 3228
- *footlights:* Defries, Coleman, 1864, 1643
Defries, Coleman, 1864, 22
Defries, Coleman, 1866, 2301
Lecoq, Louis Gustave, 1861, 1711
Pradou, Jules Emile Melon de, 1861, 1711
Schroeder, Frederick, 1890, 18265
Sloman, Bernard, 1890, 18265
Trotman, Frederick, 1872, 1411
Vincent, William, 1866, 2318
Westcott, George Richard, 1866, 2318
- *lamps:* Hunter, William Anthony, 1869, 1077

MAGIC LANTERNS:
Alston, Frank, 1894, 24655
Anderton, John, 1891, 11520
Beauchamp, Francis, 1898, 23382
Dickinson, Basil Bentham, 1894, 7673
Grottendieck, William Geldolph, 1894, 24821
Hartley, Frederick William, 1868, 46
Keevil, Henry, 1877, 2241
Moss, Richard John, 1897, 18925
Newton, Frederic, 1877, 1957
Newton, Frederic, 1893, 18440
Potter, Edward Tuckerman, 1888, 14171
Rendell, James Robson, 1890, 15292
Salomons, Sir David Lionel, 1890, 20633
Scott, Albert William, 1890, 19402
Simpson, Henry, 1892, 22151
Simpson, Henry, 1893, 24135
Solomons, Samuel, 1865, 2815
Stocks, Walter, 1890, 9934
Stroud, William, 1890, 15292
Wilson, Edward, 1876, 3867
Woodbury, Walter Bentley, 1876, 3867
Wrench, Alfred, 1889, 12860
Wrench, John Holmes, 1871, 604
- *advertising:* Parsonage, Christopher, 1898, 8286
- *bellows:* Bynoe, Frederick Oatley, 1898, 17095
Cubison, Herbert Jelfs, 1898, 17095
- *limelight:* Simpson, Henry, 1893, 4644
- *reflectors:* Colt, James Bennett, 1889, 14671
Lake, William Robert, 1889, 14671

- *slides:* Cheffins, William, 1891, 3727
Doubell, Edward Henry, 1880, 5105
Kidd, Robert Leamon, 1882, 2780
Lutticke, George Frederick, 1891, 13765
Lutticke, George Frederick, 1891, 2165
Mason, William Havelock, 1892, 4668
Morgan, William Thomas, 1882, 2780

MISCELLANEOUS:
Hall, Joseph, 1866, 1491
- *convertible bath:* Rae, Alfred, 1873, 1802
- *mechanical figure:* Pichler, Seraphicus Francis, 1876, 97
- *number indicator:* Arber, William Henry, 1898, 19240
- *surtitles:* Jones, Thomas Lloyd, 1881, 4267
Lake, William Robert, 1881, 4267

OPERA GLASSES:
Aitchison, James, 1891, 1016
Aitchison, James, 1894, 12213
Aitchison, James, 1896, 24883
Bálint, Desiderius, 1898, 23070
Barton, John Henry, 1897, 19255
Barton, John Henry, 1900, 7973
Batault, Emile, 1897, 8645
Bloch, Edmond, 1894, 20054
Bloch, Edmond, 1896, 11544
Boult, Alfred Julius, 1898, 4007
Boulter, Cornelius Alfred, 1891, 16223
Bradley, Thomas, 1891, 1016
Butterworth, Robert Harry, 1894, 3954
Cardwell, William Alexander, 1887, 17107
Carré, Ernest, 1889, 5287
Chandler, William, 1894, 21844
Clark, Henry Munday, 1892, 20137
Clark, Henry Munday, 1898, 4886
Colby, Edward John, 1889, 9955
Dallmeyer, John Henry, 1870, 2750
De Monostor, Adalbert Béky, 1898, 23070
Edwards, Edmund, 1891, 18598
Edwards, William, 1895, 14598
Engwall, Oscar Frederick, 1895, 9100
Franck-Valery, Emile, 1891, 21716
Franck-Valery, Paul, 1891, 21716
Ganem, Chakri, 1898, 21413
Gleason, William James, 1889, 10884
Green, James, 1890, 7448
Harvey, William Henry, 1894, 22211
Hasselkus, John William, 1900, 12538
Hedgman, Elward Radford, 1888, 17559
Hobson, Charles Walshaw, 1889, 540
Huet, Henri Louis, 1900, 256
Jones, Edmund Cyril, 1889, 10884
Laine, Louis, 1867, 2737
Laszky, Albert, 1898, 23070
Laszky, Sigismund, 1898, 23070
Levi, Samuel Joseph, 1889, 5287

Lüddeckens, Ernst., 1891, 18598
McDade, John Joseph, 1892, 3209
Murphy, Jeremiah, 1895, 9100
Plessey, Gabriel, 1889, 1419
Pocock, Alfred Willmer, 1891, 5922
Pocock, Caroline Spilsbury, 1889, 5218
Pocock, Caroline Spilsbury, 1891, 5922
Quinson, Gustav, 1898, 21413
Sanders, William, 1891, 2725
Schaffhirt, Otto, 1898, 4007
Schmidt, Gustav, 1897, 15723
Steward, James Henry, 1896, 9204
Stuart, John, 1897, 19255
Stuart, John, 1900, 12538
Supthut, Heinrich, 1899, 20623
Taylor, Harold Dennis, 1899, 17641
Thomas, Robert, 1872, 1570
Tiden, Charles Abraham, 1895, 9100
Villiers-Stead, Frank, 1888, 17559
Weil, Isidor, 1889, 6474
Winslow, Forbes Edward, 1898, 8261
- *camera:* Wood, William Henry, 1894, 4735

PANORAMAS:
Bellet, Ferdinand, 1897, 17747
Boult, Alfred Julius, 1897, 17747
Clark, William, 1861, 1784
Cloquet, Louis, 1895, 4807
De Santa Maria d'Yberri-Fitch, Dolores, 1900, 21985
Finger, Louis, 1870, 1584
Fitzpatrick, Hugh Donald, 1895, 6468
Foucault, Théophile, 1861, 1784
Fuhrmann, August, 1888, 7067
Fuhrmann, August, 1895, 6468
Gibbs, Joseph, 1833, 6408
Hollingsworth, Charles M., 1898, 21853
Hunt, Bristow, 1870, 1584
Mackenzie, John William, 1900, 21985
Motte, Henri, 1890, 12845
Sparkhall, Edward, 1855, 313
Train, Joseph, 1894, 16326
- *diorama:* Arrowsmith, John, 1824, 4899
- *projected:* Barber, Thomas Walter, 1894, 22990
Barber, Thomas Walter, 1898, 5532
Chase, Charles Arthur, 1895, 16070
Friese-Greene, William, 1893, 22954
Sanson, Raoul Adrien Grimoin, 1899, 1382
Tubini, Theodore, 1890, 7479

SAFETY CURTAINS:
Abel, Charles Denton, 1882, 1468
Barnett, Frederic, 1887, 12640
Booth, Lawrence, 1887, 13025
Clark, Alexander, 1882, 2935
Clark, Alexander, 1883, 2601
Clarke, Maximilian William H., 1887, 12817
Duplany, Claude Marius, 1887, 13740

Emerson, James Ezekiel, 1887, 6882
Fisher, Joseph Alfred, 1887, 13025
Geddes, William, 1887, 12304
Haddan, Herbert John, 1882, 902
Heath, William Edwin, 1887, 12304
Imray, John, 1882, 437
Justice, Philip Middleton, 1882, 4073
Justice, Philip Middleton, 1899, 13026
Lee, Robt. Bristow, 1888, 3708
Long Arm System Co., , 1899, 13026
Melville, Andrew, 1887, 12328
Midgeley, Thomas, 1887, 6882
Nagel, Junius, 1882, 1468
Pfaff, Karl, 1882, 437
Pickhardt, Gustav, 1883, 1078
Racey, George, 1872, 498
Seyde, Francis Napier, 1883, 5221
Stead, Thomas William, 1888, 7962
Stones, John, 1887, 14556
Taylor, Edmund, 1894, 17830
Trivier, Telesphore, 1882, 902
Vankeerberghen, Victor, 1882, 4073
Wiles, John Fletcher, 1888, 77
Wilson, Jas., 1889, 7241
Wirth, Frank, 1883, 1078
Young, George Adam, 1867, 3523
Young, James, 1872, 498
- *control:* Boult, Alfred Julius, 1887, 10402
Shaffer, William Cass, 1887, 10402
- *plates:* Nagel, Junius, 1884, 2154

SCENERY:
Berlyn, Frederic Harman Peter, 1891, 13683
Ramspacher, Théodore, 1860, 187
Schmidt, Christophe Frédéric, 1860, 187
Williams, George, 1891, 13683
- *decoration:* Cooper, William, 1846, 11512
Myers, George David, 1846, 11512
Walmsley, Frederick, 1900, 13529
Wansbrough, James, 1846, 11512

SEATING:
Armour, James Glencairn, 1897, 4400
Ballance, William, 1899, 6534
Bramham, Philip, 1888, 2192
Cattreut, Louis, 1884, 10358
Chandler, Henry, 1860, 2080
Chèradame, Antoine Leopold, 1872, 2053
Dalman, James Charles, 1899, 3072
Dean, Albert Reuben, 1894, 4407
Dougall, John Wilson, 1896, 5473
Farini, Guillermo Antonio, 1887, 1906
Farrell, Henry Havelock, 1896, 580
Garthwaite, Charles Wheatley, 1881, 2022
Granger, Louis Edwin, 1889, 15496
Gudgeon, Robert Horsley, 1890, 3150
Harrison, Thomas, 1881, 2022
Hatch, Oswald Birch, 1896, 5473

Hayward, Suter King, 1893, 5936
Hempson, Amis, 1860, 2080
Hipwell, Daniel Edward, 1895, 13926
Horst, Marius, 1899, 6526
Hosmer, Arthur, 1899, 4613
Jensen, Peter, 1883, 5307
Jensen, Peter, 1884, 10358
Lacey, Horace Harry, 1899, 5055
Lake, William Robert, 1872, 2053
Le Dreux, Alexander Eugène, 1872, 2053
Lyons, Lawrence Nathaniel, 1894, 5155
Mac Kaye Manufacturing Co., , 1883, 5307
MacKenzie, Neil Kennedy, 1900, 16687
Martin, William, 1894, 243
Nicholls, Thomas, 1890, 9752
Nolan, Patrick William, 1873, 2648
Ober, William Young, 1887, 16744
Oursel, Victor Charles Jules, 1872, 2053
Potter, Thomas, 1898, 23508
Ramminger, Albert, 1891, 14423
Reinold, Johann, 1897, 12735
Reinold, Peter Joseph, 1897, 12735
Robertson, James, 1900, 1182
Schleicher, Wilhelm, 1889, 12547
Schlosser, Eduard, 1888, 13361
Silliman, Charles Herbert, 1899, 4613
Smith, George Henry, 1875, 3726
Southorn, Charles, 1897, 4400
Steene, Leopold van, 1884, 10358
Stetter, Konrad, 1891, 14423
Terlinden, Gerhard, 1892, 6924
Tinet, Charles, 1867, 2902
Vilén, Nils, 1891, 9221
Walters, Austin, 1896, 19251
- *shelf:* March, Edward, 1900, 15377
- *stools:* Dufossé, Eugène, 1860, 1318

STAGE MACHINERY:
Boisset, Albert Hotton, 1895, 21101
Boisset, Frank Mendoza, 1895, 21101
Boisset, William Welch, 1895, 21101
Cawdery, John William, 1890, 5771
Chantler, Henry, 1885, 1373
Dando, Walter Pfeffer, 1890, 16699
Gardner, Edward Vincent, 1875, 4486
Gibson, James Hume, 1884, 9604
Glazier, William, 1884, 9604
Hengler, Albert, 1897, 6389
Kilham, John Thomas, 1888, 7498
Kiralfy, Imre, 1894, 18083
Petter, James Bazeley, 1887, 12197
Pichler, Seraphicus Francis, 1875, 4486
Porter, Philip, 1867, 2631
Rodeck, Carl Georg, 1892, 16120
Sachs, Edwin Otho, 1898, 27000
Spectatoria Co., , 1893, 1546
Spencer, James Robert, 1885, 1373

Stephenson, Rowland Macdonald, 1840, 8404
Wise, William Lloyd, 1893, 1546
- *aquatic:* Hengler, Albert Henry, 1890, 9047
- *batten:* Boughton, John Waters, 1898, 13837
- *brace:* Courtneidge, Robert, 1896, 11013
Rossman, John Gillespie, 1900, 13072
- *curtains:* Lytton, Edward, 1896, 3249
- *flying:* Conquest, George A. Oliver, 1899, 24539
Conquest, George Augustus Oliver, 1896, 23549
Kirby, George, 1898, 8559
Neale, Wm. Bevoir Buchanan, 1895, 2746
Scudamore, Fortunatus Augustine, 1895, 976
- *grooves:* Edwin, Walter, 1865, 131
- *hooks:* Ormerod, Joseph Bamford, 1897, 26387
- *hydraulic:* Brown, Andrew Betts, 1875, 3593
Abel, Charles Denton, 1882, 2889
Dengg, Carl, 1882, 2889
Gwinner, Robert, 1882, 2889
Kautsky, Johann, 1882, 2889
Roth, Franz, 1882, 2889
Oller, Joseph, 1886, 3920
- *revolve:* Downes, Edward, 1900, 23203
Wulff, Eduard, 1898, 16378
- *ropes:* Betts, William John, 1890, 19642
Crowe, William James, 1890, 19642
Phillips, Herbert Thomas, 1890, 19642
- *tie-bars:* Grieve, Thomas Walford, 1873, 294
- *trap:* Oliver, George, 1875, 3366
- *trucks:* Jacobsen, Bernhard Holger, 1900, 4879
TELEPHONES:
Booth, Harold Sims Joseph, 1892, 5528
Hermann, Charles, 1892, 5528
VENTILATION:
Barnett, Frederic, 1889, 13153
Bell, Henry, 1878, 3862
Bell, James, 1878, 3862

Bell, James, 1879, 2970
Bellini, Henry Linari, 1875, 3215
Cabanes, Henri, 1867, 722
Coleman, Joseph James, 1878, 3862
Coleman, Joseph James, 1879, 2970
Defries, Coleman, 1864, 2393
Dinsmore, John Henry Richardson, 1888, 5247
Gillett, William Frederick, 1885, 1173
Holbrook, Benjamin, 1887, 2315
Knott, Kennard, 1877, 3607
Lacomme, Jean Marie Auguste, 1879, 92
Lake, Henry Harris, 1887, 2315
Lion, Alexandre Léon, 1899, 7790
Mann, Henry Nepthali, 1887, 2315
Marsden, Charles, 1856, 28
Moreton, Henry Burrell, 1885, 1173
Morgan, Jacob, 1881, 1769
Morgan, William, 1881, 1769
Newton, William Edward, 1867, 722
Pennefather, De Fonblanque, 1888, 5247
Rosher, Charles Henry, 1893, 22866
Shaw, William, 1895, 11729
Stewart, David, 1801, 2549
Stott, James, 1896, 26795
Thomas, Walter John, 1895, 9914
Tollerton, Joseph, 1895, 20208
Tongue, John Garrett, 1879, 92
Vaughan, Thomas William, 1890, 19808
Villiers, Robert Edwin, 1877, 4581
Watts, Thomas Hodgson, 1873, 692
Wrightnour, John Spratt, 1900, 8946
- *heating:* Clark, William, 1863, 3015
Subra, Bernard, 1863, 3015
VENTRILOQUISM:
Harradine, William Newton, 1888, 13105
Mia-Mia, , 1891, 21887
Millis, Frederic William, 1891, 21887

Venue Index

Works Index

Theatresearch has a substantial archive of material relating to the history of theatre architecture and theatre technology.

A significant part of this library is made up of full specifications relating to the theatrical patents contained in this book.

If you would like to obtain full specifications of any of the book's patents you can order them by writing to

Theatresearch
c/o Society for Theatre Research
The Theatre Museum
1e Tavistock Street
London WC2E 7PA

Alternatively, you can order immediately by *faxing* your order to the following number:

(UK) 01423 780497

Please state clearly the year, number and name of the patentee for the patent required

Theatresearch also undertakes major theatre history research commissions, supplies information for films containing historical theatre scenes and provides a full scale theatre consultancy service for the restoration of historical theatres.

DID WE MISS ANY OUT?

If you think we have missed out any entries, please let us know. You can use a photocopy of this form. Any suggestions for new entries should, of course, fulfil the criteria defined in the introduction to this book.

Patent Details:

Surname   Christian name(s)

Patent No: Year   Class No

Profession of Patentee:

Title of Patent:

Was it ever manufactured, or used in a theatre?

Further information about the patent or patentee:

Please return this completed form to

British Theatrical Patents 1801-1900
c/o Society for Theatre Research
The Theatre Museum
1e Tavistock Street
London WC2E 7PA